BIKE RACING FOR JUNIORS

A GUIDE FOR

Riders, Parents, and Coaches

Kristen Dieffenbach, PhD
with **Steve McCauley**

VELO press

Boulder, CO

1830 North 55th Street
Boulder, Colorado 80301-2700 USA
303/440-0601 · Fax 303/444-6788 · E-mail velopress@insideinc.com

Distributed in the United States and Canada by Publishers Group West

Library of Congress Cataloging-in-Publication Data
Dieffenbach, Kristen.
    Bike racing for juniors : a guide for riders, parents, and coaches /
Kristen Dieffenbach and Steve McCauley.
        p. cm.
    ISBN 978-1-934030-22-6 (pbk.)
    1. Bicycle racing. 2. Bicycle racing—Juvenile literature. 3. Bicycle racing—
Training. I. McCauley, Steve. II. Title.
    GV1049.D54 2008
    796.6'2—dc22
                                                         2008022129

Cover photo by Beth Seliga
Cover design by Andy Clymer
Interior design by BackStory Design

For information on purchasing VeloPress books, please call 800/234-8356 or visit
www.velopress.com.

08 09 10 / 10 9 8 7 6 5 4 3 2 1

CONTENTS

INTRODUCTION

There are lots of books about training theory and how to become a faster, stronger cyclist. Training science provides an excellent foundation for improved performance. But training is also an art, especially when it comes to the Junior athlete, who is growing and changing physically, emotionally, intellectually, psychologically, and socially on an almost daily basis. This book provides insight into both the art and the science of training for the developmental (or "devo") athlete.

If you are a Junior athlete, the fact that you have picked up this book tells me that you have probably already discovered that cycling can be an exhilarating sport. And if you have already begun training seriously or entering races, you may be starting to understand the level of dedication, hard work, and quality training time that it takes to reach higher levels of achievement and personal satisfaction in cycling. Now, perhaps you want to go further and set higher goals—train harder, eat right, and maybe even work with a coach. If you've already researched the subject, however, I suspect it has not been easy to find the information you need, because the books and magazines tend to focus on training for adults, especially those who are already seasoned racers trying to perfect their technique.

This book is for you: I provide the information you need to get started as a serious young cyclist, from purchasing equipment that is right for you to setting up a great training program for your level of skill. Chapter 1 goes into the history of Junior racing, Chapter 2 gets you going, and Chapter 3 is a primer on Junior racing in different genres—whether you plan to try road racing, mountain bike racing, track cycling or time trials, or BMX or cyclocross. In Chapter 4, you can determine the best way to develop your athletic talents and abilities. Chapters 5 and 6 discuss important nutrition topics. The basics of training are in Chapter 7, and Chapters 8 and 9 explore bike skill development and strength training and flexibility. Chapter 10 emphasizes the role that your mind plays in being a competitive cyclist and ways you can use mental skills to your advantage. Chapter 11 covers unique injury concerns that riders need to be aware of, with an eye to both prevention and treatment. Female athletes' concerns are discussed in Chapter 12.

The next section of the book provides specific information for coaches and parents. Chapter 13 addresses parents and their role in the competitive cycling experience. Chapter 14 is geared for coaches and how they can facilitate successful training for Juniors and Espoirs. Finally, we provide tips on racing as a Junior and explore high school and collegiate racing. The appendixes contain additional helpful information and resources.

Throughout the book I will encourage you to set realistic goals for yourself and to keep your aspirations high, but don't forget to enjoy the miles along the journey. Use this book to understand yourself and your needs as a cyclist and you will never stop learning and improving as a racer. And even more importantly, you will find that cycling will always be a healthy and satisfying part of your life.

If you are a parent and your child has suddenly become obsessed with the sport of cycling, or maybe has been obsessed with it for years, you no doubt have many questions about the sport and how to advise him or her about how to proceed. On the one hand, you may be delighted that your child has a healthy enthusiasm for the sport and want to encourage that. On the other, you may wonder whether too much of a good thing can be harmful, or about how to protect your son or daughter from physical stresses and injuries. And you may not have much knowledge about cycling yourself, since it is not a part of our cultural identity the way baseball or football is. Having a child interested in becoming a bike racer leaves many parents at a loss. Even if you are a racer yourself, you may not be sure what level of training is advisable for a developing young athlete. Where to start? What is bike racing all about? Is it safe?

If these questions sound like an echo of the thoughts you've been having over the past weeks and months, you've come to the right place. This book will provide you with a foundation for understanding not only the sport but also how to help create a safe, supportive, and enjoyable experience for your young rider. You will learn more about your role in helping your child build a long and healthy relationship with the sport of cycling. This book will provide information on equipment as well as on training and nutrition specific to young riders. It will explain the bike-racing culture and opportunities for improvement that can help riders move from one level to another.

And who knows, maybe you will discover the joys of riding along the way too. At the very least, you will soon find yourself designing your family's menus with your child's training and racing needs in mind, looking at cycling equipment in a new light, and cheering on the sidelines of races as the cyclists come into view, peering through the crowd for your son or daughter.

If you are a coach, a team director, or another adult involved in youth cycling, be assured that this book will fuel your passion for cycling and your desire to pass that torch on to the next generation. You will want to show this book to young racers and their parents to give them a concise source of helpful information, and you may well find tips here to increase your own understanding of the sport and the young people you work with. As a coach, you will find the emphasis on skills and drills for sound bike-handling fundamentals and the discussion of the unique needs of Junior and Espoir riders to be especially helpful.

Unfortunately, our culture often demands immediate results, treating young athletes as if they were adults. Not only does this pressure increase the risk of long-term injuries, it may also cause young men and women to leave the sport permanently. A bad sport experience can leave a negative impression that lasts a lifetime. This book highlights the unique development concerns that young athletes face so that the adults structuring their training and racing can provide the necessary safeguards and guidelines to ensure proper development and reduce the risk of harm.

In short, this book has something for everyone. Whether you are a Junior or Espoir cyclist, a parent, or a coach, read on for tips and treasures that will enhance your sport, enable you to become your child's biggest fan, or show you how to help those in your charge have a positive experience in racing. Cycling, parenting, and coaching are all, in a sense, part science and part art. But remember, have fun along the way: A ride of a thousand miles (or ten thousand) begins with one spin on the bike—and a good helmet!

> Visit www.usacycling.org/juniors for more information about Junior and Espoir riding, tips from athletes and coaches, and photos.

1 WELCOME to the
World of Cycling

Day in and day out I religiously and happily lived the strict lifestyle that the sport dictates.
—Austin King, Jelly Belly Team

Even before paved roads and rubber tires, the bicycle appealed to people from all walks of life—rich and poor, male and female, young and old. And right from the start, it served a variety of purposes. Initially the bicycle was a novelty and then an alternative to the horse. Far from being merely a means of transportation, by the mid-1880s the humble two-wheeler had attracted the interest of pleasure-seekers, fitness enthusiasts, and people with a competitive spirit. People quickly found great joy in bicycle racing both formally and informally.

THE HISTORY OF JUNIOR RACING

Cycling boasts a long history of competitive events, starting with the early high-wheeler races on dirt roads and wooden boardwalks. The first officially recorded road race was in Paris in 1868, the first track World Championships were held in 1895, and cycling was included in the first modern Olympic Games, held in 1896. At the turn of the century, velodrome (track) racing became popular in huge arenas such as Madison Square Garden. But all of this was only a prelude to modern-day racing, a highly organized field of competition around the world and across a wide variety of cycling disciplines.

In these early races, anyone who had access to a racing bike could begin to compete. Plenty of different styles of bikes were made for children and adolescents, but smaller bikes weren't designed with racing in mind. Instead, these bikes were designed for play. Around the time of World

---

USA Cycling: Junior and Espoir Categories

10–12 years old
13–14 years old
15–16 years old
17–18 years old
Espoir (19–22 years old, currently male only;
  at 19, women join the Senior ranks)
Collegiate (racing program)

War I, American bicycle manufacturers took the idea of play further and began making bikes that were designed to suggest the look of jet airplanes or rocket ships, or even with a cowboy motif.

Early reports of bicycle-racing events don't differentiate between Junior and adult competitors, so it is hard to say when younger athletes began to compete. But early photographs of cyclists offer plenty of evidence that young men and even young women were enjoying cycling, and it isn't hard to imagine them competing as well.

The Union Cycliste Internationale (UCI), the international governing body for the sport, was founded in 1900 and has been overseeing competitive cycling since. It is based in Aigle, Switzerland, and has always recognized amateur and professional men's racing. The UCI began supporting elite women's competition in 1959. Winners of the World Championship events overseen by the UCI get to wear the coveted Rainbow Jersey.

Approximately 1,700 men and women under the age of 18 hold racing licenses with USA Cycling today. Riders can obtain a USA Cycling racing license when they are as young as 10 years old, and national

TABLE 1.1 Number of Licensed Racers in the United States in 2008

	Male	Female	Total
10–16 years old	883	189	1,072
17–18 years old	590	46	636
Espoir (boys only)	1,598	N/A	1,598

Elite Junior and Espoir Events

Alison Dunlap Series: A mountain bike series of events with designated Junior racing categories

Lance Armstrong Series: A road race series of events with designated Junior racing categories

Tour de l'Abitibi: The only UCI stage race for Junior males 16–18 years old in North America

Point Premium Root Beer International Cycling Classic (aka Superweek): Week of elite Juniors events and two weeks of professional racing

USA Cycling Road Festival: Road, criterium, and time trial age-group national titles for racers 10–23 years old

USA Cycling Track Nationals: Age-group national titles in track events for racers 10–23 years old

USA Cycling BMX Nationals: Age-group national titles for racers 10–23 years old

NORBA Mountain Bike National Championships: Event for racers 10–23 years old

USA Cycling Collegiate Road National Championships: College students only

USA Cycling Collegiate Track National Championships: College students only

USA Cycling Collegiate Mountain Bike National Championships: College students only

Pan American Games: World events for road, mountain bike, and track championships that include Junior and Espoir categories

championship titles are up for grabs in track events, road-racing events, and mountain biking in several Junior categories. BMX racers start even younger, with events for young boys and girls ages 4 and up that consider both age and experience levels.

U.S. cycling has a rich history of talented cyclists, even though most Americans are only familiar with the accomplishments of Lance Armstrong. But before Lance became the king of the Tour de France, he got his start racing as a Junior. Many other top riders got an early start as Junior cyclists as well.

Today, Juniors compete in nearly every event that adults participate in, but with their own special categories. And Juniors are discovering the same fitness and personal benefits that adults have noticed, gaining skills in teamwork, in setting and achieving realistic goals, and in taking good care of themselves, which will carry over into their adult lives.

A LOOK AT EVENTS

Today cyclists compete in events from sprints lasting mere seconds to ultra-endurance cycling races that last days or even weeks. Athletes compete on velodromes (specially designed bicycle tracks), dirt paths, paved roads, cobblestones, and everywhere in between. Some disciplines are about power, others rely on quick reflexes and skill, and still others place a large emphasis on endurance and determination. Depending on the style of racing, cyclists may go it alone in solo competition or may have to work together as a team to best the odds. Cycling offers something for every interest, with competition ranging from local grassroots opportunities through World- and Olympic-level competition. Each of the different cycling disciplines offers opportunities for young athletes to participate, although mountain biking and BMX are usually the ones that draw in new riders. Chapter 3 explores the difference kinds of cycling that exist today.

BENEFITS OF CYCLING FOR JUNIORS AND ESPOIR

Cycling provides benefits such as cardiovascular wellness and weight management, the development of important life skills, and social growth through team building and camaraderie. It can be a lifelong activity for everyone, from the recreational enthusiast to the most elite competitor. But for now, let's focus on the benefits for the Junior or "devo" rider.

Physical training will strengthen your heart so that it can move blood more efficiently with less work. It will also improve your endurance abilities so you can ride longer, and make you stronger so that hills will become easier to climb. All of these things translate into becoming a great athlete and eventually a healthy adult.

Benefits of Cycling

Cardiovascular benefits	Improved focus and concentration
Low impact on joints	Enhanced self-confidence
Improved body composition	Increased energy
Enhanced muscular strength	Lifetime health
Enhanced endurance	Teamwork
Good sportsmanship	Time-management skills

But the benefits of cycling go far beyond just the physical ones: Sports will build your character, too. Like other sports, cycling will provide you with opportunities and challenges that will help you learn to make good decisions. People with good character are well thought of by other people because they are trustworthy. The skills you learn as a cyclist will not only help make you a respected athlete but will also transfer to other areas of your life, and they will be useful all through your life. Exactly how does riding a bike do this? As a bike rider you will be faced with easy days and challenging days. Good coaches, your parents, teammates, and opponents will all help you learn how to stand up to the challenges and take success in stride.

Along the road to becoming a talented young rider, you are going to learn how to corner fast, ride with a pack, climb hills, and race smart. You will also learn how to focus and concentrate as you progress in your workouts (and how to focus on your homework, so you will get through it faster and have plenty of time to ride). Other skills, like managing anxiety and managing your time, will take practice and hard work, just like your training, but these skills will be very valuable both on and off the bike. Chapter 10 will explore the key mental skills for peak personal performance.

Being a cyclist is a fantastic lifelong pursuit. If you are interested in pursuing cycling as a competitive endeavor, then you must become a 24/7 athlete. This does not mean that all you do is ride. A 24/7 athlete is someone who understands what it means to be an athlete. Being an athlete means training smart, not just hard. It means making good choices about the foods you eat all the time, not just when you are on the bike.

Athletes make good choices daily about the opportunities they have so they don't compromise their fitness and performance capacity. And perhaps most importantly, 24/7 athletes know that even though they are living an athlete's lifestyle and are taking excellent care of themselves, there is more to life than cycling. For them, cycling makes life more fun and exciting. This book is designed to help you learn what you need to know to make good decisions in your cycling career.

2 GETTING STARTED: Bikes and Components

Being a successful cyclist is not about equipment.
—Al Gandolfi, USAC Level 1 coach

If you are interested in racing, you probably already have a bike, but depending on the type of racing you want to do, it may not be what you need to compete. Or perhaps you've outgrown the bicycle you have and want to make sure your next bike is just right for you in terms of style and fit. In either case, a good racing bike is a key investment. Although an expensive bike is not a requirement for racing, there are some things you need to consider when deciding what to purchase—or when evaluating whether your current bike is right for racing. Some bikes are better suited to certain events; for example, you wouldn't want to use a skinny-tire road bike in a mountain bike race. The rules don't allow it, and even if they did, a road bike wouldn't last long on trails.

Back in the day, bike frames were made of wood and iron, and wheels were made out of wood with a metal edge. Talk about a rough ride! Fortunately, rubber tires soon became common. The earliest rubber tires were solid rubber—still quite heavy, but providing a more comfortable ride. John Dunlop introduced the first commercial pneumatic rubber bicycle tires in 1888. Changes in frame design soon followed, and bicycle racing surged in popularity.

Frames have become lighter over the years with the use of steel, aluminum, and newer materials such as carbon fiber and titanium. The bicycle magazines and manufacturer websites seem to highlight the newest, coolest bikes and extras in each new issue and update—and, as in any sport, it's important to have the right equipment in cycling. But what is really necessary? Besides a good helmet, which is essential, what else do you need to race your bike? This chapter will help you decide what to purchase and how to choose among the dazzling array of options in bikes, helmets, components, and even clothing for the serious cyclist.

Before you run out to buy a top-of-the-line model, or try to pick up the same gadgets that your friends have on their bikes, take some time to think about what you can reasonably afford to spend on your bike. Keep in mind that as a Junior rider you are still growing, and this year's bike may not fit you next year. While adult riders often are able to get several years out of a competitive racing bike, you may grow enough to require new equipment each year to keep up with growth spurts. There are some ways to keep the costs of bike racing from spiraling out of control, and in this chapter I will share those tips with you. Although an initial investment is required for quality gear that can go the distance, keep in mind that for a developing athlete, a well-designed training plan is far more important than expensive equipment. The lightest, shiniest bike doesn't matter if you don't know how to ride safely or if you don't have the engine to go the distance. That said, let's get down to basics.

THE BIKE

There are three main considerations to keep in mind when purchasing a racing bike: (1) the style of the bike—that is, the specific cycling discipline or type of racing that it is designed for; (2) the quality of the frame and materials; and (3) the fit of the bike.

Each discipline—road racing, mountain bike racing, track racing or time trials, cyclocross, and BMX—offers a range of frame styles designed for different types of events and riding. (Chapter 3 provides more information about the different cycling disciplines.) For an entry-level bike, look for a basic, multipurpose bike within the appropriate discipline. As your skill level improves, there will be plenty of opportunity for you to acquire fancier or more specialized bikes down the road.

Walking into a bike shop can be both exciting and a little intimidating. Where do you start? It can be helpful to understand the basic general categories of racing bikes. You are probably most familiar with BMX bikes. These bikes are very popular with kids because of their small wheels and frame sizes and because they are practically bombproof. They can take almost anything a young rider can think up and then some, and they range from bikes suited to neighborhood riding to high-end racing versions. You or some of your friends may also have mountain bikes. Mountain bikes have slightly heavier frames than road bikes to withstand the bumps of trail racing. They use fat tires with heavy treads to help with traction on dirt, and have shocks in front, and sometimes in the back as well, that provide "travel" (the mountain biking word for suspension compliance) to help improve handling. Downhill mountain bikes are even more specialized, with even beefier frames and tires, and they have shocks that provide even more travel so they can handle fast, rough rides down mountainsides and ski slopes without bouncing the rider off. A mountain bike is a great first bike and can provide a lot of fun on the trails.

Road bikes and racing bikes have lighter frames and skinnier tires than mountain bikes and fall into a different category altogether. The most popular are probably the road bikes. They aren't as popular for younger riders as the "fat-tire" bikes and often are not as easy to get in small sizes. These bikes are light in weight, with curled handlebars and thin tires. Some are designed for speed, handling around sharp corners, and climbing well. Others are a bit heavier and are designed for bike touring or casual distance riding for fun. Individuals who tour, race on roads, or want to get in serious training miles will invest in the appropriate model of road bike. Serious mountain bikers also ride road bikes for training.

Cyclocross bikes fall between road and mountain bikes. They are like a road bike that is trying to be a mountain bike. The frame and handlebars are similar to a road bike's, but the 'cross bike is designed to use a tire that is a little wider and has more tread, and the frame can handle rough trails. Most people don't invest in a 'cross bike unless they are going to race 'cross.

Bikes built for track racing look a lot like road bikes—except they don't have multiple gears or brakes. These specialty bikes are called "single-speeds" and have a fixed gear. This means that when you pedal, the bike goes, and when you stop, it stops immediately. This may sound a little dangerous, but it is easy to get used to, and once you do, riding a track bike can provide great training. If you are interested in track racing, invest in a good road bike for training. Velodromes offer quality rental bikes for track beginners to learn on, so you don't need to invest in one right away. Once you know what type of racing you are interested in, you are ready to start shopping. Table 2.1 summarizes the different types of bikes.

TABLE 2.1 **Bicycle Styles and Characteristics**

Type of Bike	Type of Race and Riding	Unique Characteristics
BMX bike	BMX races	Small wheels (12"–20" depending on bike size) Small frame Very agile
Mountain bike	Mountain bike trail riding Mountain bike trail races	Flat handlebars Wide tires with lots of tread Front shock with some "travel" (bounce) Rear shock (optional) 26" or 29" wheels
Downhill mountain bike	Downhill riding Downhill races	Flat handlebars Wider tires with lots of tread Heavy-duty frame Front shock with lots of travel (bounce) Rear shock (not optional) 26" or 29" wheels
Road bike	Road riding Road races Criteriums Time trials	Lightweight frame Curled handlebars Narrow tires 700c wheels (smaller frames may have 650c wheels) Limited options for youth sizes
Cyclocross bike	Cyclocross racing	Road bike–like frame but sturdier Curled handlebars Slightly wider tires than a road bike, with more tread 700c wheels Limited options for youth sizes
Track bike	Track racing	Road bike–like frame Straight rear wheel dropout for easier chain adjustment Curled handlebars 700c wheels Limited options for youth sizes

Frames

Once you start looking at bikes, you will find that they come not only in many different materials but in many different shapes as well. Innovations are always taking place in the field of frame design as designers tinker with small changes that could make a big difference in the top echelons of racing, and these design changes often trickle down to the rest of us. Bike designers and builders need to understand the chemical properties of the different materials in order to make bikes that will give racers an advantage over their competition. (And you thought chemistry wasn't important.) In addition to the material that a bike frame is made of, the way the frame is put together, the angle of the different joints (yup—geometry matters too), and even the thickness of the frame tubes are critical. All of this is important to building a fast and safe bike. But if your head is spinning from all the choices, don't worry; you don't need to be an expert yet. For now, just focus on finding a bike that fits you well and that you are comfortable riding. Let's take a look at bike fit and a few other things, and then we'll talk about how to use all of this to make your selection.

Frames come in all sorts of variations based on the length of the tubing and the angles between the tubes. These angles determine responsiveness, stability, agility, and other key handling aspects of the bike. The science of frame building is beyond the scope of this book, but when you consider different bikes, you should take a careful look at the manufacturer's materials, which will explain the specific characteristics of the bike you are interested in.

Although they often come together as a set, the frame and fork (the front piece where your front wheel fits) are actually two separate parts. The fork is held on the frame by the headset, which allows the fork and front wheel to turn. The wheel fits into the "dropouts" at the bottom of the fork. The fork can have straight or curved legs and can be made of any of a wide variety of materials. Some are designed to be stiff and responsive, whereas others help dampen road vibration and reduce rider fatigue.

The front forks of mountain bikes are designed as shock systems to reduce rider fatigue and improve handling. Because mountain bikers encounter more extreme conditions and situations than riders who stick to the roads, they require more from their forks. Although a front shock makes the fork heavier, the trade-off is well worth it. Front shocks provide cushioning in different ways depending on the brand and the style. Some of the more common shock options are air, oil, and plastic elastomers (spongy plastic pieces that compress under load and then return to their original shape). The type and amount of front travel or shock absorption you will need depend on the type of terrain you will be riding and your size. Many front shocks have a lockout feature that allows you to turn off the shock when you don't need the travel. For example, if you are going to ride your mountain bike on fast fire roads, you might not want to have your forward energy wasted in the bounce of the front shock. Your local bike shop should be able to help you find the right choice for your needs and set it up properly.

While we are talking about shock absorption, we should mention that some mountain bike frames also have rear suspension. These frames provide more cushion and control for handling tough trails. Some, like the Moots YBB frame, give you mild rear suspension for smoother cross-country riding; others, like some Santa Cruz frames and other downhill bikes, are more extreme, providing many inches of wheel travel. Rear frame suspension systems may use elastomers, springs, air, oil, or other means to achieve this purpose. Some frames offer a lockout on the rear shock so that a rider can choose when to have rear travel and when not to have it.

Frame Materials   Bike frames can be made of many different materials, each of which offers different benefits and drawbacks. Here I'll describe some of the more common materials used to build bikes, and the pros and cons of each.

Steel is the most traditional material. It's strong, it's durable, and it offers a stiff ride. This means the bike will respond quickly. Unfortunately, steel—especially lower-quality varieties—can be heavy, and it can rust if not taken care of properly. On the plus side, steel holds up well over time (it has a long fatigue life), and it can usually be repaired when damage occurs. Reynolds 853 tubing is the top-of-the-line steel and is used in many top racing bikes. Moderate- to high-grade steel is an affordable and sound investment for a first-time bike buyer.

Aluminum has been a common frame material since the early 1990s. But this is not your soda-can aluminum—it's an aluminum alloy that is specially blended and forged for strength and durability. It's also lighter than steel and uses thinner tubes that can be manufactured in aerodynamic shapes. Although it doesn't rust, it has a shorter fatigue life than steel and cannot be repaired as easily. Aluminum bikes, like steel bikes, start in the moderate price range. Many excellent entry-level aluminum bikes are available for all kinds of riding.

Prices jump a bit when you start to look at carbon-fiber and titanium frames. Both are high-tech materials that were originally developed in other industries. For example, titanium is a very popular airplane material.

A carbon-fiber frame is made by mixing carbon fibers with epoxy (glue) and weaving the fibers into sheets. These sheets are wrapped and molded into tubes and glued together to form a frame. Look closely and you can see the weave. Once only available at the highest end of the market, carbon fiber is now available at more moderate prices. Carbon-fiber bikes are very light and ride nicely; however, they should be inspected carefully after any crash. Although individual carbon fibers are incredibly strong, the places where the tubes are sealed together can become damaged by an impact.

Just like airplane designers, bicycle builders are using titanium to build lightweight bikes that can take the bumps and bruises of the road and keep coming back for more. Titanium, while not quite as light as carbon fiber, is still a lightweight material that makes a strong, resilient bike that can last for years. The biggest drawback to titanium is often cost. (For a comparison of the different materials, see Table 2.2.)

Bike Fit

Once you know the style of bike you need for your discipline and the type of frame you want, it is important to choose a bike that fits you well. What exactly does that mean? Bike fit refers to how well the size of the bike fits your height, the length of your arms, and the length of your legs. Proper bike fit is essential for safe and successful riding. A bike that is too big for you will make it harder for you to corner or to handle rocks and roots. It

TABLE 2.2	Pros and Cons of Frame Materials		
Frame Material	**Pros**	**Cons**	**Other Considerations**
Steel	Long lasting Very strong Doesn't damage easily Dents can often be repaired Stiff (good for riding) Available in the moderate price range	Cheaper, lower-quality steel is heavy Can rust if not properly cared for Higher-quality steel is still a bit heavier than other high-end materials	A very traditional frame material Ranges from low-end and very heavy to high-quality 853 Reynolds steel A great choice for a first bike because it is so durable
Aluminum	Not as dense as steel (lighter) Provides a stiff, responsive ride Can be shaped to be more aerodynamic Doesn't rust Reasonably priced	Shorter fatigue life Thinner tubes mean more damage in a crash Dents can't be repaired as easily	A very lightweight frame material Can be a good option for a bigger rider (because it is lighter than steel)
Carbon fiber	Can be molded into all types of shapes Good fatigue life No rust	Expensive Can be prone to crash breakage Hard to repair	Actual individual fibers are very strong, but frame strength depends on the glue (epoxy) used to hold them together
Titanium	Best combination of durability and weight Lightweight Resilient	Expensive More flex than steel Hard to repair	Yup, this is the same stuff airplanes are made of

will also force you to overstretch certain joints, such as your knees, which can lead to overuse injuries. A bike that is too small won't let you use all of your power and strength, which will affect your racing speeds.

Before buying a bike, you need to see how it fits you. Trying on a bike isn't quite the same as trying on a new pair of jeans. With jeans you just put them on in the changing room, pose in front of the mirror, maybe walk around a bit, and then decide if they are cool enough. With a bike, it is important to do more than just see how you look in the mirror with it. Your local shop will help you figure out a frame size to start with. Most will let you take the bike out for a spin to try it out. Bikes don't usu-

Parents Beware: Avoiding a Common Mistake

As a parent, avoid the urge to buy a bike that your son or daughter will "grow into." An ill-fitting bike will lead to poor bike-handling skills, making for dangerous riding as well as a variety of overuse and improper-alignment injuries. Watch your child's growth carefully. Growth doesn't mean a whole new bike is necessary right away, however. Work with your local shop experts to determine how your child's bike can safely be modified so that it can grow with your child until he or she is ready for the next frame size. Adjustments might include changing the height of the seat, using a shorter or longer crank arm, and using a shorter or longer stem. Keep in mind that all of these adjustments are relatively minor, but a bike that is too small or too large for your child can present safety hazards from poor positioning problems and handling difficulties.

ally fit right off the floor. The staff at a good shop will also know how to measure proper fit and make any needed adjustments.

Mountain bike frames are usually measured in inches, while road, track, and cyclocross bikes are measured in centimeters. Frame size is determined by the length of the "seat tube," the tube that runs from the seat all the way down to the bottom bracket. These numbers will help you pick a starting point, but each manufacturer measures a little differently. So it is essential to look at more than just frame size when you get ready to test a bike.

For an initial quick check, the bike shop employee will have you stand over the frame to make sure you can stand safely over the top tube. If you find that you are sitting on the top tube, the bike is too big for you. If the frame seems right, he will hold the bike steady so you can put your feet on the pedals and sit up on the saddle. It is important that he hold the bike steady or set it up in a stable stand so you can put both feet on the pedals. This will help him determine whether the seat needs to be adjusted up or down. And he will look to see how comfortably you can reach forward to the bars. A few minor adjustments, and you should be ready to take a test ride. When you shop for a bike, wear your riding

Elements of Bike Fit

There are many different theories on proper bike fit. Some are based on tradition, some on experience, some on science, and some on a combination of these methods. The exact details of how a bike should fit will differ depending on the type of bike you are buying. There is no one right way, because no two bodies are exactly the same, but here are a few basic starting points:

Stand-Over Height You should be able to stand over the top tube with both feet flat on the ground and have at least 1 inch of clearance.

Foot Position Each foot should be positioned so the ball of the foot is directly over the center of the pedal and the toes are forward. Often the person who is performing the fit will also make sure that when the pedal is at the 3 o'clock position, the front of the knee is over the ball of the foot. He or she may use a plumb bob or a string and a washer to check this.

Knee Angle At the lowest point of the pedal stroke, if you stop pedaling and hold your foot in a normal riding position, your leg should not be totally straight. A slight bend of the knee is important so the knee isn't overstressed. Be sure to check both legs. Many people have one leg that is longer than the other, and it is important that neither knee be straight.

Reach When sitting comfortably in the saddle, the athlete should be able to reach the handlebars without needing to stretch. The elbows should have a slight bend to avoid any unnecessary strain on the elbows, shoulders, or neck. On a mountain bike this reach is pretty straightforward. On a road, track, or cyclocross bike the athlete should be able to reach all three hand positions comfortably—the top, the brake hoods, and the drop or curved part of the bars.

clothes so you can take the bike out around the neighborhood. Test-ride a few different styles to see what feels most comfortable to you. Don't do anything risky, especially since you're not used to this bike yet (and be sure to wear a helmet), but try to make your test ride more than just a ride in the park with Grandma. Take a few corners, stand up and ride, go up a hill, and ride on some dirt (if you're testing a mountain bike). This will help you decide if you like the bike.

Once you have picked out a bike, you should do a more detailed sizing to get the right bike fit. Some shops will do a free bike fit when you purchase a new bike; others charge for the service ($30–$150, depending on the detail and time involved). A knowledgeable bike shop employee will take a close look at how your foot sits on the pedal, your knee alignment, and the reach between the saddle and the cockpit (handlebars). For a basic fit, all the adjustments can be made with a few simple tools, while computer and even laser technology may be used for a very scientific or advanced fit. As a beginning rider, a basic fit is all you need. It may take a little while for the employee to get your fit just right, so be patient. This is normal, and the longer you ride, the more you will personalize how you like your bike to fit.

Even if you feel that you understand all the guidelines about how to get a good fit, it's best to enlist the aid of an experienced rider or a reputable shop that carries and services racing bikes when you go to shop for

Adjusting the Saddle

There are several ways to adjust the saddle to help improve your fit. Once you have determined a good starting point in a bike fit, all changes should be done in small increments to avoid injuries caused by poor position. Once you have your new bike at home, it can be helpful to take a few simple tools with you when you are out riding so that you can make small adjustments and test them for comfort. When you do make adjustments, be sure to tighten things up properly before you ride again.

Saddle Height The saddle can be moved up and down to change the reach to the pedals. Use a piece of black electrical tape or a thin permanent marker to mark your seat height. This will help you make small adjustments and return to prior settings if necessary.

Forward and Back The saddle can also be moved forward and backward (aft) on its rails (the metal pieces that run along the underside of the saddle). Be careful when you nudge your saddle forward or back. Changing this can also impact your reach to the pedals, and you may need to readjust the seat height. Also be careful that you don't change the saddle tilt (see next point) unless you intend to do so.

Nose Up or Down Keep the saddle level when you slide it forward or back. When the saddle points down at the front, you will feel like you are sliding forward, and if it points up, it can make for a very uncomfortable ride.

a bike. Avoid general sporting goods outlets or big-box stores that may not have a knowledgeable staff. And when you're getting started, avoid ordering via the Internet. With the Internet, you may get a good price, but you're missing out on the opportunity to get expert help with fit; as a result, you may end up with injuries you could have prevented. A good shop has employees who are passionate about riding and who have raced themselves, and their advice can be invaluable, saving you money and disappointment in the long run.

Why the Local Bike Shop Is Better

Big-box stores are large stores that sell everything from groceries to lawn mowers to bedsheets to sporting goods. You probably have one or two near your home. While these stores often offer inexpensive options, they are not the best choice for purchasing quality racing equipment. For many reasons, it is better to purchase your bike from a local bike shop instead. Here's why:

- Your local bike shop will carry higher-quality bikes, helmets, and components. Even if a big-box store carries the same brand name as your local shop, it will rarely carry the same models. Typically, big-box stores carry the lowest end of the manufacturer's line. These bikes are designed for recreational use and wouldn't hold up to the stress and strain of racing.
- A bike shop will have staff who know bike racing, the local racing scene, and the pros and cons of their merchandise. Big-box store employees rarely know much about these things.
- Bikes in big-box stores are usually assembled on an assembly line, not by certified bike mechanics. For safety, it is best to have a bike that has been put together and checked by a well-trained mechanic. A bike that is not assembled properly will not perform well and could even lead to injury.
- Building a relationship with your local shop can help you find a team or sponsor.
- Frequenting a local shop will help you establish a relationship with a mechanic you know and trust. With a good mechanic, you can make sure your bike stays in top shape and you can learn how to maintain it.
- Bike shops are often the center of a thriving cycling community. If your town or city has a local cycling club, the local bike shop is most likely the hub of its activity and can inform you about group rides, match you up with a training buddy, recommend local coaches, and the like.

IMPORTANT COMPONENTS

To get the scoop on the latest components, such as brakes, gears, seatposts, handlebars, and wheels, all you need to do is pick up the latest issue of any good cycling magazine or check out a cycling blog on the Internet. Companies are continually producing sleeker, lighter, and more exciting components. While these light and efficient parts can be wonderful, the lightest, most expensive equipment will not make up for inexperience. Nor can fancy components speed up the progress for developmental athletes. Your money is better spent on a high-quality frame and modest components during the early phases of training. Still, it is important to at least know what equipment is on your bike. Let's go on a quick tour of the components.

The Gruppo

Collectively, the components on a bike are commonly called a *gruppo*, which is simply the Italian word for "group" (cyclists picked up the word because Campagnolo, an Italian company, was one of the first to make a complete family of parts, or gruppo, for bikes). Bikes usually come with all of the parts installed. Most young riders start off with a pre-assembled stock bike. This is easier to manage at this point, since you

Who makes the gruppo?

Just like any other product on the market, bike components are made by many different companies. For road bikes, two of the biggest companies are Campagnolo and Shimano. Both offer complete kits, from entry-level to very elite. Many other companies, far too many to name, specialize in making different parts for different kinds of bikes. Most racers ride bikes that incorporate a variety of different components from different manufacturers. Actually, traditional road riders usually have components of the same gruppo on their bike, while mountain bikers are known to mix and match parts more. Track riders don't use nearly as many components and usually don't worry about the gruppo as much. As with frames, bike components can be made of a wide range of materials, such as steel, aluminum, carbon fiber, titanium, and different kinds of plastics.

probably don't know a lot yet about how to make a customized bike or how to put it together, and we recommend it as the best way to start out. Then the fun of changing and upgrading the different components can begin. Later, when you have more experience and know what your "dream bike" would be, you can buy a frame and a gruppo and build a bike, or purchase a frame and all the elements of a gruppo separately. Let's run through the different parts of a gruppo.

Stem and Headset The stem is the piece that connects the handlebars to the fork. Stems come in different lengths (measured in millimeters). A shorter stem means a shorter reach from the saddle, and a longer stem stretches you out. Some stems have a slight angle that may raise the handlebars as well. There are many different stem styles, depending on the type of bike you get. This is a part you shouldn't change unless you are working with someone who knows a thing or two about stems.

The headset, another piece that you shouldn't change as a new rider, consists of a series of bearing races that fit at the top and bottom of the head tube of the frame. These rings hold the fork on the frame securely. Modern headsets are a standard size and require a special tool to install properly. A well-maintained headset helps ensure smooth turning, whereas a loose headset will make for a shaky and uncomfortable ride and can be dangerous. Headsets need to be checked occasionally to be sure that no wiggle has developed. If the headset does loosen, the free play has to be taken out. Routine tune-ups by a qualified mechanic should fix this potential problem. Talk to a mechanic at your shop to determine the right maintenance schedule for your bike.

Handlebars Depending on the type of racing you want to do, the handlebars can be straight or curved. Flat or straight handlebars are common at all levels of mountain biking and on BMX bikes. They provide good control on uncertain and fast-changing terrain. Mountain bike and BMX bars may also have a slight rise from the center to the ends to help the rider change position. Rubber or a composite material is used to create grips for the ends of this type of bar. These grips dampen vibration, which helps reduce upper-body fatigue and makes for a more comfortable ride. Most grips come in simple black or gray, although a few companies make some fun variations.

Handlebars that have a flat top portion and then curve forward and under back toward the rider are found on track, road, and cyclocross bikes. This style provides a variety of different hand positions, and changing your hand position is crucial on long rides to help maintain blood flow to the hands and prevent numbness. Different positions are also used for different riding styles. For example, riding on the top of the bars is great for long, steady riding. Dropping down to the lower section of the bars provides an excellent aerodynamic position when the rider stays tucked and low, and a great power position when a rider lifts out of the saddle to sprint. Handlebar tape can be made of vinyl, cork, plastic, or other materials. Some types are very thin, others are a bit thicker, and some are even spongy or soft. The bars should be wrapped carefully to ensure a smooth wrap. It improves grip, dampens road vibration, and can provide a bit of cushion to your hands over the miles. The type of tape you use depends on your own preference. If you find that thin tape does not provide enough cushioning, try a thicker variety. Handlebar tape also comes in a wide range of colors that can be matched to your bike's paint theme.

As you might expect at this point, there are many different brands and styles of handlebars. Let's consider the curved style of bars first, as there are several important factors. There are bars designed just for track riding and sprinting, for example, and bars designed for comfort on long endurance rides. Junior riders with smaller hands may want to ask about curved bars with a more shallow curve that will make it easier for them to reach the brake levers. Bars also come in a variety of widths. Typically, bike manufacturers try to use the handlebars that are best suited to the style and size of the bike. However, this is a part of the bike that you may want to consider changing. Discuss this with your salesperson at the bike shop to see if the best fit and riding style for your body type require a change of this sort. Handlebars should not extend out past your shoulders on either side.

Sizing Your Handlebars

Measure your shoulder width when sizing handlebars. Handlebars are measured from outside to outside or from the center of one tube to the center of the other (depending on the manufacturer). The manufacturer usually stamps or marks this measurement in centimeters on the bars. This measurement should be slightly smaller than the width of your shoulders. If you go wider, the bike will be harder to handle. If you go too narrow, it will be hard to produce a lot of power and you will feel pretty cramped and uncomfortable.

For mountain bikers, the choices in handlebars are not as complex as for road racers. There are, of course, different materials to choose from (aluminum, steel, and carbon fiber). But you won't need to worry about this until you are on your second or third bike at least, and by then you'll have a feel for these different materials. Some bars are completely flat, and some have a mild to moderate bend that will raise you up a bit. As with road bars, the most important consideration in mountain bike bars is their width. Unlike road bikes, however, most mountain bike bars don't come in different sizes because the bars can be easily cut down to size. This isn't something you should do by yourself. Ask your local shop to help you out. It will have the proper saw and guide to make sure the bar's strength isn't compromised. And be sure to leave enough room for bar ends if you want to use them.

Brakes Road bike braking systems include the hoods and brake levers placed at the front of the curve on each side of the handlebars, the cables, and the actual front and back brakes. The hoods are covered by a soft rubber sleeve that makes a comfortable resting place for your hands and a good leverage point for squeezing the lever. You should be able to reach and squeeze the brakes both from the hoods and from the drops (the lower part of the bars). On a road bike, you cannot brake when you ride with your hands on the top, flat part of the handlebars.

On most road bikes the left-hand brake pulls a cable and activates the brake on the front wheel, while the right-hand brake does the same for the rear brake. On road bikes, brakes used to be just brakes. But now brake levers also incorporate the gear levers. These are carefully designed so that you won't get the two actions confused. To brake, you pull back on the levers. Gear levers operate in different ways depending on the specific design. However, all of them are very easy to use.

Companies like Shimano offer small levers that can be helpful for smaller hands. Unfortunately, these are usually an upgrade from the brake levers that come on a new bike. Ask your bike dealer if it is possible to switch out parts if you feel the smaller levers would be a good idea for you.

Brake with Caution

Always brake with caution. Squeezing the brakes too fast or too hard can stop the wheels too abruptly, causing you to crash. If your front wheel stops too fast, it will cause the bike's rear end to fly forward, and you will pitch off the front. If your rear wheel stops too fast and locks up, you may skid and lose control. Always ride at a speed you can control, and apply pressure to the brakes carefully.

Your parents may remember an older style of road bike brakes that incorporated both the hood brake levers and a second lever that ran parallel to the top part of the handlebars. Sometimes called a "panic brake," this lever allowed the rider to brake with his or her hands resting on the top of the bars. Unfortunately, this braking system didn't provide much power and could be dangerous. You won't find this system on road bikes made today. Cyclocross bikes, which have brakes like a road bike's, may have a second top brake lever similar to those your parents remember, but it is not designed to stop the bike; instead it helps the rider shave off speed as needed.

There are two common styles of mountain bike brakes. One type works the same way that road bike brakes do. The brake levers are mounted on the bars, and when you pull the lever back toward you, the cable tightens and the brakes squeeze together against the rim. There are side-pull and center-pull brakes. These brakes will stop you, but they require a good squeeze, and their performance can be compromised by mud and grit. The second type is the "disc brake." It uses the same hand-lever system, but instead of pulling together pads on either side of the rim, it has a disc system that uses pressure to squeeze the pads against a rotor mounted on the wheel to provide stopping power. Traditional brakes work fine for most riding. Disc brakes have greater stopping power and cost a good bit more. Which kind is better? It depends on what you need. Traditional brakes cost less and weigh less. Disc brakes cost more and are heavier, but they offer more consistent braking power and handle muddy conditions better.

Brake levers aren't covered on mountain bikes the way they are on road bikes, since a mountain bike rider doesn't rest his or her hands on them the same way that a road rider might. But like newer road bike systems, some mountain bike brake systems incorporate gearshift levers. Pulling the brake levers back toward the bars works the brakes. Pressing the levers down shifts gears.

Track bikes do not have brakes. Because they have a fixed gear without a freewheel, traditional brakes aren't needed. The chain is directly related to the speed of the rear wheel: When you pedal, the wheel turns, and when you stop pedaling, the wheel stops—immediately. To stop safely on a track bike, you must smoothly decrease your pedal cadence.

Gears One of the most intimidating components of a bike is probably the gearing system. Racing bikes commonly have eighteen to thirty gears (except track bikes, which have only one gear). Do you need all of them? Yes and no, depending on where you are racing. You will have plenty of time on your training rides to experiment with the gears.

What do you need to know when you are just starting out? On modern road bikes, the shifters are tucked into the brake levers. On mountain bikes, they're either combined with the brake levers or located nearby on the handlebars. Don't worry, they are designed so that you won't brake when you are trying to shift or shift when you want to brake. It is a very smart design, and you will pick up on how to use it right away. The gears you shift on your left side go with the front derailleur, which is located on the frame down by the front chain rings. The front derailleur is responsible for shifting the front gears. These are the big adjusters. The shifters on the right side activate the rear derailleur, which is located at the very back of your bike frame near the center of the rear wheel. The rear derailleur is responsible for shifting the rear cogs (or gears).

Here's how the gears work. When you pedal, you directly turn the big chain rings in front. Both the front chain rings and the cogs in the back have small metal teeth that catch the chain. This allows the movement of the front chain rings to cause the turning of the rear cogs, which are attached to the rear wheel. The number of teeth involved in the process determines how easy or hard it is for you to turn the pedals. The front and rear derailleurs allow you to move the chain from one chain ring or cog to another and help keep the chain tensioned as it moves. The tension keeps it from slipping off.

There are many different combinations for chain rings. Road and cyclocross bikes often have 2 big chain rings in front and 7 to 10 cogs in the back. Some road bikes come with 3 chain rings in front, which can come in handy on steep climbs. Mountain bikes usually have a 3 and 7 to 10 setup. The number of teeth is used to label the chain rings and cogs. Common front ring sizes on a road bike are 32, 42, 50, and 52, and common sizes on mountain bikes are 24, 34, and 44. These can be changed when damaged or if different combinations are needed. The rear cogset can be a series of separate rings or a fused block of gears. Their count can go from 32 down to 11.

At first this might seem a little backward, but with the rings in the front, the greater the number of teeth, the bigger the ring and the bigger (harder) the gear. In the back set of rings it's just the opposite. Bigger rings (the ones closest to the wheel) are easier to turn. So if you want to be in a super-easy gear, shift to the smallest ring in the front and the biggest cog in the back. And if you want to be in a super-hard gear (to produce, say, a lot of power in a sprint or when going downhill), click to the biggest ring in the front and the smallest in the back. How do you decide which gear combination is best? That is why you train and practice using different gears. And again, don't fret—after a few rides shifting gears will come naturally, and you'll gradually learn which gears to use in different situations through experimentation during your workouts.

Simple Shifting Tips

- Take your time learning how to play with the gears. Experiment riding with different gear combinations so you know what each feels like.
- Avoid "crossing the chain." This occurs when the chain is in the biggest ring in the front and the biggest cog in the rear, or vice versa. This puts a lot of tension on the chain and twists it in a way that can lead to chain slip or even breakage, often at the worst possible moment.
- Try to get into the habit of anticipating when you will need to shift so you can do it smoothly and efficiently. For example, it is much easier and better for your equipment to shift to an easier gear right before you start a steep hill than to wait until you are struggling to climb.
- Whenever possible, reduce the pressure that you apply in pedaling momentarily when shifting gears in a stressful situation. If you are just riding down a steady road, you can shift as needed. But when riding is difficult, as on a steep climb, you are putting a lot of stress on the chain. Trying to shift when there is a lot of tension on the chain will cause it to slip or even snap. And a broken chain can end a race and will mean a messy repair.

There is one more very important gear point for Juniors. UCI and USCF rules regulate what gear combinations and choices young road and track riders can use. We will take a look at current specific regulations later. Basically, what this means is that these organizations have decided that riders under 18 can't use some of the very small rear cogs. These rules have been made to help protect the knee structure of developing bodies. Training on your bike will have positive effects on your growth and development if you train safely. But if you aren't careful, it is possible to push your growing body too hard and damage it in ways that can be permanent. We'll look at a few of the more common issues in Chapter 11 as we examine overuse injuries. You will not be allowed to race if your bike has illegal gearing combinations, so work with your local bike shop to make sure you have the right gear options. Some Juniors train with adult gears and race with the proper Junior gears. This is not the best plan, because it doesn't give you a chance to practice using the gears you'll be racing with. More importantly, gear restrictions were created to help protect developing bodies, particularly knees. Pushing too big a gear too early, before your body is ready for it, may be okay in the short term, but it increases the risk of joint problems in the long run. Some Juniors are afraid that if they don't ride Senior gears, they won't be able to keep up or race successfully. But keep in mind that all European Juniors train and race on restricted gears, and they can often still keep up with Seniors riding adult gears without any problem.

Bottom Bracket and Cranks The bottom bracket and cranks allow the movement of your legs—the physical energy of your muscles—to be translated into mechanical energy in the bike to propel you forward. The bottom bracket is a self-contained, sealed piece that is set into the bottom of your frame. Its ball bearings allow for smooth movement when you push the pedals and push the crank arms. Remember, those front chain rings are a part of this as well, so turning the cranks turns them. You used to have to do a lot of maintenance to keep a bottom bracket working smoothly, and old-timers will talk about cleaning and repacking bearings every off-season. Bottom brackets no longer require much maintenance, but you do have to make sure that they are secure.

The crank arms are set 180 degrees apart and are attached to the bottom bracket. This offset allows you to continually put power into the drivetrain and keep the bike moving forward. The longer the lever (or crank arm) and the more power you can put into the drivetrain, the faster you can go. In theory this works great. However, we have to take into account the size of the rider when determining the length of the crank arms. Too long and you will struggle to turn them smoothly and lose power. Too short and you will underuse your power ability. Common crank lengths are 165, 170, 172.5, and 175 millimeters. Most bikes come with a crank arm that is proportional to the size of the bike, so you don't need to worry about this much. However, if you have an unusually short or long inseam (the measurement of your inner leg), you may want to talk to the person who does your bike fit about what size crank arm is best for you.

Wheels

In addition to a modest gruppo, your bike should have sturdy training wheels. No, not the kind of training wheels a child uses for balance when first learning to ride, but sturdy, durable wheels for everyday riding and training that are built to last. Eventually, you will invest in lighter, more flexible racing wheels as well. Racing wheels are more susceptible to wear and tear than the ones you'll be using for everyday training. They are more expensive, and they in fact are not necessary for beginning racers. While you are still developing your bike-handling skills, it is best for your training wheels to double as racing wheels. Your local shop will be able to help you pick out sturdy wheels for training.

A high-end set of racing wheels can cost several hundred dollars or more and will need more maintenance than training wheels to remain safe and reliable. A ton of really fascinating science goes into wheel building, and wheel builders are very smart engineers. High-end racing wheels are often made out of composite materials that are selected for their strength and low weight. They may have a traditional pattern of spokes, or they may have as few as three large, flat blades that function as spokes. In any case, the spokes are the key to the wheel maintaining its round shape. They are under a lot of tension because they are screwed into the rim and the hub (center of the wheel). It is very important that this tension be properly maintained so the wheel stays both true (round) and "in dish" (doesn't wobble from side to side). Learning how to properly maintain spoke tension, particularly in high-quality wheels, takes time, practice, and patience. Enlist a mechanic or wheel builder to teach you, or take a class in wheel building before you attempt to maintain your own wheels.

Wheels come in different sizes that are suitable for different purposes. Road, track, and cyclocross bikes come standard with 700c wheels, which are roughly 27 inches in diameter. Smaller road frames may require smaller (650) wheels. Using smaller wheels with a smaller frame will help keep the bike properly proportioned. This can be an important consideration for someone who needs a smaller frame. Using the smaller 650 wheels has some minor drawbacks, however. Usually no one else in the group will have a tube to fit this size wheel, so you will have to be well stocked on your own. And when racing, the support vehicles may not always have replacement 650 wheels handy. Still, if you have to decide between a bike that doesn't fit well and a bike with 650 wheels that does fit, the choice should be clear: Pick the 650 wheels! Mountain bikes, both downhill and trail (cross-country), use a different-size wheel. The 26-inch wheel used to be the standard size for these bikes, but recently a newcomer, the 29-inch wheel, has been gaining a foothold in the market. Because a 29-inch wheel is bigger, it rolls over obstacles easier (of course, it is also heavier, so there is a trade-off). The BMX wheel is much smaller at 20 inches.

Be sure to note the type of tube that your new bike tire will take. Some of the tube valve stems will look like those on a car tire (a round rim with a pin in the center). This is called a Schrader valve. Higher-end road bikes and mountain bikes generally use Presta valves. These valves are tall and thin with a little top piece that spins open and closed. A tire with a standard Schrader valve can be filled at any gas station air pump, but this isn't a good idea. It is very easy to put too much air in too quickly and pop the tube. Presta valves require a special pump. Bike shops have pumps that can be used with both Presta and Schrader valves. They range from larger floor models that will pump up a tire quickly to smaller, more portable versions that can be attached to your bike or carried in your saddlebag or pocket. Some pumps even use small CO_2 cartridges instead of a hand-pumping action to allow for really fast, easy tire fill-up. Plan how you'll handle flats, practice your plan in advance, and take the right supplies with you when you ride so you won't get stranded.

Keep track of tire pressure and add air as needed. You should check the tire pressure before every ride to help prevent flats and ensure a safe, comfortable ride. Your tires have a recommended pressure written in psi (pounds per square inch) on their sidewalls, along with a maximum pressure, which you obviously must not exceed. Make sure the tires have at least the minimum recommended tire pressure. Road riders usually find that they benefit from keeping tire pressure high. Mountain bikers will play with pressure a little more to help improve trail traction. Lower pressures allow the tire to flatten out slightly so that more tread grips the dirt. A tire with high pressure is very hard and allows for only a small part of the tire to touch the ground, which means less friction with the ground (so physics matters, too). Less friction is good when you want to go fast; more friction is good when you want to stay upright on tricky terrain. As you ride the trails, experiment with tire pressure so you can determine what type of pressure gives you a good balance between traction and speed.

The Saddle and Seatpost

The saddle is an important contributor to your comfort level while riding, especially on long training rides, and you shouldn't necessarily just take the one that happens to come with the bike you select. A bicycle seat is rarely, if ever, described as cushy or comfy; however, it shouldn't be a device of pain or torture either. Saddles are made of different materials that range in softness or firmness, from plastic and leather to gel, foam, and spandex. They also come in different widths; as with shoes, finding the best fit is important. Narrow saddles are often more comfortable for individuals with narrow hips, and wider saddles are often more comfortable for individuals with wider hips. Extremely soft saddles make it difficult to produce optimal power while riding. However, given the number of hours you're going to spend seated on your saddle, it's worth taking the time to choose a racing saddle that is as comfortable as possible while still allowing for a powerful pedal stroke.

For proper saddle fit, the sit bones (ischial tuberosities, or the bony part on either side of the butt) should rest on the saddle, relieving the pressure on the soft tissue between. An improperly fitted saddle can lead to saddle sores (chafing wounds) or even genital numbness and related problems. Manufacturers have done a tremendous job of addressing these issues for both male and female riders with the creation of a wide range of products designed to fit different sizes of individuals, with cutouts, channels, and depressions anatomically designed to reduce problems. Companies like Terry, Serfas, Selle San Marco, Selle Italia, and Specialized are good places to start when looking for an ergonomic saddle.

Once the saddle is securely attached to the seatpost, you'll slide the seatpost into the seat tube of the bike frame and secure it with a bolt or quick-release. As noted earlier, you can mark the saddle height with electrical tape or a permanent marker for easy future reference. Seatposts come in a variety of diameters and lengths. Different seatposts will fit different frame tube sizes, so check for size compatibility before getting a new one. Make sure you know how far your seatpost can be raised, and don't go beyond this. The seatpost will have a mark etched into it at that point, and extending the post beyond that mark could cause it to snap off for lack of proper support.

In a bag mounted under the saddle, you can keep basic tools and supplies for simple repairs like fixing a flat. For training, the bike should be equipped with a tool bag big enough for a tube, patch kit, tire lever, Allen (hex) wrench, some money, a mini-pump or CO_2 cartridge, and a piece of paper with identification, medical insurance information, and names and numbers of people to contact in an emergency.

Pedals, Cleats, and Shoes

Traditional around-town bikes and kids' bikes have flat platform pedals, which work well for casual riding but aren't ideal for competitive riding. The vast majority of cyclists now use the "clipless" system, which is somewhat of a misnomer, since your shoes are still clipped to the pedal. The reason for the name is that the system represents a change from the older style of pedal prevalent in the 1980s, which had a toe cage (called a "clip") and a strap system to cinch your foot into the pedal. Clipless pedals involve a cleat mounted on the bottom of a cycling-specific shoe that clips into a pedal of matching design. To release, the athlete simply turns his or her foot to "unclip." By keeping the foot in contact with the pedal for the duration of the pedal stroke, the cyclist benefits from both pushing the pedal down and pulling it up. Using the correct type of pedal and cleat helps maintain good knee health. The chosen system should allow a good degree of float (side-to-side foot movement before the foot disengages) so that the knee can move freely as you pedal. A reputable shop can explain the pros and cons of the many styles currently on the market.

For many reasons, regular sneakers or athletic shoes make poor cycling shoes, and the cleat necessary for the clipless system cannot be properly mounted onto a traditional sport shoe. Sport shoes are too wide in the front for cycling, the heel is too built up, and there is too much cushioning. The biggest problem with a sport shoe is the soft and flexible sole. It flexes when you pedal, which causes you to lose pedal power. Cycling-specific shoes have reinforced plates in the sole just under the ball of the foot where the cleat is attached. They are narrow, more fitted, and much stiffer than traditional shoes to allow for better contact and greater pedaling power. A shoe should be loose enough so that your feet or toes do not lose circulation or fall asleep, but snug enough so that your foot and heel cannot slip. As with other athletic shoes, cycling shoes vary in terms of style, price, and fit. Try on several different styles before choosing the type you like best.

In addition, there are different styles of shoes for different styles of racing. The shoes in the system favored by track and road cyclists have a smooth, stiff sole, and the cleat is mounted in a way that forces the wearer to walk as if in reverse high heels (toes raised by the cleat). In mountain biking and cyclocross the shoes have a more rugged sole, similar to a hiking boot, to allow good traction when the rider is off the bike. Both of these forms of racing can be on rugged terrain that sometimes force the athlete to jump off the bike, pick it up, and run for a few steps. The favored riders' cleat is therefore recessed up into the sole so it will not interfere with walking and running. The cleat and pedal to fit each of these different shoe styles vary accordingly.

Any road shoe can work with any road pedal system, and the same is true of mountain bike shoes and mountain bike pedal systems. The only difference is in the style of cleat attached to the shoe's sole.

COCKPIT ACCESSORIES

Just like airplanes and automobiles, bicycles now have a cockpit. This is the term now used for the few inches of free space in the center of the handlebars, where athletes can mount all types of electronic measuring devices for power, heart rate, speed, and other data. While a developmental rider may not need all the most advanced technology, he or she will certainly benefit from a basic computer that monitors time, speed, and distance. This is a good place to start to help keep track of workouts. The small receiver and display unit is mounted on the handlebars on a base that is connected by wire (or wirelessly) to a sensor on the bike. A small magnet mounted on the wheel sends a signal every time it passes the sensor that allows the receiver to calculate and display important ride information. Some of these units include a cadence meter, which counts the number of pedal strokes per minute. This is a worthwhile addition to the basic computer because it provides athletes with valuable information about leg turnover rate, an important component for creating power.

Quality training can absolutely be accomplished without any more bells and whistles. But if your budget allows for them, some of the other items can be great training tools for the young athlete, particularly when he or she is guided by a good coach.

The next cockpit tool to consider after the bike computer is probably the heart rate monitor. These devices typically can be worn on the wrist or mounted in the cockpit; they get their signal wirelessly from a monitor worn around the athlete's chest. Some monitors are so elaborate that they combine all the basic computer functions mentioned above. Others provide heart rate only. A heart rate monitor can help you better relate the physical response of your body to your level of perceived effort. Off the bike, a heart rate monitor can be used to monitor recovery heart rate.

Power meters are one of the most recent training tool innovations. Like many heart rate monitors, power meter systems often combine basic computing functions with their raison d'être, and many include heart rate monitoring as well. Power may be measured in a variety of ways, and the receiving device may be placed in the bottom bracket, on the rear wheel hub, or somewhere else, depending on the model. A power meter is definitely an investment and can cost as much as a quality frame, and may be an unnecessary luxury for a young rider. While a power meter does provide a wealth of feedback during and after a ride, this sort of information is far more useful to a coach in retrospective analysis than it is during the ride itself or to someone who does not understand how to use the information it supplies. A developmental athlete should learn basic training skills and understand his or her individual response to training before considering the use of a power meter. Anyone who is interested in using a power meter for optimum training should see the book *Training and Racing with a Power Meter,* by Hunter Allen and Andrew Coggan, for useful tips.

Other Accessories

A few other key items should be installed on your bike for safe and healthy riding. To stay hydrated while racing and training, be sure to outfit the bike with two water bottle cages, if possible (some smaller frames will allow for only one). Traditional reflectors on the wheel or in the spokes are not recommended for racing bikes, as they can cause problems with wheel balance. However, a reflective light below the seat definitely makes you more visible on the road. A white light on the handlebars is a good idea if you will ever be training or riding at or after dusk. Some communities require reflectors and lights on any bicycle that is ridden on the road, so be sure to check your local laws.

THE HELMET

Next to your bike, your helmet is by far the most important piece of gear you own as a cyclist. It is crucial that your helmet meet approved safety standards, that it fits you properly, and that you keep it in good shape. Even if you are a very safe rider, accidents can happen. A pothole can throw you off balance, wet leaves can cause your back tire to slide out, or an unaware motorist may turn in front of you, causing you to stop short. All of these situations could lead to you hitting your head on a tree or the ground. Even a mild bump on the head can be a serious concern.

Your head is sort of like an egg. You have a hard shell (your skull) surrounding the fragile yolk (your brain). Even if you don't hit the egg hard enough to crack the shell, you can scramble the yolk just by shaking the egg hard enough. Like a yolk, our brains move around inside our heads, and a sudden impact can cause the brain to slam up against the inside of your skull. This can cause bruising or a concussion that ranges from mild to life-threatening. Even mild concussions have been linked to memory problems and learning difficulties. A serious crash can cause long-term brain damage. Every year cyclists die needlessly because they never thought they would crash so they didn't wear a helmet. A bike helmet is made specifically to absorb the impact if you get knocked off your bike or crash and hit your head.

Wear a helmet designed specifically for riding a bicycle. This may sound obvious, but there are many types of helmets available—football helmets are okay for football, but not for cycling. The first thing to look for when buying a bicycle helmet is the certification of approval from the American National Standards Institute (ANSI) and/or Snell (the Snell Memorial Foundation has been independently testing bicycle helmets for safety since 1957). These organizations use a wide variety of methods to examine how well a helmet will protect your head if you fall. Typically, if a helmet meets one standard, it will meet the other.

Helmet Safety Standards: Organizations and Websites

American National Standards Institute (ANSI): http://www.ansi.org
Snell Memorial Foundation: http://www.smf.org
Bicycle Helmet Safety Institute: http://www.helmets.org

Your local bike shop will have helmets ranging from $35 to more than $100. You might be able to find one at a yard sale or that someone is selling, but it's worth a few extra bucks to spring for a new helmet. When you buy a new helmet, you not only know that it meets the safety standards (although it's always a good idea to check to be sure), but also that it hasn't been exposed to any damage. So why the big differences in price? More expensive helmets are often lighter than the less expensive ones, and more science will have gone into making sure the helmet is aerodynamic and allows good airflow. Though the more expensive helmet may be cooler, and for an elite cyclist may actually allow small gains in speed, the higher price tag doesn't mean more protection. So don't worry if you start out with a less expensive helmet. The less aerodynamic design won't

have an effect on your speed at this stage of your training, and your head
will be well protected so long as your helmet meets the standards.

Good Helmet Fit

Employees at your local bike shop should have the training to properly
fit your new helmet. Take the time to go over proper fit with them. The
right-size helmet will fit comfortably on your head without a lot of wiggle room. Foam pads that come with the helmet can help you customize
your fit; most attach with Velcro and come in different thicknesses so
you can choose the ones that work best for your head size. The helmet
shouldn't feel tight, shouldn't feel like it's going to pop off your head, and
shouldn't feel like it's just sitting on the top of your head instead of set-
tling down snugly.

Most helmets on the market today have a retainer system that cradles
the back of your head. Adjust this so that the helmet sits properly with the
front edge of the helmet just above your eyebrows. You don't want the helmet to tip back on your head because this leaves your nose and forehead
vulnerable. Now you are ready to adjust the straps. Even if the helmet
seems to fit well without doing up the straps, don't be tempted to cut
them off or leave them loose. In a crash situation, the straps are crucial
for keeping the helmet in place. On each side, the front and back straps
should meet and form a nice little triangle just below the ear. From there
the straps will meet and buckle under your chin. There should be room
for only one or two fingers to slide between the strap and your jaw. With
wear and sweat, the strap can stretch out and move out of position. A
loose helmet will slide in a crash and will not protect you as it should, so
you must recheck your helmet fit at the start of each ride.

Caring for Your Helmet Properly

Because helmets are designed to be light, they don't last forever. Depending on how much you ride and how careful you are with your helmet, a
good helmet will last one or two seasons at the most. Inspect it regularly
for wear and tear, and replace it if it develops any cracks or other visible
damage. Replace it after any crash or other impact, even if there is no
visible damage. A helmet is designed to deflect impact away from the

skull, and any compromise to its structure may decrease its effectiveness in the next crash. If you have any doubts, your local shop should be able to help you properly inspect your helmet for damage. Here's a list of dos and don'ts:

- Don't leave your helmet out in the sun. Over time the sun's rays will break down the plastics, making the helmet less effective in a crash.
- Never leave your helmet in direct sunlight in a car window or in a hot car. The heat will damage the materials.
- Pack your helmet inside your gear bag so it doesn't bang around in the car or when you are moving your riding gear. Remember, the helmet is designed to absorb impact. It can't tell the difference between being smacked against the ground when you drop your gear bag at the car and crashing against a road surface while protecting your head in a fall. Consider buying a helmet carrying case if you travel with your helmet a lot.
- Avoid putting your helmet on the hood or roof of your car. Helmets have a nasty way of rolling off, and again, they are taking an impact even if they aren't protecting you at the moment.
- Rinse the straps and pads frequently. Not only is it really gross (and smelly) to have old sweat build up in the pads, but your sweat will add to the wear and tear.
- Never ride with your helmet dangling off your bars or wrapped around your bike stem. Your helmet will bang against the bike, taking unnecessary impact. Plus, if you crash, your helmet will not be able to protect you, and your handlebars wouldn't benefit anyway!

Helmet Safety

Helmets are a mandatory piece of gear for racing, yet following the example set by many pros, young athletes often prefer to train without helmets or with the straps dangling loose or even unclipped under their chin. A poorly fitted or unbuckled helmet is the same as wearing no helmet at all. Most cycling accidents occur when an athlete is fatigued or distracted; in many cases, however, the accident is not the cyclist's fault. A properly fitted helmet goes a long way toward diminishing the potential damage from a collision or fall. Coaches and parents should encourage, or better yet, insist, that any time their young athlete is on the bike, he or she is wearing a helmet properly. Today, helmets are light, aerodynamic, and very comfortable. Since helmets are required in all races, riders should be accustomed to wearing them each and every time they mount the bike.

Also get in the habit of looking at your helmet before each ride. Here are some key ways to examine it:

- Look over the shell. Make sure there are no visible cracks or un-tapped edges.
- Turn your helmet over and inspect the inside. There should be no cracks or dents in the foam.
- Gently hold each side of your helmet and flex it slightly to look for any cracks or movement that shouldn't be there.

Handling Sticker Shock

If your bike-shopping experience has led to sticker shock, you are not alone. But there are some ways to minimize the costs over the long haul. Keep these tips in mind:

- If you invest in good components and then grow out of the bike you've been riding, consider only buying a new frame next time around. The parts or components can easily be moved from one frame to another the next size up.
- Parents can ease their wallet pains by networking with other parents of Junior riders. It may be possible to purchase a great bike that another rider has barely used during a growth spurt.
- Talk to the staff at bike shops about trade-in programs. You may be able to trade in your bike like a used car to receive a discount on your next purchase.
- Shop at bike swaps. In some towns and cities, these are an annual event. Ask at your favorite bike shop to find out what's scheduled in your area.
- Before buying any used equipment, especially a frame or full bike, you may want to have it carefully inspected for safety by a qualified mechanic, as racing bikes have a limited racing life.

- Hold your helmet up to the sunlight or some other strong light to look for weak or thin spots.

THE WELL-DRESSED RIDER

While not as crucial as a well-fitted, properly certified helmet, the "kit," or outfit a cyclist wears, is also an important consideration. To the non-rider, the racing and training kits look a little odd, especially compared with the uniforms of other sports. However, the fabrics of a cycling kit are designed to wick moisture away from the skin, which reduces chafing and helps riders better regulate body temperature (stay cooler in warm weather and warmer in cool weather). The close fit also reduces wind drag due to flapping fabric.

It is not absolutely necessary that athletes wear cycling-specific kits for training (although there are specific clothing requirements for races). A cyclist should take care not to wear loose clothes such as sweat pants, however, which can get caught up in the chain. Clothing made of cotton does not work well for riding, as it holds moisture, making it heavy and leaving the cyclist uncomfortable and vulnerable to catching a chill.

Important pieces in the devo athlete's kit include a comfortable synthetic or wool jersey with rear pockets for carrying food during rides, at least two pairs of cycling-specific shorts with a comfortable chamois (so one pair can be washed while the other is being worn—never wear a dirty chamois), a waterproof jacket, a long-sleeved jersey to wear alone or under a short-sleeved jersey, and tights or leggings. The chamois inside of cycling shorts provides some padding, but more importantly it pulls moisture away from the body, which helps reduce chafing and risk of infection. Most chamois are made out of synthetic materials and have been given antimicrobial treatments to further reduce problems.

Selecting a Good Pair of Shorts

For someone new to riding, those little black shorts can seem awfully tight and tiny. It's a little intimidating to put on something that can feel so revealing. And many first-time cycling shorts wearers say they feel like they are wearing a diaper. Cycling shorts do have somewhat bulky padding between the legs. This padding is called the chamois and provides some seat cushioning, but more importantly it absorbs sweat and moisture and helps reduce chafing and infection.

When you first try on shorts, you may find them uncomfortable. This makes sense because the shorts were designed to be worn when you are bent forward at the waist and sitting on a bike saddle, not when you are standing around a dressing room. Once you get past the funky fashion statement, how do you decide which shorts are right for you? Are the more expensive pairs really worth all that money? Considering all the time you plan to spend in the saddle, spend as much as you can afford on two or three pairs of quality shorts (so you can rotate without doing laundry daily). Use these tips to spot quality:

1. Ask the shop employees what they wear. They may have tried many different brands and can tell you what they prefer and why.
2. Look for shorts that have antimicrobial-treated chamois. This will fight bacteria and odor buildup.
3. Find shorts that are constructed out of more panels of fabric. These will fit more comfortably. High-quality shorts are often made out of eight separate pieces of material sewn together to provide a really custom fit.
4. Consider how long the legs are. Some shorts have very long legs and others have an inseam that is only a few inches long. Shorts

---

Beginner's Tip

This may sound a little weird, but cycling shorts are designed to be worn without underwear. You keep your undershorts on when you try on the shorts at the store, just as you do when trying on a swimsuit, but once you buy them, wear them solo. In addition to causing an unsightly panty line, wearing underwear with your shorts will increase problems with chafing because the form-fitting cycling shorts will cause your underwear to bunch up and rub. If you haven't ever chafed before, it isn't something to look forward to. It is very uncomfortable, especially on long rides, and it can lead to open sores or an infection, both of which can force you off the bike.

that come down to mid-thigh or a bit longer will wear better as you ride, won't ride up, and will do a better job of reducing friction between your legs and the sides of the saddle.

Other Gear

Beyond the traditional kit, a well-prepared rider wears gloves to protect hands and glasses to protect eyes from bugs and debris. There are many styles of gloves, both short- and long-fingered. Leather or synthetic leather palms will protect your hands if you fall and will keep your hands comfortable on long rides. Glasses don't need to be fancy or expensive, but they should provide UV protection and cover your eyes well. Cycling glasses wrap around and provide both front and side protection. Glasses are even more important for individuals who wear contacts, because they protect eyes from bugs and from drying out from the air, either of which can cause contacts to become dislodged or to fall out.

Wearing sunscreen for protection from sun damage is also crucial, given the large amount of time you will spend training. Sensitive areas like the nose, forehead, neck, ears, and even the top of your head (through the helmet vents) are particularly susceptible to sunburn, and sunscreen can help prevent skin cancer from developing over time. Choose a sunscreen labeled SPF 15 or above, that is water-resistant (so that your sweat does not reduce its effectiveness), and that blocks both UVA and UVB light (the types that block both may be labeled as providing "all-day protection" or as a "broad spectrum sunblock"). Keep in mind that even sport or waterproof/sweatproof sunscreens may need to be reapplied in order to remain effective. Read the product label carefully. And when using sunscreen, don't forget your lips. Sunburned lips are uncomfortable and are prone to cracking.

CARING FOR YOUR GEAR

Your new high-tech clothes are designed to move sweat away from your body, to keep you cool in the summer and warm in the winter, and in some cases to keep down the stink. Clothes that work so hard need special care. Here are ways to help you improve the lifespan of your expensive kit.

Ready to go shopping?

Make a list of the equipment you need to start racing. Here's a list of the basics to get you going, but you may want to add other things that you've seen in the bike shop or heard about elsewhere:

- Bike that fits properly, has passed a safety inspection, and is suited to your racing discipline, with room for at least one water bottle cage
- Helmet with ANSI or Snell approval that is in good shape
- Bike shorts
- Racing jersey
- Good sports bra (for the female cyclist)
- Cycling gloves
- Sunglasses
- Cycling shoes (and pedals if bike doesn't come with them)
- Bicycle pump, spare tube, patch kit, and simple Allen key set
- Saddlebag (optional, but a nice place to store your tools for the ride)
- Lock (A racing bike is an investment, so leaving it outside is not a good idea. If you must leave it outside or if you have to leave it somewhere, even momentarily, when you are at a race, a quality lock is a must. Some people even lock their bikes inside if they are in an apartment or dorm room. Keep in mind that your bike probably has quick-release wheels and may have a quick-release on the seatpost. This means that these parts can be removed and stolen even if your frame is locked to something. A high-quality U-lock, like those made by Kryptonite, and a cable to run through the wheels will allow you to lock the frame and wheels securely.)

1. This first tip is really more about good hygiene: Always change out of your ride kit as soon as possible after you finish training. Right away. The shorts are super-comfy, but sitting around in damp spandex is not healthy.

2. Once you take those shorts off, don't just wad them up in the hamper (or on the floor). Turn them inside-out and hang them somewhere to dry if you aren't able to wash them right away.

3. Wear shorts only once before you wash them. When you work out and sweat, the clothes absorb the sweat. And that sweat contains

salt and body oils. Even if you don't think putting on clothes full of dried sweat is gross, you'll probably find that it is uncomfortable because the shorts will be stiff. It can also lead to infections and saddle sores (we'll talk about those more in Chapter 11). Over time these salts and oils will break down the materials of your riding gear. Washing your kit between wearings will prolong the life of your shorts.

4. Other riding clothing is also made of high-tech fabrics. Be sure to follow all washing instructions carefully. Some may need to be washed by hand; others may require cold water or gentle cycles.

5. Use a mild detergent specially made for hardworking workout gear, such as Win Detergent (see www.windetergent.com). These detergents are designed to help get odors out (and they can get potent!), and they prolong the life of your kit.

A NEW BIKE!

There is nothing quite as exciting as a beautiful new bike! As a teenager, I saved for months for my first racing bike, a beautiful celeste-green Bianchi (that is the company's signature color). I was so proud of it that I cleaned it with tissues and Q-tips after every ride. The following steps should help you pick out a good-quality bike that will serve you well.

Step 1 Plan on visiting at least two or three bike shops and taking a couple of weeks to think about your choice. On your first visit, just poke around, look at prices, and collect a few catalogs. This will give you a chance to read about the "specs," or details of the different bikes. Most companies make a wide range of models, from entry-level bikes that are moderately priced to very expensive models. Look at available sizes, the material of the frames, and the components. Specs can be found on the website of each bike manufacturer, too.

Step 2 Pick out several models by different companies that fit your budget and then contact a few bike shops to set up some test rides.

It's best to check first, because shops may not have the size you need, though they can often get it in a short amount of time.

Step 3 When you visit the bike shops, be prepared to test-ride. Make sure you are wearing comfortable riding clothes. You wouldn't race in jeans, so you shouldn't wear them to test-ride either. The shop should give you a loaner helmet and will put on pedals that you can use. If you have cycling shoes, bring them along, but sneakers will be fine if that is all you have right now. If possible, try to do more than a few small laps in a parking lot. Just as shoes fit differently, different bikes ride differently. Don't be afraid to take your time as you decide.

Step 4 Before you make your final decision, talk to the folks at the shop. Do they have a service policy? Will they offer you a discount on accessories? Is this a shop that you feel comfortable in and that you feel will be able to help with future cycling-related needs? If another shop three blocks away seems to provide better service or is really the hub of the cycling community, you should seriously consider purchasing your bike there so that you can begin to develop that connection. And this is a pretty big purchase, so don't let anyone rush you.

Step 5 Once you have decided what you need, talk to your parents and ask them to help you create a budget. How much can you afford to spend on a bike? How much will you need for a helmet and other accessories?

Caring for Your New Bike

Once you have your new bike, you don't need to go to extremes to take care of it like I did. But there are a few things you should do when you purchase a bike to start protecting your investment:

1. Before you leave the store, ask your salesperson to show you how to remove the wheels and open the brakes (and put them back together). This will help you fit your bike in the car and will be important to know when you have to fix your first flat (of course, you'll practice fixing a flat before you go for a long ride!).

2. Record your bike's serial number on your receipt. Ask the salesperson to show you where it is. Often the store will record the serial number in its computer system in case you ever need it, but it's a good idea to have it on file at home as well.

3. Once you get home, put your owner's manual, receipt, and any other important paperwork into a file where you can find it later.

4. Take a few pictures of your new bike and store them in a safe place in case your bike is ever damaged or stolen.

5. Your parents may want to consider using the photos and receipt to record your bike with their homeowner's insurance information in case of a problem.

6. Learn how to properly clean your bike and perform simple maintenance, and find out how often you should do these things.

7. Take your new bike back into the shop after one or two weeks of riding for a bit of maintenance. The cables of a new bike will stretch and settle in after the first few rides, and minor adjustments are often necessary. Skipping this step will hurt the performance of your new bike and can increase wear and tear.

8. Until you learn how to do a major overhaul and deep cleaning, be sure to take your bike in at least once a year for a professional tune-up from a mechanic.

Once you have the equipment necessary to ride, it's time for you to learn how to ride safely and how to train effectively. In the coming chapters, we'll explore these matters as well as how to develop your talent and use your mental skills, how to handle your bike, how to protect yourself from injuries, how to choose a coach, and how to get started with racing. Hope you enjoy the ride.

3 A PRIMER on
U.S. Bicycle Racing

Riding the velodrome, BMX, cyclocross, road, or mountain bike can all be ways
to keep things fresh and enhance a rider's skills in his or her primary discipline.
—Benjamin Sharp, USAC Cycling Junior Development Director

Maybe you have recently fallen in love with the sport of cycling, but you haven't yet decided what discipline you would like to pursue. Should you go with road racing or mountain biking? Maybe cyclocross appeals to you, or you're wondering what BMX is all about. How to decide? In this chapter, we'll provide a primer on racing in each of the main cycling categories to help you determine what direction to go. Even if you already know which cycling discipline you would like to pursue, it's a good idea to know how your specialty fits into the big picture.

In addition, as a Junior or Espoir cyclist, you may want to try out a number of these disciplines and experiment a bit to see what appeals to you most. As you train in each of these categories, your all-around strengths as a cyclist will increase, and you will learn more about where your natural talents and interests lie. You can also enter one type of race, such as road races, in the spring and summer, and another type, such as cyclocross, in the off-season. Besides, there is plenty of time for specialization later; now is a good time to explore options.

You also need to know where to go to find out what the rules are for the races you will be entering. The international sport of cycling is governed by the Union Cycliste Internationale, or UCI. This organization sets up the rules and regulations for bicycle racing at the international level and organizes, for example, the World Championships. The UCI also influences national rules and regulations for the sport in participating countries around the world. Cycling programs in the United States follow the UCI rules closely. For information about UCI rules and races, consult the organization's website at www.uci.ch.

In the United States, the national governing body (NGB) for cycling is USA Cycling (USAC). USAC is sanctioned by the U.S. Olympic Committee and is in charge of U.S. teams sent to events such as the Pan Am Games and the Olympics. Additionally, USAC runs athlete development programs and coaching education, and oversees competitions in the main disciplines of cycling competition in the United States. Each style is led by a different branch of USA Cycling. Unless otherwise noted, in this book we describe only the U.S. model of racing. As you will see in the discussion of each racing category in this chapter, even at the local level it is these large governing bodies that ultimately dictate the rules of the road (or track, trail, or course) in racing. For a listing of the racing categories, see Table 3.1. For a summary of the disciplines, see Table 3.2.

TABLE 3.1 Race Categories

	Road & Cyclocross		Track		Mountain Bike—Cross-Country		Mountain Bike—Gravity Events	
	Men	Women	Men	Women	Men	Women	Men	Women
Pro	1	1	1	1	Pro	Pro	Pro	Pro
	2	2	2	2	Expert	Expert	Expert	Expert
	3	3	3	3	Sport	Sport	Sport	Sport
	4	4	4	4	Beginner	Beginner	Beginner	Beginner
Beginner	5		5					

ROAD RACING EVENTS

All U.S. road racing events are run by USA Cycling (formerly the U.S. Cycling Federation (USCF)). Road racing involves any event where a road racing–style bike is used. Some of the more common road-based events are road racing, circuit races, criterium races, and time trials. Racers can enter these races individually or as members of teams. The road season typically begins in mid-spring and runs through the end of

TABLE 3.2 Race Disciplines in U.S. Cycling

Road Riding

Event	Type of Bike	Event Distance/ Time	Type of Course	Skills Needed	Season	Spectator-Friendly?
Road race (RR)	Road bike	20+ miles	Paved roads	Pack riding Endurance Bike handling Climbing	March–August (depending on climate)	No, only at the start and finish
Time trial (TT)	Road bike	3–26 miles	Paved roads	Endurance Pacing Being aerodynamic	March–August (depending on climate)	No, courses are typically out and back, so spectators see only the start and finish
Circuit	Road bike	20+ miles	Paved roads	Pack riding Endurance Bike handling Climbing	March–August (depending on climate)	Yes and no. More than an RR because riders do multiple laps on a course; spectators see start, finish, and a few points in between
Criterium (Crit)	Road bike	30–60 minutes	City streets or industrial parks	Endurance Speed Cornering Pack handling Tactics	March–August (depending on climate)	Yes

Mountain Bike—Cross-Country Events

Event	Type of Bike	Event Distance/ Time	Type of Course	Skills Needed	Season	Spectator-Friendly?
Cross-country (XC)	Mountain bike	1–2.5 hours	Trails, fire roads, etc.	Off-road handling skills Endurance Pacing	April–September (depending on climate)	No, spectators typically see racers only at start and finish and maybe a few more times if it is a lap course
Marathon (XXC) (not recommended for Junior or new Espoir riders)	Mountain bike	30–60 miles and 3–10 hours	Trails, fire roads, etc.	Off-road handling skills Endurance Pacing	April–September (depending on climate)	No, only at start and finish
Short track (ST)	Mountain bike	30–45 minutes	Dirt courses in open field areas	Pack riding Cornering Speed Tactics	April–September (depending on climate)	Yes

(continues)

TABLE 3.2 (continued)

Mountain Bike—Gravity Events

Event	Type of Bike	Event Distance/ Time	Type of Course	Skills Needed	Season	Spectator-Friendly?
Downhill (DH)	Downhill bike	5–10 minutes	Downhill single or double track on ski hill	Bike handling	April–September (depending on climate)	Yes
Dual slalom	Downhill bike	1–2 minutes	Similar to dual slalom skiing, shorter	Bike handling	April–September (depending on climate)	Yes
4 Cross	Downhill bike	1 minute or less	Similar to a BMX course with more drop in elevation	Bike handling	April–September (depending on climate)	Yes

Cyclocross

Event	Type of Bike	Event Distance/ Time	Type of Course	Skills Needed	Season	Spectator-Friendly?
Cyclocross	Cyclocross bike or mountain bike	30 minutes– 1 hour	Dirt, roads, trails, fields, often around a park or school	Bike handling on varied terrain Quick mounts and dismounts Carrying bike while overcoming obstacles	September–December (depending on climate)	Yes

Track—Sprint Events

Event	Type of Bike	Event Distance/ Time	Type of Course	Skills Needed	Season	Spectator-Friendly?
Olympic sprint	Track bike	1 minute+	Velodrome	Sprinting	March–August (depending on climate)	Yes

Event	Type of Bike	Event Distance/Time	Type of Course	Skills Needed	Season	Spectator-Friendly?
Kilo	Track bike	1 minute+	Velodrome	Sprinting	March–August (depending on climate)	Yes
Match sprint	Track bike	1–3 minutes	Velodrome	Sprinting	March–August (depending on climate)	Yes
Keirin	Track bike	3 minutes	Velodrome	Sprinting	March–August (depending on climate)	Yes

Track—Endurance Events

Event	Type of Bike	Event Distance/Time	Type of Course	Skills Needed	Season	Spectator-Friendly?
Individual pursuit	Track bike	3 or 4 kilometers and 3+ minutes	Velodrome	Endurance	March–August (depending on climate)	Yes
Team pursuit	Track bike	4 kilometers and 4+ minutes	Velodrome	Endurance	March–August (depending on climate)	Yes
Scratch race	Track bike	Varies	Velodrome	Endurance	March–August (depending on climate)	Yes
Points race	Track bike	Varies	Velodrome	Endurance	March–August (depending on climate)	Yes
Miss and out	Track bike	Varies	Velodrome	Endurance	March–August (depending on climate)	Yes
Madison	Track bike	Varies	Velodrome	Endurance	March–August (depending on climate)	Yes

summer, although variations occur based on the seasonal climate opportunities or constraints in different regions of the country.

Road Races

Road races are typically mass-start races held on country roads. Depending on the age and level of participants, the distance may vary
from 20 to 100 miles. Road races are often held on a large loop course
or go from point to point. Groups of athletes work together in a pack
to maximize group efficiency using drafting techniques, and team
members help one another as much as possible. Throughout the race,
riders attempt to break away from the pack to reduce the number of
riders in the lead group. The first rider across the finish line is the
winner.

Circuit Races

Circuit races are mass-start races similar to road races, except they are
commonly held on a repeating loop course of 3 to 7 miles in length. Racers may ride 20 to 100 miles on the loop course depending on racer age
and ability. Circuit races are very similar to road races, and the first rider
across the line is the winner.

Criteriums

Criteriums are shorter, more speed-based, mass-start races that are
often very exciting to watch. They are held on a closed, short course
of roughly 1 mile in length that typically has multiple turns as it goes
around several blocks in a downtown area. Depending on the age and
skill level of the participants, the event may be 20 minutes to 1.5 hours
long. Racers must be prepared for a high-intensity race with repeated
sprint-level efforts and turns in tight pack situations. The event therefore requires excellent bike-handling skills. Periodically throughout
the event, mid-race sprints called *primes* (pronounced "preems") are
offered as incentives to shake up the race. Any rider who falls off the
back of the racing pack and is in danger of getting overtaken by the
racers (lapped), or who may create a dangerous situation on the course,

will be pulled from the event by race officials, which means that his or her race is over. The race is won by the first rider to cross the line on the final lap, although riders can also pick up prizes for winning the race primes.

Time Trials

Time trials are solo start events where a single rider (in an individual time trial [ITT] or time trial [TT]) or a single team of riders (in a team time trial [TTT]) works to clock the best time possible compared with other riders or teams on a given course. The length and nature of the course can vary and may be flat, rolling, or uphill. Time trials can be as short as a few miles or as long as 40 kilometers (about 24 miles).

Racing at USA Cycling–sanctioned road events requires a racing license. The license classifies individuals by category based on experience and ability. Racers can improve their category ranking by earning top finishing spots in qualifying races. Male riders begin at category 5 (more commonly known as "cat 5"); the female ranking system starts at cat 4. Qualifying races must meet size and length specifications that are set by the USA Cycling rulebook, which is available on the organization's website at www.usacycling.org. (Click on the discipline you are interested in—road, mountain bike, cyclocross, track, or BMX—to find the appropriate rulebook.) Athletes wishing to race in the United States may obtain a license through USA Cycling. U.S. citizens who want to race internationally are required by international rules to purchase a UCI racing license and obtain a letter of permission to race in the countries on the racing itinerary from USA Cycling.

MOUNTAIN BIKE RACING

Mountain bike racing is a relatively new phenomenon. It came on the scene shortly after the development of mountain bikes in the early 1980s. Several different styles of racing now exist for the off-road enthusiast.

The types of mountain bike races that are sanctioned by the mountain bike division of USA Cycling include both cross-country (XC) and downhill events.

Cross-Country

The cross-country mountain bike event (XC) is a closed-circuit mass-start race on forest and field trails and over rocks and roots on a single or double track. A typical race lasts from about 1 to 2.5 hours, depending on the category or level of the race. The distance may vary from 10 to 25 miles. Racers need endurance, power, and the ability to navigate roots, rocks, and trails successfully.

In addition to the cross-country event, mountain bikers occasionally compete in time trials (TT) and short track (ST) races. Mountain bike TTs are always individual events and may be done on a flat to uphill course. They are typically part of a series of events that make up a full weekend of racing. The mountain bike ST is a type of dirt criterium. Like a road criterium, it has a mass start on a short, fast course with lots of corners. It is very spectator-friendly. Unlike its road cousin, the short track in mountain biking is done on a dirt or trail course. This short, intense event (usually only 30 minutes long) is run on a course shorter than a mile in length, which means the lead riders quickly catch the tail (or back) of the pack. To keep the event safe, race officials pull racers who fall off the back out of the race. This event is held primarily for semipro- and pro-level riders at national events, although some race promoters may run short track races for other categories.

The cross-country marathon is a newer discipline. The marathon is a mass-start race very similar to the XC race but may go for a distance of 37 to 60 miles (60–100 kilometers) and last for 4 to 6 hours. There is also a series of even longer events, the 100-mile mountain bike races. These events, such as the Shenandoah 100, Vail 100, and Leadville 100, are not part of the traditional USA Cycling agenda but are gaining in popularity. Obviously, the ability to develop endurance and pacing is the key here. But bike-handling skills are also important. Due to the distance and stress of the cross-country marathon, Juniors should not compete in these events. Espoirs should participate only if they have at least several years of consistent training behind them, and only after careful consideration. Training for these events may compromise the ability of young riders to compete in the races they should be doing if they want to take their racing to the next level of competition.

Downhill

Downhill mountain bike racing has expanded to include both solo timed competition and head-to-head downhill competition. Downhill races take place on steep and challenging courses, often on a ski hill, and require great technique. There are four main disciplines in the downhill category: downhill events, dual slalom, mountain cross, and Super D.

Downhill, probably the oldest event in the downhill racing category, is a gravity-based event against the clock where riders seek to be the fastest down the mountain. Downhill courses may include single tracks, fire roads, jumps, and banked corners. Riders need to have good nerves, excellent handling skills, and the ability to ride on the edge. Dual slalom is similar to regular downhill except that instead of a solo run, it involves two competitors racing against each other and advancing through heats to the final event. It is similar to slalom events in downhill skiing. Mountain cross, also called "4 cross," is a four-person event on a fast downhill course that has jumps and banked corners. This event is typically on a course that is much shorter than those used in downhill and dual slalom events and is very spectator-friendly. The exact length of a course depends on the ski hill chosen for the event.

Like road racing, mountain bike races typically occur in the spring, summer, and early fall. Racers must apply for a license from USAC, and both men and women start out in the beginner category. By earning points based on finish places, they may advance to the sport, expert, and pro categories.

CYCLOCROSS

Cyclocross is a fast, intense style of racing developed in the 1950s to help road racers stay in shape during the off-season. It has grown into a sport in its own right with both national and international championship events. Cyclocross, or CX, racers use bikes similar in appearance to road bikes on closed 1.5- to 3-mile lap courses that take them over grassy fields, sand, mud, dirt paths, and the like.

CX bikes are more rugged than road bikes but have a similar frame style. They sport slightly wider tires with more aggressive tread, higher bottom brackets, and stronger brakes to allow for the variety of terrains encountered. A 'cross bike uses 700c wheels and combines the durability of a mountain bike with the agility and speed of a road bike. Racers can use a mountain bike, provided it meets the rulebook guidelines, although at higher levels of competition this would be a competitive disadvantage. The mass-start race typically lasts 30 minutes to 1 hour depending on age and level. The intensity of the race and the nature of the course make cyclocross more of a solo effort than most road-racing events. Man-made barriers, such as small hurdles made from wooden planks, are often strategically placed around the course to force riders to dismount and carry their bikes as they navigate the obstacle before remounting. Likewise, courses incorporate natural obstacles (such as small, steep hills) and different types of terrain that test the racers' bike-handling skills. Individuals can race 'cross using a USAC or USCF racing license and category designation. Because the sport began as the off-season playground for roadies, the season typically begins in mid-fall and runs through autumn or mid-winter.

TRACK

Track cycling is the equivalent of the sprint section of a track-and-field team. In comparison with road racing, track events are shorter and require greater amounts of power. Track riders tend to be stronger and more powerful than their road counterparts. Track races take place on velodromes, specialized tracks used exclusively for this purpose.

Velodromes in the United States

Velodromes were once common, but with the advent of the automobile and the paving of America, many velodromes disappeared. Fortunately, excellent tracks still exist in numerous cities. Since almost all are outdoor tracks, they are open only as weather permits.

Because of the specialized rules of the track, velodrome facilities typically have programs to introduce new riders to the rules and requirements of track riding. Most also have a stable of track bikes available for rent. All you need to bring are your riding kit, helmet, pedals, and shoes. Most tracks charge a small fee for track time, and all of these facilities require a parent's or guardian's signature for those under 18. Some facilities have designated Junior clubs.

Home Depot ADT Events Center, Carson, California
Encino Velodrome, Encino, California
San Diego Velodrome, San Diego, California
Hellyer Park Velodrome, San Jose, California
United States Olympic Committee 7-11 Velodrome, Colorado Springs, Colorado
Brian Piccolo Velodrome, Cooper City, Florida
Dick Lane Velodrome, Atlanta, Georgia
Ed Rudolph Northbrook Velodrome, Northbook, Illinois
Major Taylor Velodrome, Indianapolis, Indiana
Baton Rouge Velodrome, St. Francisville, Louisiana
Mike Walden Velodrome, Rochester Hills, Michigan
National Sports Center Velodrome, Blaine, Minnesota
Kissena Velodrome, New York, New York
Alpenrose Velodrome, Portland, Oregon
Lehigh Valley Velodrome (aka Trexlertown), Trexlertown, Pennsylvania
The Superdrome, Frisco, Texas
Alkek Velodrome, Houston, Texas
Marymoor Velodrome, Redmond, Washington
Kenosha Velodrome, Kenosha, Wisconsin

Track racers use bikes that seem, at first glance, similar to road bikes, but in fact are highly specialized. A track bike has a more aggressive racing geometry to allow for better handling on velodrome tracks.

Track bikes do not have brakes, as they are chain driven by a single gear. Riders speed up and slow down according to their pedal rate, and gear components are often switched during the course of a race evening. The gearing may change between the warm-up and the event, for example, or even between events, to give a rider more power. It is to the track racer's advantage to become strong enough to turn the pedals fast using a high gear.

Velodromes typically have two 180-degree turns with two slightly longer straights. Most tracks are 333.3 meters around, although they can range from 133 to 500 meters. The velodrome has high, banked sides that allow riders to safely carry speed through the corners. Most have smooth wood or concrete surfaces; some are indoors, but many are outside.

Because of the brakeless bikes and the high speeds, there are strict safety and etiquette rules that riders need to learn and live by in order to race safely on a track. Most tracks provide excellent beginner training, and many even have track bikes that can be rented for practice.

Track cycling provides the widest range of events of all the cycling disciplines. Trackies typically compete in multiple events during each racing day. These events can be broken down into two main categories: sprints and endurance events.

The Sprints

Olympic Sprint   An Olympic sprint requires two teams of three riders each. Teams line up on opposite sides of the track, and on the gun they take off riding single file. After the first lap, the front rider, having done his or her job, pulls off the front, leaving riders two and three to continue chasing the tail of the other team. After the second lap, the new leader peels off, leaving the third and final rider to try to finish the final lap before the third rider on the opposing team crosses his or her line.

Kilo, or 1,000-Meter Time Trial   The kilo is an individual event where the rider races against the clock in an effort to cover 1,000 meters as fast as possible. The rider with the fastest time wins.

Match Sprint The match sprint is similar to the kilo race except that instead of racing against the clock, two to four riders race each other. The final 200-meter leg of this 1,000-meter or 1-kilometer event is timed, and the first rider across the line wins. This event is usually run in heats, requiring athletes to have enough endurance for multiple race efforts.

Keirin The Keirin, a popular style of racing in Japan, puts two riders on the track behind a single motorbike for five to eight laps, depending on the length of the track. The motorbike brings the riders up to high speed before exiting the track and leaving the riders to sprint for the finish with 600 to 700 meters left.

Endurance Events

Endurance events on the track are not the same as road or mountain bike endurance events. The name in this case simply sets them apart from sprint events on the track. Track endurance riders need power and speed, but also need to build muscular endurance and a strong engine (heart and lungs). And, like all track riders, endurance riders need to have great track-handling skills.

Individual Pursuit The individual pursuit is the endurance counterpart to the individual kilo. It is performed by two individuals, who start on opposite sides of the track and race against each other and the clock. The distance is up to 3,000 meters for women and Junior riders and up to 4,000 meters for the elite men. The race continues until one rider catches the other or one rider covers the entire distance, whichever comes first.

Team Pursuit The team pursuit involves two teams of four riders. Just as in the individual pursuit, in this event the teams start on opposite sides of the track. On the gun, teams ride single file in a rotating pace-line in an attempt to either catch the other team or complete the 4,000 meters first. Three of the four original team members must cross the line for an official finish.

Scratch Race In a scratch race, also known as a mass-start race, all riders start together and ride a set distance, typically 15 kilometers for elite men at World Championships, and shorter distances for Juniors. The object is to be the first person across the line. Typically, teams work together to improve the chances of a single rider doing well.

Points Race A points race is similar to a scratch race, where all riders start together to cover a set distance, which may range from 25 to 40 kilometers. However, points are awarded for top placing across the line at various points throughout the race. An athlete can therefore earn enough points during the event to win even if he or she is not the first person across the line after the final lap.

Miss and Out Another variation on the scratch or points race theme, the miss and out is a mass-start race. It begins like a regular scratch race, but at each lap the last rider across the line gets pulled. The field dwindles until only a few are left to fight it out for the final sprint.

Madison In the Madison, an exciting style of racing originating at Madison Square Garden during its bike-racing heyday, teams of riders set up in relay style with one member of each team on the track. After one or two laps, teammates exchange, using a handsling motion that requires the incoming teammate and outgoing teammate to link arms so the new rider can be slung onto the track with as much speed as possible. Early Madison races were sometimes hours long as part of a larger event referred to as "the six-day event." The modern Madison is 50 to 60 kilometers in length and lasts 30 to 60 minutes.

Racing on the track requires a racing license similar in format to the road racing license, with categories from beginner (cat 5) through professional (cat 1). The USCF oversees track licenses and the associated upgrade points for race results. Individual track upgrade points are collected only from track racing and do not transfer from road race results.

BMX/TRIALS

The newest of the internationally recognized cycling disciplines, BMX will be represented for the first time at the 2008 Beijing Olympics. Similar in format to the motorized version (motocross), BMX pits multiple competitors against each other on circuit courses of roughly 350 meters in length, so the race is incredibly short. Riders must negotiate banked turns, berms, jumps, and other obstacles to win or place high enough to go on to the next round, until finally a single winner emerges. Riders wear protective padding and race on BMX bikes with 20- or 24-inch wheels. Racing licenses are issued by the American Bicycle Association and the National Bicycle League.

SPECIAL GROUPS: JUNIOR AND ESPOIR RIDERS

In cycling, as in any other endurance sport, years of well-planned training go into a successful racing career. To help athletes develop properly and to provide opportunities for fair competition, age-based racing is often provided. Racers under 18 years of age are considered "Juniors." This group may be broken down into several subcategories, depending on the size of the event and the promoter's objectives in holding the race. Typically, the subcategories are divided into two-year segments (for example, 12–13, 14–15, 16–17). An athlete's racing age (at any level) is considered to be his or her age as of December 31 for the current year.

For male cyclists, and in some disciplines for female cyclists, young riders from the ages of 18 to 22 are still considered to be developmental. Riders in this Under 23 (or "U-23") category are commonly known as "Espoir" riders. *Espoir* is a French word meaning "hope." This grouping gives young riders, who often lack the depth of experience that Senior riders have, an opportunity to race with other developmental riders and to learn the skills needed at the more elite Senior level.

Junior- and Espoir-level racers are also allowed to race in the Senior ability-based groupings (such as cat 4 or cat 3), but it is important to be aware that some of the rules for Juniors, such as gear restrictions, apply even for racing outside of Junior events. Chapter 15 will provide more

Junior Racing Series and Opportunities

Lance Armstrong Junior Olympic Race Series (LAJORS): A series of road racing events around the country with age-based categories. Race directors who would like their race to be part of the LAJORS series must offer specific Junior events and register the event with LAJORS. The series includes road races and criteriums. These races give Junior riders an opportunity to earn a spot in one of the USAC Junior development camps. A current list of LAJORS-designated events and information on USAC devo camps can be found on the USAC website.

Alison Dunlap Junior Olympic Mountain Bike Series (ADJOMBS): A series of cross-country mountain bike racing events around the country with age-based categories. Race directors who would like their race to be part of the ADJOMBS series must offer specific Junior events and register their event with ADJOMBS. These races give Junior riders an opportunity to earn a spot in one of the USAC Junior development camps. A current list of ADJOMBS-designated events and information on USAC devo camps can be found on the USAC website.

U.S. National Road Festival: An annual festival that includes road races, criteriums, and time trials for Junior and Espoir riders. Racers can earn national titles in their age group. The festival is held in the summer, although the exact time and location change yearly. Visit the USAC website for current information.

NORBA Nationals: National championship races for Junior and Espoir riders in cross-country events. Racers can earn national titles in their age group. This event is held in the summer, and the exact time and location change yearly. Visit the USAC website for current information.

Junior Track Nationals: An annual event that includes track races for Junior and Espoir riders. Racers can earn national titles in their age group. It is held in the summer, and the exact time and location change yearly. Visit the USAC website for current information.

Tour de l'Abitibi International: The only UCI Junior stage race in North America. Since 1969, the Tour de l'Abitibi has been held in mid- to late July in L'Abitibi, Canada, each year. Teams from all over the world participate. Like Senior stage races, the Tour de l'Abitibi consists of ten stages over six days. Events include individual time trials, team time trials, and road races ranging from 80 to 100 kilometers in length. Visit www.tourabitibi.qc.ca for more information.

details on important race and rule differences for the developing Junior cyclist.

SIGNING UP TO RACE

In the past, finding the right races to enter could be a daunting task. A young cyclist would have to simply talk with other cyclists in his or her area and read the cycling magazines faithfully to figure out how to enter the sport. Now, however, with the use of the Internet, finding races is as easy as surfing the Web and the websites of the main cycling organizations. And signing up for the races is just as easy. Still, you will have to do some research to figure out which races to enter, and talking to local cyclists remains a great place to start. Some events allow for on-site registration, but others do not, so be sure to do your homework before you drive to a race.

Current Olympic Cycling Events

Road
Road race (men and women)
Individual time trial (men and women)

Mountain Bike
Cross-country (XC) (men and women)

Track
Keirin (men)
Madison (men)
Team pursuit (men)
Olympic sprint (men and women)
Points race (men and women)
Individual pursuit (men and women)
Individual sprint (men and women)

BMX (new for the 2008 Beijing Games)
Individual (men and women)

Since BMX and track racing can take place only at specially designed venues, racing in these disciplines requires finding a location near you. Most venues of this nature have programs to help new riders get involved.

For road, mountain bike, and cyclocross, events may be sanctioned by USA Cycling or held independently by a small grassroots or local organization. USA Cycling events typically require all racers to have an annual or one-day license. Smaller organizations may require a membership fee or a race fee. Races of all kinds are typically advertised on the Internet, in bike shops, or in bike magazines, and often registration services are provided on the sponsor's website. Large races may fill up almost instantly as soon as race registration opens. Smaller races and Junior fields may allow for same-day sign-up.

Race organizers will require you to fill out and sign an entry form that must be submitted along with your entry fee. If you are under 18, your race entry form must also be signed by a parent or guardian. Races may cost anywhere from $10 to $50, depending on the size of the event. Many races have reduced entry fees for Junior riders, so be sure to ask.

RECOMMENDED READING AND RESOURCES

The USA Cycling website (www.usacycling.org) provides a wealth of information. This should be your first stop on the Web when you are looking for the following: racing calendars and information; racing rules and regulation handbooks; information about Junior and Espoir grants, programs, and camps; coaching resources; license purchase and renewal forms; athlete rankings; and championship events.

Other Cycling Organizations:

American Bicycle Association (ABA), www.ababmx.com
International Mountain Bike Association (IMBA), www.imba.com
National Bicycle League (NBL), www.nbl.org
Union Cycliste Internationale (UCI), www.uci.ch

4 TALENT
Development

In the winters, I spent hours on the trainer in my basement as the Pennsylvania snows covered the roadways. In the summers, I cut billions of grass blades around the neighborhood to scrape up enough gas money for races.

—Jim Camut, Johan Bruyneel Cycling Academy

What is talent, and how do you know when you have it? Is it something you are simply born with? Or is it something that can be developed? And just how much talent is needed in the sport of cycling? Fortunately for young cyclists, sport scientists and elite coaches have spent a great deal of time studying these questions, and they have found some interesting answers that can help you succeed. While there is no exact formula for developing talent, you can follow guidelines to achieve your best based on what these experts have discovered. In this chapter we will explore talent and the role that parents, coaches, and athletes can play in its development.

Typically in our society, talent is viewed as an exceptional ability to perform a skill well or at a level higher than average. Many people expect talent to be evident immediately. According to this "either you have it or you don't" mentality, if someone's first painting isn't a masterpiece, then it would be pointless for that person to pursue an interest in art. She has no "talent," and so art is a waste of time for her. This example is ridiculous when you start to think about it—after all, such a pessimistic view of talent leaves no room for the wonderfully human capacity we all have to learn, persevere, and grow. This mindset is nevertheless prevalent in our culture, and particularly in sports.

Athletes and parents often expect talent to be immediately evident in the first races of the first season of competition. But talent is not an all-or-nothing deal. Instead it is something that can develop through a process, and that process involves hard work, trial and error, and learning.

For the young athlete, even one who does well initially, the true nature of individual talent will take years to surface. More goes into success than physical gifts alone. Other chapters will explore how physical growth and development, nutrition, and other factors all contribute to performance and being a total athlete. For now, let's focus on the idea of talent development, learning how to make the most of one's gifts.

THE NATURE OF TALENT

Talent rarely just happens. And in the world of sport, talent means nothing if the athlete is not properly trained, personally dedicated, and supported by key people in his or her life. In short, talent cannot be developed unless it is valued by society and the individual and has a place to grow.

You've heard the saying "It takes a village to raise a child." The same goes for the young athlete and talent development. "Society" (or "the village") can be as large as our cultural collective ideals or as small as the local cycling community. If the local bike shop and team value Junior and Espoir rider development and provide an opportunity for talent to grow, then both can become keys to fostering it. Talent needs to be recognized and nurtured, no matter how little presents itself initially. Even the slightest seed of talent, which may present itself just as an interest in cycling, has the potential to blossom. The individual with talent has to have a mature personality (or at least be in the process of developing one) and a strong sense of intrinsic desire. Later in this chapter, you will see how the appropriate developmental stages can ensure that internal motivation and maturity have a chance to grow. And ultimately, a caring adult plays an important role in talent development. In the best-case scenario, a talented young cyclist will be supported unconditionally by one or both parents and will have a knowledgeable, supportive coach.

Just what does it take to excel in cycling? Randy Wilber, PhD, head exercise physiologist at the U.S. Olympic Committee, frequently reminds athletes in his talks about peak performance to "choose their parents well." Obviously, this is not really an option, but he makes an important point. Genetics plays an important role in athletic ability. Each individual has a unique genetic code that determines lots of things, from eye color to potential for height and the prevalence of certain types of muscle fibers. Some of these things matter more than others in sport performance. However, talent research has found that genetic ability alone is not enough to ensure elite sport achievement. We all know very gifted athletes who never seem to reach anywhere near their potential. And even elite athletes often acknowledge that initially they were not the strongest, fastest, or most gifted on the track, field, or court. So if physical attributes aren't enough to maximize talent, what else matters?

Can talent be measured in the lab?

Exercise physiology and human performance labs can conduct all sorts of tests to determine what "athlete qualities" an individual might have. These tests might be simple, like skin-fold caliper testing to determine body fat measurements and vertical jump tests to estimate muscle fiber type. Other tests are more involved, like on-bike stress testing to determine VO_2max, blood draws, and muscle biopsies (muscle core samples) to look at muscle fiber type in depth. All of these tests provide snapshots of what an athlete's body might be capable of, but they aren't crystal balls. A high VO_2max and lots of Type II (sprint) muscle fibers might help someone do well in a sport, but they are just two of the dozens of factors that come together to create a successful athlete. These include other genetic factors, but also include how we train, eat, sleep, recover, and balance our days. They include things outside of our control as well, such as good luck. Because of the complexity of the talent equation, testing to determine talent potential not only is a waste of money, it will not provide an accurate answer. Some testing can be used to help guide training efforts, but no long-term predictions should be based on them, and no emphasis should be placed on the results.

It turns out that there are many things, in addition to genetic ability and training, that contribute to athletic success. Researchers in both Canada and the United States have found that a wide range of factors help an athlete to maximize his or her innate talent—from parental involvement to coaching style, mindset, and mental skills. Studies have found that successful athletes are not perfect in each area, but do tend to be average or above average in most areas, and they tend to actively seek to become better in most of them as well.

Skills of Successful Athletes

Physical skills: Endurance, strength, stamina, speed, power

Sport intelligence: Understanding the ins and outs of the sport, having good tactical and technical knowledge

Skill automaticity: Being able to perform skills well without having to think about them

Focus: Being able to maintain a sense of concentration on the right things in competition and training

Hope: Having a positive outlook that things will go well

High optimism: Seeing the glass as half full, seeing things as challenging and as opportunities

Mental toughness: Being able to bounce back from frustration and work through tough times

Adapted perfectionism: A healthy focus on doing the best you can and striving to be the best you can, but understanding that no one is perfect all the time

Intrinsic motivation: Being driven from within by personal enjoyment, self-pride, and a sense of satisfaction

Goal-setting ability: Being able to set healthy, supportive process, performance, and outcome-based goals

Emotional control: Understanding how to handle frustration, anxiety, excitement, and other emotions in a positive and constructive way to support performance

Competitiveness: An enjoyment of the process of competition, not just the outcome, enjoying the competitive atmosphere

Confidence: Having a healthy sense of confidence based in an understanding of and belief in one's abilities

Coping ability: Having the skills and resources to handle stress, competition, training, and problems

High drive: A strong personal quest to do your best and reach for lofty goals

Determination: A sense of stick-to-itiveness to pursue goals and face challenges head-on

EXPLORING THE IMPORTANT SKILLS

Physical skill (partly determined by genetics), and the proper, systematic, healthy training of those skills, are important but not enough for peak performance. Let's run through the important skill areas that have been identified in elite sport achievers.

Elite athletes frequently discuss the importance of being "students of their sport" for achievement. This means that the athlete understands the key elements of training, the role of the mind in performance, racing tactics and the technical aspects of their sport, and the equipment he or she uses as part of the sport. This knowledge is built over years and through active learning (through reading, talking to other athletes, and listening to coaches, as well as through plenty of experience). Athletes do not necessarily have to be experts; they don't even need to possess enough knowledge to be able to coach others. But they do need to understand enough about the elements of training, and about what the coach and other experts are telling them, to make good athletic decisions and choices. Through well-designed training, these athletes develop skill automaticity as well. They learn the skill and requirements of their sport well through intentional training and practice so that in competition they can execute the skills without thinking about them. For example, a road cyclist might practice choosing lines for safe and fast cornering during specific training sessions and regular rides so that picking the best line is second nature when racing. Or a mountain biker might practice fixing flat tires quickly so that in competition he or she can get back into the race as soon as possible after getting a flat.

Hope and optimism are skills that help athletes think in a forward and positive manner about what is to come. An optimistic athlete looks for opportunities and sees challenges to work toward. A pessimistic athlete, in contrast, tends to view things as problems and feel hopeless, focusing on what can't be done or whatever is frustrating in a situation. This negative mindset makes it hard for an athlete to do the work necessary to overcome the obstacle. Let's consider an example. Kevin and Todd both get a flat tire in a race. Kevin has a more optimistic attitude and approaches the flat with the mindset that this is an opportunity to see how quickly he can fix it and get back into the race. He immediately hops off his bike and begins his repair, focusing on what he needs to do to get back in the race. Todd, who has a more pessimistic attitude, immediately begins to dwell on how much the flat has slowed him down. He thinks about how unfair it is that he got it, concludes that he has no chance of a good finish, and has other discouraging thoughts. None of these thoughts help him to focus on fixing the flat. Kevin is much more likely than Todd to fix the flat quickly and well, and he will get back in the race sooner and make the most of it.

An athlete also needs "mental toughness" and "adapted perfectionism" to succeed. These terms may sound a bit clinical, like something you'd hear in a psychology class. Luckily they both have very nonclinical definitions that most athletes can easily relate to. Mental toughness is the ability to bounce back from frustration and mistakes and to keep positive and focused on the future. Athletes who are mentally tough don't let the routine, day-to-day stuff get them down. When a problem comes up, they figure out how to handle it. In many ways it is similar to optimism. And most importantly, it is something that can be modeled, taught, fostered, and developed in athletes.

Adapted perfectionism simply means striving for excellence in a healthy way. "Perfectionism" sets an impossible standard. Perfection is very hard to reach in sports, and even when it is achieved, it only lasts for a moment. Its elusive nature can be frustrating and disheartening and can lead to very negative responses. *Adapted* perfectionism, on the other hand, is about the quest to be the best you can be with an eye on what is realistic given your circumstances and resources. People with a healthy sense of adapted perfectionism still have high expectations for themselves, but their expectations are grounded in reality. This allows them to focus more on the quest to improve and develop and less on the outcome (a perfect moment in time). Like mental toughness, adapted perfectionism is a skill that can be modeled, taught, fostered, and developed over time.

Mental skills like focus, goal setting, confidence, coping skills, competitiveness, determination, high drive, and intrinsic motivation are all important elements in achievement. Many athletes are familiar with these terms, as they are talked about casually in the sports world. While some people naturally use these skills better than others do, everyone can benefit from working on improving them. Chapter 10 will explore how these skills can specifically impact cycling performance and how athletes can work on these skills.

THE STAGES OF TALENT DEVELOPMENT

Some people show an early interest or strength in athletics, others in academics, art, musical ability, or some other endeavor. But if everyone has gifts and strengths—talents—then why are some so successful while others are not? Why does talent develop in some, while in others an early sign of talent seems to go unfulfilled? Talent development in young people may seem hit or miss, like being in the right place at the right time. While there is no formula or surefire way to maximize talent, researchers have been working hard to better understand more about the process.

One of the most respected researchers in the study of talent, Benjamin Bloom, breaks talent development into three distinct phases—the early years, the developmental years, and the elite years—and describes how to foster talent at each stage. His basic scheme has been utilized in

Bloom's Stages of Talent Development

Early or Beginning phase
Developmental phase
Elite phase

many studies of sport talent, proving to be a sound model for successful talent development and the development of key skill areas.

In the early phase, sometimes also called the "romance years," or the "beginning phase," it is important for young people to be exposed to many kinds of activities. They should have opportunities to engage in a wide range of movement and skill experiences as well as cognitive and mental experiences. This is particularly important for young athletes because their motor skills are still developing. It also allows the athlete to build a strong knowledge base. During this time there may be some structure, but the emphasis should be on enjoyment of the activity.

While it is never too early to start participating in sport, there is definitely a time that is too early to "train." Younger athletes (pre-puberty) should be allowed to enjoy the "play" aspect of participation without adult or higher-level sport rules and regimens being imposed upon them. The development of a personal sense of enjoyment is crucial for the development of "intrinsic motivation" (the internal sense of pride, personal satisfaction, and enjoyment crucial for long-term participation) and the longevity of sport participation at all levels, from lifetime recreational athletics through elite competition. It is not appropriate for an athlete at this stage to ride or participate like an adult. And in cycling, it is especially important that athletes at this stage not take on the challenges or distances of the experienced cyclist.

What does all this mean for young cyclists? Some athletes do not discover cycling until they have already participated in other sports and experienced a general sport romance phase. However, they should still be allowed a romance period when they first discover cycling. It is a time when they are developing a love for a sport that is new to them, and they should have time to do this without the stress of structure or the pressure to achieve. The teenage cyclist who is given this luxury has a chance to develop a personal connection with the sport and a sense of satisfaction that is based on his or her participation in the activity, not the outcomes alone. Persistent performance efforts are much more likely to follow, and talent can be realized for the long term, when this romance period with cycling is permitted.

There are no set rules or guidelines about how long this initial phase might last. That is best determined by the individual participant, his or her interest level, and his or her maturity level. It is important for parents and coaches to recognize that one 10-year-old child may be ready for the next step while another may not. Movement from one phase of talent development to the next is not necessarily age dependent. And if the transition to more advanced levels is driven by the desires of an adult, it does not bode well for continued enjoyment or efforts by the athlete. It must be the cyclist alone who is interested and motivated enough to pursue the sport at more competitive, structured levels. To put it more bluntly, a parent or other adult should never push a youth into racing; however, that is not to say that if the youth expresses interest, is personally motivated to begin racing, and seems ready physically and emotionally, the adult should not support and encourage that interest. (See Chapter 13 on parenting the young athlete to learn more about how to provide support and encouragement.)

Individuals who have enjoyed their participation during the romance phase often move on to the developmental years, the years when an athlete learns to train. While this phase of talent development does mark a step up in terms of organized structure and level of participation, it is important that the emphasis remain on development and fun. The "fun" of the developmental stage is not necessarily the "fun" of a younger athlete, however. Instead, "fun" begins to encompass the enjoyment of personal success and an understanding of self-satisfaction derived from setting and reaching personal goals. The emphasis should be on personal progress; specific outcomes, such as winning, are a nice side benefit, but not the main focus. In a study of talented teenagers, researcher Mihaly Csikszentmihalyi found that overemphasis on outcome and lack of personal investment were key reasons that individuals identified as talented chose not to pursue or further develop their talents.

The developmental years provide more specialized opportunities, usually in the form of more knowledgeable instructors with an increased emphasis on organized and personalized training, as the individual moves forward through the stage. Competition is definitely a part of this phase, but it is not the main emphasis. It is crucial that athletes learn how to train properly and that the emphasis is on training to train more (development, not outcome) during this phase. Even older athletes who enter a developmental stage in a new area later than their peers, or after deciding to switch talent-development areas—for example, switching from soccer to cycling—should be provided with the foundation skills of training for the new sport. It should never be assumed that the foundational elements are in place. Further, cycling is a sport where a deep and well-laid physical foundation of training is crucial for proper development and injury avoidance.

As in the previous stage, the amount of time spent in the developmental years will be dependent on the individual and his or her interest and maturity level. Many young athletes are lost at this stage due to programs that overemphasize outcome or that impose elite training mindsets or models before their time. But it is important to recognize that many more athletes stop participating during this phase simply because they develop other interests and discover new opportunities as they get older. For example, teenage athletes often "retire" during their developmental years once they get driver's licenses, begin dating, or begin to enjoy the financial power that comes with having an after-school job. If an athlete makes a decision to leave or back away during this phase, his or her wishes should be respected. Sometimes these athletes will return, especially if their initial experience with the sport was positive.

A successful transition from the developmental to the elite years is dependent on a solid foundation in fun and personal enjoyment from the early years and on a healthy understanding of how to train and continued personal enjoyment in the developmental years. The elite years are marked by a shift in the emphasis of participation. Personal development and enjoyment are still key elements and remain crucial to continued participation. However, outcome—or winning—also begins to play an important role. The local competition experiences of the developmental level will shift to a higher level, more competitive opportunities. If the early and developmental years provided the proper foundation, the emphasis on winning will be well supported. This provides the best-case scenario for successful talent development and continued efforts at the highest levels of participation.

THE ROLE OF PARENTS IN TALENT DEVELOPMENT

As might be expected, parents can play a central role in the development of their child's talent. No matter what else is going on, however, it is important for parents to remember that the talent belongs to the athlete. Across all stages of talent development, unconditional love and support from a trusted and respected adult, usually a parent, are crucial to the young athlete. This love and support need to be independent of the young person's participation or the outcome of competition. In speaking with the media, successful athletes frequently highlight the value of this support and its importance in their lives, and this is a frequent finding in sport performance research as well. Parents should strive, above all else, to provide this kind of nurturing environment for their young athlete throughout their child's athletic career, and they should make sure that their child gets the message that he or she is loved unconditionally.

Parents can encourage the development of talent in many other ways as well. In the early years of sport participation, parents should provide their children with as many opportunities as possible to engage in a variety of activities. They need to make sure that the emphasis of the programs is on fun and exploration, not on outcome. When their athlete is ready to move to the developmental phase, it is the parents' responsibility to find a proper coach and developmental environment. Typically, as the athlete moves forward into more competitive participation and the elite years, parents' role becomes less central and more supportive; however, they can still help their child balance the three key elements of their sport participation—fun, development, and performance.

Parents can also help their child develop the key skills identified in successful achievers. These skills can be taught directly or indirectly through fostering positive behaviors and modeling them. Key concepts and ideas that parents of successful people emphasize include the value of hard work and effort, discipline, high standards of behavior, a sense of personal responsibility for one's actions, and an expectation of follow-through. For example, parents can teach good sportsmanship by discussing why it is important and clearly explaining what it means, and by being good sports themselves. Unfortunately, the best spoken lessons will be undermined by poor examples. This does not mean you have to be a perfect parent, but when your actions don't match your words, it is important to acknowledge this and to indicate that you are working hard to do better. The message "do as I say, not as I do" rarely carries much weight with young people.

Beyond direct child-parent interaction, other aspects of the family environment also can have a positive impact on talent development. This environment may include siblings, grandparents, extended family, and close family friends. A supportive family environment that encourages hard work and discipline, a positive approach to problems, good communication, and unconditional support can all help foster achievement. Moreover, an active lifestyle where adults model positive behaviors and a healthy emphasis on personal effort and achievement provide a good foundation for talent development.

Whenever possible, parents of developing athletes should provide exposure to higher levels of sport. This exposure allows the athlete to be inspired by what lies ahead. Take your athlete to watch racers compete at a level just above where they are in their own development, or stick around to watch the pro riders warm up and race after the Juniors event. Look outside cycling for opportunities as well. Attend college events and look for other ways to expose your young athlete to positive athletic role models. If possible, encourage your local bike shop or club to invite successful athletes to lead a Juniors ride or speak at a club dinner. Interaction with elite-level performers helps young athletes realize that hard work in a sport can produce tangible results.

Finally, the parents of teenage or young adult athletes working their way up the talent ladder may occasionally need to provide some positive parental push. This is not to be mistaken for "stage parent syndrome," where the parents' ambitions are the driving force behind the youngster's ambitions. A positive parental push is the occasional push or pull that is necessary to help a young athlete get over a rough spot. For example, despite being very dedicated and invested in their sports, many teenage athletes have a hard time waking up for early-morning practice. A positive parental push might be applied by helping the athlete get out of bed in the morning.

One parent described her use of the positive parental push this way: "When Mike turned fifteen, he loved his sport, but sometimes he didn't feel like going to practice. We talked about it and he really wanted to keep participating, but he just would lose his momentum after a busy day at school. So I would encourage him to dress and get in the car. We would just drive over to practice, and if he still didn't feel like going when we got there, then we could come right home. By the time we got there, he was always excited and ready to go again." The main message here is that you can be an important support to your child's interest, but your push should not be the main source of his or her motivation.

Some parents report that their young rider has developed a deep, almost single-minded passion about bike racing. It is a fantastic sport with many potential benefits. But more is not always better, and like everything in life, moderation is important. As a parent or coach, it is your responsibility to help set boundaries that will protect and guide your athlete to a positive experience. You wouldn't allow your children to eat candy all the time just because they love it, and you wouldn't let them stay up until all hours because they want to. Their participation in cycling shouldn't be without boundaries either. Setting limits can be tough, but in the long run this approach will reduce the risk of overuse injuries, long-term joint damage, and burnout. Here are some guidelines for structuring a healthy environment:

- Make sure your athlete has an annual physical with a medical professional who understands sports medicine and your child's level of involvement.
- Make sure the coaches and other adults involved in your devo athlete's training have an understanding of positive development. Their actions should reflect the best interests of your child and focus on long-term health and wellness, not just short-term goals such as specific races or events.
- Set limits on the number of races your athlete can participate in during the season. Racing two or three times a week, every week across a full racing season, or in multiple seasons back to back in different disciplines, is not the best option for a developing athlete.
- Help your athlete build his or her own season plan. You may set the guidelines (for example, racing only two weekends a month), but let the athlete decide which races those will be. Your youngster can take responsibility for registering on time and compiling race information and travel directions.

- Build a sense of responsibility and self-reliance into your devo athlete. Help him or her understand what it means to be an athlete. There is a big difference between helping your athlete out and doing all the work for him or her. Just as children need to do their own schoolwork to learn from it, as cyclists they need to be in charge of getting their own gear ready, doing their own bike maintenance, and so on. Don't handicap their development by catering to them at events.
- Just because your athlete "can" do something doesn't mean he or she "should." Young riders might be able to keep up and go the distance for a century ride, but should they? Overwhelmingly the experts in adolescent physiology and devo sport agree that adult training plans and distances are not appropriate for the young athlete. They discourage participation in marathon distances in running and cycling due to the damage that can be done to joints, tendons, muscles, and ligaments, which are all at various stages of development.
- Participation should emphasize fun and personal improvement, not just the outcome. If your child has trouble handling poor performance, exhibits signs of unhealthy perfectionism, or sets unrealistic or impossible standards of achievement, it's time to intervene. Get assistance from a qualified sport psychology consultant to help your athlete refocus on healthy goals and learn positive coping tools.
- Help your athlete develop a well-rounded sense of self. Encourage participation in other activities at school or in the community. These kinds of activities are not only important on college applications these days but can help your athlete realize other strengths and build a healthy self-image. Don't allow your child to become overscheduled, but perhaps these opportunities provide a good balance in the off-season.

THE ROLE OF THE COACH IN TALENT DEVELOPMENT

Sport science researcher Dan Gould and his colleagues have looked at the role that coaches play in talent development. They found that successful athletes reported that their coaches taught them the skills needed to be successful both directly and indirectly throughout the phases of their development. Direct teaching methods included mentoring and clear instruction of both physical training and mental strategies and attitudes, such as goal setting and keeping an optimistic outlook. Indirectly, coaches helped foster talent development by modeling the skills they wanted athletes to develop and encouraging the positive and productive things that athletes did. The coach should strive to be trustworthy, positive, and optimistic, as these are important behaviors for athletes, and people frequently learn more from observation than from lectures.

Like parents, coaches will have to occasionally provide a "positive push" to help athletes with momentary glitches in motivation or other such interferences. And, just as with parents, a coach's positive push will only be effective when it supports the athlete's true underlying motivation; it should never be seen as an effective replacement for an athlete's own intrinsic motivation.

Coaches successful at nurturing talent have the ability to recognize each athlete as an individual and to personalize the training experience for the athlete. They use a challenge-based (versus a problem-based) approach and motivational techniques as needed to help athletes overcome temporary lulls in motivation or to encourage them to reach for the next level. A coach should be sure to provide the athletes in their charge with exposure to higher-level competition and with contact with more advanced athletes in order to provide incentive and a sense that those goals are being achieved by regular people who were once developmental athletes themselves.

Coaches focused on talent development express confidence in the athlete, provide useful feedback and critique, and ensure a safe, supportive, positive environment for learning. The emphasis is on fun and enjoyment, hard work and work ethic, and realistic but challenging expectations. At the most elite level, winning is important, but even then it is not the only element.

And perhaps most importantly, elite-level coaches are able to adjust their approach and focus based on the developmental stage and readiness of the athlete, rather than trying to force an athlete to the coach's level.

FOR THE ATHLETE: SPECIALIZATION IN YOUR SPORT

The decision to focus on just one sport is a tough one for many athletes. Factors such as age, opportunity, cost, maturity, interest level, and future goals will all play a role. Experts agree that at the early levels of participation, when an athlete is very young (pre-puberty) or new to a sport, specialization is not a good idea. For the pre-puberty athlete, focusing on just one athletic skill set does not provide the overall physical balance and development opportunities that a growing body needs to maximize its full potential.

Different types of movement- and activity-based skills will help you develop a well-rounded athleticism that will serve you well no matter what sport you specialize in down the road. Early specialization presents the risk of overuse injuries in joints and muscles that are not mature enough to handle the repetitive training loads associated with doing just one type of activity. Moreover, few young athletes have had a chance to develop the maturity, attention span, or cognitive skills necessary to do the type of work necessary to excel in a singular pursuit. Studies of national team members across a wide variety of Olympic sports have found that the ones with a wide variety of sport experiences in their background and who specialized later in their careers tended to have longer, more successful national team careers than their counterparts who specialized earlier in their sport.

The adolescent athlete who discovers cycling doesn't necessarily face the same physical and developmental concerns with specialization. After puberty, specialization may be appropriate, depending on the sport and the level of competition. However, specialization should not be an automatic assumption once one hits 13 or has taken up cycling. The choice to specialize should occur only after you spend some time developing a real love for the sport that is separate from competition. After all, athletes will spend roughly 99 percent of their time training and only about 1 percent in competition. Love of the race or the win is rarely enough to maintain the daily focus and concentration necessary to really excel.

Specialization is not something that has to happen all at once either. A high-school-age athlete may choose to specialize in cycling during the summer and off-season but take a break in the winter to play basketball. Cycling may be this athlete's real love, but basketball is a fun social outlet that provides some off-season fitness and activity. This type of balance is good for you. Additionally, when any athlete decides to specialize, training should follow a systematic plan that allows skills and fitness to develop gradually and in a way that does not add too much stress all at one time.

Overall, the decision to specialize should be your choice, not something you do because you are feeling pushed into it. While the most elite levels of competition will require specialization, early specialization does not necessarily guarantee future success. On the contrary, some studies indicate that early specialization leads to too much mental and physical stress too early. This results in physical injury, overtraining, burnout, loss of enjoyment, permanent dropout, and poor performance.

BECOMING AN EXPERT CYCLIST

In the quest for talent development, how does an athlete know when he or she has arrived? Elite athletes don't focus on the tall peak they climbed; instead, they are always looking for another, taller peak to climb. They take satisfaction and pride in what they have accomplished, but they also keep an eye on what they want to do next. The process of maximizing talent is about the quest to become an elite or an expert in your field. Research into the experiences and development of successful people has found that it typically takes about ten years to really develop expertise in something—in this case, a solid understanding of training and the skills and tactics of the sport. While physical talent development is not quite the same, the development of the other skills associated with peak performance might fall into this same category. Moreover, physical training is known to be cumulative in nature, particularly in endurance sports like cycling, and each successive year of training adds more to your physical base of endurance and strength. Elite Senior riders are usually in their mid- to late twenties, with a minimum of five to seven solid years of training behind them before they reach the top of the ranks. Successful male riders at their peak are in their late twenties to early thirties, and elite women riders can be found well into their mid- to late thirties.

Does this mean you have to just ride for ten years and then you will arrive as a great talent? Nope, that isn't quite the way it works. The main idea is that, once the developmental phase is coming to an end and you begin your quest to maximize your talent at the elite level, it takes time, patience, and a clear plan for how and what you are working on to improve. Having patience, determination, and dedication will be necessary for the journey. Along the way you will experience success and frustration, but with persistence you will see how far you can go.

Finally, it is important to acknowledge that even when everything is done well, elite performance can still be elusive. Even with the best genetic mix, fantastic skills, and great training, luck still plays into the equation. But with proper planning, the development of excellent skills, and a healthy definition of success, athletes can make the most of the talent that they do have to reach for their personal best.

RECOMMENDED READING AND RESOURCES

"Coaches' Roles in Olympic Championship Development," by K. Dieffenbach, D. Gould, and A. Moffett, *Olympic Coach* 12, no. 3 (Summer 2002), pp. 1–9.

Developing Talent in Young People, edited by B. S. Bloom (Ballantine, 1985).

Olympic Coach magazine, www.usolympicteam.com/12688.htm.

The Psychology of High Abilities, by Michael Howe (New York University Press, 1999).

Talented Teenagers: The Roots of Success and Failure, by Mihaly Csikszentmihalyi, Kevin Rathunde, and Samuel Whalen (Cambridge University Press, 1993).

5 **NUTRITION** for Juniors, Part 1

One cannot live exclusively on pizza, burgers, and fries!
—Kathy Zawadzki, Licensed Sports Nutritionist
and USAC Level 1 coach

Have you ever put diesel fuel in the tank of a car that is supposed to take gasoline? Unfortunately, I have. Diesel and gasoline are both types of fuels, and at first the car functioned fine. Well, okay, maybe not fine—it sputtered a little, but it drove. When the mechanic found out what I had done, he immediately had to drain the gas tank. As you can probably guess, the point is that the wrong kind of fuel worked, but it wasn't good enough for the engine to run smoothly. Human bodies are the same. Your body can run on many different kinds of fuels, but not all fuels are good for your engine. It's important for you as a cyclist to understand the basics of good nutrition to ensure that you will know how to make the right fuel choices for your body and athletic efforts.

Athletes often feel they need to follow a complicated nutrition plan to achieve peak performance. Advertisements in sports magazines and on the Web have all kinds of special products that claim to enhance performance, and these claims add to the confusion about nutrition. We will take a look at some of these extras a little later on to examine whether any of the claims might be true. But the truth is, none of those extras matter if you don't start with a healthy basic diet. In this chapter we'll focus on what good nutrition is all about. In the next chapter, we'll take a look at how nutrition applies specifically to training and racing.

THE NUTRIENTS

A solid diet includes six basic nutrients: fat, protein, carbohydrates, minerals, vitamins, and, of course, water. You are probably familiar with these basics. These nutrients are the building blocks of a diet that will provide all the things you need for both health and performance. Let's take a closer look at them to see why they are important in an athlete's diet.

Fats

Fat has a bad reputation in our culture. Many people think it is bad and try to cut all fat out of their diets. But this isn't a good idea, because fat plays an important role in a healthy diet. First, it is a great form of fuel. In fact, it is the primary source of stored energy that we use to run our bodies when we are resting or doing low-intensity activities. Some types of fat have even been found to be important for brain functioning. This doesn't mean that you should stock up on junk food, though, because not all fats are the same.

There are three basic kinds of fats in our diets: unsaturated, saturated, and trans fat. The goal is to choose foods that provide the good kind (unsaturated fat) and to consume as little of the bad kinds (saturated fat and trans fat) as possible. Unsaturated fat is found mostly in plant food sources like nuts or olives. Fish also contains healthy fat in the form of Omega-3 fatty acids. You don't have to go out of your way to find good fat if you are making healthy food choices; you just need to make sure you choose foods that don't have the unhealthy types of fats.

That means you want to try to minimize the amount of saturated fats and trans fats in your diet. Saturated fats are in foods like red meat and whole-milk products. Don't think that this makes these foods bad—it just means that it is important to get them in moderation. Trans fats, however, should not have a place in anyone's diet, let alone an athlete's diet. Trans fat was created in a laboratory. Saturated fat goes bad if it sits around too long, and this frustrated food manufacturers. It meant that cookies, crackers, and other snacks would spoil if they weren't eaten right away. After some tinkering, food chemists figured out that if they moved around some of the parts of the saturated fat molecules, they could create a fat that could sit on the shelf much longer, and voilà—trans fat was born. You may have seen recent news stories about trans fats focusing on the health concerns that people have about them. Some companies have begun to look for ways to remove trans fats from their snacks and fast foods, and some cities have even banned the use of trans fats at restaurants. As an athlete, you should avoid foods with trans fats. Replace any prepackaged snacks and fast-food items with healthier, fresh food options whenever possible. And learning to read food labels will help you keep trans fats in your diet to a minimum (more on that in a minute).

Overall, athletes should strive to have healthy fats make up about 25 to 30 percent of their daily diet. Seek out healthy, plant-based fat sources like nuts, olive oil, and corn or canola oil. Don't forget to get your Omega-3 fatty acids from fish as well. Work to keep the amount of saturated fat in your diet low, and as much as possible, eliminate trans fat completely.

Protein

People often assume that protein builds big muscles, and that because endurance athletes don't want to bulk up, they don't need protein. Let's dispense with these myths right away. Protein itself doesn't cause bulky muscles. The body only builds bulky muscle if that is what it is specifically trained to do. Everyone needs protein, because it provides the building blocks our bodies need for routine tissue repair—amino acids. There are about twenty different kinds of amino acids, and eight of them are essential for good health. Our bodies can't make them, so we have to get them from the foods we eat. Protein also helps maintain red blood cells (essential for carrying oxygen to your muscles), helps produce key enzymes and hormones that keep everything running smoothly, and helps control healthy water levels in your cells. So even endurance athletes benefit from a healthy protein intake.

Athletes should make sure that 15 to 20 percent of their diet comes from protein. Foods like eggs, meat, nuts, and dairy all contain protein, and it's easy to meet this requirement if you are a meat-eater. If you are a vegetarian athlete, you will need to educate yourself about how to compensate for the lack of meat in your diet. Vegetarians can get enough protein if they consume a variety of grains, nuts, and beans, but it can be difficult to ensure that you get the right amounts and combinations of foods. Make sure you get enough of all eight "essential amino acids." You can eat certain foods in combination—for example, rice and beans—to get the full complement of amino acids in one meal. Nutritionists used to think it was necessary to eat complementary proteins together, but more recent research shows that it is not really necessary to eat these combinations at the same meal. The body can store the essential amino acids for a short while. So long as you get all of the essential amino acids over the course of a day or two, you will be doing your job of providing your body with enough protein.

Do athletes need more protein than the average Joe (or Josephine)?

Athletes should get approximately 20 percent of their total calories from protein. This means you need about 1.0 to 1.5 grams of protein per kilogram (g/kg) of body weight. (Divide your weight in pounds by 2.2 to determine your weight in kilograms.) Only power lifters or major strength athletes need more than this, and even then, it's just a bit more (1.7–1.9 g/kg). Endurance athletes do not need this extra amount. Keep in mind that strength gains do not come from eating protein. The protein only provides the building blocks for repair and growth. And in order for the protein to be useful for strength gain, the athlete needs to be training for strength gain (which means doing lots of weight-room work and other power-based training efforts).

Carbohydrates

You have probably heard people talk about carbohydrates—or carbs, as they are often called. Along with fat, carbohydrates break down in the body and provide energy for your daily activities. Some popular diets recommend keeping carbs low, but these diets are not appropriate for athletes. You need carbohydrates to have the energy to train on your bike and to recover after training. Carbohydrates become an even more important energy source when you work out at a high level of intensity. An athlete who is low on carbs when training may experience a "bonk"— that is, a sudden feeling of fatigue. Bonking occurs when the level of carbohydrates in the body is too low for the demands being placed on the body. When this occurs, it is known as "glycogen debt," and it means you are running out of glycogen. When you begin to bonk, you may feel disoriented, tired, headachy, and even irritable or upset. Your pace will slow down so that your body can drop to a lower level where it can use fat as fuel (we have plenty of this in storage). Bonking can even occur when you are off the bike. If you have ever missed lunch and felt cranky or cross, you have experienced not having enough carbohydrates in your diet. Carbs are a key part of a healthy athlete's diet, and there are many dietary sources of carbs. It is essential to choose wisely.

Carbohydrates are found in a wide range of foods, including breads, grains, fruits, cookies, crackers, chips, and vegetables. Carbs are really starches and sugars that the body breaks down into glycogen. The glycogen can be used right away, or it can be stored in the body for later use. Some people worry that carbs will make them fat. But it isn't the carbohydrates that make people fat; it is too many carbohydrates, or carbohydrate sources that are high in bad fats, that cause problems. Ultimately, weight gain comes from eating more calories than you burn. Some foods have simple sugars (for example, fructose, sucrose, or glucose), and others are more complex. Both simple and complex carbs are valuable. For a healthy daily diet, choose carbs that are not highly processed and that have nutritional value beyond just being carbohydrates. This means you want foods that are more natural (an apple rather than processed fruit snack bits, and multigrain bread instead of white bread).

Healthy carb choices such as fresh fruits and whole grains also provide fiber. Just as the commercials say, fiber keeps us regular by aiding digestion and moving things along. And it isn't just the elderly folks in the commercials who benefit: Everyone—young and old—needs fiber to maintain a healthy digestive system.

The majority of your diet—approximately 55 to 65 percent of it—should come from healthy carbohydrates. When you choose your carbs, strive for a mix of different kinds—some simple and some complex—with as many natural foods as possible.

Vitamins

Vitamins are nutrients that your body uses for a wide variety of functions. Some vitamins are needed for cell repair, while others are needed for the release of energy, for proper nervous system functioning, or for any of a large number of other things that go on in your body every day that you are not even aware of. You get them mainly from the foods you eat, which is one of the reasons why variety in your diet is so important. If you have too few vitamins, your body won't run at an optimum level. For example, if you don't get enough vitamin B, you could have problems with energy production, which would leave you feeling fatigued. There are thirteen different vitamins that are considered "essential" for your body to function properly. See Table 5.1 for a summary of these nutrients.

It is also possible to get too much of a vitamin. But this is almost always caused by taking a vitamin in supplement form. Vitamin pills sometimes contain more of the vitamin than you need every day; it also can be very dangerous to take more than the recommended daily dosage of a vitamin pill, or to take a multivitamin and also routinely eat energy bars that contain high dosages of vitamins. Vitamins are found in relatively small quantities in foods. That's why it is generally safer to get your vitamins from a good diet; in fact, it's pretty hard to get too much of a vitamin from foods alone. Vitamins can either be water or fat soluble, which just indicates how the body works with and stores each kind. If the vitamin is water soluble, and you take in more than the body needs for that day, the body simply excretes (or pees out) what it can't use. There is usually no harm in that, except as far as your wallet is concerned: If you go to the health food store and buy an expensive jar of megadose vitamin C, you will be spending a lot of money on something that will just go in one end and out the other. The other type of vitamin, the fat-soluble ones (vitamins A, D, E, and K), sticks around when you consume more than you need and gets stored in your fat cells (and even skinny people have fat cells). This makes it more likely that you will experience negative side effects. Too much vitamin A can cause fatigue or hair loss, for example. So keep an eye on the amounts of the different vitamins in your supplements and special energy foods, and make sure you are not getting a daily total that exceeds the recommended amounts.

When the importance of vitamins is discussed, usually the topic of "antioxidants" comes up. Antioxidants are substances that inhibit an oxidative reaction that can occur in our cells due to pollution, stress (from everyday life or from hard training), and normal wear and tear. These

TABLE 5.1 Essential Vitamins and Amounts Needed for Junior and Espoir Males and Females

Water-Soluble Vitamins	Functions	Where to Find	Amount for Boys 14–18	Amount for Espoirs, Males	Amount for Girls 14–18	Amount for Espoirs, Females
Vitamin B1 (Thiamin)	Releases energy from protein, fat, and carbs; aids in nervous system functioning	Whole-grain breads and cereals, fortified breads and cereals, dry beans	1.2 mg/day	1.2 mg/day	1.0 mg/day	1.1 mg/day
Vitamin B2 (Riboflavin)	Releases energy from protein, fat, and carbs; aids in healthy skin development	Milk, leafy green vegetables, whole-grain breads and cereals	1.3 mg/day	1.3 mg/day	1.0 mg/day	1.1 mg/day
Vitamin B3 (Niacin)	Releases energy from protein, fat, and carbs	Meat, fish, poultry, eggs, milk, whole-grain breads and cereals, fortified breads and cereals, nuts	16 mg/day	16 mg/day	14 mg/day	14 mg/day
Vitamin B6	Releases energy stored in muscle; aids in red blood cell formation	Whole-grain breads and cereals, dried beans, leafy green vegetables, bananas, meat, fish, poultry	1.3 mg/day	1.3 mg/day	1.2 mg/day	1.3 mg/day
Vitamin B12	Aids in creation of new cells, red blood cell formation, and nervous system functioning	Meat, dairy products, fortified cereals	2.4 mg/day	2.4 mg/day	2.4 mg/day	2.4 mg/day
Vitamin C	Aids in immune system functioning and iron absorption; acts as antioxidant	Citrus fruits like oranges and grapefruit, strawberries, broccoli, peppers, tomatoes, cabbage	75 mg/day	90 mg/day	65 mg/day	75 mg/day

(continues)

TABLE 5.1 (continued)

Folate	Aids in creation of new cells and in red blood cell formation	Leafy green vegetables, whole-grain breads and cereals, dried beans, fortified breads and cereals, orange juice	400 µg/da	400 µg/da	400 µg/da	400 µg/day
Pantothenic Acid	Releases energy from protein, fat, and carbs	Whole grains, eggs; trace amounts found in most foods	5 mg/day*	5 mg/day*	5 mg/day*	5 mg/day*
Fat-Soluble Vitamins						
Vitamin A	Promotes general cell health, proper vision, and bone and tooth growth; acts as antioxidant	Spinach and other dark leafy green vegetables, orange fruits and vegetables, liver, fortified milk products	900 µg/da	900 µg/da	700 µg/da	700 µg/day
Vitamin D	Aids in bone growth	Fatty fish like salmon and tuna, fortified milk products, sunlight	5 µg/day*	5 µg/day*	5 µg/day	5 µg/day*
Vitamin E	Aids in proper red blood cell formation; acts as antioxidant	Soybeans, almonds and other nuts, sunflower seeds, wheat germ, olive oil	15 mg/day	15 mg/day	15 mg/day	15 mg/day
Vitamin K	Aids in blood clotting, bone growth	Green leafy vegetables	75 µg/day*	120 µg/day*	75 µg/day*	90 µg/day*

NOTE: Vitamin recommendations are based on the Daily Recommended Intake (DRI) reports (www.nap.edu) from the National Academy of Sciences. Asterisks indicate amounts that have been determined to be adequate intakes (AIs). Other values are RDAs (recommended dietary allowances). Please note that RDAs and AIs for some nutrients change for females if they become pregnant.

antioxidant vitamins help protect cells and tissues from any damage that might occur in this oxidative process by stopping the free radicals. Free radicals are sort of like Super Balls: When you throw a Super Ball into a room, it bounces around fast, hitting lots of things, and it may do some damage. Free radicals can damage your cells, but antioxidants catch, slow down, and stop the free radicals before they can cause a problem. There is a lot of research being conducted by nutritionists to better understand antioxidants and how they work. Currently, vitamins A, C, and E have all been found to be important antioxidant vitamins. Make sure your diet is rich in these vitamins, but remember not to get too much, especially of the fat-soluble vitamins A and E. The research does not support taking extra supplements, as it is possible to experience negative effects from too much. You won't have a problem with this if you are eating whole foods. You have to worry about getting too much only if you take supplements or eat too many fortified foods.

Measuring Vitamins and Minerals

If you have ever looked at the side of your cereal box, you know that the quantity of vitamins and minerals contained in a serving are listed in grams (g), milligrams (mg), or micrograms (mcg or μg). These are very small amounts, and they are difficult to measure. But don't worry, you don't need to measure them yourself. Food labels and many different websites (for example, www. mypyramid.gov) can help you figure out the levels of nutrients in different foods. And a sports nutritionist or an online nutrition tracking program can help you record what you eat and analyze your overall diet to make sure it is balanced and healthy and that it supplies the right amounts of vitamins and minerals.

The amount of each vitamin you need depends on your gender and age. In general, young adults need a little more than adults do because they are still growing. It is possible to receive the proper amount from the foods you eat if you are eating a diet that has a lot of variety and that includes healthy choices. Table 5.1 provides suggested amounts for each vitamin.

Minerals

Minerals, as you know from science class, are organic substances found in rocks and dirt; they are also found in the foods we eat and are needed in very small amounts in our bodies. Scientists have figured out that each of us has just under $2 worth of raw materials—such as calcium, magnesium, phosphorus, sodium, and even copper—in our bodies. And even though we need only the tiniest pinch of most minerals, they play a crucial role in running our bodies. Twenty minerals that are key to human well-being have been identified. Some are called *macrominerals* because we have a good bit in our bodies; others are called *microminerals,* or trace minerals, because they are found in such tiny amounts in our systems (see Table 5.2).

TABLE 5.2 Minerals Found in the Human Body	
Microminerals (Trace Minerals)	**Macrominerals**
Boron	Calcium
Chromium	Chloride
Cobalt	Magnesium
Copper	Phosphorus
Fluorine (aka fluoride)	Potassium
Iodine	Sodium
Iron	
Manganese	
Molybdenum	
Nickel	
Selenium	
Silicon	
Vanadium	
Zinc	

Eating a well-balanced diet with plenty of fresh foods will provide most of the minerals you need. Some athletes may find they need to take extra sodium, potassium, and magnesium when training hard or in high temperatures. We'll take a look at extra mineral needs when we look at ergogenic aids in Chapter 6. Table 5.3 provides an overview of the amounts of minerals you need in your diet and where you can find them.

Fortified for Your Health

If you have ever read your cereal box over breakfast, you have seen "Fortified with essential vitamins and minerals." But just what are they adding to your cornflakes and why? Food manufacturers often add extra vitamins and minerals to everything from bread to cereal to improve the food value. Sometimes they are replacing nutrients that were removed in processing, and sometimes they are just adding an extra something that doctors and scientists feel most people don't get enough of.

Is this a good idea? Yes and no. The concept is a very good one: Who wouldn't want the foods they eat to have more food value? However, just because a food has been fortified doesn't mean it is a super-food. Vitamins and minerals are best absorbed and used by the body when they are digested from natural food sources. Some of the added nutrients do get absorbed by the body, so fortified foods can help you get more of the important nutrients you need. If you have a choice between a fortified product and a nonfortified version of a product, such as bread or cereal, go ahead and choose the fortified one. However, if you have a choice between a less processed, more natural product that isn't fortified and a processed product that is fortified, choose the more natural product.

Water

Water may be the last essential nutrient we are discussing here, but that does not mean it is any less important. Approximately 60 percent of your body weight is water. Without adequate water, a person can easily become very ill. Water fills each of our cells as well as the spaces between cells; it helps lubricate joints, regulates internal temperature, and helps food, oxygen, and waste products move in and out of our cells, as well as through our bodies via the lymph system and the circulatory system. Water is also a major component of sweat, which helps us stay cool on a hot day or when working hard. We also excrete water several times a day in the form of urine, which helps our bodies get rid of waste products. Without water, our blood could not circulate well and many systems would fail. So it is crucial that we take in enough water to maintain a healthy life balance.

TABLE 5.3 Essential Minerals and Amounts Needed for Junior and Espoir Males and Females

Mineral	Type	Functions	Where to Find	Amount for Boys 14–18	Amount for Espoirs, Males	Amount for Girls 14–18	Amount for Espoirs, Females
Boron	Trace	Aids in cell metabolism	Green leafy vegetables, some fruits	17 mg/day*	20 mg/day*	17 mg/day*	20 mg/day*
Calcium	Macro	Aids in bone and tooth development, muscle contraction, nerve conduction, and secretion of hormones and enzymes	Milk products, green leafy vegetables, fish with bones such as sardines, fortified orange juice and soy milk	1,300 mg/day**	1,000 mg/day**	1,300 mg/day**	1,000 mg/day**
Chloride	Macro	Helps maintain fluid balance	Table salt, fish, meat, milk, eggs	2.3 g/day**	2.3 g/day**	2.3 g/day**	2.3 g/day**
Chromium	Trace	Enhances insulin sensitivity; plays a role in carbohydrate, fat, and protein metabolism	Whole-grain breads and cereals, mushrooms	35 µg/day*	35 µg/day**	24 µg/day**	25 µg/day**
Cobalt	Trace	Part of vitamin B12	Any animal product that has vitamin B12	N/A	N/A	N/A	N/A
Copper	Trace	Aids in creation of hemoglobin in blood	Seafood, seeds, nuts, whole grains, some green leafy vegetables, dried beans	890 µg/day	900 µg/day	890 µg/day	900 µg/day
Fluorine (aka fluoride)	Trace	Helps strengthen bones and teeth	Fluoridated water	3 mg/day**	4 mg/day**	3 mg/day**	3 mg/day**
Iodine	Trace	Aids in creation of thyroid hormone	Saltwater fish, iodized salt, eggs, mushrooms	150 µg/day	150 µg/day	150 µg/day	150 µg/day
Iron	Trace	Key part of hemoglobin; aids in immune system functioning	Meat, especially liver, poultry, clams, and oysters; also in dried beans, dried fruits, and fortified grains, but not as well absorbed by the body from these sources as from meats	11 mg/day	8 mg/day	15 mg/day	15 mg/day
Magnesium	Macro	Aids in bone formation; key part of many enzymes	Green leafy vegetables, nuts and seeds, dried beans, legumes	410 mg/day	400 mg/day	360 mg/day	310 mg/day

Mineral	Type	Function	Sources				
Manganese	Trace	Plays a role in bone formation; helps with carb, protein, and fat metabolism	Whole grains, dried beans, nuts, some veggies	1.6 mg/day**	1.6 mg/day**	2.3 mg/day**	2.2 mg/day**
Molybdenum	Trace	Part of several enzymes	Whole grains, legumes, nuts	45 µg/day	43 µg/day	45 µg/day	43 µg/day
Nickel	Trace	Unknown; may be part of some enzymes and may help the body absorb iron	Whole grains, legumes, nuts	1.0 mg/day*	1.0 mg/day*	1.0 mg/day*	1.0 mg/day*
Phosphorus	Macro	Part of bone and ATP; helps to maintain normal pH in cells and aids in cell metabolism	In lots of foods, especially animal products	700 mg/day	1,250 mg/day	700 mg/day	1,250 mg/day
Potassium	Macro	Aids in proper cell functioning	Orange juice, bananas, melons, potatoes, green leafy vegetables, dried beans and peas, nuts	4.7 g/day**	4.7 g/day**	4.7 g/day**	4.7 g/day**
Selenium	Trace	Part of antioxidant enzymes	Plant products	400 µg/day*	400 µg/day*	400 µg/day*	400 µg/day*
Silicon	Trace	Unknown; may help in bone formation	Grains, water, vegetables	N/A	N/A	N/A	N/A
Sodium	Macro	Helps maintain fluid balance in cells	Table salt, most processed foods	4.7 g/day**	4.7 g/day**	4.7 g/day**	1.5 g/day**
Sulfur	Macro	Helps create many substances in the body, such as insulin and various proteins	Foods containing protein	N/A	N/A	N/A	N/A
Vanadium	Trace	Unknown	Mushrooms, black pepper, parsley, shellfish	400 mg/day*	N/A	400 mg/day*	N/A
Zinc	Trace	Aids in proper immune system and cell functioning; present in many enzymes	Meat, milk, whole grains	40 mg/day*	34 mg/day*	40 mg/day*	34 mg/day*

NOTE: Mineral recommendations are based on the Daily Recommended Intake (DRI) reports of the National Academy of Sciences (www.nap.edu). Most of the figures represent recommended dietary allowances (RDAs). A single asterisk indicates that no RDA or adequate intake (AI) has been set. In these cases, the National Academy of Sciences has made recommendations about the maximum amount people should get daily. Taking in a greater level of any of these nutrients could result in toxicity or overload to your system. Double asterisks indicate AIs. N/A indicates that an amount is not yet determined. Please note that RDAs, AIs, and upper-limit recommendations for some nutrients change for females if they become pregnant. Be sure to consult a physician.

Did you know that a body weight loss of as little as 1 to 2 percent due to dehydration can result in decreased endurance performance? With a 3 percent loss, almost all athletes will experience endurance performance decreases. And with a 5 percent loss, decreases in strength and power take place, so there goes your hill climb or your sprint. This isn't just important when you are racing hard. Your hydration status matters all the time, even in the off-season when you are just training. Think about it: If you are dehydrated in training, you can't produce your best effort and your body cannot make adaptations to training.

In addition to the performance problems, poor hydration can have very serious short- and long-term health consequences, including serious medical conditions like heat exhaustion and heatstroke. Mild dehydration can cause headaches and disorientation. More severe dehydration can lead to collapse, coma, or even death. Learning how to get and stay properly hydrated is essential to both performance and your health and well-being.

Don't Trust Your Thirst!

Too many people wait until they're thirsty before they drink fluids, relying on the thirst mechanism to tell them when it's time to rehydrate, just as they listen to stomach rumbles to signal that it's time to eat. Unfortunately, thirst isn't a very good predictor of when our bodies actually need fluids. The thirst mechanism is on a sort of delay; by the time your brain gets the signal to drink, you are already a bit dehydrated, and once you are dehydrated it is very hard to catch up until you are off the bike and have had time to recover. It is important that you take an active role in staying hydrated all the time, especially when you are training, so you can stay ahead of your thirst mechanism. A great way to do this is to always carry a water bottle with you and to drink frequently throughout the day. (Just make sure you wash or change out your water bottle daily so that dirt and bacteria don't build up!) And on your long rides, plan carefully to make sure you can refill your water bottles.

How do you know if you are drinking enough fluids? The easiest way is to monitor your urine output. This may sound a little gross, but it is an effective way to keep on top of your hydration status, and being an athlete means being in touch with all of the systems in your body. The lighter your urine is in color, the better your hydration status. If your urine is dark yellow, it usually means you are not well hydrated; you are seeing more concentrated waste products because your body didn't have water to spare. If your urine is pale yellow or almost clear, you are well hydrated. (Keep in mind that a colored toilet bowl may influence the color you see.)

Ultimately, you want the color of your urine to resemble pale straw or be even lighter, with little to no odor. Certain vitamins and foods can change the color and smell of your urine, but by monitoring it on a regular basis you will become familiar with what is normal and what isn't. If you have any questions or concerns, be sure to ask a doctor, your parents, or your coach.

Without proper hydration levels, the body cannot cool itself properly, and when core temperature goes up, the body reduces force and work outputs. In addition, the risk of heat exhaustion and heatstroke, which are potentially deadly, goes up as hydration levels decrease. These extremes aren't usually a problem in training because we are able to stop and refill bottles whenever we need to, but the risk increases in competition when everyone is so focused on the outcome that they neglect hydration. It is very important to practice good drinking habits while training so that when the pressure is on, you automatically drink fluids because it is second nature. Don't think that your body is so well trained that it can handle fluids more efficiently than it could if you were less well trained. This is a myth; top athletes know how to stay hydrated. Drinking lots of fluids will help reduce your risk of hydration-related problems when competing and will give you a great advantage over competitors who don't know how to take care of their hydration needs.

In addition to getting enough water, it is very important to maintain the right electrolyte balance in your body. Certain substances in the body carry either a positive or negative charge. When these charges build up on the opposite sides of a cell wall (for example, positive on the outside and negative on the inside), they create a gradient that helps things move around. The positives want to go where the negatives are and vice versa. Sodium (Na^+), potassium (K^+), calcium (CA^{2+}), and magnesium (Mg^{2+}) are all positively charged, whereas chloride (Cl^-), bicarbonate (HCO_3^-), and phosphate (PO_4^{3-}) are all negatively charged. This movement is important for all sorts of cellular activity, such as those that occur in muscle contractions. The charged elements are called electrolytes, and your goal should be to maintain a good balance of electrolytes to water.

Coaches and athletes used to worry only about sodium loss, but we now know that all of the electrolytes are important. Most people don't need to worry about their electrolyte balance because a healthy daily diet will maintain a proper balance. However, athletes, especially those who are heavy sweaters, or those who work out in very hot (or hot and humid) conditions, need to pay close attention to their electrolyte intake.

Take a look at your clothes after a good training ride. Do you see faint to heavy white lines? Sometimes there will be multiple lines, kind of like rings in a tree. What about on your face and neck? Do you see white lines or feel crusty, gritty crystals on your skin? These white lines are dried salt (sodium) and other electrolytes that we lose when we sweat. If all we drink is water to replace our sweat, we aren't replacing the electrolytes that we lost. Athletes who experience an electrolyte imbalance may have problems with muscle cramping. Athletes who have a serious imbalance can develop hyponatremia (also known as "water toxicity"), and this condition can lead to heart problems and, in extreme cases, even death. Developing this condition is rare but is serious enough to mention.

Fortunately, maintaining the right water and electrolyte balance is pretty easy to do. Drink mixes that have been designed for athletes to use while training contain electrolytes (and sometimes other things, such as carbs for energy, which we'll discuss in the next chapter). There are also many other products on the market that provide additional electrolytes in pill, gel, or solid form. For training rides of under an hour, it's okay to drink plain water, but on rides of over an hour or on extremely hot and humid days, drink a beverage that is specially designed for athletes. These drinks will help replace the electrolytes you lose through your sweat while also providing carbohydrates for more energy.

Learning to Track Your Hydration

Did you know that even well-trained cyclists who are used to riding in hot environments (that is, who are "heat acclimatized") lose from 1.5 to more than 3 quarts of sweat per hour? Even though the body cannot process water fast enough to keep up with the highest levels of loss, it is critical that these athletes try to maintain good hydration levels. And it's also critical for you, even if you are not sweating at the maximum rate. It is normal to finish a long effort or a race with a small deficit, but we want to work to minimize the deficit as much as possible. Remember, the greater the dehydration, the more negative the impact on performance and health.

So what is your sweat rate? Of course, the most obvious sign that you are a heavy sweater is that you are drenched in wet, soggy clothes after you work out or have lots of heavy white sweat rings. But remember, most of the fabrics designed for training are also designed to wick the sweat away from your skin (to help you cool off) and to dry quickly. At the end of the ride, it can be hard to determine how much you actually sweat because your high-tech fabrics will be pretty dry—and the post-training stinky factor doesn't tell us much about an athlete's sweat rate, either. Your sweat rings will give you some idea, but a simple calculation will give you a more accurate picture.

Make sure you do this calculation on different days and under different conditions so that you can get a feel for how your body responds.

1. Check your weight before and after training to calculate your weight loss. For example, if you weighed in at 160 pounds before exercising, and 158 pounds after exercising (or, in kilograms, you went from 73 kg to 72 kg), then you had a weight loss of 2 pounds during training (or 0.9 kg). (To obtain weight in kilograms, divide weight in pounds by 2.2.) Make sure you pee before stepping on the scale so your bladder is empty, since this water doesn't count in your hydration status.

2. Keep track of the amount of fluid that you consumed during training. Fifteen ounces of fluid weighs about 1 pound (or 1,000 milliliters of fluid equals 1 kilogram). You can also weigh the bottle before and after your training session to see how much the fluid you consumed weighs (but remember to subtract the weight of the bottle itself). For example, if

(continues)

(continued)

you drank 60 ounces (1,800 ml) of fluid during a three-hour ride, you would have consumed 4 pounds of fluid (1.8 kg).

3. Add the answers from 1 and 2 together (to determine what you lost and what you lost but replaced with new fluids) to help determine how much you should have drunk on your ride. For our example, you would add the 2 pounds of weight loss during training plus the 4 pounds of fluid you drank during training, and would have 6 pounds of fluid loss (or 0.9 + 1.8 kg = 2.7 kg).

4. To plan how to keep better hydrated, consider the amount of fluids you lost in the form of sweat divided by the amount of time you rode. This is your average sweat rate per hour. In our example, the 6 pounds lost equals 90 ounces of fluid; if you divide that by a three-hour ride, you can see that you lost 30 ounces of sweat per hour (or, in the metric system, 2.7 kg equals 2,700 ml of fluid; divide that by three hours to determine a sweat loss of 900 ml/hr). Thus, you sweated about 30 ounces, or 3.75 cups, of fluid per hour. On your next ride under similar circumstances (similar training effort and weather), you would want to try to consume 30 ounces per hour.

Following the steps to monitor your sweat loss for different types of workouts and conditions will give you ballpark figures to strive for. Of course, this is just a basic equation, and it doesn't account for some factors. The procedure is still the simplest way to keep track of hydration needs.

After exercising, make sure you drink 16 to 20 ounces (approximately 600 ml, the equivalent of a small water bottle) for every pound lost during training that was not replaced during the workout. You want to be back to healthy hydration quickly so that you can recover prior to your next ride. Try not to gulp it down, though, as this can be very uncomfortable for your digestive system and can actually be counterproductive. Post-ride fluid replacement does not have to be plain water; it can be in the form of a sport or recovery drink, as this will help you replace electrolytes and carbohydrates as well.

Maintaining Proper Hydration

Here's what you can do to keep up with fluid needs:

- Carry a water bottle with you at all times. Strive to drink small amounts continuously throughout your day. And when training, try to drink every 15 to 20 minutes. Try to swallow two or three big mouthfuls.
- Monitor your daily urine output. Remember, you want the color of your urine to resemble pale straw or be even lighter, with little to no odor.
- Always take two full large bottles for all rides longer than 1.5 hours, and plan your ride so you can refill when needed.
- Know your personal hydration needs. Use the calculation method in the sidebar ("Learning to Track Your Hydration") to determine how much fluid you need, and then design a plan to make sure you get enough.

Sweat Rate Factors

Things that will affect your personal sweat rate and training hydration needs include the following:

- Intensity and duration of exercise.
- Your level of heat acclimatization (how used to the heat you are) and training status (your water needs will change as you get used to riding and training in any environment).
- Outdoor temperature (or indoor temperature, if you are training at the gym or on an indoor trainer).
- Humidity level. (Don't be fooled into thinking that just because the humidity is low, as it is in the desert or in winter, your water needs go away. It is possible to get dehydrated anytime and in any environment.)
- What you are wearing. (Are you overdressed? This will increase your sweat rate and your hydration needs).
- Prehydration status. (Did you start out your ride well hydrated?)
- Sleep loss.

This means your fluid needs will change depending on the situation. Pay attention to these needs and how well you replace your fluids. Don't worry about what other riders need, because everyone's body is different. And don't listen to anyone who tells you to train your body to go without water. That is hogwash. Over time and with training, your body will get more efficient at sweating and using water, so your needs may change, but depriving your body of what it needs will only cause problems and can hurt your health.

OTHER NUTRITIONAL CONSIDERATIONS

What About the Food Pyramid?

How do the key nutrients fit into a daily diet? Most people are familiar with the food pyramid. The U.S. government created the pyramid to help people eat the right nutrients and lead healthier lives. The pyramid provides guidelines for making healthy dietary selections that provide enough of the six key nutrients for individuals based on both age and gender. The key nutrients are the building blocks that make up the foods in the six food-group categories of the pyramid. Following the pyramid guidelines makes it easier to eat the right amount of each category of food to ensure that you get enough of each of the nutrients. The current government nutritional recommendations provide suggestions for grains, vegetables, fruits, milk, meat and beans, and oils.

The website www.mypyramid.gov provides lots of great resources and information sheets to help you learn about good nutrition. You can use links like "MyPyramid Plan," "MyPyramid Menu Planner," and "MyPyramid Tracker" to build and examine a healthy diet. Keep in mind that the site is designed for the average person, not for the competitive athlete. But it does provide sound, safe, and important basic nutrition information.

Keeping Up with Good Nutrition

These websites provide accurate and reliable information about nutrition:

- American College of Sports Medicine, www.acsm.org
- American Dietetic Association, www.eatright.org
- National Agricultural Library and the U.S. Department of Agriculture, www.nutrition.gov
- Healthfinder, www.healthfinder.gov

What Is a Calorie?

Even when you're just hanging out on the couch watching TV, your body is using energy and burning calories. Everything you do, from breathing to digesting your dinner to sprinting across a soccer field, has an energy cost. Your body meets its energy needs by burning calories, and you get these calories from the foods you eat.

Energy is stored in food, and we measure this stored energy in calories (C) or kilocalories (kcals). Different types of food store different amounts of energy. Each gram of fat has 9 stored calories. A gram of carbohydrates and a gram of protein each have 4 stored calories. When we digest food, the energy gets released, but it can either be used immediately or be stored in our cells for later use. Our brains and muscles both need this fuel to function. This is why eating right is important not only for sport performance but also for everything else in life, including doing well in school.

Daily calorie needs are different for every individual, depending on each person's age and size, basic metabolism, and activity level. To figure out how many calories you need on any given day, you must take all three into account. Let's start with your basic daily energy needs, or *basal metabolic rate* (BMR). This is what it costs you in calories just to sit around and breathe. Your BMR is mostly determined by your genetic makeup, but it can also be influenced by your size and body composition. Muscle and other lean body tissue burn more energy than fat tissue does, so someone who is lean and strong will usually burn more calories than someone who is the same size but has less muscle—even when both of them happen to be just sitting around breathing. Then, in addition to your BMR, to calculate your energy needs for the day you must add in the number of calories you will spend doing various activities, including working out.

We can calculate your BMR in a lab, or we can estimate it using an equation. The sidebar "Equation for Determining Calorie Needs" shows you one equation that can be used to estimate the number of calories you need daily. Keep in mind that unless you are working with a specialist, the calculations are just estimations. This means your actual calorie requirements could be a little higher or a little lower. Plus, your activity level will change from day to day. So counting calories and trying to account for every single thing you eat are pretty much just a big hassle if you try to do it all the time. Don't worry about the numbers too much or try to manage your intake exactly or excessively. The point is to draw general principles from nutritional information and make good choices, and to know roughly how much you need to eat to cover your training needs for the day. You want to make sure you get enough nutrients and calories to allow your body to keep growing at the right pace, to train efficiently, and to recover adequately between workouts. If you don't get the calories your body needs, your performance may not be the best it could be on your bike. If you consistently get too many calories, or eat empty calories that do not contribute the nutrients you need, you will not be performing at your best either.

Think of your daily calorie needs as a daily money allowance. Each day, you have to purchase the basics (the nutrients) for good health with your allowance. The goal is to minimize the unhealthy things (high sodium, saturated fats, trans fats, calories that don't have any food value) while making good purchases with your allowance (vitamins, minerals, unsaturated fats, Omega-3 fatty acids, fiber, and so on). If you use up all of your allowance buying games (or eating junk food), you won't have enough left over to buy gas (good fuel).

Let's say you've calculated your daily energy needs for days with different types of workouts. How could you use this knowledge? Suppose you have calculated that you need 2,500 calories on a day when you train moderately. You decide to go out to lunch with your friends at a local fast-food place. The nutrition chart on the wall tells you that the sandwich-and-fry combo you are considering has 1,100 calories. Add a large soft drink, and now it goes up to 1,300 calories. (We'll ignore the alarmingly high sodium content of the saturated fats and trans fats for now.) This is just over half of the calories you need for the day. And we know that the burger, fries, and soda do not offer a lot of other nutrients. So if you decide to eat the combo meal, you then have to decide how you are going to get all the nutrients you need with the remaining 1,200 calories that you will consume throughout the day. This doesn't mean that the combo meal is a forbidden food—once in a while, you might want to go ahead and have it. But knowing what your body needs and how a certain meal stacks up in terms of calories and nutrition can help you take more control over what is going into your body and provide it with the best fuel possible. Now consider this same meal on a recovery day, when you might need only 1,900 calories. How would this combo meal affect your daily calorie budget then? Be sure to adjust your eating according to your energy needs for the day.

The Food Is Different in Europe

In the United States, we talk about calories or kilocalories (they are the same thing), but most other countries talk about the energy stored in foods in terms of kilojoules (kJ). To convert from calories to kilojoules you need to do a little simple math: Just divide the item in kJ by 4.2. This means, if something has 4,200 kJ, you divide it by 4.2 (which gives you 1,000, so the item has 1,000 calories). This bit of trivia may come in handy if you ever go to Europe to race. If you were in Europe and you were planning a moderate training day when you needed to consume 2,500 calories, you could bring out your handy calculator, punch in the numbers, and quickly determine that you could have 595 kJ. After all, when you find the grocery store, you'll want to try all those new kinds of snacks!

Balancing Act

What you eat provides the energy you need daily, and maintaining a healthy weight is about keeping a good balance between the energy in (the food you eat) and the energy out (the calories you burn). When energy in equals energy out, your weight doesn't change. If you take in more energy than you use up, your body will store the extra, and you gain weight. And losing weight happens when you burn more than you take in.

As a young rider, your biggest concern should be making sure that you are consuming enough food (calories) and enough nutrients to maintain a healthy weight and to have the energy necessary for training. Your growth and development during your teenage years are critical. Don't try to lose weight—and definitely do not lower your calorie intake below 2,000 calories a day—without consulting with a qualified nutritionist or a physician. Chances are, you're still growing, so obviously you will be gaining weight as you grow taller. As you train,

Equation for Determining Calorie Needs

The Harris Benedict Equation provides a way to estimate your BMR, or basal metabolic rate. Once you know the calories you need to just keep your body going while at rest, you can determine your daily calorie needs. To do this, you'll multiply your BMR by your activity level. Remember that the result of the multiplication problem is just an estimate for the number of calories you need to be healthy and to maintain your current weight. Coming up with a number does not mean you should count every calorie; it should just give you an idea of what your body needs.

BMR is determined a little differently for women than it is for men. Follow this procedure if you are female:

[655 + (4.35 x weight in pounds) + (4.7 x height in inches)] − (4.7 x age in years) = BMR

Do your calculation here:

[655 + (4.35 x _____ pounds) + (4.7 x _____ inches)] − (4.7 x _____ years) = _____

Follow this procedure if you are male:

[66 + (6.23 x weight in pounds) + (12.7 x height in inches)] − (6.8 x age in years) = BMR

Do your calculation here:

[66 + (6.23 x _____ pounds) + (12.7 x _____ inches)] − (6.8 x _____ years) = _____

Now, try the following worksheet to get some rough estimates of your calorie needs for different training days. You'll be multiplying your BMR by a number that is assigned to each activity level.

- If you are sedentary (little or no exercise), multiply your BMR by 1.2:
  _____ x 1.2 = _____ calories needed.
- If you are lightly active (light exercise/sports 1–3 days/week), multiply your BMR by 1.375:
  _____ x 1.375 = _____ calories needed.
- If you are moderately active (moderate exercise/sports 3–5 days/week), multiply your BMR by 1.55:
  _____ x 1.55 = _____ calories needed.
- If you are very active (hard exercise/sports 6–7 days a week), multiply your BMR by 1.725:
  _____ x 1.725 = _____ calories needed.
- If you are extra active (very hard exercise/sports and physical job or two training sessions), multiply your BMR by 1.9:
  _____ x 1.9 = _____ calories needed.

you will also become stronger, and muscle does weigh more than fat. A professional can help determine whether weight loss is necessary or realistic, how it can be done in a healthy manner, and what you can do to ensure that changes in your weight don't interfere with your ability to train and race well. We'll talk a little more about your racing weight in the next chapter.

Food Value

The idea of food value keeps coming up, so perhaps it's time to make sure you understand the idea thoroughly. We evaluate the value of a food item based on the nutritional punch that it packs. A sugary dessert like ice cream has only sugars (carbohydrates) and fat (usually the saturated kind), but it probably has very little in terms of food value—no fiber, few vitamins and minerals—even though it is a dairy product. Compared with other foods that are rich nutritionally, like a banana, ice cream is pretty empty of food value. A banana gives you a whole bunch of the essential things you need to get in your daily diet, and with far fewer calories. Each food has different combinations of things we need, and often things we don't. All of these things are taken into consideration to determine food value.

Having stuff we don't need doesn't make a food bad or forbidden. Weighing the good against the bad will help you decide how each food fits into your healthy diet. A cookie may not have the greatest food value, but it is yummy and it will provide some energy, and maybe even a little fiber and a few basic nutrients. In moderation, cookies can fit into a healthy diet. That is the key word: moderation. One or two cookies—okay. The whole bag, probably not such a good idea. Remember, to maintain a healthy weight and to fuel your body properly for training and improvement, you need to provide it with the right fuels. Being a healthy athlete is an all-day, everyday project, not just something that happens when you are training. Any old fuel will keep it going, but only a well-balanced diet that provides all of the key nutrients will ensure that you grow the way you need to and that your body is primed to make the most of training and competition. The next section will help you learn how to evaluate the value of different foods so you can decide how to spend your calories wisely.

Reading a Food Label

The U.S. government requires that all packaged foods—and even many restaurant foods—provide the nutrition facts for consumers. This is to help us make good food choices on a daily basis. For packaged foods, this information must be right on the packaging. For restaurants, this can sometimes be found on posters in the restaurant or online at company websites. Grab your favorite snack and take a look at the label.

There are a few important things to keep in mind when you read a food label. While the company does have to comply with the government rules and regulations, its top executives are still going to work as hard as they can to make their product appear as nutritious as possible. So try to ignore all the colorful and bold claims they stick all over the packaging, and focus your efforts on the food label itself.

Start by considering the serving size when reading a food label. You may be surprised to find that it is really just a small portion of what is in the package. For example, a serving size might be just two or three cookies—it's not the entire sleeve, as many believe. And for some snacks, even though items come in twos (for example, packaged breakfast pastries), the serving size may be only one of the pastries. This is important because the information on the rest of the food label refers only to the serving size indicated.

You also need to consider how many calories that serving contains. One hundred calories is considered to be a moderate amount. Don't automatically eliminate higher-calorie-per-serving choices or assume that fewer calories means it is a better choice. This is just a starting point. There are several different things to consider when choosing foods.

To help the consumer figure out how a food fits into an overall diet, the label shows how a serving of the product would fit into the daily diet of someone who is following a 2,000-calorie diet. It is up to you to make adjustments if your calorie needs are a little higher or lower than 2,000 a day. You really don't need to do any math, though. Instead, you can follow a general rule of thumb and make sure that saturated fats, trans fats, sodium, and cholesterol all register at 5 percent of DV (daily value) or less.

The label also provides information about nutrients you should strive to get. These include dietary fiber, vitamins A and C, calcium, and iron. Ideally, you want these to be 20 percent of DV or higher. Obviously, not every food is going to be perfect. But these guidelines will help you make good choices, especially when you are choosing among several different options.

Finally, take a look at the list of ingredients. Look for shorter lists and words you can easily pronounce. Typically, more natural foods have shorter lists, while more processed foods have longer lists. Look for lists that start with whole grain or the actual food ingredient (for example, apples if it is apple juice). Try to avoid foods that have ingredient lists that start with high fructose corn syrup or bleached flour. At first this might seem a bit overwhelming, but with practice, reading labels will become second nature. The website http://vm.cfsan.fda.gov/~dms/food lab.html will walk you through different examples of food labels. If you want to be able to read labels more proficiently, going through this exercise provides good practice.

A healthy diet provides the foundation for fitness and should become one of your top priorities, especially as you grow and train as a cyclist. This chapter will give you a good start toward building a sound nutritional lifestyle. To be an athlete, you will need to think a little more than the average person about what you are using to fuel your body. Remember that car at the start of the chapter: It would run on diesel fuel, but not very well. It would run well on regular fuel, because that's what it was designed to do. But if you really wanted high performance out of that engine, then you'd take extra special care of it—you might even use premium. Now that you have a good sense of how to fuel your engine properly on a day-to-day basis, let's take a look at some of the specific nutritional needs for endurance-based cyclists.

RECOMMENDED READING

The Cyclist's Food Guide, by Nancy Clark (Sports Nutrition Publishers, 2005).

Eat Smart, Play Hard, by Liz Applegate (Rodale Press, 2001).

Nancy Clark's Sports Nutrition Guidebook, 4th ed., by Nancy Clark (Human Kinetics, 2008).

Nutrition Periodization for Endurance Athletes: Taking Traditional Sports Nutrition to the Next Level, by Bob Seebohor (Bull Publishing, 2005).

Sports Nutrition for Endurance Athletes, by Monique Ryan (VeloPress, 2006).

6 NUTRITION for
Juniors, Part 2

It's not what you start with, but what you have left in the tank that makes the winner!

—Jeremiah Bishop, Trek/Volkswagen Racing Team

In the previous chapter, we talked about the basics of good nutrition. Eating well should be a day-to-day priority for any serious athlete. Without a good nutritional foundation, it is hard to train or race well, and if you pay attention only to your nutrition and hydration during training or on the night before races, you will be missing a great part of your potential performance. But it can be difficult to eat well, even when you have the best of intentions. Like anyone else, athletes are busy with school, jobs, and other demands that are placed on their time, such as having to do chores. It can be difficult to find the time to plan out your meals, and all too easy to grab a quick snack that may not be the best choice. Going out with friends to get pizza, or going to parties where lots of junk food is served, presents another type of challenge for Junior and Espoir riders.

And to add to all this, athletes are bombarded by ads for many supplements and for all sorts of products claiming to enhance performance. For the most part, if you don't have good nutrition, no special mix, potion, pill, or concoction will make up for it. Athletes need to be very careful about taking supplements, not only because many of them do not do what they say they will or can be harmful to your health, but also because many of them are illegal, both by law and according to sports organizations such as USA Cycling. This chapter is designed to provide more advanced information about nutrition that applies specifically to the concerns of cyclists and other athletes.

> ### When should I eat?
>
> Athletes are often unsure of the best way to eat. One of the best models for both good health and good performance is "grazing." This means many small meals spread out over the course of the day rather than three widely spaced meals. This type of diet helps keep you from getting really hungry and eating too much at one time. Eating small meals every few hours also helps you maintain a steady flow of energy to your body.

MAINTAINING YOUR WEIGHT

Wondering about your weight is not a bad thing—many athletes are interested in the topic. After all, our athletic performance depends to a great extent on how healthy our bodies are, and weight is a component of that. However, as a devo athlete, there are many more important things you need to be concerned with, such as your bike-handling skills, your grades at school (you wouldn't want your parents to decide you needed to cut back on cycling and focus more on your studies, so you'd better do well!), and your basic endurance fitness. We will talk a bit about weight management in this chapter, but before you try to change your weight, be sure to consult with a doctor or sports nutritionist. Nutritional decisions you make now can have an impact on your growth and a lifelong impact on your health.

Unless you are working with a specialist, it is important that you not try to lose weight during the racing season. Losing weight could hurt your performance, even if you aren't doing it on purpose. So eat enough to maintain your weight, and while you're at it, make sure that those calories you are taking in have all the nutrients you need (see Chapter 5).

Is there an ideal body weight? Yes and no. Certain body types are typically more successful in certain sports than others, but just because you don't seem to fit the mold doesn't mean you won't be able to accomplish as much as someone else with the body shape usually associated with that discipline. In general, elite roadies tend to be lean. Mountain bikers and cyclocross riders are often a little more powerful in their build, but in the elite ranks you will see a wide range of body types. Trackies, who

How often should I weigh myself?

Don't put too much emphasis on weight as an indication of fitness, especially during your devo years. It is easy to get caught up in numbers, but remember that they tell you only a very small part of the story. While you are growing, getting taller, and gaining muscle, you will find that your weight changes. This is healthy and normal. Focus instead on how your clothes fit, how you feel, and your fitness level. Weighing yourself can have some pros, though. For example, if you know your weight before a ride, you can compare it with your post-ride weight to determine whether you are hydrating properly (see Chapter 5, "Learning to Track Your Hydration" sidebar).

Even though all those TV infomercials would have you believe otherwise, the secret formula for weight management is no secret. When the calories you consume are equal to the calories you burn, you will maintain your weight. If you tip the scale and eat more than you need, your body will store the extra pounds and you will gain weight. And, of course, if your intake is less than what you need, you will burn up stored stuff and lose weight. While the equations below look simple, there is a bit more to it. Otherwise, people wouldn't struggle so much with weight. In this chapter, we'll look more closely at each of these equations:

$$\text{Energy In} = \text{Energy Out} \rightarrow \text{Maintain weight}$$
$$\text{Energy In} > \text{Energy Out} \rightarrow \text{Gain weight}$$
$$\text{Energy In} < \text{Energy Out} \rightarrow \text{Lose weight}$$

specialize mostly in power-based efforts, tend to be muscular. But keep in mind as a devo athlete that you aren't elite yet. A true cycling build takes many seasons of training to develop. Don't worry about ideal body weight or body type. And don't let anyone discourage you from pursuing your sport. Basketball great Michael Jordan was cut from the varsity squad at his high school, and yet with hard work and dedication he went on to have a pretty good career.

You rarely hear cyclists talk about wanting to gain weight. But let's go over this one anyway. There is no reason to bulk up for riding the way football players and other athletes sometimes do for their sports. However, sometimes cyclists are concerned with getting stronger, especially if they are involved in sprint cycling efforts. Building bigger and stronger muscles becomes important for these athletes. Some try protein shakes and similar products, taking a bet on the manufacturers' claims that these products will build muscle. This isn't exactly true. Protein does provide the body with amino acids, which the body uses to build muscle. But eating protein doesn't make your body build more muscle. Instead, you need to put in some hard work in the weight room. Power-based work, together with ingesting sufficient protein and more calories than you burn, should help you build muscle. Your diet provides your body with the materials for muscle recovery and growth, but you still have to work for it. You want the growth to be slow and steady to prevent your body from gaining extra fat while it is also adding muscle. If you are putting on more than half a pound a week, you may be gaining too much too soon.

On the other end of the spectrum, cyclists, just like everyone else, sometimes get caught up in the "I need to lose a few" mindset. This goes for both male and female riders. In general, this should not be the first concern of a devo athlete. If your coach feels that being lighter would help you perform better, consult a professional—a physician or dietician—who can help you do so safely with the smallest impact on performance. As mentioned above, you never want to try to lose weight during your racing season. Your body needs the calories to race and recover properly, and you don't want to risk not getting enough nutrients. If you are working with someone to reduce your weight, your emphasis should be on losing about a half pound per week—and absolutely no more than 1 pound per week. If you find you have lost more than this in a week, you may actually be seeing water loss; you are probably dehydrated. And dehydration has a very negative impact on performance. Additionally, when you lose weight at a fast rate, you may lose both fat and lean (muscle) body mass. The fat is what you want to lose, but when you lose muscle mass, you also lose power. This means that, yes, you will be lighter going up the hill, but you will have less power to get yourself up the hill, so you won't see a net improvement.

A Better Way to Monitor Weight

Body composition provides a good alternative to using weight as the sole predictor of fitness and race/training readiness. Body fat testing is about

Eating Breakfast to Do Your Best

Your mom is right—breakfast is the most important meal of the day.

Sometime before you go to sleep you have a snack, or maybe the last food you had was dinner. Then you sack out for seven, eight, or maybe even ten hours. During that time, your body still needs energy to function: You need to breathe, your heart still needs to pump blood, and so on. Some repair work is even taking place to help you recover from training. So while you snooze away, your body is busy digesting and consuming fuel. When you finally wake up, your immediate energy reserves are pretty close to empty. You still have energy stored in your liver and fat cells, but this is reserve energy and your body will not release it right away. It needs circulating energy (the stuff that you used up all night sleeping) to help burn it.

Even a small bit of breakfast with 50 to 300 calories can help jump-start your system the right way. If you don't like to eat in the morning, consider making a smoothie the night before and keeping it in the fridge, or grab a simple granola bar. This is important whether you are going for an early-morning training ride or just going off to school. Your brain needs circulating fuel to think properly, and your muscles need this same circulating fuel to do a quality workout.

"But wouldn't I burn more fat if I trained on empty?" you might ask. This is a common nutritional myth that has led many athletes to try to go out for a ride before breakfast. The theory is that by riding without any immediate energy available, you will force your body to dig into fat stores and thus burn more fat. This is one of those things that looks great on paper, but to date, the research hasn't supported it. Without circulating energy in your system, there is no fuel to keep the fire going. This actually makes your body concerned about not getting enough fuel, so it may be even more likely to hold on to its energy reserves tightly. The same thing happens if you consume too few calories throughout the day.

determining how much lean tissue and how much body fat you have. Everyone needs to have some body fat to be healthy. Body fat cushions our organs and helps us stay warm. A very low body fat percentage (less than 3 percent for males, and less than 11 percent for females) can lead to serious health concerns for both men and women.

You actually have two types of stored body fat. Have you ever cleaned a piece of chicken before you cooked it (or watched your mom or dad do this)? The yellow lumpy stuff that is just under the skin or attached to the meat is called *subcutaneous fat*. And guess what? You have it too. Humans tend to build it up on their thighs, tummies, and many other places, particularly just under the skin and on top of the muscle. Most of this fat is just extra storage fat. We also have a little bit around our organs to cushion them and keep them warm. Now think about the last steak you had. The white marbling you see in the steak is called *interstitial fat*. This type of fat can be healthy.

Scientists and fitness specialists can help you determine your body fat percentage using different methods. The gold standard is a *DEXA scan*. This is an expensive test that needs to be done in specialized facilities, and it provides the most accurate information on body composition. Some facilities have a machine called the BodPod that is very accurate for assessing body fat percentage. *Hydrostatic weighing* (sitting on a special scale while you get dunked underwater to be weighed) is also an accurate way to determine body fat, but there are not many places that do it. Many labs and fitness facilities use *pinch calipers* or other tools to determine your body fat. These tools can actually do a fairly good job of estimating body fat and are a good place to start. A local fitness center or YMCA may provide this type of body fat testing. There are also scales that can measure your body fat composition in addition to weight. However, it can be hard to get accurate readings from these scales unless you are optimally hydrated.

Having a high body fat percentage has been linked to many different lifetime health problems, such as diabetes and heart disease, and it is definitely detrimental to performance. Being too lean is just as worrisome. Too little body fat can hurt your immune system and your performance and has been linked to other health problems. For female riders, a body fat percentage that is too low has been linked to bone loss and problems with menstruation (see Chapter 12).

Now that you understand the most important general principles of nutrition and weight management, you are ready to think about how to put them into practice. Next we'll look at how to apply these principles to training and racing in your sport.

NUTRITION FOR TRAINING

Eating after training seems sort of like a no-brainer. Training makes you hungry, so you eat. But it's a little more complicated than that if you want to make the most of your training and recovery periods. When you train, your body's systems speed up in order to help move glucose (that key energy source) into your cells faster, and this helps fuel those muscles that are working so hard. When you stop training, this system stays sped up for a little while longer. While this system is working at double time, you have a great window of opportunity to replenish everything you burned up during training. It lasts for about two hours. The first half hour is a crucial time for replenishment. It is sort of like having extra workers on hand to restock the shelves for the first two hours after the store closes: They work the hardest in the first half hour, and then they slow down the closer it gets to quitting time. You want to make sure that the supply truck (good healthy food) arrives while all the extra workers are around to help put it all away. If you wait until they have all gone home, it will take the normal work crew much longer to do the same job.

To maximize the post-workout replenishment window, strive to get in at least 100 to 150 grams of carbohydrates and a little protein during the first thirty minutes after a training session. A peanut-butter-and-jelly (or banana) sandwich on whole wheat or a turkey-and-cheese on twelve-grain bread are great post-training or post-race snacks. Think about your post-ride replenishment plan before you even go out to train, especially for any effort over an hour and a half long. If you drive to join a group ride and your drive home will take more than fifteen minutes or so (not including post-ride hangout-and-talk time), make sure you pack something in the car or your bag to eat after the ride. Your immediate post-ride meal doesn't have to be food. There are plenty of different post-ride mixes on the market for replenishment drinks, or you can

On-the-Bike Training Foods

There are lots of products available for on-the-bike eating: gels, bars, gel blocks, and even jelly beans that have been specially formulated for training nutrition. Companies like Clif, Powerbar, and Hammer all make bars and gels designed for easy on-the-bike consumption. Clif makes Clifshots, little Jell-O-like squares, and Jelly Belly makes a special energy jelly bean. These products can get pretty expensive, however, and they aren't your only training options. For lower-cost alternatives, consider:

- Bananas—the perfect prepackaged training food.
- Granola bars (just make sure they aren't candy coated).
- Peanut butter sandwich on whole wheat. Cut it into halves or quarters to make it easier to get out of your pocket (skip the jelly, since it would be messier).
- Fruit snacks.
- Gummi bears (one of my favorites)—yes, they are just simple sugar, but they are great in a pinch and so yummy. Just make sure that you follow them up with something a little more substantial, like a banana.
- The bottom line is that your pocket fuel should be something that provides you with quality energy (so avoid the quick-energy candy bars) and is also nutritious. Dieticians will tell you that it doesn't matter how good your fuel is if you don't eat it.

No matter what you choose—prepackaged or homemade—make sure everything is bite-sized and easy to handle on the bike. On the bike is the one place where prepackaged foods are a good choice (while in daily life we try to opt for whole, less processed foods). Foods that are hard to open or awkward to handle on the bike are not safe options.

make your own healthy smoothie by blending together low-fat yogurt, bananas, and your favorite berries (fresh or frozen).

Practice What You Eat

Training is hard work and requires energy. You can do most mild to moderate workouts without additional fuel, but your workouts may be more productive when you are fueled properly. Your body has only about an hour's worth of training-level energy that is easily accessible, so for a longer workout bring along some extra fuel to keep you going. Your goal should be to consume 100 to 250 calories each hour that you exercise. You don't want to eat it all up at once, as this might cause stomach cramps or, worse yet, "bike burps." Instead, take a few bites every fifteen to twenty minutes to ensure the steady stream of energy you need.

The fuel you take in during training doesn't have to be solid food. For some people, eating while riding can be tough, and it can be easier on some courses than others. Most riders use a mix of foods and liquids to make sure they get in the right level of nutrition. These mixes come both premixed and as powders you can add to water. They are specially formulated, based on all sorts of research, to provide you with just the right amount of carbohydrates and electrolytes. These drinks shouldn't be carbonated. Most of them use forms of sugar like maltose that are easy on your stomach. (For many people, fructose, another form of sugar, can cause an upset stomach if taken in when training.) There are lots of mix options out there, and they all taste different. Most companies sell small packets of their products so you can test them out, both for flavor and to see how well the formula works for you. Experiment a little and make sure the formula you choose for race day is something that agrees with your digestive system.

It is important to fuel on the bike in training for another reason as well. If you don't pay attention to nutrition when training, it will be difficult to

Can I water my drink down?

If you need to water your sports drink down so it doesn't upset your stomach, go ahead and do so. Many athletes find that tastes they like off the bike are too strong and intense when they are training, especially as they become tired. Your sense of taste actually changes a little with exercise. Energy drinks and mixes that are truly made for athletes (as opposed to those fruity drinks in bright colors that are located near the soda in the store) take this into account and aren't flavored as strongly. However, if you still find the mix in your bottle too strong, add some water. Just keep in mind that when you water down the taste, you water down the energy and electrolytes too.

change your habits when you race, when nutrition matters even more. Quality training on empty is hard to accomplish, but it is even harder for your system to function properly when you ask it to put in an all-out effort in a race without proper fuel. Even if you fuel properly in a race, if your system isn't used to training hard and processing food at the same time, you are unlikely to be able to do both effectively. During training, practice fueling up with the same foods and habits that you will use in a race.

NUTRITION FOR RACING

Ideally, good nutrition should be something you pay attention to all the time. But as a race day approaches, there are some special considerations to take into account to make sure you're at your best.

In the days before the race, be sure that you are getting enough sleep at night. Without sleep your body can't do what it needs to do to use the great nutrients you have provided it. While you are sleeping, your body is making repairs and helping you get ready.

Also, in addition to eating well after each training ride, be especially careful about staying hydrated. You don't want to go into the event with any sort of deficit.

On the day of the race, have a good breakfast or meal four to five hours before the event, depending on when the race starts. Plan ahead according to your start time. For example, for an early start you may need to have a bottle ready to drink as soon as you wake up. But be realistic. If an event starts at 7 A.M., don't get up at 3 A.M. to eat. Have something simple as soon as you do get up and then plan to eat well during the event. This meal, along with a good diet on the days leading up to the event, will ensure that you start the race with good glucose stores and have plenty of energy in your system. Try to consume at least one full (16 oz.) water bottle two hours before the event. Use a mix if your stomach can tolerate it. Don't gulp it down all at once, though.

If the race starts later in the day, eat something two hours prior to the event. A light carbohydrate source (30–50 gm) that your stomach will be okay with—such as a banana or a bagel—is ideal. If your stomach can't do solids when you have pre-race jitters, you will be okay with the mix in your bottle.

You don't have to worry about taking in a lot of fluids in the ninety minutes just prior to the race if you are well hydrated. For some people, drinking during this time just means more trips to the bushes. However, don't be afraid to drink during this time.

Take in about 10 ounces of fluids (half a bottle) fifteen minutes prior to the start. Drink more only if you know from experience that it won't be sloshing around in your stomach.

Work on timing your warm-up to end ten to fifteen minutes before the start of the race. A warm-up that ends too soon is not as helpful as one that takes you closer to race time, but that doesn't mean you should skip it. Keep track of your warm-up routine so you can refine it for different types of races and different conditions.

During a race, shoot for a minimum of 16 ounces of water per hour (about a large bottle). Try to avoid waiting until you are thirsty, because by this point you are already dehydrated, and even a 1 to 3 percent change in hydration level can hurt performance. Consider ahead of time where you will be able to drink along the course, especially on rough mountain bike courses. You may need even more fluids on a hot or humid day.

For long events, it is important to get in carbohydrates as well as water during the race. The easiest way to do this may be a liquid form; however, gels and bars are okay, too. Try to ingest 30 to 50 grams of carbs per hour when the event is more than ninety minutes in length. Start taking

When to Avoid New Products

Race schwag (the goodies bag you get when you register for a race) often includes samples of energy bars or drinks donated by event sponsors. It is always a bad idea to try these things or anything else new during a race. New products that your body isn't used to might not settle well in your stomach. This can lead to a sour stomach or gastrointestinal cramps. It is often difficult to find a port-o-potty mid-race, and ending a race due to a bathroom emergency is no fun. So save the schwag bag and try out the product during a training session.

in carbs as early as thirty to forty minutes into the race. Taking in carbohydrates during a shorter race wouldn't hurt, either—it is just much harder to do in high-intensity situations.

Eating While Traveling

Being a bicycle racer requires frequent travel—and the more serious you become about the sport, the farther afield you'll want to go to seek out new challenges. It's likely that you'll be putting in some "windshield miles" as you begin to participate in regional races. But traveling can do more than take you out of your own comfortable bed. For one thing, it can disrupt your normal eating patterns. It's easy on the road to chow on convenience store foods or rely on fast-food meals. Obviously, these are not good sources of nutrition. And worse yet, when you eat this way you deny your system the good things it is used to. Not only does this impact your health, but it can really hurt your performance.

Plan ahead for road travel. Stock the car with healthy snacks so you won't be tempted to eat junk on the road. In a cooler you can pack granola bars, bagels, peanut butter, apples, healthy crackers, and bottled water. (Don't forget the silverware and some napkins! Peanut butter is very hard to spread without a knife—not impossible, just very messy.) If you

---

But Pizza Is Soooo Good!

The post-race nosh on pizza, especially at an all-you-can-eat pizza place, is a standard among athletes, particularly collegiate riders. You might argue that the crust provides good carbs and the cheese provides protein. Although this is true, that doesn't mean it is a good choice. Pizza crusts are usually made of white flour, not whole grains, and the oils and cheeses used, particularly in fast-food pizzas, are loaded with saturated fats (the unhealthy kind). In addition to being bad for your heart and general health, saturated fats slow down healing and reduce your body's ability to deal with the muscle and joint inflammation that occurs with hard efforts. So pizza and other fast foods may satisfy your hunger after a race, but they also actually slow down your recovery and can hurt your ability to race again the next day. Shoot for healthy, whole-grain foods. And if you must have pizza or fast food, have it in moderation, and save it for days when you haven't trained especially hard.

will be staying overnight in a hotel, consider packing a breakfast kit with some instant oatmeal or something similar. You certainly shouldn't rely on the donuts and sugary muffins at the hotel buffet, which could have a negative impact on your performance. Often, early race-start times require you to check out of the hotel before the breakfast even begins. A nice bonus when you pack ahead is that it will save you money that you can put toward your next bike instead.

SUPPLEMENTS

Getting a balanced diet can seem complicated and time-consuming, especially when you are busy and on the go all the time. So it's understandable that some athletes turn to supplements like vitamins or protein powder. They can seem like a great option, and supplements are a very common part of sports culture today. But you must be very careful about the supplements you take. Instead of compensating for a bad diet and giving you the balance that good nutrition can supply, supplements can actually throw your system off balance and create problems—especially if taken in high dosages.

In theory, if an athlete has a well-balanced diet, there should be no need for supplementation. However, getting a well-balanced diet can be a challenge, especially when you are traveling, if you don't like certain foods or have food sensitivities or allergies. Supplements can help you get the nutrients you need in these cases. But many of the vitamins and minerals the body needs are not absorbed as well in supplement form as they are from natural foods. Athletes shouldn't rely on them to replace a poor diet.

Despite what the ad—or the clerk at the vitamin store—says, some supplements are unnecessary at best and harmful at worst. Even though our bodies need these things for good health, in some cases it is possible to take too much. Side effects can range from gastrointestinal distress to more serious concerns. For example, iron is an important mineral that helps to transport oxygen from your lungs to your muscles. If you don't have enough iron in your diet, you could become anemic (see "Anemia" in Chapter 12). Under a doctor's supervision, taking an iron supplement in this case may be the right thing to do. However, if you take iron supplements when you don't need them, you may experience stomach cramps and diarrhea. And iron is not the only supplement that can cause problems when taken unnecessarily. The fat-soluble vitamins (A, D, E, and K) are stored in your fat cells when taken in excess, and this can cause unintended and often unhealthy side effects.

Some supplements are simply a waste of money. For example, the nutritional recommendations call for the average teenager to take in 75 to 90 milligrams a day of vitamin C. Your body cannot store excess vitamin C because it is water soluble. So any extra vitamin C in your system simply gets flushed out daily. If you megadose on vitamin C, your body will have the same amount as someone who is consuming the right amount. The only difference will be that you will have a lot more vitamin C in your urine, which isn't very helpful.

The bottom line? Shoot for the daily recommended dosages of the different vitamins and minerals, and obtain them, if at all possible, from your diet. But be very careful before taking any supplement, especially one that provides more than the recommended dosage. Make sure you thoroughly research any supplements you are considering before you purchase them. Check with reliable sources (such as http://www.supplementwatch.com) before you make a decision. And talk to your physician as well, just in case there are any health issues that would pertain to you personally that should be taken into consideration. Make sure you understand the potential side effects as well as the potential benefits.

ASKING A PROFESSIONAL

Athletes often consult with nutrition specialists to help them sort out how to fuel properly. But whom should you consult? Not all nutritional specialists have the same qualifications. Your family doctor might be able to help, but he or she is trained to treat illness and may not be up-to-date on athletes' nutritional needs. Your doctor may be able to recommend someone else in your community who can help. The American Dietetic Association (ADA) has a registry of certified individuals, and its website (www.eatright.org) has a "Find a Nutrition Professional" link that can help you find a qualified dietitian with an office near you. The ADA even has a specialization, "Board-certified specialist—sports dietetics," that professionals can earn. Your local hospital will have registered dietitians on staff, and local universities and colleges may have professors who teach and study nutrition. Be sure to ask about their qualifications to work with athletes, as our needs are a little different from those of more sedentary folks.

Lots of people who claim to be sports nutrition specialists are not registered dietitians. This does not mean they are not good at what they do, but it does mean they may not have met the equivalent of the national standards that the ADA has set. Not all states regulate the type of training an individual must receive before claiming to be a specialist. Be sure to ask (or have your parents ask) about a nutritionist's qualifications, and check out his or her credentials, before you decide to consult. Did the nutritionist attend a college program or become certified by a reputable organization like the American College of Sports Medicine (ACSM), or did he or she get a certification for $19.99 over the Internet? Do a little research on the Internet. Many certifying organizations will allow you to verify someone's credentials on their websites.

You also want to be careful about anyone who tries to sell you special vitamins or nutritional supplements as vital for your health or performance. A good nutritionist will focus on using food to satisfy your body's needs and will turn to supplements only as an additional idea. Further, if a qualified nutritionist does recommend some type of supplementation, he or she will offer several different options. Be careful of someone who tries to get you to buy something that he or she sells to make extra income.

If the cost of the consultation is a concern, consider contacting your local college or university nutrition program. There may be students in the program who will work for a reduced fee or even for free in order to get practice working with athletes. Their work is usually supervised by a professor who is an expert in nutrition. Some schools even have community fitness or wellness programs that have these sorts of programs at very reduced fees.

Nutritionists typically work sort of as doctors or consultants. You go in for an appointment to talk about your diet. The nutritionist gathers information about how you eat and your needs, then makes suggestions about things you can do to improve your diet. He or she may ask you to keep a food diary or a journal for several days to record what you eat and drink, how much, and when. Many use a computer program to help determine what nutrients you are getting in sufficient amounts and what nutrients you are lacking.

Ergogenic Aids

Supplements, by definition, are substances that help bring your diet up to speed. As we saw in the first part of this chapter, some can be helpful in some situations, but others can be harmful or just a waste of money. Ergogenic aids are in a different category. These are things that are supposed to help you improve your sports performance. (There is some overlap, however, between the categories, since numerous supplements are also considered ergogenic aids.)

Ergogenic aids can be things that are normal parts of your diet, or they can come in pill, powder, or liquid form. They can be natural substances like herbs, or they can be medicines, drugs, or other chemical substances. Some of them work and some don't, and some are perfectly legal whereas others may be illegal or banned from sports. They can even be things we use, such as time trial bars and aerodynamic helmets. However, for the sake of this chapter, we will focus on the things you might ingest, such as over-the-counter or prescription medicines, drugs, and the like. In an earlier section, we talked about the pros and cons of taking basic supplements, so we will focus here on the other types of ergogenic aids.

If you have paid attention to pro sports, over the past year or two you have heard a lot about athletes and the use of ergogenic aids. It seems like every time the Tour de France is in the news, there are controversies about the use of banned substances among the athletes. So you know that there are serious safety considerations when it comes to their use as well as ethical and legal considerations.

A continuing controversy is over "blood doping." Blood doping involves taking a drug (EPO) to increase the number of oxygen-carrying red blood cells in the athlete's system, or even taking out the athlete's

What about my medicine? Can it be banned?

The short answer is yes. But read on, because you may be able to get permission to take a banned substance if you truly need it for medical reasons.

Some over-the-counter and prescription medicines do appear on the list of substances banned from certain sports. This means that medicines you take for a cold, for asthma, or for other health problems may be prohibited. It is important that you check all medicines you take against the USADA list to see if any of them are included. But don't just look for brand names. Many over-the-counter cold medicines have ingredients that are banned, so be sure to check the ingredient list on the medicine container and go through the list of banned items carefully.

Elite athletes must be very careful about what they use from the local drugstore if they want to test clean. In the case of a cold, you can just suffer through the symptoms, drink lots of fluids, and get plenty of rest, just as the doctor says, and you'll get over it. This is not always the case for other illnesses or conditions. Some medicines on the prohibited substances list are essential to an athlete's life—for example, an athlete with asthma really does need that inhaler. This does not mean that people with asthma have to make a choice between cycling and taking that lifesaving medicine, however. Cyclists who need to take a certain medication on the list may use a "Therapeutic Use Exemption" (TUE) form to apply for permission to use the banned substance. This paperwork takes time and requires your doctor's signature, so be sure to fill it out ahead of time. The USADA website provides all the necessary information for filling out a TUE.

As a beginner, you do not need to worry about this. But when you start competing at the level where testing becomes a reality, it is a good idea to be familiar with the rules.

own blood, spinning it down to isolate the red blood cells, and then putting the red cells back into the athlete's bloodstream. The purpose is to increase the athlete's ability to carry oxygen to the muscles so that they can work harder. However—and this is a very important "however"—blood is supposed to be a fluid, and those little red blood cells are solid. The more of them there are in the blood, the more the blood becomes less like water and more like sludge. This is very risky because blood cannot flow well under these conditions. Those little cells start to stick together and the athlete can have a heart attack, a stroke, or some other serious cardiac event. In fact, many athletes have died experimenting with this particular ergogenic aid.

Legal Versus Prohibited Substances

Some ergogenic substances are illegal according to state and federal law. This means that possession and use of them are criminal offenses and that violators can be arrested and charged with a crime. Marijuana, synthetic testosterone, and cocaine, for example, are against the law just about everywhere. You know that criminal matters have serious consequences, so we won't dwell on this. But as an athlete, you also need to consider that some ergogenic substances may be banned by sporting organizations even if they are legal according to state and federal law. The United States Anti-Doping Agency (USADA) publishes a detailed and up-to-date list of substances that are banned or prohibited for each sport (see http://www.usantidoping.org/). This list includes substances that impact performance, substances that can be harmful to an athlete's health, and substances that violate the spirit of sport. It is updated annually based on new research and as new drugs are released to the market.

Who Gets Tested?

In the sport of U.S. cycling, the USADA oversees all the testing for banned substances. Initially, as a beginner in the sport, you are unlikely to have to undergo testing. However, the higher you go in competition, the more likely it is that you will get tested. Athletes get tested in two different ways. During racing season, they are tested at major competitions. At designated events, the winner and several other racers selected at random will be tested immediately after the competition. Individual athletes are put on the designated athlete list once they've reached a certain level of competition, and once that happens, they may be tested at any time. Testing involves peeing in a cup following a very strict procedure to ensure your safety and the integrity of the sample you provide. The USADA website provides great informational videos that explain the process and tell you what to expect.

At a competition where athletes will be tested, it is the responsibility of the race promoter to let competitors know where the post-race testing list will be posted. Athletes are required to show up immediately for their test and will be provided with a testing escort. They are allowed to change out of their race gear into dry, warm clothes. They are also allowed to have an advocate (a friend, parent, or coach) accompany them to the testing site. If you do reach the level of racing where testing becomes a possibility, I would strongly recommend that you bring an advocate with you. You may be tired after the race, and your advocate can help make sure that the testing is done properly. You will have to stay with the testing officials until you are ready to urinate. This can sometimes take a little while, especially if you are a bit dehydrated from the race. There will be paperwork, of course, which is where your advocate can help out. Then, when you are ready to urinate, you will choose a selection kit (a sterile, sealed set of jars for collecting your urine and sending in your sample) from a box and fill the collection vial with half of your sample urine. A same-sex testing official will be required to witness your sample. This may sound a little creepy, but it is done to ensure that your sample is really yours (you wouldn't believe what some athletes have done to cheat!). Then you pour the other half of your sample into a second container (this is so there is a primary sample and a backup sample) and seal both. The seal helps to ensure that no one can tamper with your test. At this point you are done, and the sample gets sent off to the lab. The off-season testing that elite athletes must undergo is similar, except that the testing agent comes to the athlete's home at random times.

What happens when you test positive?

Testing positive is a very serious matter. A positive test can result in sanctions, sport suspension, or even a lifetime ban from competition. Even for athletes who get suspended, who serve their time out of the sport, and who return, the taint of having been a cheater is always with them. It influences how people treat them and can hurt their ability to get a decent sponsor (the bread and butter of making a living as a competitive rider).

All anti-doping organizations take the stance that remaining clean is always the athlete's own personal responsibility. This means that you are responsible for any substances you ingest—an athlete cannot make the excuse that it was his or her coach's fault. Nor is ignorance of the rules an excuse. Even if you take something inadvertently that causes you to test positive for a banned substance, you can still get in trouble. As a Junior athlete climbing the ranks of elite performance, your likelihood of getting tested increases as you move up in levels. Carefully consider any supplements or other substances you want to take.

It is possible to take a substance completely by accident. Vitamins and other supplements are made in factories on assembly lines. The same line is often used to make different kinds of supplements. In between, say, a batch of weight loss pills and a batch of vitamin C, the machine will probably get cleaned. But if the cleaning isn't perfect, then a little of whatever was used to make the weight loss pills might find its way into the vitamin C pill you took. If the weight loss pill contained something on the banned sport substances list, you might fail your drug test. Granted, the likelihood of this happening is pretty remote, but it is something you should try to avoid nonetheless, because the consequences are serious. Look for companies that use the Good Manufacturing Practices (GMP) seal. Sport governing bodies do not consider the possibility of this kind of contamination to be an acceptable defense for a failed test. Remember, ultimately it is your responsibility to remain clean as an athlete.

USADA and WADA (World Anti-Doping Agency) are committed to preserving the rights of athletes, the right to safe and healthy competition, the rights of sports, and the rights of society as they relate to safe, fun, and fair sport competition. Under these organizations, a substance is banned or prohibited if it meets two of the following three criteria:

- Has the potential to enhance performance
- Poses a health risk
- Violates the "spirit of sport"

But if you are sure there are no health risks associated with a substance and that it is legal, take a moment to consider whether it really works. Many companies make claims that aren't quite true. Some web-sites (for example, http://supplementwatch.com) do a great job of explor-ing the pros and cons of different supplements. Manufacturers' websites may talk a mean game about how great their products are, but take a close look at the research they cite. Before you take anything, be sure to check it out carefully. There are often far better things you could spend your money on, like new bike parts. Why waste it on a pill or potion that doesn't really work?

Key questions to ask before taking any drug or supplement:

- Is it legal?
- Is it banned?
- Is it ethical and does it fit with the spirit of fair sport?
- Are the claims based on sound research?

When evaluating the research behind the claims, think about the following:

- Who conducted the study? Was it someone paid by the manufacture? This can really influence the results.
- Was only one study done or is there a lot of supporting evidence?
- Who was tested? Sometimes things are tested on "average" folks who aren't active, which means they might not have the same impact on an athlete.
- Was it tested on humans? A lot of products tout all sorts of claims but forget to tell you that all the results were seen in rats!

There are lots of other questions you might ask, but this should get you off to a good start.

RECOMMENDED RESOURCES

The World Anti-Doping Agency, or WADA (http://www.wada-ama.org/en/), sets the inter-national standard for safe and legal sport.

In the United States, the United States Anti-Doping Agency, or USADA (http://www.usantidoping.org/), is responsible for overseeing drug and ergogenic aid education, testing, and sanctioning for all U.S. Olympic sports.

7 TRAINING
101

Decide honestly how far you want to go with cycling, set a long-term goal, and never forget it. Every single day, take a little chunk off of the block that stands in your way.

—Nick Ranno, 2nd place, 2005 Collegiate Nationals

Athletes in every sport train. At some levels, training is very informal and the focus is on having fun—for example, intramural sports. At other levels—such as pro football or elite cycling—training is highly specialized and organized. As a Junior or Espoir athlete just beginning your career, you are probably somewhere in between these two extremes. Cycling is still exciting and fun for you, but you may feel you are ready to start taking your training more seriously. This chapter will give you a basic knowledge of the science of training so that you can take that next step. Think of training as an investment in your future health and your ambitions as an athlete.

Researchers who study exercise physiology, kinesiology, and human movement have learned a great deal about how our bodies respond to training and how we can best train the body for peak performance. Coaches and athletes study the things that the researchers report in an effort to train smarter. It is important to keep in mind that every individual is different. Understanding the basic science of training will give you a great foundation, but you will still have to carefully consider how to apply all that training science to your own situation. Your unique physical and genetic makeup and any special health concerns you may have will influence your training needs and your body's responses to training. This means that you can't just do what some other athlete does in training; the unique needs of your body and your situation require that you tailor your training. As a devo rider, one of the smartest moves you can make is to be actively involved in the whys and hows of your training program. A coach, your parents, your doctor, and other riders can all help you learn more about safe and effective training and how to personalize it. Let's begin your journey to becoming a smarter rider by exploring basic training concepts and ideas.

CONSISTENT TRAINING

Training offers so many benefits. You know that training enables you to become a faster rider, but it does so much more than that. For endurance athletes, the primary purpose of training is to build a better engine (stronger heart and lungs) in order to go farther faster. Other training benefits include:

- Less fatigue over time (which means you can ride stronger for a longer period of time)
- Faster recovery
- More efficient delivery of blood and oxygen to working muscles
- Greater power
- Less muscle soreness
- Better ability to focus on skills and tactics
- Reduced susceptibility to injury, and faster recovery from injury

All of these things add up to better performance and more personal success. Keep in mind that just riding your bike and putting in miles aren't the same thing as training. You may be riding several times a week, but this doesn't mean you will be improving in a way that will translate into better performance. Training means having a well-thought-out plan that brings about physical adaptations that lead to specific improvements. It is critical that you train smart, not just train.

Sport scientists have developed a four-stage model of training for developing athletes. This model is based on what we know about talent and elite performance. (To read more about talent development, see Chapter 4.) When someone first starts to ride, he or she may still be learning physical fundamentals. People start out at different levels at this point; each person has a slightly different set of skills to bring to the cycling experience.

Most young people have had some sort of exposure to physical activity and movement before the age of 10; this is when kids have an opportunity to learn how to run, skip, throw a ball, learn to swim, balance on a beam, and balance on a bike. These are all fundamental skills for being athletic and having a healthy, physically active future. These experiences also lay the foundation for sport performance and talent development. Don't despair if you didn't get much of this; it just means that you may have to work a bit harder to develop your athletic self by seeking out different types of sport skill-learning opportunities.

In most organized sports, the activity becomes a little more structured after the children reach the age of 10 or so, particularly in the early teenage years. By then, most young people have mastered the basic elements of many athletic activities. They can move safely, and they can safely learn to train at a more serious level. This means that a coach or mentor can guide them to help them better understand how to physically improve. Young athletes can now understand what their body is doing and why and how it changes in response to training. Athletes may compete in this phase, but the main goal should be to learn what training is all about and what it means to be an athlete.

From the "learning to train" phase, riders move on to the "training to train" phase. In this stage, they set down a solid base of physical, psychological, technical, and tactical skills and abilities. Although they were working on these things before to some extent, training now becomes more focused. As an athlete in this phase, you will be competing, but the purpose of competition is to help you learn what you need to work on and identify training elements to emphasize. This will put you in the best possible position for the final phase.

There is no set time limit for how long athletes should spend learning to train and then training to train. Often these areas overlap and blur together. This is fine as long as you are aware of what you are doing and what is being learned. However, the final stage, training to compete, shouldn't start until an athlete has spent at least two solid years riding (this is just a rough guideline, as some riders take longer and that is perfectly okay) (see Chapter 15 for more details). "Training to compete" means that an athlete has a strong base in terms of fitness, has good skills, and knows the tactics and technical fundamentals a cyclist needs to go after races in a smart and planned manner.

> ### Stages of Becoming an Effective Bike Racer
>
> 1. Fundamentals/Learning to be athletic
> 2. Learning to train
> 3. Training to train
> 4. Training to compete

The 24/7 Athlete

When we talk about athletes in everyday conversation, most of us immediately think of the competitions an athlete takes part in—the big games, the record-setting home runs, and just being in the spotlight in general. Or we think about the hours and years of grueling training that Olympic athletes have engaged in to get to the high point of their career. But as an athlete, you need to be aware that it means so much more. For a true athlete, one who is striving for peak performance, being an athlete is a 24/7 endeavor. In training, athletes train with intent. They know what they need to accomplish and apply themselves with focus and dedication. They also know that being an athlete goes far beyond what happens in training. Here are a few things athletes need to consider on the road to being the best they can:

- *Nutrition:* This means nutrition all the time, not just before, during, and after competitions. What you eat and drink prepares your body for training and competition and plays a huge role in your ability to recover from training (see Chapters 5 and 6).
- *Sleep:* Both quality and quantity matter, not just the night before a competition, but all the time. Athletes know they regularly need to get high-quality, undisturbed sleep to allow the body to repair and refresh itself after training. Most people need seven or eight hours a night, and teenagers often need nine or ten. But training may increase the amount of sleep you need. Shortchanging your sleep and burning the midnight oil will only add stress to your body and reduce your ability to get stronger. Lack of sleep will also reduce your

reaction time, compromise your ability to make good decisions, and impair your focus.

- *Life Stress:* Believe it or not, a stressful life can have a very negative impact on training and racing, even if the stress is unrelated to cycling. Practice good time management with your schoolwork so you aren't up late rushing to finish a paper or cram for a test. Talk to your parents, friends, or teachers when you are stressed so they can help you find ways to reduce it.

- *Lifestyle:* This is how you live in general. Athletes, particularly elite athletes, are successful for a reason. Because you need to train, have good recovery and nutrition, and get your schoolwork done, you may not have the time or energy to hang out the way your non-cycling friends do. This doesn't mean you never have any fun; it just means you need to make good decisions and think about how different things might impact your goals. For example, going to the movies may sound like fun, and you may choose to go; but you might opt to go home after the movie instead of hanging out with your friends until midnight, because you have a group ride at 8 A.M. and you want to be well rested to perform well.

Common Mistakes for Beginners

Beginning riders often make their biggest mistakes when they are impatient with themselves. When they feel they are not making progress fast enough, they push harder in training. But overtraining can cause injuries, decreased performance, and even burnout. It is important for riders to understand that the effects of training are cumulative over time and cannot be sped up. As a cyclist, you must keep the big picture in mind and remember that you are working toward long-term goals. Step back from your day-to-day concerns once in a while and look at how one year will build into the next year. This is always the recipe for elite success in endurance-based sports. (See Figure 7.1)

Another common training mistake is to try out every new training program you come across. Riders sometimes switch programs because they are frustrated with their rate of progress or lack training knowledge, or just because they are so enthusiastic about riding that they want

FIGURE 7.1 Effects of Training over Time

to try out every new trick or theory. However, changing your training strategy several times across a season, before any one program has had a chance to be truly effective, will undermine your ability to improve. It is important to set goals, choose a training plan, and then stick to the plan to give it a chance to work. Every training plan needs to be flexible, to take account of the inevitable twists and turns of the season, but radically changing a training plan too often is not beneficial. It creates a situation where you are not getting the consistency necessary for long-term strength and endurance gains.

PERIODIZATION

Training is all about systematically stressing different physical systems. This stress occurs when you change the volume, frequency, and intensity of the work you do during practice. For example, one day you might ride 40 miles at 17 mph. This is the volume (you went 40 miles) and intensity (how hard you worked—17 mph pace) of your effort. If this is a little more than what you are used to, it will stress your body, and if you allow yourself to recover properly (more on this in a moment), your body will get stronger.

How do you get the greatest possible benefit from your training program? Reliable research tells us that something called "periodization" is the key. Periodization is all about shifting volume and intensity of training in a systematic way over time. Athletes used to just train hard all the time, but we found that this led to injuries. The athletes didn't improve as

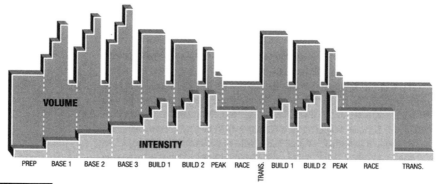

VOLUME

INTENSITY

| PREP | BASE 1 | BASE 2 | BASE 3 | BUILD 1 | BUILD 2 | PEAK | RACE | TRANS. | BUILD 1 | BUILD 2 | PEAK | RACE | TRANS. |

FIGURE 7.2 Classical Model of Periodization

much as might have been expected. In periodized training, athletes cycle through harder days and then easier days, harder weeks and then easier weeks. And it turns out that when they do this, they get stronger faster in a systematic and planned manner. There is not just one way to periodize training—which is part of the fun—but this can also make it a little harder for the beginner. The classic model of periodization looks like Figure 7.2. In this model, the work (volume or intensity) builds up over a series of weeks, and then there is a rest week before it starts again.

Don't become overwhelmed by all the detailed theories about periodization at this point. When you first begin to train using periodization, start small. Just concentrate on having a pattern of hard days and easy days. The more serious you get and the more you develop as a rider, the more complex your periodized training plan will become. Eventually you will include all the elements for peak performance (see Figure 7.3).

Principles of Periodization

There are eight key principles in periodized training that are well established. I have added a ninth element in the description below to explain a relatively new concept that is just beginning to be recognized by sport scientists:

1. *Overload:* You have to stress the body in order for it to get stronger. Too much stress, and you get injured; too little stress, and you don't improve much, if at all. Learning how much overload is "just

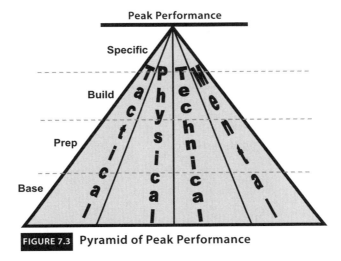

FIGURE 7.3 Pyramid of Peak Performance

right" takes a bit of trial and error. This is where an experienced coach can be very helpful.

2. *Progression:* If you did the same thing every day, week after week, you would get bored, right? Well, your body can get bored, too. If you always go the same route at the same pace, your body learns exactly what it needs to do and doesn't bother to change anymore: There isn't any need to improve. Progression—the changing of volume and intensity of riding over time—helps you keep improving and keeps you from getting bored (see Figure 7.4). Remember, these aren't just random changes; they are changes based on your goals and the physical goals (gains in speed, power, endurance, and so on) and other goals (improved tactics, skills, and the like) that you are trying to reach.

3. *Specificity:* If you want to become a better bowler, you need to practice bowling. If you want to become a better bike racer, you need to ride your bike. The specificity principle says you have to train the systems you want to improve.

4. *Use it or lose it:* This one probably makes a lot of sense. Sometimes it is also called the "reversibility principle." It means that if you stop training, you will lose your fitness. This doesn't happen overnight, so missing a day of training isn't going to ruin your fitness; it takes

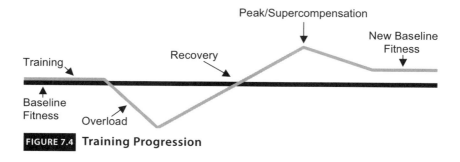

FIGURE 7.4 **Training Progression**

awhile to lose it. Generally, however, after ten to fourteen days of doing absolutely nothing, athletes will start to notice a drop in their fitness level. And even after just a few days of little to no activity, you may begin to feel stale and out of shape.

5. *Diminishing returns:* Some athletes feel that if some training is good, more is better. This is only partially true. If you train two days a week, then training four days a week will help you do better. The principle of diminishing returns says that as you increase your training beyond a certain point, the gains you make get smaller and smaller. So with four days of training you will definitely get stronger than if you would if you trained for only two days, but if you trained for six or seven days, the gains you make would be smaller. In fact, the extra little bit you might gain from these two additional days is so small that it is outweighed by the increased chance of injury you have if you train hard for six or seven days a week.

6. *Moderation:* As in nutrition, in training moderation is a great principle for health and wellness. This principle draws attention to the importance of being balanced. Keep in mind that doing too much of any one thing is probably going to set you up for injury or illness. This means that doing same workout, taking the same ride, or the aiming for the same intensity day after day will not allow you to make many gains. (See Figure 7.5.)

7. *Individualization:* Just like snowflakes, every individual is different. Your training program may be similar to someone else's, but to be truly effective, it must be tailored to your body's unique needs. Listen to your body and learn what it needs so you can

always make sure that your training program is well adapted to your own needs. Individualized training gives you a better shot at maximizing your potential. Following someone else's plan will rarely enable you to perform to the best of your ability.

8. *Variation:* Doing the same workout over and over again can lead to injuries. You may overtrain some muscles at the expense of others, and you will get bored with the program, just as you would if you were not changing the volume and intensity of your training. Variation in speed, distance, terrain, and even workout routine can help to prevent overtraining and ensure a well-rounded, interesting training program.

9. *Rest:* Finally, there is the rest phase. This is perhaps the most crucial but most overlooked, or at least undervalued, principle of periodization. Training will not do much for you if you do not have proper recovery. Training tears you down, but you must have good resources for recovery (sleep, food, hydration, quiet time, for example) and actually utilize them to get the full benefits of periodization and training. Just as rest following a hard effort on a training ride allows you to do another one, rest following a training ride will allow you to ride strong on your next training ride and achieve more in your training rides over time. Sometimes you may need only a day's rest; other times, you may need a few days of rest, or even a few weeks of rest at the end of a season. It all depends on what your plan is and what your goals are.

MONITORING YOUR TRAINING

To keep track of training progress and recovery, coaches and athletes have found it useful to monitor and record details about training. Some of the things that are good to keep track of are heart rate, power, and rate of perceived exertion, or RPE.

Rate of Perceived Exertion

Swedish scientist Dr. Gunnar Borg created a scale that athletes can use to rate how hard or easy a training effort is. You can use this scale to rate the intensity of your training. All of this information helps you to evaluate your progress, fine-tune your training program, and make changes as you improve.

The Borg scale is a scale of perceived effort that ranges from rest to maximal exertion using numbers from 6 to 20. Although the numbers are given specific descriptions (for example, "very light" for 9, or "extremely hard" for 19; see Table 7.1), it is up to the individual to determine what each level feels like. This means that the numbers you assign to a workout will be somewhat subjective. But by keeping track of your perceived exertion in your training log, you can see improvement over time. For example, if a particular effort at a certain speed used to be an 18, and now it feels more like a 16, you know you have made an improvement. Seeing this kind of progress can be a strong motivator.

A different version of the Borg scale that goes from 1 to 10 is also sometimes used, often by fitness clubs. It works in basically the same way as the 6 to 20 scale, with 1 being the easiest level and 10 being the hardest.

TABLE 7.1 Borg's RPE Scale	
RPE Rating	Exertion Level
6	No exertion at all/rest
7	Extremely light
8	
9	Very light
10	
11	Light
12	
13	Somewhat hard
14	
15	Hard (heavy)
16	
17	Very hard
18	
19	Extremely hard
20	Maximal exertion

Heart Rate Monitors in Training

Heart rate is a popular means of monitoring exercise intensity, especially because heart rate monitors are so widely available. Heart rate is measured in beats per minute, or bpm. The average person may have a resting heart rate (that is, the rate of heartbeats per minute when completely at rest, such as in the morning before getting out of bed) in the mid-60s. Athletes, however, frequently have lower resting heart rates because their hearts are stronger and able to do more work with fewer beats per minute. We also all have a maximum heart rate, which is the highest number of beats per minute we can each achieve when working at high intensity. This max rate is determined partly by your genetics and partly by your age (and it drops as you get older).

There are several different mathematical formulas for determining your max heart rate, but most coaches and scientists prefer to use a riding test to make sure the figure is accurate. Tests can be done in a lab to determine your true max, but it requires a pretty involved procedure, typically under the supervision of a qualified senior exercise physiologist or medical professional. Most coaches and exercise physiologists use a sub-max testing protocol, such as a twenty-minute time-trial test, because it is easier to do in the field and easier to repeat later to see progress over time. Once a max or sub-max heart rate has been determined, this information can be used to set heart-rate training zones to guide the intensity of your workouts in a periodized training plan. The training zones in periodized training are described using percentage of max heart rate. For example, the recovery zone is often defined as the zone where you are working at 65 percent of your maximum heart rate or lower. This percentage can be used to determine a range of beats per minute that you would use as a guideline for your workout effort on a recovery day.

You can measure your heart rate by taking your pulse during your workout, but this is pretty impractical while you are training, and it is also not very accurate. As soon as you slow down to take your pulse, your heart rate starts to decrease. Many companies have developed heart rate monitors. They usually have a chest strap that picks up the heartbeat and transmits the signals to a wristwatch or handlebar-mounted receiver. The higher your heart rate, the harder you are working. Using heart rate isn't a perfect way to measure training, but it is affordable, and it is a great way for you to gain a better understanding of what is going on in your body when you train. Learning to listen to your body and estimate how hard your heart is working can only benefit you and help you train more effectively.

Measuring Power in Training

The current trend in cycling is to use a power meter to keep track of training workload and intensity. This is one of the most accurate ways to

Morning Heart Rate

Get in the habit of taking your heart rate each morning. Tracking your resting heart rate over time will help you monitor your body. If your resting heart rate is higher than normal, this might indicate that you aren't yet fully recovered from a series of hard workouts, or that your body is fighting off a cold. It is best to take your resting heart rate when you've woken up naturally; if you were startled awake by an alarm clock or the family dog, it may have caused a spike in your heart rate. You should be lying down and feeling mellow. Use a digital clock or an analog clock with a minute hand, find your pulse, and count. You can either place the first two fingers of your right hand against the right side of your neck to feel for the pulse of your carotid artery (or the first two fingers of your left hand on the left side of your neck), or you can use the first two fingers of one hand to find your radial pulse point on the inside of your wrist (on the thumb side).

Make sure you use your first finger or two, not your thumb, as your thumb has its own pulse and will just confuse your count. Press very gently. You want to be able to feel the beat, but you don't want to squish the artery and slow down the blood flow. Count the beats for an entire minute. Some people prefer to count for 10 seconds and multiply by 6, or to count for 15 seconds and multiply by 4. This will give you your beats per minute (bpm), but if you miss a beat in a short count and multiply, you could be off by as many as four to six beats.

If you have trouble taking your resting heart rate in the morning, try taking it in the evening. Wait until you have been lying down for at least half an hour, then take your pulse. The key is to be consistent in how and when you take your pulse, so that you can compare one day with the next or one week with the next.

monitor and measure training and is certainly a trend that is here to stay. Power is measured in watts and provides athletes with a specific number indicating how much work has been done. Your fitness and strength level determines how much power you can produce and for how long. The more power you can put out, the faster you will go. And being able to put out high power over time indicates that you can ride farther faster. Keep in mind that while power is important, it is not the only factor in the equation. You also need to practice your bike-handling skills and know about the basic tactics of racing.

To determine your power output, you will need access to a power meter. There are a number of different models on the market, and they are expensive. It is not a tool that you really need to have in your first or second year of training. But as you get more serious, it is definitely a worthwhile investment. Remember, in your first season or two you are learning how to train properly and just starting to build a base. Having a power meter isn't that helpful at that point.

Knowing your maximum power output will allow you to set power-based training zones. If you don't have regular access to a power meter, you will not be able to design workouts around power. However, you can still test yourself occasionally on an indoor trainer designed to measure power. A teammate or coach may also let you borrow a power meter. These checks can help you monitor progress by evaluating power changes for different levels of effort.

There are several companies that make power meters. The top meters on the market measure power using sophisticated electronics and strain gauges sealed into the rear wheel hub or bottom bracket of your bike; both report the data to an electronic computer that sits on your handlebars. The unit can be detached from the bars, and the data can be downloaded to desktop software for analysis. If you are going to invest in a power meter, do your homework first. Be sure to read *Training and Racing with a Power Meter,* by Hunter Allen and Andy Coggan, two of the top bike power specialists out there. In their book they discuss the theories regarding training power and provide a nice overview of using a power meter effectively. They also discuss the pros and cons of the various power measurement devices available.

TABLE 7.2 **Measuring Training Zones**

Training Zones	RPE	Heart Rate	Power
Recovery	6–10	<65% max HR	<55% max power
Endurance	10–15	65–80%	56–75%
Tempo	16–17	81–85%	76–85%
Threshold	17–18	86–95%	86–99%
Max/Red Line	19–20	96–100%	100%+

Training Zones

Coaches and athletes can use the science of training zones to help design practice. Training zones enable you to break your efforts down into different categories so that you can train different systems in the body. There are many different theories about training zones and ways to determine and use them. Some programs use five zones, whereas others use four, six, or seven. Every approach has certain things in common, however.

Almost every zone system agrees about the first (or easiest) level, for example. This is when you are riding easy at a slow pace, your heart isn't beating very hard, your RPE is low, and you aren't putting out much power. It is the recovery zone, where everything is easy and the body isn't getting taxed or producing waste products. As you pick up the pace, at some point you move into the next zone, and RPE, HR, and power all increase. This continues up through your maximum (or Red Line) effort, when you are maxed out with regard to perceived effort, heartbeats per minute, and watts. Keep in mind that training is always on a continuum; it is sort of like a dimmer switch instead of an on/off switch. So there is some overlap as you move from one training zone to the next in all of the systems.

It will be up to you, or you and your coach if you have one, to determine which monitoring system you want to use and which training zone theory you will follow. While all of the heart-rate and power technology is nice, remember that athletes trained successfully for the Tour de France and other big races for almost 100 years without any of these bells and whistles. Learning to ride based on how your body feels and learning good bike-handling skills are also valuable, and many cyclists around the world continue to train successfully without all of the technological extras. Don't feel like you have to have all the technology right away in order to be successful.

KEEPING A LOGBOOK

In addition to using perceived effort, heart rate, and power meters when training, athletes can benefit from keeping track of the work they do in training. Keeping a training log will allow you to monitor your training and all the important details that go with it. It will provide a way for you and your coach to review your progress, look for patterns, and assess your training plan. Logbooks can also be a great source of pride and motivation. Your logbook will help your coach to evaluate the direction and design of your training and your responses to training. Even if you don't have a coach yet, someday you may, and when you do, a good logbook will help him or her get to know you and your training history quickly and objectively.

How you keep your logbook is a very personal decision. You may want to keep it as a computer file, or you may want to keep a paper-and-pencil log in a notebook. You could create personal log pages on the computer, then print them out and put them in a binder. There are even online training logs you can use (see www.trainingpeaks.com, for example). These allow you to upload key workout data and provide you with charts and graphs of your progress. Your logbook will only be as useful as the information in it, so be sure to choose a format you are comfortable with and then use it regularly. *The Cyclist's Training Diary* from VeloPress is a logbook with a useful standard format.

What to Put in Your Logbook

Include the following in each entry:

- The date
- What you were supposed to do for the workout and your training goal for the session
- What you actually did for your workout (this may be different from what you had planned to do, so be sure to note the reason for any change from the plan)
- Warm-up and cool-down information
- Any other activities you did as part of the workout (for example, strength training)
- How long and/or how far you went for your workout
- The intensity of your workout (create your own scale to rank how hard you perceived the workout to be)
- How you felt (good, got the sniffles, sore quads, etc.)

Optional things you might want to include are:

- The weather
- Resting heart rate that morning
- Mood
- Other things going on in your life that could affect your workout (work stress, school stress, etc.)
- How you slept the previous night (how many hours, quality)
- Any other information you want to include—many people also journal in their training log, for example
- Race details

RECOVERY: THE OTHER HALF OF TRAINING

Recovery is a key element of proper training. But it's not the whole story. As Dr. Randy Wilber of the U.S. Olympic Committee puts it, training plants the seeds: What you do after with rest—nutrition, recovery activities, and so on—is what allows the garden to grow. Understanding the recovery side of the training equation is what can put top riders ahead of the pack, or make the difference between a bad season and a great one. A lot of attention gets paid to training: what to do, how much, when, and so on. Unfortunately, what many athletes don't realize is that this is only half the training equation. During training, you tear your body down, and during recovery you need to provide it with the resources it needs to repair and grow stronger. When your body doesn't get a chance to recover properly, this can lead to overtraining, insufficient recovery, decreased performance, injury, loss of enjoyment, and even burnout from a sport you really love. (See Figure 7.5)

Not allowing recovery to happen is the most common mistake among riders, especially among beginners. Many athletes train under the misconception that if some training is good, then more is always better. Using this logic, whenever they have a bad race or training day, they respond by doing more hard work. Although training hard and pushing your limits are crucial steps to becoming a better rider, you will not

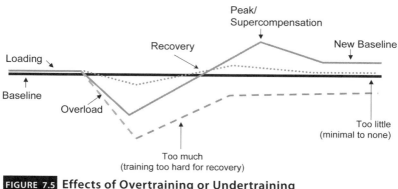

FIGURE 7.5 **Effects of Overtraining or Undertraining**

make gains unless you allow for adequate recovery. Recovery, both during your days off and during active recovery workouts, provides the
body the time and the resources it needs to adapt to the stress placed
on it during training. It is the adaptations to training stress that occur
during recovery that allow a rider to improve. Short-term overtraining
is okay and a natural side effect of training, but it should only last a few
days at most. Long-term overtraining can ruin a season.

Building rest and active recovery days into a training plan is a crucial aspect of effective training. Though most of the training plans we
see from struggling athletes build in days off the bike and easy ride
days, we typically discover, upon further investigation, that the rider
isn't honoring these days properly. Days off need to be taken advantage
of, not replaced with another activity (for example, don't go running
on your day off from cycling). Active recovery rides must be done at
recovery pace. For most riders, this pace feels agonizingly slow, especially when compared to regular training days. However, it is essential
that recovery rides remain mellow if gains are to be made. Monitor
yourself on active recovery days (paying attention, for example, to
heart rate, perceived intensity, and cadence) to ensure that you keep
the intensity within your recovery parameters. Avoid doing recovery
rides with individuals who do not understand the recovery concept
or who constantly feel the need to challenge the pace. And make sure
you understand what recovery means in terms of your own training,

because recovery, like most aspects of training, will vary from one individual to the next.

Logging Recovery

We already talked about keeping a good logbook to track the workouts you do and your body's response. You can also use your logbook to track recovery efforts. Things you might keep track of include hours and quality of sleep, recovery days and/or recovery rides, and general recovery from your previous day's workout. For this third bit of information, you can use a rating scale of 1 to 5, where 1 means you were not at all recovered and 5 means you were totally recovered.

You can also use a scale like the "Recovery Cue," designed by Michael Kellmann and his colleagues, to track your recovery on a weekly basis. They recommend including responses to the following questions:

1. How much effort was required to complete my workouts last week? (Use a scale of 1–5, where 1 means "excessive effort" and 5 means "hardly any effort.")
2. How recovered did I feel prior to the workouts last week? (Use a scale of 1–5, where 1 means "still not recovered" and 5 means "feel energized and recharged.")
3. How successful was I at rest and recovery activities last week? (Use a scale of 1–5, where 1 means "not successful" and 5 means "successful.")
4. How well did I recover physically last week? (Use a scale of 1–5, where 1 means "not at all well" and 5 means "very well.")
5. How satisfied and relaxed was I as I fell asleep in the last week? (Use a scale of 1–5, where 1 means "not at all satisfied and relaxed" and 5 means "very satisfied and relaxed.")
6. How much fun did I have last week? (Use a scale of 1–5, where 1 means "not much fun at all" and 5 means "a lot of fun.")
7. How convinced was I that I could achieve my goals during performance last week? (Use a scale of 1–5, where 1 means "not at all convinced" and 5 means "very convinced.")

There are no right or wrong answers when you evaluate your recovery. This is just a tool to help you learn more about your training and how your body responds to it. It will help you maintain a healthy balance in your training and help prevent overtraining or burnout.

Preventing Overtraining

Without proper recovery time, athletes are at risk of overtraining, which can have a serious impact on the quality of racing and training. Symptoms of overtraining include physical or emotional exhaustion, disruptions in sleep patterns, and lingering or frequent colds, persistent soreness, and lots of little injuries that do not seem to heal as quickly as they normally would. Overtraining can have psychological effects, too, such as increased irritability or moodiness, decreased ability to cope with stress, a feeling of isolation from teammates and family, and decreased enjoyment in riding or in other areas of life.

Because overtraining can ruin a whole season, athletes work hard to prevent it from occurring. Some of the things you can do to prevent this are:

- Setting short-term stepping-stone goals (see Chapter 10)
- Communicating with your coach about how you are feeling
- Building time to relax (mentally and physically) into the training plan
- Keeping a positive outlook
- Evaluating training regularly so you can catch problems before they become a big deal
- Avoiding training tedium by building in variety
- Keeping your training fun
- Paying attention to stress in school, life, and training so you don't overload your system

Remember, "rest" may be a four-letter word, but it is not a bad one. Plan and respect your rest time. Don't skimp on your sleep, and take naps, if necessary, to stay well rested.

USING TESTS APPROPRIATELY

A wide variety of physical tests are used to set benchmarks and parameters for training in cycling. Unless the testing method is highly sophisticated and done repeatedly over time so that results can be compared, testing is not the best way to determine someone's potential as an athlete. There are so many factors that come into play. However, testing, if done correctly, can help determine starting points and measure your progress over time. Some take place in the lab, while others are conducted in the field; of the two general types, laboratory testing is often the more accurate because it factors out stray variables (like changes in weather) that can otherwise interfere with results. Some of the more common tests are threshold tests and body-composition tests.

Threshold tests can be done either in the field or in the lab. Some methods estimate where lactate threshold occurs using sub-max tests; others require a lab technician to draw blood from the athlete to determine this point more precisely. Knowing your lactate threshold can help you set up accurate training zones for heart-rate or power-based training. However, you should read much more about periodized training in other sources or have a coach help you if you are going to try to use these figures to design your training plan.

Body-composition tests can be done to determine how much of your body is fat mass and how much is fat-free mass (or lean tissue). As a Junior or devo athlete, you will experience changes in your body composition due to the physical changes related to puberty. Do not worry too much about your weight or body composition while you are still growing. It is much more important to emphasize a healthy weight and good nutrition.

CROSSTRAINING

When you engage in activities other than biking, you are "crosstraining," using other activities to enhance or maintain fitness. Crosstraining can be beneficial in a healthy program, particularly for Juniors, who are still developing physically, and it is especially important in young riders who are still developing their basic athleticism. During racing season, occasional crosstraining can supply cardiovascular benefits and reduce your chances of suffering from overuse injuries. It can also decrease your risk of injury in general. In the off-season, crosstraining is a great way to break out of your usual routines while still maintaining fitness. For a cyclist, crosstraining activities might include running, swimming, aerobics classes, weight training, or using a fitness machine like the elliptical trainer. The more serious you get and the higher you go in cycling, the less you will probably use crosstraining. But initially it will help you develop a well-balanced body.

TRAINING ALONE VERSUS TRAINING WITH OTHERS

There are pros and cons to training and riding with other people; basically, whether it will be beneficial to you depends on what you are trying to accomplish. Group rides are a great place to practice pack-handling skills or drafting, for example. These rides can be fun and motivating and provide you with a pace challenge. But group rides also mean that someone else is usually setting the pace, which may be too fast or too slow for what you need to do for your training. Consider your training goals as you decide whether or not a group ride fits your training needs. And keep in mind that group rides don't have to be with a big crowd; a ride with just one other person can be beneficial from time to time.

Communication between riders is extremely important for the safety of everyone in the group. Learn the customs and expectations of rider communication so that you can be a responsible member of the group. There are some common verbal cues that riders use on group rides and in races. The people at the front of the group have a responsibility to the rest of the group to be alert for potential hazards on the road, and the people at the back can let everyone know if there is an overtaking car. If you hear someone call out an obstacle, relay it to the rest of the group. The following cues are used by riders almost universally:

- "Car up"/"Car back": If the road has been quiet and a car is coming toward the group, call out "Car up," and if a car is coming up from behind, call out "Car back."
- "Sand"/"Glass": If safe enough, use a hand signal to indicate where the sand or glass is when you call it out.
- "Rider up"/"Runner up"/"Walker up": Call this out before the group overtakes the rider, runner, or walker. This both alerts the person getting passed and lets the members of a riding group know they need to slide over a bit.
- "Hole": One of the most dangerous things that a rider can do is to swerve in a group, but just as dangerous is to hit the hole. If you see one ahead, don't hesitate to let everyone know.
- "Stopping"/"Slowing": Calling out the group action can help give those in the back a heads-up in case they aren't paying attention the way they should be.

TRAINING WITH A PURPOSE

Sometimes a ride is just a ride. But when you have goals for the season and you intend to reach them, it is important to train with a purpose rather than just go with the group flow and hope to get there. That is sort of like driving around aimlessly and hoping to end up at Disneyland.

Training with intent doesn't mean hammering on every ride, but it's more than just following a training plan and putting in the miles. Training with intent means that every time you get on your bike, you have a purpose and you know how it fits into your overall plan. It means that at the end of each ride, you have a clear idea of what you have accomplished and how it will bring you closer to your goal.

Daily training rides that are done with intent provide the stepping-stone gains you need to improve. Training with intent also provides you with the information necessary to make progress evaluations and training adjustments more accurately, both during the racing season and post-season.

So how do you train with intent? Start by asking yourself the following questions about your season. Be as specific and detailed as possible with your answers.

How to Ride with a Group

When you ride with a partner or a group, it is important to know and practice good pack-riding etiquette:

- Be a safe rider. Remember that your actions and reactions on the bike affect everyone else in the group. Don't do anything suddenly or anything that is unexpected.
- Point out obstacles like sand, glass, and potholes. Physically point them out when you can do so safely with a finger or a waving motion of the hand.
- Stay alert. Riding in a group isn't an excuse to zone out.
- Do not use your cell phone, change clothing while riding, or do anything else that might make you less stable on the bike when you are in a paceline or at the front of a group. If you need to do these things, drop to the back of the group.
- Learn how to hold a wheel and how to eat and drink safely so you can do these things and maintain a steady pace.
- Maintain your place in the paceline; don't overlap the wheel in front of you. This is extremely dangerous for both you and the other riders in the group.
- Know the expectations of the ride: Is it a no-drop ride (no one gets left behind), or does the group start out mellow and pick up speed as the ride progresses, with an understanding that those who fall off the back will have to fend for themselves?
- Come prepared. Bring your own flat repair kit, food, and water. Don't rely on someone else to take care of you.
- Be on time. Don't make the group wait for you. Group rides have a set time and will not wait for latecomers. Your best policy is to arrive early so you can get your bike ready.

1. What do I want to accomplish this season? What are my main goals?
2. What is it going to take in terms of skills and fitness to accomplish my goals?
3. What training activities will help me learn the skills and gain the fitness that I need to accomplish my goals? (This information should directly impact the nature of your periodized training plan.)

4. How will I evaluate my skill learning and fitness gains, both daily and over the course of training?

The answers to these questions provide you with all the information you need to enter each week of training with a clear sense of purpose. Based on your long-term goal and the week's focus, you can determine what you need to accomplish during your ride each day. You will know what skills and fitness components you are working on, and you will be able to evaluate your efforts at the end of the ride. If you want to focus on group-handling skills and general fitness, then you need to ride accordingly; the ride you take to work on these objectives will be different from a ride you take while focusing on sprint placement and higher-intensity fitness. Likewise, if your daily training focus is to improve your aerobic efficiency, then you may decide that a solo or small-group ride is the best choice, whereas if you want to learn how to ride comfortably in a group, a large-group ride would be in your best interest.

Training with intent will give you a clear sense of purpose every time you get on your bike. Each ride plays a role in the big picture. And perhaps more importantly, training with intent will increase your confidence in your training and will help you get more from your hard work and logged miles. Of course, sometimes a ride is just a ride, but in a well-designed training plan, even these rides are done with intent.

A Complete Workout

Every workout or training session should have a clear beginning and end. A quality warm-up will be at least 10 to 20 minutes long, depending on what your body needs and the intensity of the workout that you will be doing. During this time you should ride at a slow, comfortable pace. This prepares you both mentally and physically for the ride ahead. The warm-up is the time when you begin to let go of the stresses and concerns of the day so that you can focus on training. It also allows your body to get prepared by pulling blood out into the working muscles and improving the lubrication in the joints, and this helps to decrease the risk of injury.

The end of your workout should include at least 10 to 15 minutes of a slower cool-down pace. During this time, your body has a chance to flush out some of the toxins and waste products that you built up during your workout. This begins your recovery so that you will be ready for your next workout.

Scheduling Your Days

How many hours are in your week? Every single person has the same amount: 168. But for most of us, that seems like 10 or 15 hours fewer than we need to accomplish all that we have planned. It's all too easy for good intentions to go awry; maybe you've discovered that sometimes the end of the week arrives before you've had a chance to carry out that wonderful training plan you devised. Take time at the start of the week to schedule in your workouts just as you schedule other appointments or classes. Don't just assume they will happen sometime during the day. Just expecting to find the time for a workout is a sure way for it to get lost in the chaos of your daily life. And if things do happen and you can't fit in your regular training during the week, don't try to cram it all in at the end. Training should be a pattern of work and rest. Trying to put all of the work together in a jumble will not bring about the improvements you are working toward.

TRAINING SAFE

Biking, like most sports, has its dangers. The best way to avoid these and to stay safe while training is to be aware of the hazards and what you can do to protect yourself. An accident on the bike can have much more serious consequences than just impacting your training or dampening your enthusiasm for the sport. It can cause severe injuries or even death.

We've already discussed the pros and cons of riding alone or with a group for training purposes. But there is another benefit to group riding. Riding alone, particularly on country roads or on trails, should be done with caution. All riders, young and old, should be sure to let someone know where they intend to train and their estimated return time.

Carry a charged cell phone, and plan your rides carefully so you don't get lost by yourself. Carry some cash with you in case of emergency, and always bring along identification, a card with emergency phone numbers, and a complete repair kit (such as a multitool that includes a chain repair piece, a spare tube, a patch kit, a tire lever, and a tire pump or CO_2-filling device).

If riding outside isn't an option due to waning daylight, weather, or concerns about riding alone, you can definitely get a quality workout inside. There are a variety of options for indoor riding. For example, you can use an indoor trainer that props up the rear wheel of your bike and provides resistance. Or you can use a roller, a device with three drums that you balance and ride on. Rollers don't provide as much resistance as indoor trainers, but they are great for balance and endurance riding. These are both great options, and both are easily portable for pre-race warm-ups as well. There are also many different types of stationary bikes designed to model real road riding.

Personal IDs

Carrying identification with you on training rides is a good habit. Even if you always ride with other people, having personal information handy will help ensure proper medical care in case you are ever hurt or injured. Your ID can be a homemade laminated card, your driver's license, or a professionally made ID. (Check out www.roadid.com for an excellent selection of athlete ID bracelets and charms.) Your ID should include your name, blood type, emergency contacts, and any known allergies, at a minimum.

As you get more serious about riding, your training will require you to be out on the roads or trails more often. This means you probably will not be able to select only the sunny and warm days to ride (unless, of course, you are lucky enough to live somewhere that is always warm and dry). Riding in the rain isn't that bad, if you are properly prepared:

- Use fenders if you ride with a group. Constantly being splashed with road spray off a wheel is not a pleasant way to ride.

- Have a rainproof, packable jacket that you can carry in a pocket for surprise showers. Many companies make excellent shell vests and jackets that are breathable and water-resistant or waterproof. These can keep you warm when a sudden shower or downpour hits.
- Watch the roads and temper your speed. Rain, especially when it first starts, can raise the oils that cars leave on the road, causing slick spots. Road paint lines and gravel also become more hazardous when wet.
- Be prepared for slower braking times due to wet rims.
- If riding on a trail, be aware that roots, rocks, and leaves all get slicker with rain.
- Wear clear or yellow lenses in the rain. They will help enhance the contrasts in the lower light of a cloudy day.
- Be alert. Drivers don't usually expect to see people out exercising in poor weather.
- Be smart. If there is lightning or hail or the roads start to get icy, seek shelter and call for a ride home. Do not set yourself up for a serious accident.
- Stay warm. Fatigue, dehydration, and the chill of a rainstorm can increase your risk of getting hypothermia, even in good weather.
- Don't ride through puddles on the road, no matter how tempting. You never know how deep they might really be. In addition to destroying your rims, this is a good way to tempt a crash.
- If riding in the rain or at dusk, it is a good idea to have lights on your bike. A small white light on the front and a blinking red light on the rear under your saddle will help drivers see you. A wide variety of very small but bright battery-powered red and white LED lights that you can carry in a pocket are available. Bring these with you for extra lighting.

You will probably also face a wide range of temperatures over the course of your training year. For hot and humid days, be sure to plan carefully and bring enough water. Plan your training routes so you can refill as often as necessary, and avoid training in the heat of the day. Watch the humidity and pollution index, especially if you have allergies or asthma, and don't train when these indexes are high.

You need to be just as aware of your hydration status when it is cold as you are when it is hot. It is possible to get dehydrated even when it is cold, and sweating isn't necessarily the most reliable gauge of how much fluid you need to replace. Learn how to dress properly for the weather. Use layers and the proper fabrics to stay warm and dry. The proper fabrics are those designed to wick moisture from your skin and to keep warmth in. This means no cotton or other fabrics that retain moisture. Make sure you keep your head and ears, hands, and feet warm as well. Frostbite is a dangerous condition that can occur even on moderately cold days if you are outdoors for a long period of time, such as when you are on a long training ride. Make sure you check the windchill levels and the forecast before you head out, and have in mind an alternative, shorter route home in case the weather gets worse.

Most beginners realize that riding in the dark can be dangerous. What they may not know is that the angle of the sun in the morning or evening can pose a danger as well. Remember that drivers may not see you because the sun is in their eyes. Even in the best weather conditions or lighting, there will be drivers who misjudge how fast your bike is moving. Even pedestrians may walk out in front of you because they are not looking for cyclists or misjudge your speed.

And then there are the various four-legged and two-legged critters that can be potential road and trail hazards. Through my years of riding I have heard, seen, or experienced rider encounters with squirrels, chipmunks, horses, dogs, cats, turtles, cougars, chickens, deer, a bear, a wild boar, a bat, and even a cow. And if you talk to other riders, you will be sure to hear about even more to add to the list. Sometimes the encounters are no big deal, but sometimes they result in a crash. Any crash of this type can cause injury.

Encounters with critters are especially dangerous when the animal runs out in front of the bike, leaving the rider no time to stop, or when the animal runs into the wheel or the rider. Sometimes an animal becomes aggressive or hostile. Road riders need to be particularly aware of dogs that haven't been well trained or that are not properly contained. Do not stop to face off a dog that is chasing you. First, focus on riding away.

Rules of the Road

Whenever you ride on roads, you must remember that you are sharing the road with others. Roads have many potential hazards, but being aware of the potential problems and rules will help you stay safe and enjoy your ride.

- Don't dominate the road. If you are riding solo, stay as close to the white line on the right side of the road as safely possible. If you are in a group, the group should stay as far over to the right as possible as well. Dominating the road so that cars have trouble traveling will only create hostility.
- Signal at all intersections. Don't assume that drivers can read your mind. Legally you are required to signal, and for your own safety, it is important to be predictable.
- Know the laws. Even if you don't drive yet, as a rider on the road you are responsible for knowing and obeying the traffic laws that apply to you.
- Don't ride on the sidewalks or against traffic. You must never ride your bike on sidewalks (unless you are riding through a town where it is briefly required) or against the flow of traffic, especially at training speeds. Be careful on the local bike path as well. Do not try to do training efforts on the bike path—use it for warm-up and cool-down on your way to and from your training rides.
- When you are leaving a driveway or parking lot, be alert for drivers who don't expect you to be there.
- At yield signs and yellow lights, slow down and stop. Drivers are often very anxious to "go" when they get the green and may not see you.
- If you are riding on a street with parked cars, watch for cars that have someone on the driver's side who may open a door as you approach. A head-on collision with a door—or swerving to avoid a door—can cause serious injuries.
- Practice defensive driving. Drivers are often distracted, busy, and in a hurry. Don't assume that they see you or that they know the speed you are traveling.
- Be courteous when overtaking others. Don't pass runners, riders, or walkers without letting them know you are coming.
- If you are a mountain biker, you should be aware that respecting the environment is part of the code of the sport.

In a loud and commanding voice, tell the dog "Stop" and "Go home." This is sometimes enough to make the dog at least pause, giving you a chance to get ahead. If the animal seems very aggressive, make a report to your local police or animal control division when you get back home. Most communities have regulations about loose animals that pose a hazard to people. Riders on the trail need to know what wild animals are in their area and how best to handle these situations. (See Chapter 8 for more information on wild animal encounters.)

RECOMMENDED READING

The following books explain the science of periodization and other training theories and provide specific details about how to apply them:

The Cyclist's Training Bible, by Joe Friel (VeloPress, 2003).

Effective Cycling, 6th ed., by John Forester (MIT Press, 1992).

The Mountain Biker's Training Bible, by Joe Friel (VeloPress, 2000).

Periodization: Theory and Methodology of Training, 4th ed., by Tudor Bompa (Human Kinetics, 1999).

8 SKILL
Development

You should always be able to control the bike and perform technical and tactical skills with minimal interference from your brain.

—Michael W. Heitz, USAC Level 1 coach

Training is more than just putting in lots of miles, and it's more than brute force—speed and strength. To race well—and even just to be safe on the road, track, or trail—you need to develop your basic riding skills. This means working on your bike-handling skills, cornering, climbing technique, braking, drafting safely, and the like. You need to develop tactical knowledge, understand how to read a race, and learn when to sprint. In racing, etiquette is more than just being polite: If you don't know the etiquette of racing, you put yourself and other riders in danger.

Learning good riding technique is the first step toward improving competition results, and it should be one of the primary goals of any new rider. Learning how to handle the bike confidently in all kinds of situations and terrain will not only serve to decrease the number of accidents you are in but will also improve the quality and results of the time you spend training and racing. In this chapter, we will look at some of the basic skills in each discipline. We cannot cover every aspect of skill development, of course, but we have tried to provide a solid introduction to the subject. Many of the skills we cover here also transfer from one discipline to the others, so if you are concentrating on one discipline, you should still read through the whole chapter to pick up useful tips. For example, the section "Awareness on the Track" could apply equally well to racing on the road.

There are other books that focus on advanced skill development for specific disciplines, and once you have mastered the basic skills presented here, you should seek out those resources. Continue to push your limits through regular practice and good coaching. And above all, always make safety your top priority.

ROAD SURVIVAL SKILLS

Focused traffic-safety training should be something that every new rider takes very seriously. Understanding the traffic law, and how bikes are accommodated in the traffic law, isn't optional: These are your survival skills on the road. Every rider should practice emergency braking; know when to yield to traffic at the intersections of driveways, sidewalks, and cross-streets; and learn how to ride defensively in order to avoid drivers who fail to yield the right-of-way. These are the prerequisites, the things that must be second nature before you can safely develop your other riding and racing skills through regular training rides.

Cyclists often feel that they have the same rights as drivers of cars and other motorized vehicles. Technically this is true. We travel in the same direction and are obligated to follow the same road signs. Many cyclists follow only the rules that are convenient. For your safety—and because it is the law—follow the traffic laws. This means always traveling in the direction of traffic, and no scooting through red lights or stop signs. The more unpredictable you are on a bike, the less motorists will know how to react and the more frustrated they will get with cyclists. This puts you at risk and makes the roads more dangerous for everyone on two wheels. You may feel you are in the right, but cars are bigger than you.

No matter how good your bike skills are, many unpredictable things happen on the roads that can create dangerous situations. Potholes, glass and sand, car doors that open in front of you, rocks kicked up by car tires, suicidal squirrels that jump into your spokes, and drivers who pass you only to make a quick right turn in front of you without using a turn signal—these are just some of the possible hazards. This is why it is key that you always wear your helmet and that you are always alert when you ride (no cell-phone conversations or music headphones).

One other word of caution: Remember that riding on roadways in low light conditions such as dusk or dawn is extremely dangerous. There are lots of shadows, drivers can't see as well as in the daytime, and if the sun is rising or setting, motorists can be blinded by the light in their eyes. Using lights on your bike—for example, a flashing rear light and a bright front light—is highly recommended if you must train or commute on your bike during these times, and is always essential at night.

Once you're sure you have a solid grasp of the traffic laws, how they affect you as a cyclist, and what your responsibilities are, you are ready to click your shoes into your pedals and get started on skill development.

GENERAL SKILLS

Entering and Exiting the Pedals

Before practicing anything else, you must be able to easily clip and unclip your cycling shoes from the pedals. It is not uncommon for new riders to carefully come to a nice slow stop only to discover they have forgotten to unclip, which usually means a slow-motion plop to one side is about to ensue. These kinds of falls are usually more damaging to your ego than to anything else. An easy way to master the skill of unclipping is to practice on a stationary indoor trainer (the type that allows you to use your own bike). You can also lean your bike against a wall or fence that allows you to feel nice and stable as you practice. A coach or parent can help hold you up if you feel more comfortable that way. Try repeatedly entering and exiting the pedals with both feet. Whenever you change pedals or clipless systems, or even change the position of the cleats on your shoes, do this exercise again until unclipping comes naturally. Most riders get the hang of clipping in and out very quickly, as the movement is very natural. The hardest part for most is just remembering they need to do this as they slow down. But don't worry, you'll pick it up quickly.

Balancing the Bike at Slow Speeds

After mastering pedal entry and exit, start working on basic balancing skills. Balancing the bike involves body position, small shifts in weight, and constant adjustment of the front wheel, which during slow-speed riding means actually turning the handlebars to maintain control. When you ride at higher speeds, these constant adjustments become unnoticeable; experienced riders make the corrections without thinking about them most of the time.

When a rider is sitting on the saddle and coasting, with no pressure on the pedals, the center of gravity will be higher on the bike, and thus balancing the bike is more difficult. Exerting pressure, or torque, on the pedals actually lowers the center of gravity of the rider and makes the balance effort easier. The decrease in pressure on the pedals transfers the center of gravity to a higher point, which means that balancing the bike requires rapid and often dramatic turns of the handlebars.

So how do you eliminate the crazy wobbling and occasional panic you often see in riders at very slow speeds? The answer is brake application, with continued pressure on the pedals. At slow speeds, a simple way to create more torque on the pedals is to apply the rear brake while pedaling against the brake action. This is actually the skill that will lead to what is called a "track stand," maintaining a complete stop without touching your feet to the ground. You've probably seen experienced cyclists do this while they wait for a red light to change at an intersection: The rider is able to balance with hard rear brake pressure, pressure on the forward pedal with back pedal adjustments to maintain the pedal pressure, and slight turns of the handlebars to adjust the balance point.

Many a rider may look good at speed on the bike only to fall apart when trying to ride at very slow speeds, typically because they have not learned to use the brake in conjunction with forward pressure on the pedal. These skills apply to road and mountain bikes, but with the track bike there is no way to turn the cranks backward because there is no freewheel. When track riders perform a track stand, they actually pedal and move the bike backward slightly, if needed, to maintain balance and static position, since the gear is fixed.

Emergency Braking

Effective braking requires adequate use of both brakes. The front brake is the most effective of the two, even if it does have a bad reputation for bucking riders off as if it had a mind of its own. If your front brake catches before your rear brake, you can create a dangerous situation where the back of your bike is traveling faster than the front, risking a type of crash known as an "endo" (as in "end over end"). Sitting up on the saddle, not pedaling, and being completely unprepared for the sudden weight transfer almost always leads to an ejection from the saddle. Practice leading with your rear brake an instant before you apply the front brake.

To maintain good control of your bike during rapid decelerations, drop your shoulders closer to the handlebars, lower your back, and slide back on the saddle to distribute more of your weight to the pedals. Hold the pedals at the 3 and 9 o'clock positions to create a platform to stand on. Using both brakes forcefully to gain maximum stopping power is a learned skill that must be practiced. Try it in a safe place, starting out with stops at slow speeds and gradually increasing the speed at which you stop as you master the technique.

Climbing

Ascending a hill requires proper gear selection and a steady pace. It's easy to go into a climb too hard and then discover that you can't make it in the gear you've chosen without standing in the pedals, slowing down, or becoming so bogged down that you can't continue—which is not always a great idea. Standing up may be appropriate at times to negotiate an obstacle when mountain biking, but often the rear wheel will spin out if you take your weight off the saddle and the rear wheel. Staying in the saddle as much as possible is recommended on most climbs on trails.

Learning how to select the proper gear when you climb will come with practice. And the proper gear selection will depend on how you are feeling and the nature of the hill you are climbing. When in doubt, always gear down to a slightly easier gear. How you change gears when climbing is just as important as gear choice. Practice anticipating upcoming climbs, and if you are going to shift gears, do so before you increase the pressure on the pedals and your drivetrain. If you wait until you are pedaling harder, you are asking your chain to move under greater stress. This makes it more likely that you will drop the chain or even break it. If you have to shift gears while climbing, don't stop pedaling, but let up on the pedal pressure momentarily as you continue to turn the cranks to allow the chain to move without the load. (If you don't pedal, the chain can't shift.)

The steeper the climb, the more you may have to adjust your body position on the bike to accommodate the grade, sliding forward on the saddle and keeping your shoulders low to the bars. That little trick of using the rear brake can actually help you when climbing: If you encounter a technical spot that causes you to slow, applying a little rear brake while maintaining pedal cadence may help you keep your balance and continue moving up the climb without stopping. If you are just starting out on a mountain bike, find a trail where you can practice easy climbs, then locate more challenging climbs to practice on. As your skills improve, practice managing different sorts of obstacles while climbing. During your training rides, experiment with different gears until you have a sense of the gears you'll need to use for different types of climbs.

For the Coach: "Tell, Show, Do" Instruction

A simple three-step approach can be used to help a young athlete learn new handling skills. Coaches can start by explaining the skill to be practiced and the reason why. This will help the athlete begin to understand the skill. Next, provide a simple demonstration. You can demonstrate the skill yourself, but it is often much more effective to have someone else demonstrate it so you can point out key elements while the athlete watches. Last, provide opportunities for skill practice that are appropriate to the athlete's current skill level and that afford him or her an opportunity to be successful. Avoid the temptation to provide overly complex skills or describe more complicated aspects of the skill. Additional levels of challenge can be added as the skill and confidence level of the athlete improves.

Practicing on an Obstacle Course

When you were younger, you may have had the experience of riding an obstacle course on your bike. Some programs designed for elementary school children use this technique for teaching beginning riding skills. But this method can also be useful for more advanced riders who want to improve their handling technique. So before you head for the road, try setting up your own obstacle course to practice cornering and other skills at slow speeds. You can use cones, spare water bottles, or other markers in a large paved area that is not being used, such as a school parking lot on the weekend. If you want to practice mountain bike or cyclocross skills, use a grassy or dirt surface. But don't try this on a rainy day, when the slick, wet surface would make the maneuvers more difficult to carry out. Also, have an adult help you carefully check the parking lot for loose gravel and other debris that can cause you to lose traction. If possible, bring a broom so you can sweep away any debris that might present a hazard.

Obstacle courses can be fun and you can get creative with the layout, depending on your practice area or terrain. You might want to get some friends together to do this with you, so that you can think of different things to try. And if you are a coach, you can use an obstacle course to teach certain skills in a controlled setting. The International Police Mountain Bike Association has a forty-hour entry-level training course for new police bike officers that is built around an obstacle course that everyone must master at slow speeds before advancing to high-speed skills. The program includes actual time trial competitions using a slow-speed cone course and a high-speed obstacle course over varied terrain. It is amazing how quickly advanced skills develop when a rider is pushed to do repetitions of various basic skills—especially in a competitive environment. The new bike cops spend one week of intense skill training on the bike, and graduate looking like expert cyclists.

ROAD BIKE SKILLS

You will need both a paved parking lot and a grassy field to practice some basic skills on your road bike. A large field with hard, short grass is a great place to practice bump skills. Though a paved empty parking lot will also work, the grass is much easier on the body when you fall off the bike, and this will inevitably happen when serious basic skills work is undertaken. Wet turf or grass that is too deep to easily pedal should not be used.

Before you begin to practice the skills listed below, be sure to practice the ones listed above under "General Skills," which apply to all the disciplines. You should feel comfortable entering and exiting your pedals, balancing the bike, and braking before doing bump drills and practicing drafting and cornering. And also be sure to read through the section "Track Cycling Skills" later in this chapter, because many track skills are applicable to cycling on the road.

Touching and Bumping Drills

After practicing slow- and high-speed braking, practice riding at close quarters with other riders in the grass. We will use two exercises: bumping and shoulder touching. Each drill can be performed with two riders working together, but it is even better if you can try the drills with several partners so that you get used to people with different riding styles. Shoulder touching is simply riding next to a partner at a slow speed, close enough to reach out and touch each other's shoulders while both of you are still rolling forward. You can practice with your hands resting on the hoods or in the drops, but most riders who do this keep their hands up on the hoods. This drill takes just two riders, and it works like this: First, one rider reaches across while riding to touch the other lightly on the shoulder, then keeps that hand on the shoulder while riding for 5 to 10 seconds. This rider then puts both hands back onto the bars while the other rider tries the same exercise. Next, both riders touch each other's shoulders at the same time. If you panic, remember that you can brake with the hand remaining on the hood; if you are the rider on the left, you will be grabbing the front brake, because your right hand is touching the rider next to you. This skill simply improves your comfort level for close-in pack riding. It helps you get a feel for the effect that touching the rider next to you can have on your line of travel. Riders sometimes assist each other by holding on to a shoulder or placing a hand on the lower back, depending on the situation.

Bumping drills are useful because there are many situations in racing and in training where you will be riding very close to other riders; it's something you'll have to get used to. The drills work like this: Two riders begin by simply riding next to each other at slow speed, hands in the drops, and then gradually come close enough to touch. Don't panic and hit the brake when you make contact with the other rider; keep pedaling, and apply brakes only for speed control. Practice this until both of you feel comfortable riding with constant elbow contact and can hold to your lines. Then, more aggressive bumping can be undertaken: Remember, though, the goal is not to knock down your partner but to protect your space—and keep him or her out of it—while holding your line. This is a skill one has to master before riding in a large group or a peloton. Eventually, you can graduate to a paved lot and higher speeds. After all, road races and many other types of bike races are on hard surfaces.

Bumping skills come in handy when you line up two abreast in a group to do a road training ride, or when you practice movement and gaining position in the peloton. When you are ready to practice on a paved surface, find a nice, quiet road with wide shoulders and very little traffic so you can legally ride two abreast. Do this with several other riders, and perhaps include one or two people who have practiced enough to go on to this next step. Send someone to the back, and have this rider slowly work his or her way up the middle of the pack. Take turns doing this. Everyone should be in their drops. No one should be aggressive at this point: You do not want to crash the group, but rather to learn how to capitalize on the movements of other riders that give you an opening and allow you to gain better position in the group.

For another exercise in the group setting, on a quiet road try placing your hand on the lower back of the rider next to you and giving him or her a gentle push. Control your steering with your other hand, and slowly increase your pace while holding your arm steady on the rider next to you. You essentially increase the other rider's speed by doing some of the work for him or her. The other rider must be ready for the push and should keep pedaling. The most common use of this technique is to help a rider who is suffering from the pace and having trouble keeping up.

A large Junior or collegiate team can easily practice all of these skills in a very practical way during a large group ride. For these drills, bring riders of all abilities, and have the most experienced and fittest athletes of the bunch direct the pace and work to keep everyone together. The top riders take turns pulling the group in the front and pushing slower riders in the back who are struggling to hang on. This is a great team-building experience and a very good workout for everyone involved.

Drafting

Drafting is an essential skill in a road race when the going gets tough. It is also a valuable component of long training rides because it allows a group of riders to work harder than they could solo, and for longer stretches of time. The technique is based on the simple fact that bike racers create a draft when pedaling at higher speeds. In other words, the first rider in a group pushes the air out of the way, creating an area with less wind resistance directly behind his or her bike. A rider who follows close to the rear wheel of the front rider can thus expend less energy to stay at a given speed. A rider in a good draft may work up to 40 percent less than the front rider, and the larger the group, the better the draft. With riders spread out in front of you, you can conserve energy and save your big effort for a breakaway or final stretch. Drafting allows the members of a team to work together at top efficiency. Often the members of a team take turns in the lead.

When speeds pick up and a group strings out into a long line of riders, it becomes even more critical to stay in the draft. Riders have to work hard to hold their wheel and maintain a space on the road, especially if there are crosswinds from time to time. Crosswinds can push drafting riders off to one side or the other of the lead rider, and if the lead rider moves close to the edge of the road, the sweet spot of the draft may be eliminated. "Putting everyone in the gutter" refers to this tactic: Riders must struggle for a protected position on the edge of the road when the leader moves as close as possible to the right side with a left crosswind, or moves left with a right crosswind. The rider immediately behind the leader may gain a bit of draft riding in the gutter behind the leader, but everyone else begins to feel the full force of the wind, just like the leader.

When a team forms a draft, the lead riders must learn to provide good communication and warning signs regarding obstacles, traffic, and upcoming stop signs or red lights. The rear rider should practice pulling up as close as possible without touching his or her front wheel to the rear wheel of the leader. Applying the rear brake while still pedaling provides better speed and position control than simply braking without pedaling, which can quickly create a gap or cause an accident. If others are trying to follow you and you hit the brakes unexpectedly, trouble is very likely to follow. Crashes can also occur when the front wheel of one rider overlaps with the rear wheel of another. Practice drafting with just one other rider until you feel comfortable, and then increase the group size, preferably on a quiet road with little traffic and wide shoulders.

Cornering

Cornering skills are best learned firsthand from a good coach. Corners are where many of the accidents happen during road races and criteriums, in part because many riders are weak in this area. Off-camber corners, or inconsistencies in the pavement such as those caused by utility covers or rainy or wet conditions, only make matters worse. To begin your cornering practice, use a slow-speed obstacle course. Set up an imaginary corner of cones or half tennis balls, then do some practice runs around it with increasing speed. A coach can demonstrate the desired skill; if you don't have a coach or can't afford one at this point, try to find an experienced cyclist to demonstrate technique for you. If you can, attend a USA Cycling race clinic. There you can learn from an experienced rider how to brake on approach, when to pedal through and when not to, how to manage the corners when in a group, and how to maintain a proper body position, particularly when surface conditions are wet or slick.

MOUNTAIN BIKING SKILLS

Mountain biking is a great cycling discipline for riders of any age to begin competitive racing, and skill instruction is readily available around the country from coaches who specialize in off-road riding. Summer mountain bike camps are available in most areas that have off-road trail networks. In some states with good off-road access to trails and racecourses, there are mountain bike race leagues with organized coaching specifically geared to high-schoolers.

Starting with slow-speed practices is a prudent course on any bike. The fat-tire bike is a bit easier to balance—and more forgiving in varied terrain—than its skinny-road-tire cousin, making it a little easier to learn on at first. Practice the basic balance and handling skills described below on a grass or dirt cone course before taking them to beginner-level trails.

Keeping Momentum Up

Momentum and gravity are a cyclist's best friend if you learn how to work with them: On a mountain bike, learn to let your speed coming down a descent carry you into the next climb. This means constantly adjusting your gear depending on the terrain. Don't just cruise downhill; choose a high gear and keep pedaling. Then as you approach a climb, choose the correct low gear and shift into it before placing too much torque on the chain as the climb heats up. It especially helps to carry speed into technical trail sections like rock gardens. Going too slow can make negotiating the obstacles much harder. Practice using momentum to good effect as you transition from downhill stretches to climbs.

Choosing Your Line

Choosing a good line of travel means always looking ahead, constantly choosing the best possible part of the trail for easiest passage. It's easy to focus on obstacles that may be approaching, but if you focus on them too much, you can end up riding right into the thing you wanted to avoid. Look where you want to go, and you will tend to go there. Try riding some trails while consciously looking for the best line of travel.

Cornering

The turns on a mountain bike racecourse may be quite diverse, ranging from tight turns in trees on single tracks to steep uphill or downhill switchbacks. Wide-open fire roads or trails with two tracks may have much wider turns. To get a feel for the turns you will encounter on a course, pre-ride the course slowly before tackling it more aggressively. In your training sessions, practice many types of turns. Try different ways to handle them until you feel comfortable with your technique for each type.

While racing a mountain bike course, you will generally want to try to carry as much speed as possible into a corner or a sharp turn. This requires assessing the situation quickly, because you don't want to misjudge the corner and lose control because you were going too fast. Try braking at the absolute last moment before entering a turn and letting up on the brakes during the turn, then get right back on the pedals before you lose too much speed. During tight turns like those on a single-track switchback, you may have to feather the brakes and pedal to keep the bike upright, especially when you are headed uphill. Try to stay off the front brake in tight turns in wet, loose, or rocky conditions, using only the rear brake.

Wild Animal Alert

Mountain biking means you are often riding away from civilization. Although this means you don't have to worry about cars, you do have to be aware of wildlife.

Different types of wildlife present different hazards depending on where you live. In some areas rattlesnakes are a concern. In others, surprising a bear can be dangerous, particularly if it is a mama bear with babies. Cougars can also be potentially hazardous to the cyclist on the trail. Elk and moose are very large obstacles, but they usually get out of your way. And surprisingly, deer often pose more of a risk than their larger counterparts because they are prone to spooking and jumping out in front of riders on the trail, causing bike/deer collisions. Riders rarely cross paths with skunks unless they are riding at dusk, but it does happen, and the result can be very stinky. One friend of mine even had a collision with a bat on a trail at dusk.

None of this should discourage you from riding, but stay alert when riding in the woods. Always ride with a partner and carry your cell phone. Consider putting a small bell on your bike. The noise will alert the animals that you are coming and they will usually flee. Most of them do not want to encounter you any more than you want to encounter them. Educate yourself about the wildlife in your area, the time of day they are most active, and what to do if you encounter them. Avoid riding at dusk or dawn when it is cooler and many animals are out and about. Check the website for your local national park or contact park rangers. They will be able to provide information about animal dangers and any ticks or poisonous plants to look out for in the area.

Descending

Going downhill is the easy part of cycling, right? Well, not exactly. Although your muscles don't have to work as hard on the descent as they do on the climb, going downhill effectively takes very skillful riding, especially in mountain biking when there are uneven surfaces, turns, rocks, and other obstacles along the way. But descents, like other bicycling skills, are made easier with practice and repetition.

Once you decide to work seriously on your downhill technique, the first order of business will be to find an area where you can practice many types of descents. If you live near a ski area, check the trail system once the snow is melted. Some ski areas even offer lift services in the summer for easy trail access; if this service is available to you, you will be able to practice descents without wearing yourself out first on the way up. Or you could do a hard workout on the mountain without the lifts to get in a good training session, then switch to the lifts for downhill practice.

At first, find downhill runs that do not have a lot of loose stones; riding on loose stones may require you to do a "power slide," a more advanced skill that you can try after you have enough experience with basic downhill riding. And if you plan to attempt the expert trails at a ski area, wear *all* the protective gear recommended for a downhill rider. We are not going to cover downhill racing and freeriding in this book, two subdisciplines within mountain biking (freeriding involves jumps from natural or man-made objects onto landings, dirt jumping, and other stunts); if you develop an interest in those specialties, check for resources on the Internet and at your local bike shop. The type of downhill practice you will be doing as a beginning mountain biker is for cross-country mountain biking, which includes varied terrain and climbs as well as descents.

As you practice on the ski runs or other downhill trails, learn to use your brakes efficiently and with proper body positioning. Get to know the technical sections of each descent by riding the course at an easy pace first. You can usually pre-ride a course before a race as well, which makes race day safer and much more enjoyable.

As you begin to pick up speed on descents, practice using slight weight shifts from side to side with your hips to control the bike and head it in the right direction. For super-steep sections, take the back position on the saddle with your shoulders low to the top tube (the same position described above for emergency braking). This will help keep your rear wheel on the ground, giving you more control. Keep your head up, look ahead, and be ready for each change and transition.

Power Slides During Descents

Sometimes there are loose stones on the trail that can cause your bike to slide. In these situations, it may be necessary to drop a foot to gain a three-point stance and do a controlled slide. This is called a "power slide." Flat track motorcycle racers do a similar maneuver. You drop the inside foot (the direction the bike wants to lean) and keep the outside foot planted firmly at 6 o'clock on the pedal. Keep the ground foot forward, toward the front wheel. Rather than keeping the front wheel lined up with the rear wheel and trying to steer the bike through the loose section, you will have to turn the bars seemingly in the opposite direction that you want the bike to go. This is an acquired skill, and it takes finesse to judge how much to turn the bars out to keep the bike upright. To practice the power slide, find a loose descent with some wide-open turns or wide fire-road switchbacks. Be sure to put on old tires that you don't mind tearing up, as inevitably you will skid the rear tire. To get started, you can force the slide by laying on the rear brake.

Descents Made Easy: Do a Pre-Ride

If at all possible, always pre-ride your racecourse slowly before riding it at a faster speed while trying a new technique. You want to be confident of your ability to handle and execute the needed skills before you do it at speed. If you encounter difficult sections during a descent that you are unable to ride, hop off, turn around, and either ride back up or push back and try to practice the section again after studying the best line.

Studying the hard sections of a racecourse can be a huge help. It may give you an advantage, as riders who show up late or do not take the time to check out the course first will be left pushing their bikes as you fly by. Pre-riding the racecourse is essential to knowing how long the climbs are and how hard you can attack them and still have gas at the top. Knowing where the technical sections are, what gears you need to be in to maximize your speed on all sections of the course, and where you can safely pass slower riders is critical to achieving good results in any cross-country mountain bike race.

Counter-Steering in the Flats

If you live in an area where it gets snowy or icy on the roads, you probably already know that in a skid the driver of a car must turn into the direction of the skid to recover from it and regain control of the vehicle. If the car skids right, the driver must turn the steering wheel to the right. In mountain biking, you need to be able to do the same thing when you are riding in slick or slimy conditions. This is called counter-steering. Cyclocross riders do it frequently; experienced motorcyclists are also familiar with the technique. The trick to counter-steering on flat terrain is to keep pedaling and not panic. As soon as the rear end starts to kick out, you must quickly counter-steer, or turn into the direction the bike is kicking out toward, and keep pedaling. (If the rear wheel kicks out right, turn toward the right.) You have to learn just how far to go: Too much counter-steer and you'll drop a foot or hit the ground. If you hit the brakes and stop pedaling while the rear end is kicking out, you'll definitely have to quickly drop a foot to avoid falling. Counter-steering is also used in other situations; we'll discuss those later.

It's best to avoid skids whenever possible (see next section). However, they are not always avoidable and sometimes take you by surprise. If you practice the counter-steering technique, you will be able to handle slick conditions with more confidence. Try finding a muddy section of trail and practice counter-steering in a skid. Remember to use old tires; skidding causes a lot of wear and tear.

Avoiding the Skid

Skids are best avoided whenever possible. A skidding rear wheel not only tears up the trail, but tears up your tire as well. On a road bike, skidding can quickly ruin a thin tire, creating a flat spot or even wearing a hole right through to the tube; the damage may not be so dramatic with mountain bikes, but it is still there.

You will go into skids from time to time, however, no matter how much you try to avoid them, if you do a lot of mountain biking. Steady, hard application of both brakes using proper body position can stop the bike very quickly, but in emergency braking situations this means it is easy to lock up the tires and go into a skid. When a rear wheel skids or slides out during braking or on descents, it is generally because there is not enough weight on the wheel and it wants to lift off the ground. Compensate by sliding your rear end farther back until it is off the back of the saddle, by easing up on the brakes, or both. A good rule of thumb in hard braking is to place one finger on the left (or front) lever, and two on the right (or rear) lever. This should keep you from applying too much pressure on the front brake. Again, if you want to practice skids to get a feel for the bike in that situation, use old tires that you don't mind tearing up.

Dismounts

There are many occasions for jumping off the mountain bike, especially when riding unknown terrain and on very technical sections of a trail or racecourse. Skidding can also sometimes translate into an emergency dismount. In all these situations, it is a good idea to know how to eject yourself from the bike. In a nonemergency dismount, there are a few ways to come off the bike, such as swinging one leg over the rear wheel and then stepping off the other pedal when the first leg makes contact with the ground, or pulling the leg over the top tube and doing the same (although this method is a bit more awkward than the first one and requires good flexibility). See "Cyclocross Skills," later in this chapter, for more details on these dismounts and tips on how to carry the bike if you must run with it through a section.

Emergency dismounts may be necessary in situations where you are losing control of the bike and simply need to land in a manner in which you will not be injured. Unclipping as your rear wheel heads skyward and leaping straight out to the front can be effective, but if the speed is high, it is difficult to do; you may be better off tucking, while trying to protect your head and neck, and rolling with it. In a very steep descent, unclipping and letting the bike go forward while jumping off the back is far preferable to a forward dismount. Remember that anything is better than an "auger"—or heading straight into the ground head-first. If you want to play around with "falling" off the bike, do it in a grassy area free of any obstacles or debris that could hurt you when you hit the ground.

Downhill Equipment

Keith Darner, manager of the Race Performance Management (RPM)–Yeti mountain bike team in Nathrop, Colorado, has been running the RPM team for Junior riders for almost a decade and is an expert on gravity racing. He promotes the Chalk Creek race in the Mountain States Cup Series. He recommends that Juniors use full protective gear for downhill racing, especially since their skills are still under development:

Helmets Make sure you use a full-coverage helmet that is approved by the Department of Transportation (DOT). Beware of the new carbon-fiber helmets that some of the pro-gravity riders use, which are not DOT approved. A helmet with full facial protection is essential for beginners.

Body Armor All downhill riders should wear body armor that includes at least coverage for the shoulders, elbows, and back (spine). This protective gear typically comes as a set. A knee-shin combo is also required equipment, and this should cover both legs from the knee down. You can also acquire bib shorts and other pants that have protective plates built into them for the hips.

Gloves and Goggles Full-fingered gloves and good eye coverage are a must. Remember that there is no substitute for good protective equipment designed specifically for the sport.

TRACK CYCLING SKILLS

Young riders have warm-weather opportunities to learn track riding at almost every velodrome in the United States, and year-round opportunities exist at the ADT Events Center velodrome in Carson, California. Different types of entry-level programs are available at velodromes, and in some cases specific club teams specialize in the instruction of track riding and racing. The three USA Cycling Official Track Training Centers (Carson, California; Colorado Springs, Colorado; and Trexlertown, Pennsylvania) utilize specific club/team programs for instructing Juniors on the track. Almost all of the track skills and tactics discussed here are applicable to road bikes, and in some cases to mountain bikes, cyclocross bikes, and BMX bikes as well.

Track bikes don't have conventional brakes; instead they have a fixed gear, which acts as the braking system. This takes some getting used to, but it works on the track for a couple of reasons. First, all the riders on the track are in the same boat, so no one makes extreme changes in speed. Second, the direction of travel is always the same (turn left). Third, for training purposes there are lanes that dictate the speed of travel and the expected actions from riders. Fourth, there are rules of etiquette and action that allow riders to predict each other's movements. After exploring these rules, we'll describe specific track skills.

Four Rules of Etiquette

These rules of etiquette are the unwritten rules of riding, training, and racing at the track.

Always Pedal. On a fixed-gear bike, there is no coasting or freewheeling. Beginning riders must remember the importance of pedaling; forgetting to pedal can cause you to be thrown off the bike the same way that front braking can. There are three basic types of pedaling on track bikes: (1) pedaling for bike propulsion, the most common type; (2) back pedaling, the slight back pressure on the pedals used to slow the bike (a very subtle, controlled effort); and (3) soft pedaling, used for speed maintenance, where no real effort is made either to propel the bike forward or to slow the speed of travel. Besides pedaling for your own good, you must pedal to avoid surprising someone behind you with an unexpected stop.

Be Predictable. Riders on the track must ride straight lines, move between lanes at expected times, and in general move around the track in ways that are predictable and expected by other riders. With experience, riders learn how to predict other riders and act predictably. Many rapid movements on the track are carried out in predictable ways: for example, moving uptrack in the turns, winding up at the rail, and moving across the straights to enter the pole at speed (see Appendix B).

Be Aware and Look Before Moving. Riders must be aware of each other on the track. When initiating any action, a rider must pay attention to other riders and consider how this action will affect them. Making sure your actions or movements are safe means looking before changing your line of travel, performing mental calculations to compare direction and speed of travel, and taking note of any other factor that could affect your safety or the safety of others. For Miss Manners, the point of good etiquette is always to be considerate of other people; the same is true when sharing the track with others, except that in the case of cycling, the result of improper etiquette could be physically dangerous for all concerned.

Communicate. Essential communication takes place between riders both before and after entering the track. It takes two main forms: verbal communication and body language. Talking with other riders before getting on the track can help you predict how these riders will act. Riders also talk from time to time on the track itself. Short phrases and one-word cues are best for on-track communication, and these must be stated loudly and audibly. "Stick" and "Stay" mean the same thing: *Hold your line.* "Rail" is a request for riders to clear the rail, the very top lane of the track next to the handrail, because someone is winding up or picking up speed behind them. To read the body language of other riders on the track, you must be aware of their signals. For example, a rider might "pop an elbow" to the side to indicate that he or she is pulling off the front of the paceline. Or a rider wanting to pull off the front of a paceline might move half a bike's width uptrack on the straight before pulling off. Either movement indicates that the rider is ready to relinquish the front of the line. Riders traveling with their hands on the tops can usually be expected to continue their line and speed of travel. Riders in the drops might be a bit more serious about their activity; perhaps they are getting ready to change their line of travel or their speed. Time and experience will teach you to read other types of body language, communicate quickly and properly, and in general follow all of the rules of etiquette.

A final point, but not a rule of etiquette, is that although these rules often apply to racing, they do not apply the same way to all racers across the board. The more advanced the racing, the more relaxed the rules are. As a beginner, you are expected to follow them; elite international competitors can break the rules within acceptable limits. And it is common to see riders who are skilled enough to break the rules of etiquette do so gradually. In both training and racing, crashes occur most often when riders do not adhere to the rules of etiquette. So think safety first, and practice the rules of etiquette until you are advanced enough to know when it is safe to make exceptions.

Three Lanes

Every track is marked with the same lines that carry the same meaning. Starting from inside and moving outward, the track is divided into the following areas and lanes. The "apron" is the flat surface that exists inside the thick blue band called the "Blue Band" or the "Côte d'Azure." The apron is not part of the track's riding surface; it is for accelerating onto the track or decelerating as riders come off the track.

Above the Blue Band is a black line called the "Black Line" or the "Measurement Line." Ninety centimeters above the Black Line is the "Red Line" or "Sprinter's Line." Between the Red Line and the Black Line is the Sprinter's Lane, the first lane of riding on the track. If a rider is traveling fast or performing a timed effort, it is okay to be in this lane. If a rider is rolling slowly to warm up or for some other reason, he or she should not be in this lane.

A few feet above the Red Line is the Blue Line. This line is different from the Blue Band. It marks the bottom of a lane designated for moderate- and slow-speed rolling, warming up, paceline work, and the like. The lane is about the width of one or possibly two riders, though riding side by side to chitchat is not acceptable in training if the track is busy. Riders in this lane must pay attention to their surroundings because the most variability in activity occurs here.

There are no lines above the Blue Line, but at the end of the track is a wall called "the rail." The rail marks the edge of a windup lane that should be reserved for riders accelerating for training efforts, timed efforts, or efforts in the Sprinter's Lane with speed.

So there are three lanes of travel at the track, and the spaces between these lanes should remain clear so that they can be used as passing lanes. If used properly, these three lanes and the four rules of etiquette will ensure a safe and fun experience.

Awareness on the Track

Developing awareness on the track is a key skill for beginning riders. There are several levels of awareness. At one level, there is awareness of what is going on with your body. Internal information is constantly being generated (for example, you should be aware of how hard you are riding, how much harder you can ride, the need to smooth out that pedal stroke, and so on). At another level, you must be aware of everything going on around you. Gathering external information is a skill that you can develop (for example, you will learn to pay attention to where you are in the field, where you want to be, how you can effect that change, where close riders are, whether they look fatigued, whose wheel you are on, how far away the break is, who is in the break, whether it is clear for you to attack, and the like). Learning to use the constant sensory input—information that your eyes and ears relay to you—is critical to safe riding. Knowing where other riders are around you, how fast they are going, what is happening on the entire track, and what is happening on the infield with coaches and/or officials is all critical to staying out of trouble.

Your track awareness will develop naturally as you spend time training in groups and as you experience racing. As you train on the track or road, try to develop this awareness by focusing on what is going on around you, especially when training with a group, so that you can develop this skill. Good awareness on the track will ultimately lead to better tactics, higher performance, and fewer accidents. Initially, there may be too much information for you to fully comprehend and act upon. This is why it is important for cycling organizations to have a graduated program for young riders that does not place them beyond their skills in race or group situations on the track. As riders become more comfortable with the information they can see, process, and turn into action, they can take in more information and perform at a higher level.

Anticipation

Anticipation refers to the ability to know when something is going to happen on the track around you and how to react to that action in an appropriate manner—to your benefit, if possible. It is developed with time as riders learn what normal riding behavior is and is not. For example, if you are in a line of riders that is transitioning or rotating from front to back, you must anticipate when your turn in the front is about to occur; adjust your speed, if necessary, as you move to the front; and prepare for your transition out of the front. Or, if an attack is imminent, you should be able to anticipate where it will come from and be in a position to respond to the attack. Anticipation requires a lot of awareness (see previous section) as well as the ability to think ahead and plan your moves accordingly. Experience and feedback from your coach will also help you learn how to anticipate.

Transitioning

Transitions occur when riders at the front of a paceline pull off the front and uptrack (to the right) in order to move to a position farther back and in the draft. Every rider needs to be able to do this smoothly. Though sprinters and individual pursuit specialists will use it less than team pursuit and mass-start riders do, it is an important skill for all to learn, including new young riders. Because of the height and steepness of the track, you will decelerate as you go uptrack, pulling off the front, and accelerate as you return to the paceline. Become familiar with how it feels to do this solo before trying it with a group. You will also need to learn how high to go and what angle to use based on the size of the paceline behind you. Be sure to look before pulling off so that you don't pull up into an attacking rider and thereby cause a crash (although technically it is the attacking rider's job to see and expect the transition and react appropriately). In mass-start races, riders flick or move an elbow to signify to following riders that they intend to pull off in the corner. Finally, riders must learn to look back to the left as they ascend to help gauge their return. When transitioning, it is always better to be early than late on the return.

Judging Speed

The ability to judge your own speed is another skill that requires repetition and feedback. Training drills that incorporate gradual accelerations or sustained speeds are ideal for developing this instinct in a rider. One good exercise is to ride 5 kilometers at a set, sustainable pace and check your time as you complete each lap. You can have a friend, a more experienced rider, or a coach call out your times, or you can check your cyclocomputer after each lap. Another way to develop the skill is to do your first lap at an easy pace and then amp up your speed with each progressive lap. With this kind of feedback, you will begin to understand how the effort you are applying is affecting your speed. Don't become dependent on your cyclocomputer, however. Instead, the idea is to develop your instincts about speed. You should be able to tell from internal cues whether you are putting out an 80 percent effort or a 90 percent effort, and you should be able to judge what you can do and what you can't do. You should know what level of effort you can sustain for a given amount of time, and you need to get a feel for how far 333 meters, or 250 meters, is. If you are 250 meters from the finish, can you hold top speed long enough to win a sprint, or will you need to wait a bit before beginning your attack? Sprinting involves a tight relationship between the body's ability and the rider's awareness of that ability.

Drafting

Just as in road biking, track work requires the ability to draft; however, on the track you have the added difficulty of riding on a fixed-gear bike without brakes. The sport of cycling feeds off the fact that riders can gain shelter from the wind by hiding behind other riders (teammates or opponents). However, riding so close and regulating speed without brakes make some riders, and certainly new riders, uncomfortable. With a fixed-gear bike, you cannot simply brake if you get too close to the rider in front of you. So you will need to learn how to adjust the speed of your bike using your legs. To speed up, you gently apply just a bit more pressure to the pedals, and to slow down, you hold back just a bit. These are very fine micro-adjustments, not big fast adjustments. Don't move up on or off of a wheel too quickly. On an outdoor track, you may also have crosswinds. You must learn how to make micro-adjustments in your position and other movements to ride smoothly through these.

Bumping

Some bumping and nudging among the riders occur in every discipline of cycling, but especially in track racing. The riders are not trying to make each other crash; the bumping simply is unavoidable because riders are often in such close proximity to each other when they are drafting. To do well in racing, you will need to become comfortable with bumping other riders and being bumped by them. This is a bike-handling skill that requires a lot of balance practice—but it is one thing to be able to balance at very slow speeds and another to balance at top speed while being nudged. Bumping drills with gradually increasing speeds can help you develop this ability. See "Touching and Bumping Drills" under "Road Bike Skills" for specific drill suggestions.

Speed Regulation

When it comes to regulating speed, there are really just three things you can do: accelerate, maintain a steady speed, and decelerate. Obviously, acceleration on a fixed-gear bike is accomplished the same way it is on any other bike, with forward pressure on the pedals. Maintaining speed involves the management and control of that forward pressure, and deceleration involves the careful, subtle application of pressure on the pedals during the upstroke, or return (7 o'clock to 11 o'clock positions on the pedals). Understanding the amount of force to apply in the appropriate direction and at the appropriate time is, again, a matter of experience, education, and feedback. Be sure to spend some time on your fixed-gear bike performing each of the three skills. A simple way to practice acceleration and deceleration is to make repeated entries and exits from the track, each time bringing your speed up to a decent training level, and then decelerate and exit the track.

High-Cadence Pedaling

Learning to pedal at high cadences requires regular practice, patience, determination, and, if possible, the attention of a good coach for feedback and instruction. An important component of high-cadence pedaling is the pedal stroke. Let's approach the pedal stroke as a clock, with the forward crank being the minute hand and the power portion of the stroke falling roughly between 1 and 5 o'clock. This range of the circle produces the vast majority of the power that causes propulsion. If you want speed, as produced during high-cadence work on the track, you must focus on the 2 or 3 o'clock position through the 7 o'clock position. You probably are used to exerting the most pressure on the pedal when it is between the 1 o'clock and 5 o'clock positions, since this seems to come naturally to most people. As you change the focus of your pedal stroke, you may notice slight changes in muscle use (or *muscle recruitment*). This means your muscles will learn to activate and deactivate, or recruit, in new ways. Under the new way, you are making better use of the potential power of the upstroke. And the end result is increased cadence and greater speed.

Drills to accomplish this change in pedal stroke are many and varied. The skill is only partly learned without load and fatigue. Practice skills may include pedaling while traveling downhill and undergeared (if required) on a road bike, doing intervals on the rollers, and using other methods of achieving high cadence without the muscular fatigue associated with riding under a heavy load (that is, high power). The progression leads to high pedal cadence under a high load. (For example, individual pursuit elite riders require 110 to 115 revolutions per minute [rpms] and approximately 500 watts. Matched sprints between top athletes recorded on a power meter reached 175 rpms, with an average wattage for 200 meters at over 700 watts over a 10.7-second period.)

Riding in control during high-cadence sprints on the track bike also requires a great deal of handling capability: The rider must be able to safely control the bike while spinning under load, and this includes the corners. Finally, training to improve peak rpms while under load is absolutely necessary. An elite rider who can produce 246 rpms on the rollers may be unable to ride faster than 10.8 seconds in the 200-meter while under load (a time that is simply too slow for international competition standards in the matched sprints and keirin events).

Madison Technique

Racing the Madison event in a productive manner involves mastering all of the aforementioned skills and then some. This American home-grown event is complicated: It is hard to ride, hard to score, and great fun to watch. The safe transition of riding partners in and out of the racing involves the handsling. This is the track cycling equivalent of passing the baton, only instead of passing a plastic or metal stick from one rider to the next, riders briefly grasp hands as they pass so that one rider can use his or her momentum to "sling" the other rider forward. This procedure must be practiced under the guidance of a skilled instructor. In a handsling, the riders must position their weight appropriately to prepare for the change in momentum (forward for the racing rider and backward for the relief rider). The riders must be comfortable grabbing hands and pulling on one another. The fact that it is performed amid the traffic of other riders makes it even more difficult. (See www.frontrangers.org for tips.)

Tactical Race Strategies

Understanding endurance race tactics involves understanding the dynamics of a race paceline. Let's consider this scenario: If there are twelve riders in a points race, and the speed is at least at tempo speed (that is, not creeping along, but not going flat-out either), the best riders will want to secure a position in the draft and will try to stay there without hitting the front unless they have a specific reason to be there (for example, positions 4–7). Good riders will choose forward positions over positions farther back (positions 1–5). And the riders who are a little bit lacking for the field they are in will typically be found at the back (positions 8–12). Thus, the best riders will let the riders in front pull, transition, and reenter the paceline in front of them by opening a gap and making it easy for them to get into line. If they don't want to be behind a certain rider, they will make it difficult for that rider to enter the paceline in front of them. This is one of the dynamics of the paceline and is based on rider strength, technical ability and handling skills, and respect.

Another dynamic of the paceline is easier to understand if we consider the Madison event (described above under "Madison Technique"), where half of the riders from each team are high on the track, going slow, and half are in the paceline racing. The fact is that every rider in the paceline is expending energy. The riders at the back are expending the most energy because they are riding a longer line around the track and must navigate up and down the track to go through traffic and around exchanges (a nuance of the race we haven't discussed). If they want to score points, they have to first ride past all of their opposition, and there are eleven other teams in the race. The riders in the front are spending time in the wind, but they are spending energy to save energy, because they get time in the draft to recover. And they expend this energy in a fairly straight line and low on the track. The best riders are spending energy to protect their positions; this involves constantly sizing up what is happening in the race, deciding whom to let in and whom to leave out, and performing small accelerations to get and hold wheels. They are close to the front and therefore to points and breakaways, but they are actually expending the least energy in the race.

Gaining Position

Gaining position when another rider wants to give it to you is a simple thing. He or she opens the gap, and you ride into it with the proper acceleration to fit directly into line. Gaining position when another rider wants to be where you are is a very different thing indeed. It requires aggressive riding. In order to get that position, you have to move into the position you want. But how? It must be done gradually, and *gradually* cannot be stressed enough. Asking the rider to give you the position will never work; you must take the position and be a better bike handler than the other rider to get it done. Meanwhile, you have to take care not to break the rules by engaging in improper or excessive contact.

Usually, the rider whose handlebars are more forward is in control of the other rider. For example, let's say that two riders are fighting for position behind a desirable wheel. One rider is directly behind the wheel and in position, and the other rider is coming down into the position from uptrack, with his shoulders at the first rider's handlebars. In this scenario, because of the importance of the handlebars in steering, it is the uptrack rider who has the dominant position. The downtrack rider's handlebars are not free, so she is being squeezed out; the uptrack rider has an advantage because of his ability to steer. Some riders are very good bike handlers and cannot be controlled in this fashion, but they are the exceptions. However, mastering the skill of gaining the position you want takes time; your confidence will build with experience. And even if riders are vying for position aggressively, they must not get into a bumping match, which can be very dangerous. Ask your coach or track mentor for help in preparing for this type of situation.

Protecting Your Position

Protecting your position on the track requires confidence, good bike-handling skills, and determination. If a rider is moving in on a position you want, gently touch her hip and/or say something to indicate that you want the position and have it. This occurs all the time in a larger peloton on the road and is certainly acceptable and helpful if a rider does not realize she is moving into your line, or lane of traffic. The rider may decide to hold the line she was in already, and try again after moving in behind you, or she may decide to try to take your position. If the rider takes the latter course of action, then both of you have another decision to make: Is it worth the fight? And if so, how far are you willing to go in that fight until it is no longer worth it?

If you want to protect a position, you must not open a gap—not even a small one. Gaps are invitations for riders to try to steal desirable positions, and provide them with the "foothold" they need to steal those positions successfully. If you are in a good position, the best way to protect it is to stay tight on the wheel of the rider in front of you. That is one reason why it is so essential to practice being in the paceline.

If the pace slows and the group wants to bunch up, there is a different technique that comes into play. You can see this happening when riders pull out of line and next to one another, forming a wall as they become stacked on top of one another. This makes passing difficult and puts riders in the stack in a better position to fight for the spot they want. The riders who try to sneak in from a lower position on the track to steal a position during this time are at a disadvantage.

Being caught behind a rider who is slowing, with riders immediately to your right, is typically a bad situation to be in, especially if the end of the race is approaching. This is called being "boxed in." When you are boxed in, there is little you can do about it unless the rider to your right opens up some room for you, or the rider in front of you accelerates.

Taking Laps

Taking laps, or "lapping the field," is important in points races and Madisons and can easily determine the outcome of the race, if successful. Gradual accelerations are not effective because the field will follow 99 percent of the time. Instead, riders must attack, and the forward—but not front—positions are best for this. A rider attacking from the back provides notice to the field that he or she is winding it up, and everyone can see a rider attacking from the front. Attacking sharply from third wheel uptrack on a straightaway allows you to apply serious power when riding "uphill," while also giving you the advantage of moving "downhill" into the turn to catch some speed and move away from the field with a gap behind you. The gap forces other teams to work together to catch up. See the USA Cycling Track Rules for specifics on points and taking laps in a Madison or a points race.

Blocking

The term "blocking" is commonly misunderstood in cycling. If a rider is "blocking the field," this does not mean he is physical blocking the lane or stopping the forward progress of the opposition. Instead, it refers to a subtle way of influencing or persuading the field of riders in an effort to control progress. At the track, the field is very susceptible to influence. If a rider shows the field that it should accelerate, oftentimes it will. If a rider shows the field that it should decelerate, it may very well do so. Thus, blocking is simply the effort of a rider or group of riders to lure the field into doing something, which is usually bad for the rest of the field. For example, in a field where every racer is for himself, except for two riders who are from the same team, one rider may attack while the other goes to the front and rides a very gradually decelerating pace without pulling off the front. The rider on the front is blocking by slowing the pace of the chase.

Controlling the Sprinter's Lane

By rule, the Sprinter's Lane is controlled by the rider who is in front and below the Red Line (Sprinter's Line). This means that getting this position is a little hairy for the rider coming downtrack. By rule, the lower rider has the right to the position. The rules do not typically allow riders to come down on other riders who control the Sprinter's Lane, and the rider who controls the Sprinter's Lane cannot be passed on the left even if there is room to pass. The rules forbid this. However, you can move in on the rider in the Sprinter's Lane as long as you do it gradually. Riders attempting this will often ride as close to the Red Line as possible in order to use up the extra track and make it harder for other riders to pass them. Also, a limited amount of lateral movement is allowed all riders, and this position lets riders take the best line through the turn.

CYCLOCROSS SKILLS

Cyclocross is a rigorous sport where athletes must often dismount their bikes smoothly and carry them while jumping over sets of barriers or running up steep hills; once over the obstacle, they remount their bikes with ease and ride on the sections that are rideable. The competitions are performed on a course that may include dirt, grass, mud, sand, or even ice, typically in the fall and winter.

Riders from other disciplines often do cyclocross in the fall and winter and their other discipline in the spring and summer. 'Cross provides a change of pace and plenty of incentive to keep training hard. It does use some unusual skills that riders from other disciplines will need to practice, however. If you are interested in trying cyclocross, you will need to be able to dismount and remount your bike as confidently and smoothly as possible. You will also have to get used to carrying your bike over obstacles and up very steep grades, and to riding in mud, snow, and ice. Other important 'cross skills are picking lines through obstacles, shifting your bodyweight to advantage on difficult hills and turns, and counter-steering your machine.

Dismounting and Remounting

Dismounting and remounting your bike may sound simple enough—you do it all the time, right? But there is definitely an art to it. If you do it clumsily in a 'cross race, you are wasting precious time.

Let's start with getting off the bike. First, try unclipping your right foot and bringing it around the rear of the bike; next, unclip your left foot and step off the bike; then lift the bike and take off running. Get comfortable with these moves. Begin by trying them at low speeds and then ramp it up, trying it faster each time.

However, you'll need to take dismounting to a different level to do it the way the experts do. Watching a first-class 'cross racer go through the motions is like watching a finely tuned machine at work. The real pros will smoothly bring their leg around the back of the bike, then bring the leg forward so they are standing on one pedal with the other leg right next to it on one side of the frame. In this way, the best 'cross racers set themselves up to get their first step in very quickly, and those who don't do it this way lose crucial seconds. That said, as a cyclocross racer you can't count on dismounting this way every time; you need to be ready for anything, because course designers are not always going to put barriers or obstacles on flat straightaways. You need to be able to get off your bike in many different ways.

Remounting efficiently is also a more complex skill than you might imagine. It can be fun to watch riders remounting at a race: It is a thing of beauty how smoothly and quickly a world-class 'cross racer can remount and accelerate out of the obstacle, but rookies can be equally entertaining. They often stumble over themselves and crash, or take a giant leap of faith onto the saddle and miss. Here's the secret for remounting like a World Cup athlete: Start slow and work your way up. That is, start by just walking alongside your bike and swinging your leg onto the saddle, trying to land on the saddle with the backside of your thigh and sliding onto your saddle from there. Once you get the hang of that, you can move up to a small jump. You don't need to launch yourself into the air just hoping to land on the saddle. Jump only high enough to just clear your saddle. There is no reason to expend a lot of energy trying to jump way into the air just to slam down on your saddle a moment later. Finally, try landing on the underside of your thigh and sliding onto your saddle. Start slow and build up to speed, and find a nice grassy hill so you have a soft landing if you crash. Have confidence that you *will* get it, and keep practicing; it takes years to get this down, and the more practice you get, the better you will get at it.

Getting on and off your bike is one of the most important skills you can have in cyclocross. The more comfortable you are with these skills— in any condition, especially bad weather and difficult surfaces—the better able you will be to choose the best strategies for different sections of a course. Sometimes you will want to ride a sandy or muddy section, and sometimes you will want to get off the bike and run. But your choice should not be dictated by your lack of skill in dismounting and remounting; it should be dictated by what's best for the conditions at hand. Having those options could make the difference between winning and losing a race.

Managing a Slick Course

Cyclocross races test more than just your fitness: Just being able to go the fastest in a straight line on the road or track is almost meaningless when the ground is muddy, snowy, or icy. Technical skills will play a big role in your performance.

One of the most important things to remember in the mud is to stay light on the front wheel. Keep your weight farther back than usual and let the front wheel track naturally. Keep in mind that mud can hide holes big enough to swallow your front wheel whole, and if you ride into one, you may go over the handlebars. Snow and ice can also be a problem, particularly late in the cyclocross season. Be cautious anytime you ride on snow, as ice can be lurking below. As with mud, keep your front wheel light so it can track where it needs to go.

Counter-Steering

You can use counter-steering in cyclocross in a variety of situations, especially in slick conditions when you are starting a skid, and in cornering. To initiate counter-steering, nudge your handlebars slightly into the opposite direction from the direction you actually want to go. Let's say your bike begins to slide out to one side; to solve the problem, turn the handlebars into the direction of your slide to regain control. You are turning into your slide while pedaling to straighten yourself out and keep moving on course. To use the technique in cornering, come into a corner fast, and then slide out the rear of your bike while counter-steering to keep your balance. You can carry more speed out of the corner this way and produce faster lap times. This technique can be used in all types of courses and situations, not just slick mud.

The Pits

Cyclocross rules allow pits on the course, where you can have someone waiting to fix a flat tire or make other minor repairs for you. Generally the pits are located alongside the course, and you are allowed to change bikes for any reason, whether for mechanical failure, a flat tire, gear problems, or because your bike has so much mud on it that it weighs a ton. So it's best if you can have two bikes for 'cross and a friend who is handy with repairs (or an actual bike mechanic). You simply ride into the pits and get a fresh bike or make your changes, then get back on your bike to be on your way. Some races are so muddy that it is faster to get a new bike on every pass than to sludge your way through the course twice with the same bike. Simply have your mechanic clean one bike while you are riding the other, and do a quick handoff when you come through again. If you need a repair, switch bikes and let your mechanic know with a quick word what the problem is. The pits can be a great benefit if used correctly with a good support team.

To use the pits to best advantage, you should have the correct equipment there: tools, any replacement parts that may be needed, and a source of water. Professional teams have at least one extra bike in the pit, and sometimes two. If you have an extra bike, set it up exactly the same way as your primary bike. You do not want to have one super-nice ride and another junky bike "just in case"; in the case you do need that bike—and you will—you want to be confident that you can be just as fast on it as you are on the other one. However, you can set the two bikes up with different tires, or with different tire pressures, to cope with changing course conditions. Keep both bikes in tip-top shape. You prep for a race all season and put in hours and hours of training and hundreds of dollars in traveling and racing expenses. Why not put in a few more hours to make both bikes work properly?

Every race promoter will set up a water source for cleaning bikes differently, depending on what is available. They will typically try to set up a water station specifically designed to help riders or their support crews quickly hose off bikes. This will often be in a designated area with a hose or several hoses. Riders wait their turn and clean bikes as quickly as possible.

BMX SKILLS

Entry-level competition on the BMX bike is a great way for young riders to learn bike-handling skills in a relatively safe environment, and BMX tracks are available in many communities. Age-specific competitions begin for children as young as 3 to 5 years old. When these kids are old enough for mountain bike or road bike competition, they will have a significant head start, but many decide not to change disciplines as they progress through the BMX competitions.

BMX racing is a sprint event of short duration and does not offer the best opportunities for a rider more physically suited to endurance racing. A child's natural inclinations toward sprinting or endurance may not become evident until he or she has begun to mature in early adolescence, but certainly the BMX venue provides a great resource for any young rider to develop great handling skills. Many riders physically suited to this sprint event may never leave the competitive world of BMX racing, and with the entry of this discipline into the 2008 Summer Olympics, there is much incentive to progress in the well-organized competition schedules of BMX in the United States.

If you are interested in BMX, or have a child who would like to try it, we highly recommend that you go to the track and watch the racing. Find a local pro to learn from.

RECOMMENDED READING

Bicycling Magazine's *Complete Book of Road Cycling Skills: Your Guide to Riding Faster, Stronger, Longer and Safer*, by Ben Hewitt (Rodale Press, 1998).
Cyclocross Training + Technique, 3rd ed., by Simon Burney (VeloPress, 2007).
Effective Cycling, 6th ed., by John Forester (MIT Press, 2005).
Mastering Mountain Bike Skills, by Brian Lopes and Lee McCormack (Human Kinetics, 2005).

Here are additional resources for mountain bike skills and equipment:

Alison Dunlap's website, http://www.alisondunlap.com/. Alison is a great coach and her website is a useful resource.

Dirtrag, an online mountain bike magazine, http://www.dirtragmag.com/.

Gravity mountain bike e-magazine, http://www.pinnedmtb.com/. This site provides news and resources.

Mountain bike resource page, http://www.leelikesbikes.com/. This site also has a link to Lee McCormack and Brian Lopes's mountain bike skills instruction book and other skill-related books like *Pump Nation.*

USA Cycling's official pages on mountain-bike-related racing topics, http://www.usacycling. org/mtb/.

For manufacturers of equipment for downhill racing, including body armor, see http://www. azonicusa.com/, http://www.sixsixone.com/, http://www.foxracing.com/us/en/fox/, and http://www.dainese.com/eng/home.asp.

For more skill building, see *Racing Tactics for Cyclists,* by Thomas Prehn (VeloPress, 2004). This is a comprehensive look at road tactics and strategies, written by an expert.

The following websites are good resources for those interested in BMX:

USA Cycling's official BMX pages can be found at https://www.usacycling.org/bmx/.

For complete training programs for riders of any level, see http://www.trainingpeaks.com/ trainingplans/gregromero/.

The websites of the two race series organizations in the United States for BMX are at http:// www.ababmx.com and http://www.nbl.org/index.asp.

For the latest news on the sport, see http://www.bmxnews.com.

For a forum site with news, updates, online chats, and equipment for sale, see http://www. bmxtalk.com.

9 STRENGTH TRAINING
and Flexibility

Stretch! Kids grow fast and stretching is a good habit to avoid injury.
—Connie Carpenter-Phinney, 1984 Olympian

As we saw in "Training 101" (Chapter 7), being an athlete means training many different systems within your body. Cyclists tend to be full of enthusiasm for workouts that involve riding, because they love to ride. Going to the gym is usually not a top priority. In this chapter we will take a look at how flexibility and weight training fits into a cyclist's development.

STRETCHING AND FLEXIBILITY

As a young athlete, you may not think stretching is necessary. However, learning good stretching habits early can be a crucial part of a long and injury-free career. Maintaining good flexibility is a topic experts are pretty much in agreement on. It will help you avoid the kinds of injuries that result from overuse or overexertion on the bike. Even better, the increased flexibility and range of motion will improve your training and competition performance.

Stretching can be done anytime you feel the need to relax. The more flexible you become, the more you will enjoy stretching. There is no harm in stretching several times a day, provided that you do so safely. However, always be sure that you are properly warmed up before doing any stretching exercises. When your muscles aren't warmed up, it is more difficult to stretch them and you do not make many gains in flexibility. If you haven't had a chance to get your blood pumping before you stretch, be very conservative and don't push the stretches too hard.

There are many excellent products on the market that can help you build and maintain your flexibility. They include these helpful tools:

- *Foam rollers:* A foam roller is a long (2- to 3-foot), round piece of foam that has just a bit of give. It is designed to gently press into your muscles as you roll on it and is used for self-massage.
- *The Stick™ (at www.thestick.com):* The Stick is a handheld device that athletes use to gently massage tired muscles. The regular Stick is a flexible, 1-foot-long stick with handles. The main part of the Stick is made of a flexible plastic rod covered with ceramic beads. You can press lightly or more deeply depending on the type of massage you need.
- *Stretching webbing:* Many companies make webbing straps that are designed to help athletes stretch. They often have foot and hand loops or holds to help athletes improve their stretching technique. For example, stretching webbing might be looped around the foot of an outstretched leg. The webbing is held in each hand and gently pulled. This provides a good stretch for the hamstrings and lower back.

When stretching to improve flexibility, do so following a good warm-up; after training, as part of your cool-down routine; or after a competition. You will make gains in flexibility only when your muscles have been warmed up properly and only when you complete your stretching in a careful and controlled manner.

Important Points to Remember When Stretching

Follow these basic principles for good results with your stretching regimen:

- *Never, ever* bounce when stretching. Bouncing can trigger a muscular response called the "stretch reflex." The stretch reflex is a defense mechanism that the body uses to try to keep you from stretching muscle fibers too far and causing serious damage. When you bounce, the body may misinterpret the movement as a dangerous or potentially harmful one, such as occurs in a slip or fall on ice, and in response your muscles may tighten in an attempt to protect themselves from overstretching and tearing. Bouncing is counterproductive; it actually increases your chances of pulling or straining a muscle and decreases your chances of making true flexibility gains.

- Always breathe regularly when stretching. Stretching should be relaxing, and holding your breath isn't very relaxing. As you prepare to stretch, inhale deeply, pulling your breath deep into your belly (also called belly breathing). Think about your belly expanding and filling with air. Then exhale slowly and deeply as you lean into your stretch. As you hold the stretch for a moment, continue to breathe comfortably and slowly as feels natural. Remember, no holding your breath.
- Whenever possible, change out of your damp workout clothes before stretching. It is difficult to stretch properly if you are chilled. While catching a chill alone cannot cause you to get sick, it can contribute to the stress your body experiences and play a role in lowering your defenses against germs. If you can't change right away, at least throw on a second layer and put on a hat to stay warm.
- Try to stretch on a comfortable but firm surface, such as a stretching mat or carpet. Stretching on a cold or hard floor is uncomfortable and can cause you to become chilled. Stretching on a surface that is too soft, such as a bed, is not good for stretching posture.
- When stretching with someone else, don't measure your flexibility against his or hers. Genetics and athletic history play a large role in your degree of flexibility. Paying attention to your personal gains in flexibility is a much better strategy.
- Gains in flexibility will be made over time. Stretch consistently, not just occasionally or when something hurts.
- Always pay attention to your body positioning and alignment. Good posture is important. Sloppy stretching means you are not making the flexibility gains you think you are making and can increase your risk of injury.

The Stretches

Below you will find a list of basic stretches along with descriptions of how to perform them. This is by no means a complete list of stretching activities, and each of them has several variations that you might hear about in fitness classes or read about elsewhere. Not everyone will benefit from every stretch on this list or even feel comfortable doing each one. Feel free to modify the list as needed. For example, you might wish to incorporate yoga postures or other stretching moves that you feel comfortable with. However, always follow the principles of healthy stretching. You don't need to stretch every muscle in your body every time you stretch, especially if something isn't tight. But it is important to consider which muscles are tight and to pay attention to those areas. Knowing your own body—especially the areas that are prone to getting tight and which stretches work best for you—is a key part of being a successful athlete. You should plan on spending a minimum of 10 minutes stretching after each training session. Aim to repeat each stretch two or three times and to hold each for 10 to 20 seconds each time.

Here are the basic recommended stretches:

- *Pecs and shoulders:* Stand tall with your feet shoulder-width apart, knees slightly bent (not locked out), and toes forward, then clasp your hands behind your back and gently raise your arms behind you as high as you comfortably can. Maintain body alignment, with your shoulders in line with your hips, and your hips over your feet. Stay tall during this stretch; do not lean forward or bend at the waist. Maintain this posture for the next two stretches.
- *Shoulders and upper back:* Raise one arm to shoulder height in front of your body, use the other hand to grasp it just above the elbow, and gently draw the raised arm across your body. Repeat on the other side.
- *Triceps:* Raise one arm over your head and then bend it at the elbow so your hand falls behind your back, then use your other hand to gently press down and back on the raised bent elbow. Repeat on the other side.
- *Groin:* Stand tall with your feet slightly more than shoulder-width apart, keeping your toes forward; bend one knee and shift your body weight in that direction until you feel the stretch in the groin area on the opposite side. Repeat on the other side.

- *Calf stretch, parts A and B:* Stand facing a wall or stable surface with your feet apart so that one foot is a few inches in front of the other; you should be about 6 to 12 inches away from the wall (depending on your flexibility). For part A, lean your upper body toward the wall so that your arms rest against it, keeping both feet on the ground and the front knee bent, then move your hips forward toward the wall until you feel the stretch in your calf. For part B, follow the same motion as in part A, but raise the heel of the back leg as you move your hips forward toward the wall. Repeat with the other leg in front.

- *Hip flexor:* Stand in a forward-to-back split stance with your legs about shoulder-width apart. Then, keeping your rear heel down and your torso tall, bend your front knee and gently press your hips forward until you feel a stretch in the hip region. This stretch can also be done with your front foot up on a step or a low chair. Repeat with the other leg in front.

- *Standing quad:* Standing tall, bend one knee and grasp the ankle of the bent leg behind you. Bring the heel of the bent leg up toward your butt while keeping the bent knee pointing toward the ground. Make sure you don't pull the knee out toward the side; keep your foot behind your butt. Keep your torso tall and press your hips slightly forward. Hold on to a wall or chair for stability with your free hand if needed. Repeat with the other leg.

- *Side stretch:* From a standing position with your feet shoulder-width apart, raise both arms over your head and reach for the sky; then bring one arm down to reach low across your body while extending the upstretched arm over your head, and lean in the direction you are reaching. Repeat on other side.

- *Good morning stretch:* From a standing position with feet shoulder-width apart, gently bend from the waist and press your palms down toward the floor, as if you were pushing stuff flat in a suitcase. After you have held the stretch for 10 to 20 seconds, slowly come back to an upright stance by unbending from the waist and sweeping your outstretched arms in an arc motion until you are pressing your palms up toward the sky, then slowly lower your arms to your sides.

- *Full body:* Lie flat on your back on the floor with your arms extended over your head and your legs out straight; pretend that there are strings around your wrists and ankles and that you are gently being pulled lengthwise as you stretch. Repeat with your toes pointed, and again with your heels pressed to the floor and your toes pulled back.
- *Leg lover and twist:* Take a seated position with both legs out in front of you. Bend one leg and place that foot on the outside of the straight leg, then wrap your arms around the bent knee and hug it to your body. Your foot may come off the floor. After you hold the hug for 10 to 20 seconds, place the arm opposite the bent leg so that the back of the arm is against the thigh of your bent leg (if the right knee is bent, use your left arm, and vice versa). Sit tall and gently twist your whole torso in that direction. Repeat with other leg.
- *IT band:* From a seated position, with both legs out in front of you, bend one leg and place the ankle just above the knee of the straight leg. Sit very tall (using your hands for support, if necessary) and bend the straight leg; as the straight leg bends, the bent leg will also come up. Make sure that the bent knee stays pressed forward; you should feel this in the hip/gluteus region of the leg that is bent. Repeat on the other side.
- *Seated groin:* Sitting tall, bend both legs so that the soles of your feet are lined up in front of you, and gently use your elbows to press down on your bent knees. This provides a very gentle groin stretch.
- *Proper hurdler:* From a seated position with both legs out in front of you, bend one knee and bring your foot in so it rests against the inner thigh of the other leg. Sitting tall, gently lean forward over the straight leg. Make sure you lean directly forward over the straight leg and that your torso is squared up with the foot of the straight leg. As you become more flexible, try reaching forward toward your toes with your hands. Repeat on the other side.

Specialized Stretching: Yoga and Pilates

More and more cyclists are signing up for yoga and Pilates classes and spending time on the mat as well as on the road or track. Both disciplines have significant benefits for cycling that make them well worth your time and effort. The flexibility you can gain on the yoga mat, and the core-strength improvements you can develop through Pilates, will carry over into cycling in many ways.

In yoga, you will follow the instructor through various positions that are achieved by stretching the muscles. Although yoga has its roots in the history and religion of India, basic yoga classes usually have nothing to do with religion and everything to do with the physical process of carefully stretching one's muscles to learn and perform the set poses. Yoga will teach you how to breathe properly and can help you learn how to relax when you are stressed. And once you learn proper technique, yoga is something you will be able to do anytime, anywhere, for stretching or for relaxation purposes.

Pilates is an exercise form originally developed by Joseph Pilates (1881–1967) as a method of promoting rehabilitation from injury. The classes, which incorporate a huge range of exercises using both specialized equipment and floorwork without equipment, are growing quickly in popularity across the United States. Pilates proponents claim that this style of exercising improves core strength, flexibility, agility, and economy of motion—all perfect for a competitive cyclist!

With a good instructor, you may find that yoga and Pilates are not only great sources of both strength and flexibility training, but also fun, providing a change of pace from the bike. They may produce positive performance benefits, as they seem to be good for both mind and body. Check the Web, using the key words *yoga, Pilates, classes,* and the name of your hometown or area, and you should be able to find out where the classes are offered. Most health clubs and YMCAs offer affordable classes, and some instructors have studios offering both individual and class instruction. Instruction may cost anywhere from $10 to $20 per session, depending on your area. If you belong to a fitness center, these classes are probably already included with your membership fee; if not, consider joining one, as it may offer many other classes as well, plus weight-training instruction and equipment. If you are in college, your school may offer the classes as part of the physical education program.

Just as with cycling coaches, the level of expertise and knowledge may vary from instructor to instructor. Ask what certifications the instructor has and find out about the focus and level of the class. Don't join an advanced class if you are a beginner, as you will be more likely to get injured this way. When you take a class for the first time, let the instructor know you are a beginner. A good instructor will keep an eye on you to make sure you perform the moves safely and correctly. Be sure to ask about discounts for students and reduced prices for purchasing multiple classes.

Massage

It may seem a little odd to include massage in a section on stretching and flexibility. But actually it makes perfect sense. We aren't talking about a spa massage with candles and facials, but a good sports massage. And although a massage can be nice and relaxing, for an athlete it serves a much greater purpose.

A sports massage helps athletes flush out waste products from muscles and gain and maintain flexibility. There are many different styles of massage, each with a variety of benefits and uses. The best massage therapists combine intuition and different styles of massage to provide their clients with a healthy experience.

How often athletes get a massage will vary depending on training, injuries, and budget considerations. In racing season, many athletes schedule a massage once a month during their rest week to help speed up recovery. Together with your parents, coach, and massage therapist, you can discuss your training and recovery needs to determine how often massage might be beneficial.

Finding a good sports massage therapist is key. Different states have different rules and regulations about who can practice as a massage therapist and what certifications are needed for someone to be a sports massage therapist. Probably the best way to find a good massage therapist is to ask other athletes whom they use. Once you find someone, always start off by asking the therapist about her qualifications and what work she has done with athletes. You may want to try two or three different massage therapists to get an idea of different styles. Over time, you will want to go to just one or two therapists consistently; the more you work together, the better the therapist will get to know your body and its needs. This can be especially important if you have a recurring injury or particular muscles that tend to tighten up.

A massage usually costs anywhere from $50 to $100 an hour, depending on where you live. Most massage therapists will do sessions ranging from half an hour to two hours, but one hour is typical. In addition to asking other athletes for recommendations, you can find reputable massage therapists through sports medicine doctors, physical therapy clinics, chiropractors, and massage therapy schools. Massage therapy schools often have a discount-rate clinic where their students can practice. While this can be a lower-cost option, these students are not usually as skilled in sports massage as an experienced massage therapist who has specialized in that area, and you may not be able to work with the same therapist each time.

What to Expect When You Get a Massage   When you go for your first massage, let the therapist know that you are new and that you are an athlete. A good massage therapist should ask you about any injuries you may have and will want to know how much you are training and what sorts of workouts you are doing. He may ask you if you have any preferences about the style of massage or the intensity of the massage work you would like. The more he knows about you, your training, and your health, the better. Here is some other information about massage protocol:

- What you wear for a massage depends on the setting and your comfort level. For a massage in an office or in the athlete's home, the athlete is typically nude beneath a sheet. The massage therapy code calls for the athlete to remain draped or covered except for the part the massage therapist is working on. This is to protect your modesty and to keep you warm. You do not have to be nude under the sheet if you are not comfortable with that.
- In a camp or race setting where other athletes and people are present, the massage therapist will provide massage through your clothes.

- Don't be afraid to tell a massage therapist if she is working too deeply on your muscles. Sports massage may be uncomfortable at times (especially if you have a knot or sore spot), but it shouldn't be more painful than you can handle. It is very important to communicate with your massage therapist.
- It's okay to fall asleep during massage, although this can be hard to do during a sports massage if the therapist is working on sore or tight spots.
- Some people like to listen to gentle music during a massage, some prefer to talk to the massage therapist, and others just want silence. The massage therapist will ask you about your preferences before you begin.
- Avoid getting a full massage the day before or the day of a hard workout or race. A very light massage can help flush out and ready your muscles, but deep work may leave you sore or with heavy legs.
- Always drink a lot of water after a massage. Fluids are crucial for flushing out the toxins released by your muscles. You may feel a little nauseated after a massage; this is normal and is due to the toxins.

WEIGHT TRAINING

Weight training specifically for cycling is a complicated subject, and the pros and cons of its usefulness are hotly debated among coaches. Weight training, or strength and resistance training, is most commonly performed in a gym or weight room and can include a variety of techniques. It is unclear whether these methods lead to performance benefits for cyclists: Even the scientists can't agree on their effectiveness. Sprint cyclists, who are more focused on power than, say, endurance cyclists, are more likely to spend time in the weight room. The decision to add weight training to your training routine also depends on your age and growth patterns.

Should Junior and Espoir athletes even be in the weight room? The answer, according to leading organizations such as the National Strength and Conditioning Association (NSCA) and the American College of Sports Medicine (ACSM), is yes, but with important reservations. Care must be taken not to overtrain. Junior riders vary in their level of physical maturity and development, and the level of weight training that they engage in should be adjusted accordingly. Young bodies—prepuberty or in the early phases of puberty—should do no more than body-weight-based resistance training (push-ups, pull-ups, and the like). Before puberty, young athletes lack the hormones necessary to make the gains expected in the weight room. More importantly, the body develops in different phases in the early stages of puberty. Typically, your bones will grow first. Once you have long bones, the muscles and tendons can take a while to catch up. Stressing your joints before the muscles and tendons have caught up can lead to problems and increase your risk of injury. If in doubt about whether your body has grown enough to safely train with more than just your own body weight, err on the side of caution and wait, or consult a medical specialist who can help you decide if training with weights would be beneficial for you. Keep in mind that there are experts who feel that it is best to wait until you are fully matured before beginning weight-room work.

Despite the debate over whether Juniors should engage in weight training, one thing is certain: Anyone performing weight training should use good technique while performing the exercises. Weight training, just like cycling, can be dangerous, and failure to use proper technique may result in serious injury to your body that can ruin a cycling season or cause problems for an even longer period of time. This warning is of particular importance for young, growing bodies, in which bone, muscle, and tendon growth may all be occurring at different times.

If you choose to undertake a weight-training program, it is a good idea to use a certified coach, especially when you are getting started and

The Experts Weigh in on Weight Training

The position of the National Strength and Conditioning Association (NSCA) on resistance training for young people is widely accepted among coaching professionals. It emphasizes the importance of "a properly designed and supervised resistance training program" that is safe and that enhances overall health. Such a program should not only "increase the strength of children" but also "improve the psychosocial well-being of children." To see the entire NSCA position statement, visit www.nsca-lift.org/Publications/YouthforWeb.pdf.

learning proper form. A weight-training expert has specialized knowledge and will be able to tailor a program to your specific sport needs. A coach can also make sure your weight-room program is progressing at an appropriate rate—by, for example, helping you determine when to increase the amount of resistance and the number of sets and repetitions that you undertake. In addition, he or she can help you set up a training plan that will complement your workouts on the bike. You don't want your weight-room efforts to undermine the hard work you do on the bike. Find a trainer who is familiar with the needs of the adolescent or developing body and with cycling. It is very important to make sure that your joints are protected while you grow, and improper lifting can put an unsafe load on these vulnerable areas.

As you begin your weight-training program, you will need to learn about different techniques and approaches. Traditional weight training is usually done with either free weights or dumbbells, or with specialized machines designed to work various muscles. Table 9.1 provides an overview of the pros and cons of each. Once you have decided on a general approach, you will need to learn how to manipulate the three key elements of weight training: the load, the repetitions, and the sets. The load, or resistance, is the amount of weight you will use. A repetition is one complete movement, and a set contains a certain number of continuous repetitions. For example, you might do three sets of five repetitions of a particular movement with 5-pound weights. Over time, with the help of a professional, you will learn to manipulate the load, the number of reps, and the number of sets to get the desired results. In general, higher weight with lower reps and sets is useful for making greater power gains, and low to moderate weight with moderate to high reps and sets is useful for gaining endurance. And just as with endurance training, the best gains are made when you balance the hard work you do with good rest and recovery practices.

Potential Benefits of Resistance Training

The benefits of resistance or strength training are multiple. One of the main benefits is muscle growth and increased muscular strength. But in addition to strength gains, resistance training can improve your muscu-

TABLE 9.1   **Pros and Cons of Free Weights and Weight Machines**

Weight Machines		Free Weights	
Pros	Cons	Pros	Cons

Safer, to a degree
Guide user through
  proper motions
	Must fit appropriately to
	  be safe and for user to
	  gain desired effects
	Often a poor fit for
	  younger or smaller
	  athletes
	Less variety available
	Still require supervision
		More variety
		Can specialize weight
		  more
			Greater risk of improper
			  form
			Greater risk of injury
			Vigilant supervision
			  necessary

lar endurance, enabling you to ride longer. It can also help you improve your muscular explosiveness and power, which come in handy during short climbs or surges in a race. If performed correctly, resistance training can decrease the risk of injury and strengthen all your stabilizing muscles and tendons. Other benefits are improved body composition, increased cardiovascular development, and gains in self-esteem.

Common Weight-Room Activities

There is a huge range of exercises you can do in a weight room. Ask your coach for specific recommendations.

Free weights: Dumbbells, weight bars, and loose weights that can be added as needed.

Weight machines: Machines that guide an athlete through specific movements properly, using levers and pulleys to provide the weight. Nautilus is an example of one company that makes machines for weight training.

Plyometrics: Activities that involve rapid but controlled movements to develop power and speed. Plyometrics might include double- or single-leg stair hops, for example. These are favorite exercises of track sprinters.

Speed and agility drills: Usually running-based drills designed to increase reaction time. This type of drill may be an off-season, pre-season, or crosstraining element for cyclists, particularly for those involved in track or cyclocross.

Body-weight-based exercises: Activities such as push-ups, pull-ups, and dips. These activities are suitable for all cyclists throughout the season.

Key Weight-Training Terms

Concentric muscle action: occurs when muscle lengthens

Eccentric muscle action: occurs when muscle shortens

Flexibility: the ability to move through a full range of motion (ROM)

Hypertrophy: muscle growth (often associated with resistance training)

Isometric muscle action: muscle tension with no visible joint movement

Muscular endurance: the ability to provide repeated or sustained, continuous contraction

Muscular fitness: the strength, endurance, speed, power, and flexibility to meet the demands of your sport

Muscular strength: the amount of force that can be generated in a single effort

Neuromuscular response: occurs when motor nerves send a signal to muscle cells telling them to contract

Power: strength and speed combined

Speed: getting from point A to point B quickly

Dos and Don'ts

Strength training should always be done in a controlled manner. Use these guidelines to help you develop a a safe and healthy workout program:

- Never lift more weight than you can safely control.
- Never let gravity pull a weight down; always set the weight down slowly and gently. Letting a weight go down too fast can cause serious damage to your joints and muscles. There are important gains to be made during both phases of the lift: As you lift the weight, one set of muscles contracts to produce force and move the weight; as you lower the weight, a different set of muscles contracts, pull-

ing the body back to the starting position in a controlled manner. For example, when you do a biceps curl, the biceps muscle contracts and causes the elbow joint to bend, raising the lower arm and the hand that is holding the weight. While this is happening, the triceps muscle lengthens. Then, as you lower the weight, your biceps muscle relaxes and your triceps muscle contracts, allowing your arm to straighten as you control the weight back to the starting position.

- Never hold your breath when you lift. Concentrate on exhaling as you lift the load and inhaling as you control the weight back to the starting position.

- If you use free weights where you load weights onto a bar, *always* use weight cuffs to secure the weight. Slipping weights can cause very serious injuries to yourself or others.

- To maximize your gains, take at least one day off between weight-lifting workouts, but try to avoid taking more than three days off in a row.

- To keep your muscles warm and active, the rest period between sets should be minimal—just enough time to drink a little water or stretch a bit.

- Start by lifting with large muscle groups before you do smaller groups. For example, do chest exercises before you do biceps or triceps. Both biceps and triceps are used in chest exercises; if you do the small muscles first, they will become fatigued and won't be able to assist the chest muscles. As a result, you may overstress the muscles in your biceps and not be able to lift effectively with your pectoral muscles (chest).

- Make sure your training program is balanced—that is, that you work opposing muscles. If you work your hamstrings, for example, you need to work your quads. If you work your back, you need to work your chest. This way, the muscles will make similar strength gains and work together more efficiently.

Common Weight-Room Myths

As common as weight training is in our society, there is still a lot of incorrect information floating around. Following is a list of common myths along with the actual facts.

Myth 1 *Women bulk up in the weight room.* Don't worry! While resistance training will make you stronger, it will not bulk up female athletes the way male athletes bulk up. Women don't have as much testosterone as men, so they cannot put on muscle the way guys do. And both male and female endurance athletes should focus their lifting efforts on muscular endurance (moderate weights with moderate to high reps), a strategy that is not designed to build up bulk.

Myth 2 *If you keep lifting, you will just keep getting bigger.* Again, your muscle growth depends on your body and the type of lifting you do. A good trainer will help ensure that you lift for your body type and sport demands, so this should not be a concern.

Myth 3 *Weight-training specific areas helps you lose weight in specific areas.* No matter what the infomercials or ads promise about weight-training equipment, you cannot spot-reduce. If you decide

Finding a Certified Trainer

A certified coach or trainer may also be called a personal trainer or a fitness instructor. Whatever his or her title, your coach should have excellent credentials and should be experienced in working with developmental athletes. The best experts will have a college degree (BS, MS, or PhD) in a sport, exercise, or movement science like kinesiology or exercise physiology. These individuals should have credible certifications, such as those offered through the American College of Sports Medicine (ACSM, www.acsm.org) or the National Strength and Conditioning Association (NSCA, www.nsca-lift.org). Check with your local university sport science program, YMCA, or reputable gym to find someone reliable.

Reputable certifications to look for are:

- American College of Sports Medicine (ACSM)
- Certified Personal Trainer (CPT)
- Health Fitness Instructor (HFI)
- National Strength and Conditioning Association (NSCA)
- Certified Strength and Conditioning Specialist (CSCS)

to incorporate resistance training into your program, aim for a well-balanced training plan that emphasizes muscular endurance and muscle balance. This will improve muscle tone and strength and help prevent injury.

Myth 4 *When you stop training, muscle turns to fat.* Muscles follow the principle of "use it or lose it." If you have muscles you don't use, they will atrophy or shrink. They don't turn into fat. But if you aren't eating a healthy diet, or if you are consuming more calories than you use up, your fat stores may grow while your muscles shrink, which can make it feel (and look) like fat is replacing muscle. You can avoid this by maintaining a healthy diet and remaining active in the off-season (see Chapter 7).

WHAT ABOUT THE CORE?

Core training has become a hot topic in the field of weight training. It is a relatively new way of training and is defined differently by different groups. In general, your core includes the muscles in your torso that help you balance and stabilize. Some people only talk about abdominal muscles, but your torso also has back muscles and many small muscles in your hips and glutes area that play important roles in balance. While the experts debate the finer points of the subject, however, we can talk about the basics—what you should be doing in terms of core training to help you perform at your best on your bike.

When you are on your bike, the muscles in your midsection are responsible for helping you maintain proper riding posture and balance. When your abdominal muscles (or "abs") or lower back get tired, you will slouch on the bike. As soon as you slouch (typically this is when you sort of tuck your tail and curl a little, similar to when you slide down in a chair), you change the way your muscles are being worked. This can cause a big drop in power—your ability to ride hard.

Working on your abs and lower back can be a part of your regular training. Ab work includes traditional crunches for upper, lower, and side ab muscle groups. Old-fashioned sit-ups (where you go from a position on the floor all the way up to a full upright position) are not a good idea. They put a lot of stress on your lower back, and they are too easy to do incorrectly. Stick with basic crunch variations (see next section) or, better yet, take an abs fitness class or consult a professional to learn how to do a wide variety of core exercises to benefit your overall fitness. Pilates is also an excellent means of working on creating a strong, healthy core.

Beginning Ab Exercises

When performing abdominal exercises, make sure you never hold your breath, and that all movements are controlled. As you do your ab exercises, your breathing should follow a steady pattern. As you perform the muscle contraction, or crunch, exhale. As you relax, or return to the starting position, inhale slowly and control your movements. Your ab exercises should be steady and slow. If you move too fast, you begin to use momentum more than muscle power. Go slowly enough to ensure that you are controlling your movement. Here are some variations to get you started:

- *Regular crunch:* With your hands across your chest or behind your neck, use your abs to raise your shoulder blades off the floor.
- *Reverse crunch:* Place your hands at your sides or under your lower back for support, keep your feet off the ground, and curl the muscles of your lower abs to bring your knees up toward your chin.
- *Double crunch:* Put the regular crunch and the reverse crunch together, with your hands behind your head.
- *Pull-in-knee crunch:* Stretch your legs straight out, lifting off the floor by 1 inch; draw one knee in and curl your lower abs; then crunch the upper body up and across, bringing the opposite elbow toward the bent knee. Slowly return your leg to the stretched-out position, but don't rest it on the floor. After doing one side, switch and do the other side. This isn't the fast bicycle crunch you might have learned in the past.
- *Pull-down-knee crunch:* With your legs straight up, bring one knee down and curl your hips, then crunch the upper body up, bring-

ing the opposite elbow to the lowered knee. Straighten the leg again as you lower your upper body. Do all repetitions on one side, then switch and do the other side.

- *Crunch pulse:* At the end of any abs exercise, hold the contracted position, and then do a series of small, tight, controlled pulse motions that require just a bit of relaxation of the muscles before you squeeze the contraction again.

When you start doing ab work, build up slowly. Focus on doing just one or two exercises for the first week to help reduce soreness. You may prefer to do your ab work based on time rather than count. If you have a watch with a second hand, this means you can just watch the clock rather than worry about counting. For the first workout, pick two exercises and do three sets of 20 to 30 seconds per effort. Rest for about 20 seconds between sets and take one to two minutes between exercises. After the first week, add one or two new exercises to your routine each week.

Beginning Lower Back Exercises

Lower back exercises focus on the muscles around your spine, the *spinae erector* muscles. Just as with abs, it is important that all lower back work is done in a controlled manner. The goal is not how high you lift or raise, but how well you engage your muscles.

Supermans Lying prone on the floor (facing the floor) and keeping your chin down, raise a right arm and left leg by squeezing the muscles of your back and then alternate (left arm, right leg). Do ten reps on each side.

Seal (Trunk) Raises Lying prone on the floor and keeping your arms at your sides, squeeze your lower back muscles to raise your torso 1 to 2 inches off the floor. Hold for a count of 2 to 5 seconds and lower slowly.

PLYOMETRICS

Many athletes, especially younger ones, find plyometrics an enjoyable way to do resistance, endurance, and power-based training. Plyometrics, or "plyo work," involves jumping and body-weight exercises that emphasize safe movements and controlled activities designed to improve speed, explosiveness, and power. Plyo training can involve stairs, wooden boxes, medicine balls, cones, and other simple tools. Efforts are often counted by the number of foot strikes the athlete makes during a session. The surface for plyos is very important because of the jumping involved, and beginners should be limited to 80 to 100 foot strikes per session and two to three sessions per week. It is very important to work with a trained individual when starting out with plyometrics, because while this form of exercise can be very effective, the moves also need to be done properly to keep the athlete safe and healthy. Plyos can be an excellent activity for the off-season, but they can be too much during the season, when the emphasis needs to be on cycling itself.

RECOMMENDED READING AND RESOURCES

The Athlete's Guide to Yoga: An Integrated Approach to Strength, Flexibility, and Focus, by Sage Rountree (VeloPress, 2007). This guide to yoga is written especially for athletes and carefully addresses their needs. It gives clear, easy-to-follow instructions. Includes a 15-minute instructional DVD.

Massage for Cyclists, by Roger Pozeznik (Vitesse Press, 2005). A good massage therapist can help athletes maintain health and reach peak performance. In between trips to the massage therapist's table, self-massage can help an athlete address trouble spots and stay fresh. This book provides great pictures and instruction for effective self-massage.

The Next Level: Strength Training for Endurance Athletes, Endurofit DVD, www.endurofit. com (2005). See www.startingstrength.com.

Stretching, 20th anniversary ed., by Bob Anderson (Shelter Publications, 2000). This is the classic book on stretching, first published in 1980.

Weight Training for Cyclists, by Eric Schmitz and Ken Doyle (VeloPress, 1998).

Yoga for Athletes, a DVD by Bodywisdom Media, 2002. See Bodywisdommedia.com.

10 TRAINING Your BRAIN:
Mental Skills in Cycling

The brute physical and mental demands of cycling create an environment in which the fittest, smartest, and most tactically astute survive to win.

—May Britt Hartwell, USAC Level 3 coach

Being a cyclist is hard work. Legs burn, lungs strain, you sweat a lot. When we train, we tend to focus on all the things we can do to make ourselves stronger and faster. It's easy to forget in the midst of all that effort that your brain is always along for the ride. Even when you aren't consciously thinking, your brain is at work. If your thoughts are negative or pessimistic, they can put a damper on your feelings and your fun, and can even get in the way of riding well. When they are positive and focused right, your thoughts can influence your feelings and your attitude and help you make the most of your training and skills. So how do you get your thoughts and emotions to help you out instead of causing trouble? In this chapter we will look at how athletes can benefit from training their brain and how you can begin to train smarter while you are training your body.

As we noted in the chapter on training, cycling is unique among sports because it involves so many hours of training alone. There are teams in cycling, but the bulk of training is still an individual endeavor. Maintaining the motivation and dedication to hit the road day after day, no matter what the weather, through an entire season can be tough. The hours in the saddle can be long, and it is crucial that your focus and concentration remain sharp, both in training and during races. You need to be alert for road or trail hazards. You need to know what the other riders in the pack are up to and who is getting ready to jump. Unlike with soccer, field hockey, or even track, fans are often few and far between as racecourses wind through country roads or go deep into the woods. You need to know how to cheer yourself on and how to keep your cool when things go wrong. Elite athletes develop key mental skills and learn how to use them to the best effect. Successful athletes tend to be:

- Confident but not cocky
- Focused on the task at hand
- Calm in stressful situations
- Competitive in a healthy way
- Goal oriented
- Optimistic
- Able to stay relaxed and focused at the same time
- High in positive energy
- Students of their sport, always learning
- Able to practice the way they want to compete
- Able to maintain good control over their emotions
- Able to handle and recover from distractions

Studies of elite athletes have shown that no one is born with a perfect set of skills, physical or mental. Everyone has some skills that come naturally to them and some that they need to work on. And everyone can benefit from training in their different skills, no matter what level they start at. Training your body makes you physically stronger. Training your mind can lead to improvements in many other areas:

- Your tactical awareness (race smarts)
- Your training efforts
- Your level of anxiety (learning to set it at the right level)
- Your self-confidence
- Your motivation and dedication
- Your ability to get through the tough times
- Your ability to learn new skills
- Your level of enjoyment of your sport

The best thing about training your mind as well as your body is that these skills will help you both on and off the bike. The same mental skills that help successful athletes achieve their dreams can also be used to your advantage in other areas of your life. This means that once you learn how to set useful goals or handle distractions, you will have great skills that you can use in any situation—your classes, your job, or whatever you set your mind to.

It is not uncommon for young riders to overemphasize the physical side of training. They figure that they can worry about the other stuff later. However, even beginning riders can benefit from mental skills training, and the sooner you start working, the stronger your skills will be by the time you have reached the highest levels. In fact, it's a good idea to start now, before bad mental habits become more ingrained. And at the top levels, having a strong mind can make all the difference. Many elite athletes and Olympians readily admit that they didn't win their gold medals or set records because they were physically the strongest. Instead, they say that at the top, the physical difference between themselves and their competitors is very small. What made all the difference was their own mental strengths and mental preparation. I have found this to be true in my own athletic past and in my coaching as well. This mental component of athletics seemed so significant to me that I spent almost eight more years in college after earning my undergraduate degree just so I could learn more about how our thoughts can be the key to elite success.

ARE MENTAL SKILLS A MYTH?

Maybe someone has told you that great athletes are just born that way or that "you either have it or you don't." Although we've heard that saying so often that we sometimes believe it, experience does not back it up. Mental skills training, or MST, has been shown to be helpful for athletes of all levels and to improve performance in all sorts of activities where people seek to perform at their best, including school, business, music, performing arts, law enforcement, and surgery—you name it, and there's a good chance that positive mental skills can make a difference.

Some people may not take MST seriously because it entails a new way of doing things that is different from the way they were done in the past. That's their loss. You have an opportunity to take advantage of cutting-edge training methods. Over the past thirty years (making it a relatively recent phenomenon in the world of science), more and more colleges and university professors have been studying MST. Their findings have been significant. In fact, the U.S. Olympic Committee is so convinced that mental skills training is important that it has established an entire division of sport psychology consultants to help Olympic athletes sharpen their mental skills, and in 1983 a national registry of people who are certified to teach athletes MST was developed.

Learning how to focus your thoughts and change the way you think in order to attain your peak performance is just like learning how to use your brain to do math problems or learn a foreign language. Almost everything that goes on in our bodies is due to conscious or unconscious signals from our brain. It keeps us breathing and sends signals to help us regulate temperature. It reminds us to move away from hot things that might burn us and helps us cope with stress. If your brain is like a computer program, then MST is like the help menu or the owner's manual. You can just use it straight out of the box, but if you learn a little about how it works first, you can do much more with it.

This doesn't mean that athletes never have problems that might require extra help or support from a counselor or psychologist. Of course, if something is hurting your health, well-being, or quality of life, consulting with a properly trained person can be very helpful. But MST is all about improving skills and building strengths, and all athletes can benefit from this.

The best time to practice and improve your mental skills is before you ever need them. If you make MST a regular part of your training routine, you may find yourself less susceptible to pre-competition jitters or other forms of self-doubt that can hurt your training. This doesn't mean you won't ever get nervous or face challenges, but it will make you better equipped to handle the challenges and less likely to have trouble when they arise.

Learning how to use your mental skills will help you train smarter and train more efficiently, but it can't replace training. Saddle time is very important; MST isn't some magic pill to improve performance. The one time that MST can be helpful in the absence of training is when an athlete is sick or injured. We'll talk about that a little more in Chapter 11.

SUCCESS AND MOTIVATION

What do we mean when we talk about performance, success, and achievement? Take a minute and think about it. Is success only winning a race? Or is success about making the most of the opportunities that you are presented with and the talents you have? Across all sorts of areas—art, science, business, and sports—people who do well tell us that they put a major emphasis on being the best they can be, and that this has been the key to their success. So let's start off by talking about goal setting and sources of motivation. These are two key elements to having a healthy and productive view of success. Then we will look at some of the mental skills that you can begin to work on in training.

Me and My Motivation

What exactly is motivation, and where does it come from? Motivation is why we choose to do things—or not to do things. We can be motivated by things inside of ourselves and by things outside of ourselves. The intrinsic, or internal, motivators are a sense of personal pride, satisfaction, accomplishment, and enjoyment. The extrinsic, or external, motivators are things like rewards (trophies or, better yet, cash!), living up to expectations, and status. Everyone is motivated by a unique combination of factors. Understanding your own motivation and striking a balance between intrinsic and extrinsic sources of motivation will help you keep your motivation going.

Being motivated by only external (extrinsic) sources can lead to all sorts of trouble. If you ride only to get the rewards, to please other people, or to feel successful, it can work great for a while, when you are doing well. But if you hit a rough spot or a slump (and all riders do), your extrinsic motivation needs will not be satisfied, and over time your confidence and drive to ride will suffer.

I don't mean to say that extrinsic motivation is a bad thing. It isn't. Getting up on the podium, wearing the yellow jersey, making your parents proud—these are all great things. They can give you the boost you need to train hard and make training fun. It is easy to find extrinsic sources of motivation, and when we talk about goals, these motivators can provide great outcome-focused goals. However, it is really important that you also develop intrinsic motivation. This is the motivation that will keep you going when the going gets tough; it will make the sport even more satisfying and provide you with a lifelong love of cycling.

Note to Parents and Coaches

You play a crucial role in the type of motivation that your young cyclist develops. Your words, your actions, and the things you emphasize will create an environment that will shape this process. Chapters 13 and 14 will provide ideas on how you can create a supportive, positive environment.

Unfortunately, our culture tends to place a huge emphasis on extrinsic rewards. After a competition, people ask only if you won. We don't always place a lot of value on the hard work that it takes to get there. Intrinsic motivation is all about valuing the process and taking pride in what you do. Setting effective goals will help you build up your intrinsic motivation.

SETTING GOALS FOR SUCCESS

Every New Year's Day, people set goals about things they want to improve in their lives. You have probably set a lot of goals in your life. Goals help people focus on the things they want to do. If they are done right (and yes, there is a right way and a wrong way to set goals), goals will fuel your intrinsic motivation, help you prepare properly, improve your confidence, and make riding more fun. If they aren't, they can leave you feeling that what you want to achieve is too big for you to handle or can undermine your confidence.

Goals can be divided into three categories:

1. *Outcome goals:* Goals that focus on gaining rewards or on achieving a title, with an emphasis on competition with other people. These

are a useful motivating factor but usually are long-term goals that will take a while to achieve. Examples of outcome goals include winning a particular race or upgrading to the next category.

2. *Performance goals:* Goals that stress your performance changes over time, with an emphasis on striving for incremental improvements. These can help you make progress toward your outcome goals. Performance goals might be improving your 5k time trial time or improving your watt output.

3. *Training goals:* Goals that break down all the little things you need to do in order to make improvements (also called "process" or "stepping-stone goals"). These outline the specific workouts and activities you will do that enable you to reach your performance goals and outcome goals. You might plan to do a two-hour ride in a heart-rate range of 140 to 150 bpm, or you might set a training goal to do four to six 8-minute efforts.

When you dream about the things you would like to achieve, you are actually beginning to create goals. And when you decide to go after your dreams, it is important to consciously set outcome goals. Outcome goals are the big, end-of-season-type goals, like winning a key race, signing with a pro team, or earning enough points for your license upgrade. They can be very exciting and motivating. You may close your eyes and daydream about standing on the podium with your arms raised or signing that contract. Most people have no problem setting outcome goals. The problem is that these outcome goals usually take a while to achieve, and if that is the only goal an athlete has, it can be very hard to stay focused on it over the long haul. Because they are far off, they leave you without a clear idea of how you are going to get there and no way to figure out if you are making progress.

Another potential problem with outcome goals is that you don't have any control over the people you are competing against. If your goal is to win a particular race, this might be easy, or it might be really difficult, depending on who shows up. If your outcome goal is to get signed by a team, you may find that in one year it is easy to get signed, because lots of team spots have opened up, while in another season there are no spots. In either case, you may have worked very hard and had an excellent season but still feel terrible because you did not reach your goal. In reality, the goal was unattainable only because there were factors beyond your control. This can really hurt your self-confidence and motivation. For all these reasons it is important to support your outcome goals with performance and process goals.

Once you have set an outcome goal, you must therefore set a few performance and process goals to help support your plan. Performance goals give you a way to evaluate your progress over the course of a season. These goals might be power- or time-based improvements at certain points in the season. Typically they are things you can count, and they have to do with your own improvement over time, rather than your performance compared with someone else's. Performance goals can help you decide if you are on target to reach your outcome goals and can help you adjust your training and your expectations accordingly.

Process or training goals are perhaps the most important type of goal. They are the short-term stepping-stones that you will use to improve. If you set a performance goal to improve your 5k time trial time over a four-week period, for example, you will want to set training goals that give you specific activities that help you. You might do a workout with the training goal of doing a set number of hard intervals, or do hill repeats at a set cadence. These small stepping-stones will help you focus on the daily process of improving.

Your training goals should help you achieve your performance goals, and your performance goals should help you achieve your outcome goals. Obviously, just setting these goals won't guarantee that everything happens: You still have to get out there and do the work. But proper goal

SMART Goals

S: Specific
M: Measurable
A: Action oriented
R: Realistic
T: Timely

setting is the most effective tool that people can use when setting out to achieve something.

Now that you know the three types of goals you need to set, there are, of course, some principles to help you set effective ones. Remember always to set SMART goals. The "S" stands for "specific." Make sure all goals, from process to outcome, are clear. Avoid setting vague goals such as "have fun" or "do well." It is very difficult to work toward vague goals because they do not specify what you need to do or provide a way of determining whether you have done it well. Try to set specific goals like "hold a cadence of 95 rpm for 5 minutes," or "keep my arms and shoulders relaxed."

"M" is for "measurable." The more specific your goals are, the easier it will be to measure them. If you can't keep track of what you are working on, you won't be able to evaluate whether you have achieved it. Not all goals are equally measurable. Some can be measured with a power meter, bike computer, or heart rate monitor. Other goals will require you, your coach, or your parents to pay attention (for example, do you look relaxed on the bike every time you come around in a criterium?). You may need to be a bit creative in how you measure something.

Since you are measuring your goal progress, be sure to actually pay attention to the progress you make. Evaluating how well you are doing at achieving your goals will help you make adjustments. Sometimes you may need to make adjustments to your training goals. Maybe you need to do more, or maybe you are attempting to do too much and need to do less, setting goals that specify small, incremental changes. Sometimes you may need to adjust your training environment so you have better opportunities to achieve your goals (for example, quieter roads to train on, more sleep so you are fresh enough to train). And sometimes you may need to adjust your expectations or timeline (see "T" below) based on your measurement and evaluation of your progress.

"A" means goals should be "action oriented." You want all your goals to be based on things you can do. If your goals focus on things that are out of your control, you will create a situation that does not help you improve and that will hurt your confidence in the long run.

"R" stands for "realistic." It's okay if your outcome goal is lofty. But make sure the performance and process goals you set for your training are realistic. This means they should be in line with where you are in your training now, your level of fitness, and the timeline you have for accomplishing them. If your performance and process goals are too challenging, they will feel like too much to handle, and this will hurt your motivation and your confidence as you struggle to reach them. If they are too easy, they will not be very motivating because they are boring. Your parents, your coach, and more experienced athletes can help you set realistic goals that will be achievable yet challenging. Don't worry if it takes a little trial and error to set goals that are realistic: That is just part of the process of learning how to train properly.

The last letter in SMART is "T," meaning that your goals should be "timely." If your goals are set for things that are years or even months off, it can be hard to maintain your momentum. You want your goals to help you move forward, so it is best to set them in segments. You might start by deciding what you want to achieve in a season of training. Then you can set monthly performance goals and weekly training goals. By keeping your timeline timely, you will be able to adjust your training as you go along, rather than waiting until the end of the season to realize you are off-track.

Here are some more tips for successful goal setting. Start slowly with just a few goals and goal setting will enhance your training and racing:

- Don't try to set a lot of goals all at once. Choose one key area to focus on at a time. With practice, and as you get better at goal setting, you can set more.
- Keep a training log and write your goals in it. It can be easy to forget your goals if you don't write them down. Having them in your training log will help you use them to improve and remind you to evaluate them.
- Make sure your training goals lead you to your performance goals and that your performance goals lead you to your outcome goals. You may do a few cycles of training and performance goals in your buildup to your bigger outcome goal.
- Make sure your goals are challenging but realistic. Don't put too much pressure on yourself, but don't sell your abilities short, either.

- Your goals should be your own. It's okay if a coach or a parent or someone else helps you write your goals. But you need to really want to achieve these things yourself and believe that you can. It is difficult to stay properly motivated if you are following someone else's goals for you. And it is very important for your intrinsic motivation to achieve the things you set out to achieve. Think about it this way: If you pick up a book on a topic that interests you, you read it without a problem. If a teacher assigns a book to read, you aren't as motivated to read it and often wait until the last minute before you even find out what happened in chapter 1!
- Stay flexible. It's normal and expected that goals will change across the season. Sometimes you might achieve things faster, and sometimes slower. Not reaching a goal is not failure; it just means you need to design a new plan. Training is a process that you will refine many times, and that's okay.
- Ask people to help you. Read training books and websites, talk to a coach, and talk to experienced riders and your parents. All these resources can help you in different ways.

Goal setting is really pretty simple, once you've got the hang of it. It does require you to be organized about your training and to think about how you do what you do. And it will take time and patience to learn how to set effective goals. Table 10.1 provides a few of the common problems that beginning goal setters sometimes confront and the things you can do to avoid them. Figure 10.1 is a sample SMART Stepping-Stone Goal-Setting form. A blank version of this form is supplied in Appendix F.

TABLE 10.1 **Common Goal-Setting Problems and Solutions**	
Problem	**What to Do**
Overwhelmed by too many goals	Set your outcome goal and then set just one performance goal; pick just one training element to work on at a time.
Forgetting to support your goals	Remember, you need the stepping-stones. What you do each day builds up; just as multiple stepping-stones create a path that takes you somewhere, your training goals will eventually lead you to your performance and outcome goals.

(continues)

TABLE 10.1 (continued)

Problem	What to Do
Vague goals	Sometimes it can be hard to be specific. After you set your goals, ask yourself, "How will I know if this has occurred?" and "How can I measure this?" If you cannot answer these questions, your goal is probably too vague.
Goals that are too easy	Athletes sometimes set easy goals because they doubt their abilities or they worry about not achieving them. Remember, goals are just there to help you improve. Ask someone else to help you set realistic goals if you are being too easy on yourself.
Goals that are too hard	Maybe you are being too hard on yourself, or you don't have a good sense of what you can do. If you set goals that are too hard, it will undermine your confidence. Ask someone else to help you set realistic goals that are suited to your ability level.
Not setting any goals	No goals means no plan. This is fine if you don't care where you end up. But if you want to improve, a goal plan really is the way to go.
No evaluation	If you go to all the trouble of setting goals, but then you don't evaluate them, you have only done half the job and will only get limited benefits. If you want the full power of goal setting to be realized in your achievements, make sure you evaluate your progress regularly. Many athletes find it easiest to evaluate training goals once a week (for example, Sunday night), performance goals every couple of weeks, and progress toward the outcome goal every four to six weeks.

THE POWER OF WORDS: STICKS AND STONES— AND WORDS—CAN REALLY HURT

We all have an internal dialogue. It is sort of our own running commentary on what we do, how we do it, and how we feel about it. Sometimes it is very quiet, just background rumblings. Our talk can be positive ("nice job," "way to go") or negative ("you suck," "you'll never make it"). Unfortunately, many of us don't listen to the positive comments, but when the negative voice speaks up, we not only listen, we turn up the volume. This negative self-talk, or "stinkin' thinkin'," can do a lot of damage to our confidence and performance. Fortunately we can do something about this, and we can even turn it around to our advantage.

My outcome goal for this season:

Win the 17-year-old national time trial

Goal Evaluation Date: _August_

Performance goals:

♦ _30 km in sub 42 minutes_   End of July

♦ _30 km in sub 43 minutes_   end of June

♦ _30 km in sub 44 minutes_   end of May

Training Goals for _May_

♦ Week 1 – Test to determine self-selected cadence

♦ Week 2 – Focus on cadence drill workouts

♦ Week 3 – Focus on force-building workouts

♦

NOTE: You may do other workouts each week as well, but you will focus on reaching these specific training goals and evaluating your progress. Each month, you will set new training goals depending on your performance goal progress.

Is my outcome goal . . .   **Are my performance goals . . .**   **Are my training goals . . .**

  X _Specific?_   X _Specific?_   X _Specific?_

  X _Measurable?_   X _Measurable?_   X _Measurable?_

  X _Action oriented?_   X _Action oriented?_   X _Action oriented?_

  X _Realistic?_   X _Realistic?_   X _Realistic?_

  X _Timely?_   X _Timely?_   X _Timely?_

FIGURE 10.1 SMART Stepping-Stone Goal-Setting Example

Think about a time on the bike when you have struggled. It may have been when you were going up a hard hill or lagging behind in a pack or paceline, or maybe it was when you just felt yourself getting tired. If you are new to cycling, think about a time off the bike when you got frustrated with yourself. What types of things did you say to yourself? Did you swear at yourself? Did you call yourself names? Did you say you just weren't cut out for this kind of thing? Ask yourself two key questions:

Would I say this to myself out loud around my mom or best friend? Would I say this to my teammate or my best friend?

If you response is "Of course not, my mom or best friend would tell me I was wrong," or "I wouldn't say something so negative to someone else," that's a pretty good indication that you were using stinkin' thinkin'. This negative self-talk is not helpful at all.

Another type of unproductive self-talk focuses on things that are beyond your control, like the weather or competitors' actions. "Crap, it's raining today," and "Oh, no, she's here, now I don't have a chance," are examples of this kind of negativity. By emphasizing things that you have no control over, you hurt your confidence and reduce your chances of putting out your best performance. You have no say over the weather, and unless you somehow can put up a detour sign to misdirect all the competition, like the villains in cartoons, you have no say over who shows up for a race. Why waste your time and energy on these things? You want to focus the power of your mind on more useful things.

Another common self-talk problem for athletes is forgetting to stay in the moment. Dwelling on things like "I really blew it on the last prime," or focusing on the finish possibilities of a 60-mile road race when you are only on mile 20 ("I'll never make the top ten now"), is negative and keeps you from focusing on what needs to be done right now.

When positive thinking is new to you, it's not easy to do all the time, especially if you are fatigued, frustrated, or discouraged. It's important to begin practicing positive self-talk on days when you are training and when you feel fresh. That way, you'll have good habits to build on when you are not feeling fresh and when circumstances are challenging.

Replacing Stinkin' Thinkin'

So we are agreed that stinkin' thinkin', focusing on unproductive things, and letting the past or far-off future get in the way aren't helpful. What next? With practice, you can learn to focus on positive and productive thoughts that can help you perform well.

Step 1 Pay attention to the negative, unhelpful things you say to yourself. In this step, just become aware of the kinds of self-talk that you engage in. You can't change something if you don't know it is happening.

Step 2 Practice some "thought-stopping." Pick a word or visual reminder, such as "Halt," or thinking of a red traffic light or stop sign, and use it whenever a stinkin' thought pops into your head.

Step 3 If you don't replace the stinkin' thinkin', your brain will just make up more to fill the space. Practice following up your thought-stopping effort with a positive and more productive statement. For example, you might hear yourself saying, "I'll never make it" as you climb a steep hill. Immediately say "Stop" (or whatever your cue is) and replace that bit of stinkin' thinkin' with "steady and smooth" "relaxed and strong," or some other phrase that will help you focus on the things you need to do to ride the hill, even if it is a tough one. Your replacement phrase should be positive, constructive, and specific. It should be the kind of supportive statement you might make to encourage a teammate.

FOCUS MATTERS

Every day, we need to pay attention to lots of different things. You listen to your teachers giving you assignments, you pay attention to friends, you pretend to hear what your parents say. If you have your learner's permit or your driver's license, you know that to drive safely you have to attend to many things at once. How fast are you going? Are you staying on the road? What are other drivers doing? And perhaps, most importantly, what's on the radio? Okay, I'm kidding—the radio is not the most important thing. But being able to pay attention to multiple things at the same time is a very useful skill. So is being able to stay focused for a long time. You can't (well, shouldn't) drift off in class, and you definitely shouldn't while you are driving.

The ability to keep track of several things at once and to stay focused over time also matters in sports. You must stay focused to maintain the pace you need over the course of a ride or an interval. You need to attend to important cues to notice when you have a chance to make a key break or recognize that a key turnoff is coming up on a trail (I know because I've missed both when I wasn't paying attention!) You also need to keep track of how your body is feeling so you can pace yourself well.

The first step to good focus and concentration is to understand the many things you need to pay attention to. Once you've figured out what is important, you can begin to look for ways to practice good focus in training. Practicing your focus skills on routine rides is the only way to build up this skill and ensure that you have strong skills for competition.

What to Focus On

Some of the things you must focus on as you train or race have to do with how your body is feeling. Examples of internal focal points are:

- Heart rate
- How your legs feel
- Hydration level
- Hunger level

Other focal points are external. These include:

- Gearing
- Power, speed, cadence, and distance traveled
- Your position in the pack
- Where other riders are

When you practice focus skills, start small. Take a short period of time, such as a five-minute effort, to practice shifting your focus between different internal and external cues. Can you keep on top of your effort? Can you stay focused for the whole effort? As your skills improve, gradually increase the length of time you try to stay focused. Remember, the goal is to learn how to stay alert and aware of all the important cues throughout a ride or a race. This will make your ride safer and help you ride or race at the appropriate effort level.

Overcoming Distractions

As you learn how to focus on the many cues inside and around you, you may begin to notice that a variety of things occur to disrupt your concentration. It is important to be able to refocus after distractions. Common distractions that athletes experience include:

- Stinkin' thinkin'
- Nervousness
- Worries
- Things in the environment (dogs, car horns, cars)
- Other racers
- Dehydration and/or bonking (too little water and/or food)
- Overanalyzing the race
- Focusing on the wrong things (past, future, wrong thing at the wrong time)
- Bike problems
- Boredom

What can you do about all these distractions? Well, you can ride on an indoor trainer in a closed room! But a better way is to prepare yourself to handle the distractions you might be able to predict. You can't possibly be prepared to handle all distractions, but some distractions are common, and the better you become at not letting them ruffle you, the better you will be able to handle the less predictable distractions.

If you plan how you will cope with common distractions and interruptions, you will be less frazzled when they inevitably occur. Put some thought into what you would do in various situations, and prepare for them appropriately. It's a good exercise to list the steps you will take in each situation. For example, if you were planning what to do in the case of a flat tire in a race, you might write the following:

GETTING A FLAT IN A RACE

Plan: Put a spare tire in the wheel van and carry a tube and CO_2 cartridge if it is a rough course. Say to myself, "Relax and fix it—this is just a challenge, not the end of the race."

Practice: Practice changing tubes and taking the wheel in and out of the frame quickly.

Think about the following situations and plan how you might handle each. Brainstorm ways you can practice your plan:*

- Discovering the race is on a poor course or includes less-than-ideal road conditions
- Arriving late to a race
- Finding out the race promoters have delayed the race start
- Getting off to a poor start (for example, not clipping in right away)
- Encountering bad weather
- Missing a break in the race
- Bonking
- Experiencing mechanical trouble

Visualization: Seeing with the Mind's Eye

Close your eyes for a second (after you read this paragraph) and see if you can visualize your bike. What color is it? What stickers are on it? Is it dirty or clean? Now reach out and touch it. What does the bar tape feel like? Lift it. Can you feel the weight in your hand? Being able to see and feel these things is the basis of good visualization skills.

Using visualization techniques, you can supplement your actual training by practicing physical skills mentally. Visualization does not replace training, but it gives you a chance to review physical skills in your mind until they become second nature, all without increasing the actual physical load that your body experiences. When you visualize something, your muscles actually fire on a microscopic level even though you are not actually moving your muscles. This means that when you pedal in your mind's eye, using correct visualization technique, the muscles you use when you are really pedaling fire on a microscopic level. These skills can help you become more comfortable with new skills and handling

*Adapted from T. Orlick, *Psyching for Sport* (Champaign, IL: Human Kinetics, 1986).

techniques and boost your confidence on a trail or in a pack-riding situation that makes you nervous.

Good visualization skills begin with using all five senses. You want to be able to feel, see, smell, taste, and hear the environment you are visualizing. The more realistic the situation, the better. You also want to make sure you are visualizing in real time. Don't go faster or slower than you would in real life. You can use different points of view when visualizing: You can watch yourself performing a skill the way you would watch a video, or you can shift the point of view so that it is as if you were actually doing the activity in your imagination. Both ways can be helpful. Watching an internal video lets you consider what you need to look like on the bike. When you ride in your mind's eye, you actively engage all the key muscles as you ride. Practice doing it both ways.

HOW NERVOUS IS TOO NERVOUS?

Athletes often tell me they get nervous before they race and are worried about being nervous. When I ask them how they know they are nervous, they describe physical symptoms like shaky knees, butterflies in the stomach, sweaty palms, frequent pre-race trips to the port-o-potty or bushes, and other similar symptoms. Then we talk about how they physically feel when they are really excited about something. The athletes are always surprised when they realize that their physical feelings of nervousness look a lot like their physical symptoms of being excited about something. So what is the difference? The big difference is how we assess the situation. If we think our symptoms are negative, then they will make us worry and we may become overanxious, which will hurt our performance. If we interpret these things as signs of excitement, then these same feelings tell us that we are ready to get started.

Sometimes we may feel these physical symptoms too strongly, which causes anxiety, and sometimes they may not be strong enough, which means we may not really be ready to compete. Everyone is different when it comes to how psyched up or how relaxed they like to be before a race.

Basic Relaxation Techniques

It can be difficult to regulate your energy level before a race, or even to fall asleep the night before a race. Learning a basic relaxation technique can help in both of these situations. You can also use relaxation techniques before doing visualization to help clear your mind and allow you to focus better. You want to practice relaxation *off* the bike in a quiet place with few distractions. Here's how:

- Start off in a seated, upright position (you don't ride lying down). Close your eyes and uncross your legs and arms. Initially you want to be in a quiet, calm setting free from distractions. As your skills improve, vary this practice, trying out more distracting locations, keeping your eyes open, and so on. When your skills are very good, you can even practice while actually riding (with eyes open!). This skill can enable you to see yourself handling a difficult maneuver or breakaway just before you carry it out.
- Begin by concentrating on your breathing. Focus on inhaling slowly and deeply, and then, on a slow count to three, exhale slowly. Continue doing this until your breathing becomes smooth, comfortable, and natural. If any thoughts pop into your head, let them float right through as you continue to focus on your breathing and counting.
- Once you feel that your breathing is smooth and regular, start at the top of your head and work your way to your toes. Concentrate on breathing slowly and smoothly as you find tension and stress in different areas of your body. Breathe slowly and say "relax" as you concentrate on the tension melting away or flowing out of the different areas of your body.
- Once your body is in a relaxed state, return your full attention to your breathing. Concentrate on inhaling slowly and deeply and then count to three while exhaling slowly and completely. Keep your mind free from distracting thoughts by failing to acknowledge them, letting them pass through, or mentally "putting them into a box."
- When you feel completely relaxed, slowly open your eyes.

Determining Your Optimal Race Readiness

Knowing how you perform best—calm, all jazzed up, or somewhere in between—can help you prepare yourself for races. How do you like to feel before a competition? Take the time to figure out what pre-race mental and emotional state works best for you, and plan how you can reach this state every time you compete. Try this exercise:

1. Think about your best competition. How did you feel before it began?
2. Think about a not-so-good competition. How did you feel before it began?
3. Compare the two. How are they different and how are they the same?
4. What can you learn from these similarities and differences?

If you feel that you are often too nervous or that you tend to experience too many physical symptoms, then practice relaxed breathing to help you calm down. Consider creating a pre-race routine that will allow you to stay calm. Plan carefully so that, whenever possible, you arrive at the race early enough that you are not rushed during the check-in or warm-up period. Use music to help you focus, and avoid people who may cause your feelings of anxiety to increase. Additionally, practice reframing how you think about those feelings of anxiety. Remind yourself that these feelings are normal and that all athletes have them. Also remind yourself that they are signs that your body is getting ready to perform. Embracing these signals of readiness can help decrease the worry over the fact that you feel them.

If your level of anxiety tends to be low, you may find that it is difficult to get up to the energy level necessary to do well. Perhaps you are not getting that race adrenaline rush. Normally, I feel that training with music presents more potential problems than benefits. (Riding with music on open roads is very dangerous.) However, good, energetic music with a driving beat can really help you get into race mode. Make a race mix to listen to in the car or plan a playlist for your MP3 player. If you are going to listen to your race-prep music while warming up, try to limit it to your trainer warm-up. Riding with headphones or earbuds, particularly in an area where you don't know the roads or traffic patterns, creates a very dangerous situation. You may also want to consider doing a solid warm-up to get your heart rate up. Whether you need to relax to calm yourself down or you need to jump-start your system to psych yourself up, practice the techniques you will be using until you feel confident that you can carry them out on race day.

WHEN YOU WORRY

Young athletes have a lot to think about—school, friends, training, maybe an after-school job. And the number of things to worry about seems to increase as you get older. As we saw in the training chapter, when the body experiences stress, it can take a toll on the body over time, regardless of whether the stress comes from training, problems with friends, family difficulties, or some other source.

The better you can manage the sources of stress in your life, the less likely it is that the cumulative stress will have a negative impact on you. Over time, stress can lead to all sorts of problems, both physical (colds and injuries) and mental (staleness, burnout). It can also damage your enjoyment of your sport and your ability to concentrate or perform well.

Handling Stress Effectively

Instead of being a victim of your stress, take charge of it. Here are some techniques for doing that:

- *Plan:* Use your goal-setting abilities to create a clear plan. Knowing what you are going to do when certain challenges arise, and why you are going to do it, can help reduce feelings of uncertainty.
- *Practice:* In each stressful situation that arises, focus on the things you can control and let go of the things you can't control. This will get easier with practice; don't worry if it doesn't always work just right at first.
- *Prioritize:* When you know that something important isn't getting done when it needs to get done, your anxiety level can really in-

crease. Make it a practice to prioritize your responsibilities so you can keep on top of things.

- *Share your goals:* Tell people who are close to you what you are trying to accomplish, so they will be better equipped to support your efforts.
- *Ask for help:* No one can assist you if no one knows you need assistance. If you can think of ways that your parents or your coach can help, ask if you can discuss this with them and let them know. Chances are, they will appreciate the opportunity to support you in this effort.

PUTTING ALL THE PIECES TOGETHER

Learning how to train both your mind and your body at the same time is very important for long-term success. You don't have to jump in and master every skill right away. Choose just a few new things to try, and as you feel your skills improving, move on to other new skills.

RECOMMENDED READING

Embracing Your Potential, by T. Orlick (Human Kinetics, 1998).
In Pursuit of Excellence, 3rd ed., by T. Orlick (Human Kinetics, 2007).
The Mental Athlete, by K. Porter (Human Kinetics, 2003).
Mental Skills for Competitive Swimmers: A Workbook to Improve Mental Performance, by J. Hogg (Sport Excel Publishing, 2000).
The Sport Psych Handbook, by S. Murphy (Human Kinetics, 2004).

11 ATHLETIC INJURIES
and Health Concerns

Remember that cycling can be a lifelong sport. Keeping this in mind can change what the sport means to you and how you experience wins, losses, and injuries.

—Meghan Milliron, Top 5 overall at 2002 Collegiate Nationals

Cyclists get injured sometimes. Actually, athletes in all sports get injured sometimes. When you play with gravity, go fast, or push yourself hard, sometimes you get hurt. But that isn't any reason not to train, and you shouldn't let fear of injury keep you off the track or trail. By training smart and riding safe, you can minimize your risk of getting injured. And by learning about common injuries and proper injury care, you can minimize the impact that injuries have on you. This chapter is designed to provide you with some of the most essential basic information about being a safe, healthy, smart rider.

COMMON INJURIES

Every athlete and every medical concern is unique. It is important to consult a physician or physical therapist whenever you are injured or feel concerned about a potential health problem. Some injuries are avoidable—for example, if you practice principles of safe riding, you will be less likely to be in an accident, and if you always take care to begin a workout with a warm-up and then stretch out as part of your cool-down, you are less likely to experience pulled muscles and overuse injuries. But even when you do everything you can to stay healthy, the unexpected can happen. Ideally, you will have a good relationship with someone in the medical profession before you need help. This can help ensure the care you receive is fine-tuned to your specific needs. Below we discuss just a few of the specific medical issues you may encounter as a cyclist, paying attention to both prevention and common treatments and methods of taking care of yourself.

Road Rash

When a cyclist falls off the bike, he or she typically carries some speed that may cause sliding. This sliding produces friction and can easily tear skin. Technically, road rash is classified as a burn. Mild road rash is only annoying, but more severe road rash can be very painful. In any case, it is important to clean road rash carefully. This can be difficult to do yourself. If it occurs at a race, go directly to the EMS or medical services station for assistance. If it occurs on a training ride, it may be worth it to see your doctor for assistance in cleaning out the wound. This will help healing and reduce the risk of infection.

Neosporin or a similar antibiotic ointment is essential for proper road rash care. Keeping these wounds moist and covered will help healing and keep scarring to a minimum. As your road rash begins to heal, avoid the temptation to let the scabs dry out or to pick at them, and keep the sensitive new skin out of the sun. This will minimize the scarring and changes in skin pigmentation that can occur.

Be prepared to change the dressing on your road rash every few hours and at least once a day, depending on how much the wounds are weeping. The weeping of these wounds is normal so long as the fluid is clear. It may be a little reddish the day of the crash, but after a day or two the drainage should be clear. Gauze bandages that are designed not to stick to wounds will be your best friend when you have road rash. Shaved legs will help the bandages stick better (and having shaved legs before you get road rash will help healing as well). Larger drugstores and medical supply stores also carry tube bandages, a stretch gauze that can be cut to length and used as a sleeve to hold bandages in awkward places like elbows and knees.

The first night or two, road rash may make sleeping difficult. Rolling over can cause a rude awakening as you bump the raw, inflamed areas. Often road rash is accompanied by bruising under the rash area, which makes them even more sore. This is especially true for hip and shoulder road rash because those areas tend to hit particularly hard. Road rash that is not properly covered also has a tendency to stick to the sheets due to the weeping of the wound. If your road rash gets hot or becomes red around the edges, if the color of the drainage changes, or if you develop fever or nausea, be sure to see your doctor as soon as possible. These can all be signs of an infection and should be treated immediately.

The very best way to handle road rash, of course, is not to get any. While a road-rash-free career is pretty much unheard of, getting lots of it isn't normal either. Work on your bike-handling skills, use common sense, and learn how to read the road. Try to anticipate what other riders are going to do, and pay attention to road hazards. These are all crucial elements of riding that will diminish your chances of getting road rash.

Unnecessary Injuries

Each year many unnecessary injuries occur as the result of fatigue or inattention on the bike. It is important to be alert, particularly at the end of a long, hard workout as you spin your way home. Don't check out until you are actually back in your driveway and off the bike. And avoid unnecessary distractions when still on the bike. Fumbling in your back pocket to pull out your phone, then checking the screen and answering it, is an accident waiting to happen. I know of at least three athletes who have crashed, broken bones, and ended their seasons in the effort to answer their cell phone. Text-messaging is out, too, as is talking on the phone, even with a headset or earbuds—anything that takes your focus off the road and reduces your ability to see, hear, or quickly react to hazards is a bad idea. You can take your cell phone with you—in case you need to use it in an emergency or if you're stranded with a flat on a remote country road—but leave the power off. The voice-mail messages will be there when you are ready to devote your undivided attention to listening.

Listening to music is another hazard while riding. Music is great when you are on a stationary bike, because it can eliminate the monotony and turn an otherwise boring routine into a fun workout. However, it is not a good idea when you are riding on a road or trail. Consider what happens when you have tunes blaring into your ears. Essentially, you lose one of your five senses, severely handicapping yourself. On the road, not being able to hear traffic can be a deadly proposition. On the trail, you might just be distracted enough to miss upcoming roots and rocks. So leave the music at home or confine it to the indoor trainer. On the bike it is crucial that you have all five senses helping you stay safe and well.

Concussion

In the old days, athletes used to talk about "getting their bell" rung or "taking a knock to the noggin." Whenever you receive a blow to the head or make a quick stop that causes your head to snap forward or back, your brain moves around inside your skull. This movement causes the brain to bump up against the inside of the skull in the same way an egg yolk would bang into the eggshell if you shook it. When the brain bangs against the skull, damage or bruising will occur. At the site of the bruise, there may be swelling and/or bleeding. When your elbow swells, it is uncomfortable, but when your brain swells, the swelling cannot go anywhere because of the skull. As you can imagine, a bruise on the brain isn't such a good thing. All that pressure gets placed on the rest of the brain and can have a serious impact on the vital functions the brain performs, depending on what part of your head you hit. And keep in mind that a concussion can occur even if you don't actually hit your head.

Signs of Concussion

- Nausea (actually getting sick or just feeling like you need to vomit)
- Balance problems or dizziness
- Double or fuzzy vision
- Sensitivity to light or noise
- Headache
- Sluggishness
- A feeling of fogginess or grogginess
- Concentration or memory problems
- Confusion

Even if you just suspect you have a concussion, it is critical that you go to your doctor, or, if you are in a race, to the EMS or medical tent. Tell your coach and parents about your concerns so that they can help watch for problems. A concussion can have serious consequences if it is not monitored carefully, due to the swelling that might occur, and only a qualified medical professional can properly diagnose a concussion. If possible, take your helmet with you so that the doctor can inspect it.

In fact, whenever you crash, be sure to check your helmet for scrapes and scratches, even if you aren't sure that you hit your head. Inspect it carefully, and examine the inside for cracks in the foam or tearing where the straps attach. Never wear a helmet that you suspect has crash damage. It will not protect your head well a second time because the materials are compromised. Helmets are designed to crush in the event of a crash so your head doesn't. Once it's done, it's done. Recycle it and buy a new one.

If you have been diagnosed with a concussion, even a mild one, you must not return to riding—or to any other activity that may involve impacts to your head—until you have been cleared by a doctor. It is not good enough that you feel better or that a few days have passed. Get official medical clearance. One of the most dangerous situations with a concussion is the second-impact syndrome. This occurs when someone who already has a brain bruise experiences a second blow to the head, even if it is minor. A second blow can be life-threatening.

Concussion problems can be reduced through use of and proper fitting of a quality helmet. Learning how to fall (tuck and roll) can reduce the likelihood of a nasty crash. But the most effective way to reduce the chance of concussion is to learn how to ride and react to potential crash situations safely. Practice your bumping drills and stay alert when you ride.

Allergies and Asthma

It is not uncommon for adolescents and teenagers to grow into and out of allergies during the course of their cycling careers. Adults grow in and out of allergies as well, but we are concerned with young people here.

If you have been diagnosed with allergies, follow the advice of your allergist. Keeping your lungs free and open and your sinuses clear will reduce problems with sinus infections and colds and, more importantly, will keep your lungs clear and open for maximal breathing capacity. If you have severe allergies, make sure you carry a card or I.D. bracelet that states your allergy. You may also want to consider carrying an Epi-Pen™ if you are prone to severe allergic reactions. This is especially important on long road rides in the countryside and when mountain biking on trails. I have been stung by bees multiple times while riding, once by five lovely little buggers while going downhill at 45 mph—I didn't even see them coming! The exertion of exercise can move the bee venom through your system quickly, so be sure you are prepared.

Many people with allergies have trouble with asthma as well. Having asthma should not keep you from being physically active. Plenty of active people and even professional athletes have asthma and are able to train and compete. Work closely with your doctor to determine the best medicines for helping you remain active. Always keep your inhaler with you, and be sure that your training partners know how to help you if you experience an attack.

Elite Athletes with Asthma

Having asthma does not have to limit your athletic activities. The following elite athletes have all talked publicly about how they have learned to manage their asthma symptoms to achieve peak athletic performance:

- Amy Van Dyken (Olympic gold medalist in swimming)
- Jackie Joyner-Kersee (Olympic gold medalist in track and field)
- Nancy Hogshead (Olympic gold medalist in swimming)
- Greg Louganis (Olympic gold medalist in diving)
- Isaiah Thomas (former NBA basketball player)
- Dennis Rodman (former NBA basketball player)

In addition to regular asthma, athletes can be affected by exercise-induced asthma, or EIA. Athletes at any level can experience this. People who suffer from EIA may experience coughing, wheezing, chest tightness, or shortness of breath when they exercise, particularly as the intensity of the exercise increases. The symptoms may begin while you are exercising, but for most sufferers the symptoms increase 5 to 10 minutes after the exercise session has ended. Problems may last for 20 to 30 minutes and sometimes longer, depending upon the severity of the case. A post-training hack seems normal to many athletes because they are used to it; in fact, many endurance athletes experience some difficulty with EIA. Other athletes may be impacted for up to a day after really hard exercise.

Like traditional asthma, EIA does not have to prevent you from training or competing. Because symptoms show up with hard efforts, diagnosing EIA can be difficult, however. Contact your local sports medicine professional to find a specialist who works with EIA to ensure that you are properly diagnosed and receive appropriate treatment and advice.

With asthma and EIA (as well as many other medical conditions), it is important that you keep track of your medication. As an up-and-coming athlete, you may eventually be in a position where you might be drug-tested. Many medications, particularly those used to manage asthma and EIA, are on the banned drug list, but athletes who get proper documentation and medical clearance can use their meds. You probably don't need to worry about this now, but visit the website www.usantidoping.org to learn more about who gets tested and what you may need to do when you upgrade to a 3 on the track or road, become classified as an expert in mountain biking, or decide to go to nationals to compete for a national age-group title.

Growing Pains

Young athletes, particularly as they enter puberty, can grow amazingly fast. When kids grow, long bone grows first, then muscles, ligaments,

---

Traveling First Aid Kit

Your race bag should include a small personal first aid kit. Take this kit with you when riding alone as well as to races and group rides. You can buy a kit at most drugstores, or you can build your own. This kit should include:

- Personal medications (including a backup for any asthma medicine)
- Ibuprofen or other medicine to reduce pain or swelling
- Neosporin or other antibiotic ointment
- Bandages
- Gauze
- Ace bandage
- Bandage tape
- Gloves (to protect you or others from blood or other fluids)
- Tweezers

and tendons catch up. This can put young athletes at risk of joint problems in a way you wouldn't see in older athletes. It is important to pay attention to your growth spurts and any problems that arise. Keep track of your growth, and talk with the folks at your bike shop to make sure that your bike fit keeps up with your size changes. A bike that doesn't fit well can lead to many different overuse or chronic injuries.

Overuse Injuries and Growing Bodies

Repetitive and stressful activities can put joints and muscles at risk of overuse injuries. With repetition, the body performs the same motion over and over again. Things like pedaling and running are considered repetitive activities. Over the course of a workout, an athlete will complete countless cycles of a movement. Even when everything else is perfect, this wear-and-tear can break down the body. Small imperfections in the system, such as tight muscles, muscle imbalances, and improper bike fit, can throw the system out of whack. Common overuse injuries include bursitis and tendonitis. Many knee problems can also be due to overuse.

Training is stressful, and that is a good thing. We actually stress ourselves on purpose when training to help make us stronger and faster. But like ice cream, chocolate, and just about everything else, it is possible to have too much of a good thing. Doing too much or pushing too hard can turn a good stressful workout into a too-much, too-stressful workout.

The aches and pains associated with training are normal and no big deal if they come and go. Keeping track of symptoms and soreness in your logbook can help you determine what led to the problem and how often it is occurring. Injuries that recur frequently, that hurt even when you should be recovered (for example, when you are off the bike or when you've just had a rest day), or that interfere with the quality of your riding could indicate that something is becoming a chronic problem. This can be serious: Any chronic injury in a devo rider can lead to a lifelong injury concern, especially when growing joints are involved. This is why it is so important to pay attention to how your body is responding to training and recovery and why you must take care of problems as they occur.

The "Itises"

Athletes tend to get the "itises." In medicine, when they stick "itis" on the end of a word, it indicates that something is swollen. *Tendinitis* is a swollen or inflamed tendon, and *bursitis* is an agitated bursa sac (a small, liquid-filled sac that helps cushion joints). Swelling isn't such a bad thing. It is actually the body's defense mechanism when something is wrong. If you've ever fallen and sprained your ankle, you know that it swells up pretty fast. The joint gets stiff, the area is flooded with fluid, and all of this helps to immobilize the joint that the body feels is at risk, sort of like nature's splint. Walking becomes difficult and painful. And even though the fluids may help to protect the joint, sometimes it can be too much of a good thing. It can slow down the healing process by making it hard for fresh fluids with healing cells and materials to get in and for waste products to get out of the injury site.

Both long-term (chronic) and short-term (acute) injuries can cause swelling. Immediately icing the injury site after exercise or a fall can help reduce swelling and bruising. The cold constricts blood flow, slowing down the rush of fluid to the site. Ibuprofen is an example of an anti-inflammatory medicine that helps keep new swelling from occurring as well. The nonsteroidal anti-inflammatories, or NSAIDs, like Advil and Aleve, can cause stomach upset in some athletes, so they should be taken with care and only if you have no history of adverse effects. RICE, for Rest, Ice, Compression, Elevation, is the most effective tool that athletes have for managing inflammation. Light exercise, if it doesn't hurt and doesn't cause further damage, can also help increase blood and lymph

---

Two Kinds of Injuries

Acute This doesn't mean that the injuries are pretty. Acute injuries are the ones that happen as a result of something sudden, like a fall or twisting an ankle. They are often the result of an accident or other unforeseen event.

Chronic Chronic injuries are those that last over time. They can creep up over time, or they can be created by an acute injury. Chronic injuries can be short- or long-term. Sometimes they can be cleared up completely, and sometimes they need to be managed for a lifetime.

circulation, which will help flush out swelling and aid in bringing fresh blood and repair supplies to the injury site.

For swelling due to trauma, like a fall, wait until the swelling subsides to make sure there are no other concerns before returning to training. If the inflammation is due to a chronic or recurring injury, consult with a doctor or physical therapist to see what a proper treatment might be.

Broken Bones

Unfortunately, broken bones do happen. If you break a bone or suspect you have broken a bone, see a doctor and follow his or her advice. The most common bones broken in cycling are the collarbone and the wrist. Crashes can happen fast. Sometimes it seems as if someone has magically pulled your bike out from under you in less than a nanosecond. It is only natural to stick your arms out to try to break your fall, but this defense mechanism isn't very effective. Learning to tumble and fall safely can help reduce your risk of broken bones. You may still get some road rash, but that heals much more easily than a broken bone or concussion. Practicing bumping drills in the grass will help you learn to relax in stressful situations. Ideally, if you do go off the bike unintentionally, you want to tuck and roll. The common reflex—and the worst thing you can do—is to stick out your arm to break your fall. This is how wrists and collarbones get snapped. Try to tuck into a ball and roll, and keep your chin in close to your neck or chest to minimize any face or head road rash.

If you do break a bone, don't despair. Broken bones heal and you will be back on the bike soon. Ask your doctor when you will be allowed to train on an indoor stationary bike. This can provide a safe, stable way to ride without risking further injury until you are completely healed. Although you can't jump right back into training, at least you can stay active. Also ask your doctor what other activities you might be allowed to do.

Knee Injuries

The knee is a complex joint, and an injury to the knee can stop a cyclist short. Some of the most common knee problems in cycling are patellar tendinitis, chondromalacia, ilio-tibial (IT) band syndrome, and plica syndrome. If you experience any knee pain, get properly diagnosed promptly. Unresolved knee pain can turn from a short-term problem to a long-term training deterrent. Get a referral from your doctor to visit your local sports medicine clinic. A specialized sports medicine doctor is the best choice for treating knee injuries due to cycling and can help you understand what the problem is and how to adjust your riding.

Some common knee concerns are:

- *Patellar tendinitis:* This condition is due to wear-and-tear, swelling, and buildup of scar tissue at the front of the kneecap. You may feel it when going up or down stairs, and your knee might be sore to the touch.
- *Chondromalacia:* Athletes with this syndrome describe pain behind their kneecap, especially when they first stand after sitting or when pushing a big gear. The problem occurs when the kneecap is out of alignment or when the back surface of the kneecap becomes rough.
- *Ilio-tibial (IT) band syndrome:* The outside of your thigh has a piece of tissue that starts up by your hip and attaches down on the outside of your knee. When something higher up gets tight, this portion of tissue on the outside of the knee starts to snap against the bony parts of the knee instead of floating peacefully. This snapping causes microtears, inflammation, and lots of pain.
- *Plica syndrome:* If you are part of the 30 percent of the population who doesn't have a plica, consider yourself lucky. A plica is a little piece of joint lining behind the kneecap. If it gets agitated, it becomes inflamed and causes sharp pain. Fortunately there are many treatments to try before surgery is needed.
- *Osgood-Schlatter's (OS) disease:* This one sounds much scarier than it actually is. Basically, it is inflammation of the tendon just below the kneecap and just above the lower leg. Typically individuals who develop OS have a swelling just below the kneecap that is very sore to the touch. Traditionally, young boys 10 to 15 years old who are active in sports and in a growth spurt develop this problem.

But doctors are seeing OS in more and more young women now as girls' participation in competitive sports continues to increase. The medical community believes that the problem is caused by a strong quadriceps muscle pulling too hard on a patellar tendon (the one that helps keep the kneecap in place).

Although Osgood-Schlatter's disease is typically seen in running-based sports, it is important to mention it here because many young cyclists cross over from other sports and may already have problems with OS. According to research, about 13 percent of young kids have OS. Treating OS is difficult because the swelling can be persistent. It is treated using the RICE techniques and nonsteroidal anti-inflammatories. Young

Is it true that osteoporosis can affect cyclists?

Most people associate osteoporosis with older women who fall and break a hip because their bones are so fragile. However, doctors and scientists have noticed that individuals who do not have a healthy diet may have problems maintaining healthy bone density (or strength), no matter what their gender. They figured this out while studying what might happen to astronauts when they were exposed to long periods of weightlessness in space. Researchers had healthy men and women spend long periods of time (we're talking weeks) on bedrest. These people never stood up or walked around during the study period. What they found was that all of the test subjects lost bone density—a very serious problem for long-term bone health. Researchers have also found that unless people do some sort of weight-bearing activity (such as weight training, hiking, aerobics, or running) regularly—that is, an exercise where the body experiences the impact of gravity—bone loss can occur. This bone-density loss cannot be replaced later on. Serious road cyclists who spend hours training on the road have been noted as being more likely to experience this problem. Maintaining a healthy diet with plenty of calcium (found in dairy products and dark, leafy green vegetables), and regularly including some weight-bearing activities in your program, will reduce your risk of encountering this type of problem. If you have any questions or concerns, be sure to consult with your doctor. You can even request a full body scan or bone-density test to document your bone health.

athletes may also be advised to take time off from sports. Cycling may be a good alternative activity to alleviate the stress on this joint. If an athlete feels he or she is suffering from OS, it is important to consult a sports medicine specialist and to explore treatment options to diminish the likelihood of long-term negative consequences.

These or any other knee problems should be properly diagnosed by a medical professional so that the treatment can be tailored to your needs.

Other Riding Aches and Pains

Riding puts the athlete into a rather unusual position, often for long periods of time. Cyclists on the road, track, and trail may experience muscle and joint aches in the knees, hips, lower back, upper back, shoulders, hands and wrists, and neck. These pains can be nagging and annoying. They can make riding uncomfortable, and they can even keep you from riding. When there hasn't been a crash or injury that can be linked to a pain, there's a good chance that it is due to overuse or poor form or fit.

Many of these injuries can be prevented through proper bike fit, good bike posture, and proper recovery techniques such as stretching routinely. Make it a habit to get your bike fit checked as you grow. Consider your posture on the bike, and peek into store windows as you pass to double-check that you are sitting tall.

Make it a habit to shift your position on the bike. This can help reduce strain and pain from overuse. Head and neck stress can be reduced by tilting your head from left to right as you ride instead of just riding with your chin lifted. Arm, wrist, shoulder, and hand pains can be alleviated by shifting your hand position on the bars during a ride. It also helps to wear riding gloves. Gentle shifts on the saddle can change the way the joints of your lower body are stressed. Making these small shifts a part of your normal riding routine will help reduce riding aches and pains.

Saddle Sores and Other Concerns

The one injury that is probably unique to cycling is the saddle sore. Saddle sores develop in the crotch area due to friction, and both male and female riders can experience them. Saddle sores can be small or large;

basically, they are inflamed sores that look like pimples but are actually boils or infected hair follicles. Sometimes athletes will get a rashlike problem, commonly called "monkey butt." Both conditions are painful and can force an athlete off the bike.

Saddle sores can be the result of poor saddle fit (to the shape of your butt), a poor bike fit that causes poor body position on the bike, or poor saddle position. If you are having recurring problems, consult with a bike-fit specialist and explain the problems you've been experiencing so your fit can be adjusted. Don't feel shy talking about saddle sores; they happen to every serious rider at least once during his or her cycling career. Other common causes of the sore bumps or rash are wearing wet shorts for too long, getting grit or dirt in your shorts (a common concern for those mountain biking in the rain), and wearing worn or old chamois. New riders may also experience a very specific rash where the thigh meets the torso if they wear underwear under their cycling shorts. Cycling shorts are designed to be worn without underwear, and the extra fabric can cause a lot of friction. If a saddle sore doesn't seem to be healing within a reasonable amount of time, or if you think it might be infected, see your doctor. He or she may prescribe an antibiotic to heal and dry up the sore.

If you develop a saddle sore, take a few days off the bike to let it heal. For a rash, or monkey butt, going commando (no underwear) may or may not be helpful. Baby powder or another talc can help dry and soothe the area as well (or use diaper rash products). Companies like Chamois Butt'r and Assos make products that are designed to be rubbed into the short chamois or the skin before a ride. These creams reduce friction over time and reduce rash and saddle-sore concerns. If you have actual sores, *do not* pick at or try to pop them. The risk of infection is high, and an open saddle sore is so much worse—trust me. If you really have to ride, you can experiment with making a little donut cushion to take the pressure off the spot, or try wearing two pairs of shorts for extra padding. Neither is a very comfortable solution, but it might help in a pinch.

Let's face it, riding your bike means you are sitting for a long period of time on some pretty sensitive stuff. In particular, you are putting a lot of pressure on your scrotal sac and the area surrounding that tissue. Guys often experience discomfort on the bike and may even have a period of numbness or diminished feeling after a ride. While this isn't uncommon, it is something to pay attention to. Some medical professionals have raised concerns about the long hours that cyclists spend on the bike and the damage that this long-term nerve pressure might do. There is no evidence that this problem is linked to cancer, despite the myth, but repeated nerve trauma is always a concern for comfort and health reasons. So what is a guy to do?

There are two things that can help alleviate the problem (although it may never go away completely). First, move around when you ride. You want to shift your hips gently now and then when in the saddle to change the pressure points. Standing up for a few pedal strokes can be helpful because it removes the pressure altogether. This will help reduce the continuous nerve pressure in any one area.

Saddle choice can also help. Saddles come in many different sizes and are made of many different materials. Ideally, you want your sit bones (the bony part of each butt cheek) to sit on either side of the saddle so the important stuff in between is raised up just a bit. Some saddles make this easier to do because they have a channel or groove down the middle, and some go even further by having a cutout in that area. Take a look at Specialized Body Geometry saddles, which have been designed with this problem in mind. Try different saddles. And don't be afraid to talk to the staff at your local bike shop or to other riders. Knowledgeable cyclists will know what you are talking about, as it is a common concern among riders. They may be able to give you advice on saddles that worked for them. If you continue to have problems, notice any changes in your testicles, or experience numbness after a ride that takes a long time to go away, be sure to talk to your doctor. (For information on saddles for women, see Chapter 12.)

More serious problems can occur due to improper saddle pressure. In Chapter 12, we'll discuss some of the problems female riders might encounter. Male riders need to know that genital numbness or problems with peeing during or after a ride (due to inflammation of the prostate gland) may occur. None of these are "normal," and they should not be treated as though they were just something to put up with. Don't suffer in silence. Experiment with saddles made of different materials or with different shapes. Some saddles have a cutout area to help reduce the pressure. Getting your bike fit assessed is crucial in the treatment of these problems as well. And again, there's no need to be embarrassed. The person helping you with your fit will have helped many other athletes with similar concerns.

Who are you?

Even if you ride with other people, it is a smart idea to always carry your vital information with you on the bike. Consider creating and laminating a little card to carry in your pocket. You can laminate things at most office goods stores and copy stores. Avoid putting the information in your saddlebag, as it may get overlooked in an emergency. If you are in an accident, your bike will not go into the emergency room with you; the doctor has a better chance of finding it if it is in your pocket. The information on your card should contain:

- Your full name, address, and phone number
- Key contact people and phone numbers
- Date of birth
- Any allergies or medical concerns
- Blood type
- Insurance provider, policy number, and insurance company phone number

You can also get professionally made identification cards from companies like Road ID (www.roadid.com) or MedID (www.medids.com/RoadID.html) that are designed to last under sweaty conditions and provide emergency personnel with all the crucial information they need.

HEAT AND ICE

Icing is an important part of pain and injury management. You can safely ice two or three times a day. Each time you ice, plan on sitting still for a while so the ice stays directly on the injured or swollen spot. Here are some more tips on icing an injury:

- Use crushed ice or small ice cubes in a secure resealable plastic bag, ice packets from the pharmacy, or a bag of frozen vegetables. Frozen veggies like corn and peas work particularly well because they wrap nicely around injured areas, especially awkward joints like elbows, ankles, and knees.
- Never place any ice packet directly on the skin. Although deeper tissue will benefit from the cold, surface tissues can be damaged in this way. Use a T-shirt or towel between your skin and the ice.
- Never apply ice to broken skin or road rash.
- Use an elastic bandage or cloth to tie the ice firmly in place, if necessary.
- Keep the ice pack on for 10 to 15 minutes. If you like, you can then let the area warm up for 20 to 30 minutes before you ice again. You can repeat this up to three times a day.

Ice is not the only way to go when you are trying to heal. Sometimes heat can be used to help bring blood to an injured site after icing. An increased blood flow brings all sorts of good things that aid in recovery and help flush away waste. When an injury first occurs, ice is your best friend. But 24 to 48 hours later, if no new swelling has taken place, heat can be used to help loosen up the area and further the healing process. Use heat carefully, and do not use it if you have broken skin or new inflammation from training. Here is how to use heat successfully:

- Use a covered heating pad with a control device or a covered hot water bottle. With a control device, start with a low setting to see how you react to the heat.
- Avoid putting the heat directly on the skin. Most heating pads have a flannel covering, but if not, use a towel or other cloth. As with ice, the heat will do the muscle good, but too much on your skin surface can cause trouble.

- Apply heat to the affected area for 10 to 15 minutes at a time. You can remove the heat, let the area cool down, and then reapply it for 10 to 15 more minutes. You can repeat this up to three times a day.

CAN I RIDE WHEN I AM SICK?

The number one goal for a successful athlete is to be a healthy athlete. This makes sense, as being healthy is the best way to achieve peak performance. Seasonal colds, the flu, strep throat, and other minor illnesses come and go, and no matter what precautions you take, you will most likely get the sniffles now and then. But what can you do to keep yourself as healthy as possible?

- Wash your hands frequently. The antibacterial gel you can buy is helpful, but nothing beats good old-fashioned soap and water.
- Make it a habit not to touch your eyes, nose, or mouth during cold and flu season. These are prime ways that bugs get in.
- Stay well hydrated.
- Get plenty of sleep, especially during times of stress or when colds are going around.
- Minimize negative stress. The more stress you experience, the harder it is for your body to fight off bugs.
- Stay warm. While not wearing a hat wouldn't cause you to get sick, getting cold does force your body to dedicate resources to warming you up. This can reduce the resources you have to fight off bugs. A simple hat and warm-up jacket should do the trick.
- Eat right. A diet full of whole grains, fruits, and vegetables will provide you with the key vitamins, minerals, and antioxidants you need to stay healthy.

If you do get sick, you may need to cut back on your training. See Table 11.1 for some rules of thumb about training when you are not in top form. However, when in doubt, talk to your parents and/or doctor. If you are really unsure, it is never wrong to err on the side of caution.

TABLE 11.1 **Training with Symptoms of Illness**

Don't Ride	Ride Easy
Fever	Stuffy head
Vomiting or diarrhea	Runny nose
Full-body chills, aches, or pains	Mild symptoms of a head cold
Pink eye	Headache
Strep throat (before starting on antibiotics)	
Sinus infection	
Yeast infection	
Bronchitis	
In these cases, don't ride for at least 24 hours after your symptoms have disappeared or for at least 24 hours after starting antibiotics, unless you have received medical permission to ride.	In these cases, keep your pace and effort mellow to allow your body to spend its energy fighting off whatever is attacking you. If you feel worse while riding, go home and rest. Consult your doctor if you have some other illness and are not sure if it's okay for you to work out.

Beating the Common Cold

To date, science doesn't have a way to beat the common cold, at least not completely. Some limited research has indicated that proper levels of vitamin C help maintain a healthy body, and zinc has received limited support for helping shorten colds. But there are things you can do to lower your risk, and you can reduce the severity of your symptoms. Your best bet is to get plenty of rest, wash your hands frequently, drink lots of fluids, and eat a well-balanced diet.

WHAT TO DO WHEN YOU ARE INJURED

Sometimes, despite our best efforts, injuries keep us off the bike. Sometimes staying off the bike is a no-brainer. Athletes usually don't have too much trouble accepting a couch position when they experience broken bones or sharp pain. They don't like it, but they can accept it. Other injuries, those that are less dramatic or hard to see, can be harder to accept. This is especially true of the little nagging injuries that creep up and become bigger injuries, and then eventually become injuries that sideline you. But accepting an injury and allowing the body to heal are part of being a great athlete; it's far better than being one who never completely heals and sort of limps from one injury to the next.

When you have an injury and aren't sure whether you should train or race, ask yourself the following questions:

- Will I make this injury worse by continuing?
- Does this injury make me change how I move (like a limp), which could cause me to injure another part of my body because I am moving differently?
- If you are injured while racing, is finishing the race worth jeopardizing your ability to train and compete next week, next month, or even next year?

There are no easy answers to these questions. Talk to your parents, your coach, and/or your doctor to help you make your decision about whether to go forward with training or racing.

Sometimes, your body will help you make a decision. Anytime you get hurt and there is a pop or a snap; the pain is sudden, sharp, or stabbing; your breath gets taken away; or you must limp or change how you move while riding, you are getting a really loud signal that says "*Stop Now!*" Swelling, tenderness to the touch, and bleeding are all signs that you should seek medical advice sooner rather than later. Ignoring a sudden pain is never a good idea. Attempting to train through a sudden or acute pain can increase the severity of the problem or lead to secondary injuries. It is frustrating to stop, but failing to do so could mean it will take even longer before you get back on the bike.

For more routine injuries and training aches and pains, it may be harder to decide what to do. It may be difficult to remember exactly when something started to bug you or to assess whether it has gotten worse. Keeping a logbook is a great way to keep track of the little things. Make notes in your log about your training aches, rate them on your own personal scale (for example, 1–10, where 10 means it was so bad you cut your session short, and 0 means you barely noticed it), and note what you did (stretch, apply ice, take ibuprofen, etc.). Your log can come in handy if you decide to talk to a physical therapist or sports medicine doctor. And over time you may be able to see patterns that will help you prevent future injuries.

Treating Injuries with RICE

Rest Allow the injured area some downtime.

Ice Applying ice to your injury helps reduce the swelling. Ice it for no more than 10 to 15 minutes at a time, and be careful not to put the ice bag directly on your skin (this can cause painful ice burns). A bag of frozen corn or peas makes a wonderful ice bag and is less likely to cause a burn.

Compression Gently wrapping the injured area will remind you to be careful and can help reduce swelling. Just take care not to wrap too tightly. Check the fingers or toes of the wrapped limb to make sure they are receiving enough blood.

Elevation Whenever possible, keep the injured limb elevated. This will help your body reduce swelling. This is your permission to put your injured ankle up on the end of the couch.

HELPING AN ATHLETE HEAL: FOR PARENTS AND COACHES

Nothing is more heartbreaking than a sick or injured child. As a parent or coach, you want to protect him or her and make it better. When working with devo athletes, it is inevitable that you will have to handle these situations. Anyone working with sports, particularly devo sports, should strongly consider maintaining current certifications in first aid, CPR, and sports first aid. This will help prepare you for emergency racing or training situations. And a well-stocked first aid kit is a must.

In addition to the physical damage that can occur when an athlete is injured, there may be psychological consequences. The level of emotional impact depends on the severity of the injury and the degree to which it hinders the athlete's ability to train and compete. Keep in mind that different athletes react differently. An injury that one athlete easily shakes off may have a lasting impact on another athlete. And even chronic training injuries like shin splints or growing pains that don't require a rest from training can take their toll on an athlete.

Common reactions to both chronic and acute injuries (for example, broken bones, road rash) include:

- Decreased confidence in one's skills and abilities
- Irritability and mood swings
- Poor academic performance
- Increased anxiety (particularly if the injury occurred as a result of training)
- Decreased performance due to holding back
- Feelings of isolation, anxiety about being left behind, or fear of falling behind
- Loss of athletic identity (which can be particularly difficult if the athlete feels he or she has no other talents or skills)

When an athlete is injured, the coach's reaction can play an important part in recovery. If you are a coach, stay in contact with your injured athletes to provide support and informational resources. When athletes feel isolated from teammates, their coach, and their sport, it can contribute to feelings of sadness and depression, which in turn can lengthen healing time and undermine the coach/athlete relationship. Injured athletes, particularly those who aren't allowed to ride or race, may find it difficult to attend events as spectators or volunteers, so you may not see them during the recovery period. Technology such as text-messaging and e-mail can be a great tool for staying in touch with your athletes in these situations.

Just because athletes can't train on the bike during a recovery period doesn't mean that they can't be productive. There are probably things they could be doing to stay as healthy as possible until the doctor says it is safe to begin cycling again. For example, an athlete with an injured knee may benefit from swimming, or one healing from intense road rash might work on improving his or her nutrition habits. An athlete can

Helping the Injured Athlete

- Be empathetic—listen to the athlete's concerns and provide support.
- Encourage the athlete to seek expert advice from trained professionals for serious or chronic injuries. Help him find the right resources, if necessary.
- An injured athlete can keep track of her rehab/recovery activities in a log-book. Encourage the athlete to do this. This will help her see progress in what often feels like a very slow process. It will also serve as a reminder of a successful recovery that can be an encouragement in future times of recovery and healing.
- Reevaluate season goals and readjust them as necessary.
- Listen for concerns or fears about returning to the bike or competition and begin to discuss them. Don't hesitate to consult a sport psychology professional early in the process if you are concerned about an athlete's return.
- Talk with your athlete about what to expect during recovery. Clear expectations will help reduce anxiety. Be honest and realistic about the injury and the recovery process.

even practice changing tires to reduce the amount of time it takes to fix a flat in a race. Brainstorm with your athletes to help keep them invested in their own recovery rather than just dwelling on the loss of training.

Unplanned downtime can be an excellent time to practice skills like goal setting or relaxation and visualization skills. Goal setting provides the athlete with a powerful tool during rehabilitation. Strong, positive visualization skills can allow an athlete to practice skills and bike handling in a safe and controlled manner. The use of imagery to practice skills can even help rebuild damaged confidence. Finally, if visualization is used to practice rehabilitation exercises, it may improve the recovery process.

RECOMMENDED READING AND RESOURCES

Andy Pruitt's Complete Medical Guide for Cyclists, by Andrew L. Pruitt, with Fred Matheny (VeloPress, 2006).

Tour de Life, a book by Saul Raisin with Dave Shields, is a must-read. It tells the inspirational true story of an incredibly talented young cyclist and his return to competitive road cycling following an injury that almost ended his life.

Asthma Action America, http://www.asthmaactionamerica.org

Asthma and Allergy Foundation of America, http://aafa.org

See the following websites for more information on first aid training. To locate CPR and first aid certification courses near you, check with your local chapter of the American Red Cross or call your local hospital's community education department.

- American Red Cross, www.redcross.org/services/hss/courses/
- American Heart Association, www.americanheart.org
- American Sport Education Program (ASEP), www.asep.com

12 WOMEN on Wheels

Never be afraid of being the only woman on a ride.
—Sarah Uhl, 2001 Junior World Champion,
Track Match Sprint

When I was a young athlete, it wasn't easy to find cycling gear that was sized specifically for females. It seemed like manufacturers had decided that all they needed to do to make something for women was to add a dash of pink. I remember feeling very frustrated when the only cycling shoes that fit me were the ones that were grey and pink! As the saying goes, "We've come a long way, baby!" Manufacturers have finally realized that women are active and that they are more interested in the performance of gear than the colors. We also know a lot more about the specific fitness needs and concerns of women who ride. In this chapter we'll take a look at some of these issues and concerns.

First and foremost, let's clear up one important issue. Everyone is unique, and even though we tend to stereotype characteristics as male and female, this doesn't mean that everyone automatically fits the stereotype. For example, in general, women tend to have longer legs and a shorter torso than men of the same height. This is just in general, so there are plenty of women who don't have longer legs and plenty of guys who do. So, just because you are a girl doesn't mean you automatically need "women's-specific" gear; by the same token, guys shouldn't steer away from gender-labeled equipment just because it has been labeled. Try different things and find what works for you.

If you are a male, and you have ventured this far into the chapter, please keep going. Although some of this information is specifically about girls, you might find some of it useful. During your career you will have female training partners and friends. You never know when this knowledge might come in handy.

GEAR AND EQUIPMENT

One of the best changes in cycling gear in recent years is the sizing of jerseys and shorts to fit smaller riders. In general, female athletes have narrower shoulders and wider hips than their male counterparts. Jerseys that are cut with a princess seam and a better female fit don't flap in the wind and tend to feel more comfortable. Women's shorts not only have a slightly more curved fit in the hip than men's shorts, but also often feature a chamois that is seam-free down the middle, the area that is most sensitive to chafing for women. Don't automatically assume you need the female cut, but don't rule it out either. A well-fitting kit is a crucial element to comfortable riding over time.

Gloves and shoes have also been sized for smaller hands and feet. Companies like Specialized have taken fit issues further by not just downsizing their fit but also studying women's bodies to make other modifications. Their products are ergonomically designed for women's bodies. Other companies, such as Terry and Serfas, have also made great women's-specific products after conducting research on women's cycling needs.

And though it has taken a while, bikes and parts have begun to catch up with the needs of female riders as well. This is great news for young female riders (and can be helpful for Junior males as well). Brake levers have been made smaller to accommodate the reach of smaller hands; 650c wheels (a slightly smaller wheel size than the standard 700c size) are available to allow shorter riders to ride full-sized frames more comfortably; and frames have been tailored to female geometry with shorter top tubes and come fitted with components sized appropriately.

While we are on the subject of comfort, it's worth noting that saddles, particularly racing saddles, are very uncomfortable if they don't suit your body well, especially as you put in more and more miles. Getting used to a saddle takes some time. However, a saddle shouldn't hurt, cause bruising, or create sores or chafing. Saddles come with different levels of

Finding a Good Sports Bra

A sports bra is an important component of your competitive kit, and there are dozens of great styles and brands on the market. Although cycling isn't generally a high-impact sport, selecting a supportive sports bra is key. A sports top is designed to minimize chest movement. If you tend to experience some breast soreness or tenderness during or just before your period, cycling without a sports bra can exacerbate the problem. In addition, breast tissue is relatively delicate. It is basically fatty and connective tissue that is on top of your chest muscles. If it isn't properly supported, the skin will stretch over time. So wear a good sports bra for support. This may not seem like a big issue when you are young, but as you get older you'll be glad you did.

Try on a lot of different styles to find the one that is most comfortable for you. Some lift and separate the breasts, and others compress the breasts against your chest. Some are short like traditional bras, and others are torso length. Some are pull-on styles, and others fasten in the front or back. If you are looking for the type that compresses, you want to make sure that you can breathe comfortably and not feel constricted. If a bra has fasteners, make sure they don't dig into your skin, as this can cause chafing and sores. Consider the fabric as well. Many sports tops, especially those designed as fashionwear for the gym, are made of cotton or are cotton based with some synthetic fiber. These might look cute, but they are a bad choice for cycling. Cotton holds moisture and is slow to dry, especially in comparison to the wicking fabrics available today. A cotton garment up against your skin will feel cold and clammy as you sweat and may make you feel chilled or uncomfortable. Opt for the fabrics that wick. And keep in mind that not all sports tops need to look like bras.

padding, are made of different material, and feature different styles. Gel saddles are resilient over time but tend to be a little heavier. Saddles with cloth or foam padding might not feel as cushy, but they do hold up well over time.

Perhaps the biggest innovation in saddle fit is the shape of the saddle itself. Some saddles have wider rear areas, and others are narrower.

Women with wider hips will be more comfortable on wider saddles, and individuals with narrow hips may find that a narrow saddle suits them better. Ideally, your sit bones (the bony bits in your bottom where your pelvis bone is) should be on either side of the saddle. Some saddles are solid, and others have a cutout area or softer area in the middle that can help protect delicate tissue from pressure. (Similar saddles with anatomically appropriate cutout features have also been designed for males. See Chapter 2.) Try testing some of these saddles to see if the design fits your body and offers the fit that is right for you. Some bike shops will let you try different saddle styles before you decide to make a purchase. Talk to other riders for their recommendations or ask to try their saddles.

HEALTH ISSUES

Women's sports and fitness experiences have been filled with myth and misunderstanding. Until the 1960s, the Olympics organization didn't let women compete in anything longer than the 200-meter race in track and field for fear that it was "too much exertion" for women to handle, and even some doctors in the late 1800s warned women against riding a bike, citing fears that their uteruses would fall out! Today, we know these ideas are ludicrous. Unfortunately, other myths about women's participation in sports still exist.

Sometimes women are afraid that exercising or lifting weights will make them get big and bulk up like guys do. Don't worry. This just isn't the way it works. Men have more testosterone in their bodies than women do, and this hormone contributes to how big they get when they exercise. Plus, to get really big muscles you have to do very specific exercises and spend a lot of time lifting weights. You are going to be spending most of your time on your bike. You will get muscles, but being fit and toned is much better than the alternative.

Despite plenty of evidence to the contrary, some people are still concerned that participating in high-energy, stressful sports like cycling may have a negative impact on a woman's ability to have children. To the contrary, fit and healthy women have been found to have easier pregnancies and healthy babies, and they have an easier time losing the baby weight after their child is born. If you are a Junior or Espoir rider, having kids is probably not on your top-ten list of things to do right now, but someday you might want to. If you ever do venture down that road, you will be able to continue being physically active. The American Medical Association and other key health advocates report that women who are active before their pregnancies can safely continue to remain active throughout the experience. You might not be able to go as hard or as fast as you used to as you get bigger, and you will probably want to opt for stationary riding, swimming, or other alternatives toward the end of the pregnancy, for both comfort and safety reasons, but unless your pregnancy involves complications, you can still exercise. And there are lots of high-level women in sports like basketball, soccer, track and field, and cycling who have returned to very successful sports careers after having a child.

Of course, it is always important to work closely with your doctor whenever your health status changes, so find a good provider for your prenatal care as soon as you decide to start a family. This might be a traditional OB/GYN, a family practice physician, or a certified nurse midwife working under a doctor's supervision. Whichever type of prenatal care you choose, consult with this person as soon as you suspect you are pregnant, or even beforehand. This will give you a chance to discuss personal health concerns, questions related to continuing your training throughout a pregnancy, and other matters before you are caught up in the excitement of becoming a mom. Follow the instructions that he or she gives you. Although most women can exercise throughout pregnancy, there are always exceptions: If you are blessed with triplets, develop pregnancy-induced hypertension, or have other special considerations, you may have to stop cycling for a while for your safety and the health of the baby (or babies).

One of the scariest myths, because of the very real and serious health concerns that can be connected to it, is that not having a period is a normal sign that a woman is a highly trained or elite athlete. Not having periods is *not* a normal or healthy part of being an athlete. An interrupted or stopped menstrual cycle can have very serious consequences for your long-term bone health. We'll discuss this issue more fully later in this chapter in the section "Female Athlete Triad." For now, let's just bust the myth that it is good, healthy, or normal for a girl or woman to stop having her period. Missing more than one or two cycles in a row is always a reason to visit the doctor.

For Parents and Coaches

Many young women may be uncomfortable discussing menstruation. Puberty is a very personal experience, and sexuality and all things related can be a minefield to navigate. Not everyone is raised in a home environment where this is dinner conversation, and not all adults are comfortable with the subject, either. So when educating young women about such things, proceed with care, but definitely proceed. It is crucial that they have accurate information about puberty and how it impacts their bodies in general and, more specifically, as young athletes.

If you are a coach, you may want to start by gathering information about concerns that girls might have (besides this chapter, look for information from the National Collegiate Athletic Association [NCAA]; it has fantastic Female Athlete Triad resources at www.femaleathletetriad.org that you can share with athletes and parents). By providing parents with the same information you give your female athletes, you help reduce any concerns of having had an inappropriate conversation. Providing printed information also allows your athletes to learn at their own pace and comfort level. Then they can come to you with questions, and they will better understand why you might ask certain questions. And to protect yourself, when you do have a conversation with a young woman, keep it focused on the facts as they relate to health and wellness. It isn't a bad idea to have a physician or medical professional you can consult with as questions arise.

The Female Knee

As the old song goes, the knee bone's connected to the thigh bone, the thigh bone's connected to the hip bone. There is some real wisdom in this when it comes to the female knee; you cannot fully understand how it operates until you understand how it operates as part of your skeleto-muscular system. Typically, a female's hips are wider than a guy's, particularly after puberty. This means that the alignment of muscles and tendons from the hip to the knee is a little different. This contributes to the fact that we tend to see more knee problems in female athletes than in male athletes. Cyclists aren't as troubled by tears in the knee as some other kinds of athletes—such as soccer players, who must twist and turn the knee joint—but knee pain can still occur in cycling. Chapter 11 covers the most common knee problems and other injuries that cyclists experience. But as a female cyclist, just bear in mind that when you keep up with your stretching routine, make sure your bike fits properly as you grow, and maintain good muscle balance, especially through puberty as your body is changing, so you are protecting your knees and ensuring that knee problems won't keep you off the bike while you spend valuable time healing.

Puberty

Puberty can be uncomfortable, from the time it starts when you are 11 or 12 until your physical development is complete and you are considered an adult. And it's no wonder. During puberty, a whole new system—the reproductive system—is getting activated in your body. Some people experience growth spurts of as much as an inch or more in a matter of weeks. These spurts can actually be painful; they are often called "growing pains" because of the aching joints and muscles associated with them. When we grow, our bones grow first, and then the muscles, tendons, and ligaments have to catch up. Before things even out, your body will feel the stress and strain. Not everyone begins puberty at the same time. Some people start sooner and some a bit later. However, if you haven't begun to change—especially if you have not yet gotten your period—by the time you hit 16, it is very important to consult with the appropriate physician.

When puberty occurs, both boys and girls develop their secondary sex characteristics. Body hair changes texture in some places and sprouts up in others, and body shape changes. All of these things are due to hormones released in the body. For girls, the change in hormones such as estrogen will lead to breast development, a change in how fat is distributed in the body (which is why little girls are built like little boys and women are more curvy), and menstruation. None of these things should interfere with your riding. And don't let anyone tell you that the changes in your body will alter or end your ability to be competitive. Our history logs are full of fantastically strong and successful women riders.

Being physically active can help reduce problems from cramps and other discomforts associated with your monthly cycle. Using tampons is perfectly safe when you are riding, provided you follow the manufacturer's recommendations for using the product. If you're not sure how to use tampons, talk to your mom, your doctor, or a trusted female friend. Pads can also be used when riding, but they tend to be uncomfortable in cycling shorts and don't stay in place well.

In some segments of our culture, it's okay for young girls to be active and play sports, but teenage girls and women are discouraged from being competitive or involved in serious athletics. It goes against the norm in some communities, and female athletes can even be mocked. Fortunately, this is becoming less common, and in most of the United States young women have the same opportunities as their male counterparts, and even the same kind of recognition and encouragement. If you like riding your bike and like competing, don't be afraid to be different. There are thousands and thousands of women out there who remain active and competitive even into their senior years. A few years ago at the National Cycling Festival, I met a fantastic woman in her seventies who was racing in the time trial. She was just as enthusiastic as any other racer I met there. You may be in the minority in your racing club or area, but don't let that discourage you. If you feel that you are not getting the support and encouragement you need, turn to the Web for some great all-women's riding resources (see "Recommended Resources" at the end of the chapter).

Anemia

Anemia occurs when the body is low in iron, and it is not uncommon among young women who are athletes. Iron plays an essential role in red blood cell (RBC) production, and RBCs transport oxygen to your muscles. Without proper oxygen, an anemic athlete will feel tired and have trouble training or racing well.

Common signs of anemia include:

- Fatigue and loss of energy
- Unusually rapid heartbeat, particularly with exercise
- Shortness of breath and headache, particularly with exercise
- Difficulty concentrating

If you are experiencing these symptoms, you will need to visit a doctor for a blood test to find out if anemia is the reason. The blood test is pretty simple; it involves having a small amount of blood drawn by a doctor to be analyzed at a lab. It is important to request that the doctor order an iron profile and serum ferratin. These are not part of a standard blood test, but they enable the doctor to determine whether you have anemia or if you are at risk of getting it. If you do have anemia, you will be given iron supplements, and the test may need to be repeated periodically to monitor your progress. There are different levels of anemia, from mild to severe. Your doctor will help you find the right formula of iron supplementation and dietary changes to get your iron level back to the normal range. If you do develop anemia, don't despair. Simple dietary changes or a small iron supplement can help you get back to normal, and plenty of athletes, both male and female, continue to have successful careers with the right treatment.

Don't try to self-diagnose anemia and take an iron supplement on your own because you are worried. Taking iron supplements when you don't really need to can lead to some pretty uncomfortable gastrointestinal side effects (think explosive diarrhea), and if you are wrong about the cause, you will continue to be tired. Additionally, a mildly anemic athlete can become a more anemic one (and have more performance problems and health concerns) if the problem isn't treated properly. Be sure to address any concerns with a physician right away.

Is anemia preventable? In many cases, yes. Some people may be more likely to develop anemia than others because of their genetics, but diet plays a big role in maintaining healthy iron levels. We get iron from red meats and some dark green leafy vegetables, such as spinach (Popeye knew what he was doing). It can be very difficult to get enough iron if you are a vegetarian, and iron is one of those supplements that isn't absorbed as well in pill form as it is from foods. If you are a vegetarian, be sure to choose foods that are rich in iron. Even if you aren't, make healthy daily choices from the list below to stay full of energy. And stay away from junk food, which is rarely rich in iron.

Iron-Rich Foods

- Iron-fortified cereals, pastas, and breads
- Lean red meats, including beef, pork, and lamb
- Liver
- Dried fruits, such as raisins, prunes, dates, and apricots
- Seafood, such as oysters, clams, tuna, salmon, and shrimp
- Beans, including kidney, lima, navy, black, pinto, soy, and lentils
- Leafy green vegetables, such as collard greens, kale, mustard greens, spinach, Swiss chard, and turnip greens
- Tofu
- Some vegetables, including broccoli, asparagus, parsley, watercress, and Brussels sprouts
- Chicken and turkey
- Nuts
- Egg yolks

Female Athlete Triad

The female athlete triad is a combination of three conditions that are often interrelated in complex ways: disordered eating, osteoporosis, and irregular or missed periods. The American College of Sports Medicine released a new position statement on the female athlete triad in 2007, and a growing body of research shows that we should pay attention to this important area of concern.

People used to think that it was normal and actually good for female athletes to miss their periods. We now know this is false. Young women, regardless of their training level, should not miss periods or have irregular periods (also sometimes called amenorrhea). Most girls begin their period between the ages of 12 and 16. Some start sooner and others later, but it is key that you start. If you are 16 or older and have not begun to menstruate, be sure to check with your doctor or gynecologist. Why is this such a big deal? When you get your period, a whole lot more is going on than just menstruating once a month. The cycle of menstruation includes the release of different hormones that play roles in bone development and healthy growth. When a woman stops menstruating or has disturbed cycles, her bone strength can suffer.

That's why the second part of the triad is osteoporosis. Irregular menstrual cycles have been linked to decreases in bone mass and bone strength. This can lead to stress fractures and can cause bones to break more easily. For an athlete, this means that simple falls can be a serious matter. And, even more seriously, young women who develop this condition are at risk for lifelong bone-health problems and osteoporosis later in life. In fact, in young women with a history of irregular menstrual cycles, bone density can be very poor, in some cases matching that of someone two or three times their age.

Disordered eating is the third element in the triad. For a long time, the concern was that women were training too much, and people worried that females just weren't designed to handle training. Of course, people also used to believe that the world was flat and that women who lifted weights would bulk up (just for the record, both are false). Fortunately, we now understand that the training volume or intensity isn't the problem; the main problem is inadequate calories. It is crucial that developing young athletes get enough calories to sustain their growth, daily activities, and training activities. Athletes do not need to have recognized eating disorders such as anorexia (self-denial of food) or bulimia (bingeing or purging) to be at risk of problems with the disordered eating part of the triad. Disordered eating, or not consuming adequate nutrition or calories, can be due to poor nutrition education or concerns about weight gain or body image. No matter what the cause, poor nutrition behaviors take a huge toll on the health of the individual, and professional nutritional help is essential for overcoming them. If body image, weight control, or fear of weight gain is a concern, proper care by a specialist in eating disorders is advised.

Although most people associate eating disorders with teenage girls, these problems can occur in males and females of all ages. Many different factors can contribute to eating disorders, and there are two main classifications that doctors use when diagnosing them.

- Anorexia nervosa is a set of behaviors where an individual reduces calorie intake and may be very restrictive about amount, type, and timing of meals. Even when they are very thin, individuals with anorexia nervosa may view themselves as fat and continue to try to lose weight. This is a very serious condition and can have a severe impact on health and wellness.
- Bulimia is often thought to be on the opposite end of the spectrum. Individuals suffering from this disorder purge the food they eat by vomiting or using medicine designed to soften the stool. Like anorexia nervosa, bulimia can have severe health consequences.
- Both anorexia and bulimia have criteria that doctors use to diagnose them. But even if an athlete doesn't meet the medical criteria, she may still exhibit a pattern of disordered eating. This means she is practicing unhealthy eating habits that put her at risk for developing further problems.

Keep in mind that the three elements of the female athlete triad are interrelated. An athlete who is not consuming enough calories is setting herself up for triad-related concerns. As mentioned, the athlete may not have an eating disorder like anorexia: Perhaps she is just watching calories, hoping to lose weight, or "too busy" to take the time to eat as much as she should. Training can use up a lot of energy, and it can be difficult to get all the foods you need, especially when you have a busy training schedule on top of school and maybe a job as well. But when the calorie imbalance between energy in and energy out becomes too great, for whatever reason, the body thinks that something is wrong and begins to conserve. When this happens, it begins to shut down nonessential systems. These nonessential systems can include menstruation.

Researchers feel that eating enough (both in terms of quality and quantity) is a crucial element of helping to prevent the slide into the female athlete triad; eating right is also important for good performance and long-term health.

But if I take the pill, I get my period, so I'm covered, right?

Some athletes and coaches assume that taking the birth control pill will eliminate the possibility of getting amenorrhea (missed or absent periods) and the risk of developing the female athlete triad, because the athlete will get her period on a regular basis that is dictated by the hormones in the pill. Unfortunately, this isn't the case. The female athlete triad is all about the body not getting enough fuel to sustain all the activities the athlete is engaging in as part of training for her sport on top of all the normal biological things that are part of living. The hormones in the pill may regulate the menstrual cycle, but the underlying problem of improper nutrition is still there. This doesn't mean that the pill isn't a good option, but it is critical that nutritional concerns are addressed as well. The athlete should have a conversation with her doctor, weighing all the options both as a young woman and as an athlete, before making her decision.

Warning Signs for Female Athlete Triad

If an athlete exhibits one or more of these signs, this doesn't automatically mean she is experiencing the female athlete triad. It does mean that it would be worthwhile for her to consult with a physician who is familiar with the triad. For help finding a local doctor who knows sports medicine, contact the head athletic trainer at your local college or university.

- Noticeable weight loss
- Signs of disordered eating (for example, restrictive diet, emphasis on eating or not eating, secretive eating, counting calories, lack of enjoyment in food, unable to socialize and eat)
- Cold hands and feet
- Dry skin
- Hair loss

- Absent or irregular menstrual periods
- Increased risk of injury
- Delayed injury-healing time
- Stress fractures
- Mood changes
- Poor concentration
- Depression

An athlete experiencing the female athlete triad may not exhibit disordered eating. You may notice, however, that an athlete expresses other unhealthy training and performance behaviors as a dysfunctional way of coping with stress and other problems. As a parent, coach, or teammate, be aware of the training habits and beliefs of the young athletes you work with and watch for unhealthy patterns. If you suspect a problem, seek assistance from a medical professional as soon as possible. The sooner these issues are addressed, the sooner the athlete can continue a healthy pursuit of performance goals. Unhealthy exercise or training behaviors might include

- Exercising even when injured
- Hiding injuries
- Experiencing excessive or unrealistic feelings of guilt or anxiety when unable to train
- Avoiding other responsibilities to train
- Basing one's overall happiness on how training or competition goes
- Basing one's self-perception and self-esteem on how training or competition goes
- Hiding or lying about weight or weight changes
- Hiding training or seeking out extra training in an effort to catch up or "punish" oneself for perceived weakness or poor performance

Helping Someone with an Eating Disorder

The most important thing to realize when you are concerned about someone's health and eating disorders is that this is not something a person does on purpose. An eating disorder is a serious problem that requires support, education, and patience from many sources in order to help an athlete return to wellness. If you suspect that someone you know has an eating disorder, the first step is to talk with a medical professional, nutritional expert, or counselor who has experience with eating disorders. He or she will be able to help you determine the best way to reach out and help. You can often find specialists through your local hospital or listed in the yellow pages. You do not want to confront or try to help an athlete who may have an eating disorder without the proper support and tools. For the athlete, admitting there is a problem may be scary and difficult to do. You want to make sure you have access to the right resources so that you can get her the help she needs to become healthy. Your role, whether you are a parent, coach, or teammate, is to be supportive, no matter what. Here is a list of dos and don'ts when working with an athlete who you fear might have an eating disorder.

- Don't judge the athlete or her behavior.
- Do provide unconditional support.
- Don't confront the athlete and accuse her of being sick.
- Do express your concern for her happiness, health, and well-being.
- Don't lose touch with her when she begins to seek treatment.
- Do stay in contact, even if the athlete cannot train or compete for a while.
- Don't let an athlete continue to participate if you feel she is at risk until you have medical clearance.
- Do support the athlete and let her know that getting healthy is the road back to great performance.
- Do understand your own assumptions and prejudices regarding weight.
- Don't recommend dietary changes or weight changes without the assistance of a qualified athletic trainer, medical doctor, or dietician.
- Don't overemphasize weight in training or competition discussions, particularly with young developing athletes.
- Do emphasize nutrition education and healthy eating patterns.
- Don't make an individual's weight a public issue on a team, for good or bad.

- Don't assume that lower weight or body fat will enhance performance.
- Do understand the psychological connection with food, weight, and eating.
- Do know the signs and symptoms of disordered eating.
- Do provide accurate information about nutrition, healthy weight, and performance.
- Do emphasize performance and health risks of low body weight.
- Do refer to a trained specialist in disordered eating issues.
- Don't banish the athlete from the team, but don't let her continue to harm herself, either.
- Do model healthy eating and watch how you talk about weight and eating behavior (don't put yourself down for weight concerns).

RECOMMENDED RESOURCES

Interested in learning about women's cycling organizations and cycling gear? Looking to connect with other women who share your passion for riding? Many companies and groups are dedicated to female cyclists. Here are just a few of the resources available on the Web:

Adventure Chix, www.alisondunlap.com
Bay Area Women's Cycling Association, www.bawcycling.com
Betty Bike Gear, www.bettybikegear.com
BikeSutra, www.BikeSutra.com
Cycling Sisters (Chicago), http://cyclingsisters.org
Desert Foxes, www.desertfoxescycling.com
Harlot, www.harlotwear.com
Luna Cycles, www.lunabicycles.com
MTBChick.com, www.mtbchick.com
Northwest Women's Cycling, www.nwwc.org
Sweet Pea Bicycles, www.sweetpeabicycles.com
Team Estrogen, www.teamestrogen.com
Team Speed Queen, www.teamspeedqueen.com
Terry Bicycles, www.terry.com
Velo Bellas, www.velobella.org
Velo Girls, www.velogirls.com
Women's Offroad Mountain Bike and Tea Society (WOMBATS), www.wombats.org

13 BEING a PARENT of a
Young Cyclist

Support your children in their efforts, but let them take a high degree of ownership and responsibility.

—Bill and Cindy Schultz, Parents of U23 National
Mountain Bike Champions Sam and Andy Schultz

Ready or not, you are on your way to becoming a cycling parent. Cycling will provide your child with a world of opportunities and experiences. Being a sport parent is a tireless yet very rewarding job. You will provide financial support, transportation to events, time, an occasional positive parental push, and a shoulder to lean on. But perhaps the most important thing that you will be able to give your child is unconditional love and support as he pursues his interests. This chapter will provide you with ideas and information to help you be the best sport parent you can possibly be.

Your child can gain so much from his cycling experience, especially if caring adults are there to help create a healthy environment. Children who participate in sports with the guidance of caring adults have the opportunity to

- Learn an appreciation for lifelong fitness
- Become more self-confident
- Develop team and social skills
- Build character
- Learn how to value their own effort and personal success

In addition to being valuable skills for sport performance, these are the same abilities that will make them successful in adulthood.

In Chapter 14, we will discuss the motto of the American Sports Education Program: "Athletes first, winning second." Using this motto, the

The Essential Elements of Talent Development

Athletic talent cannot be developed unless

- It is valued by society, and most importantly, by you, the parent
- It is recognized and nurtured by caring adults
- There is a place for development to occur
- The athlete has intrinsic motivation (self-pride and satisfaction)
- The athlete has internal discipline (not external discipline enforced by someone else)
- The athlete has a mature personality (or at least a developing one)
- The athlete has caring adults in his or her life

Other key elements include:

- Unconditional support and love from at least one key adult
- Positive push as needed
- Exposure to elite and successful achievers
- Good role models (the more, the better)
- Multiskill emphasis
- Focus on effort and development

emphasis for devo sport is on helping the athlete be all that she can be—physically, socially, psychologically, and emotionally. Coaches are expected to help youth athletes achieve success, but never at the expense of their personal development. As a parent, you, too, will play a starring role in your athlete's development. Your crucial role involves keeping the main emphasis on the development of your young athlete.

Every parent believes his or her child is special. And you are, of course, correct. Every child is a unique individual with talents, skills, and potential different from anyone else's. The key is to help your child feel special while also instilling an understanding of his or her roles and responsibilities in society.

While scientists argue the nature-versus-nurture debate, parents will tell you that both are true. Even identical twins are born with unique personalities. Some kids are naturally more resilient, some are shy, and some are bubbly. This is their nature. The environment around them is crucial to helping them make the most of what nature has given them and for developing the key skills they will need to be successful in life. Since they already have what nature gave them, the focus now should be on how they are nurtured.

It turns out that science can help us in this task. Research into how children learn and develop talent has provided a wealth of information about nurturing growth and talent. Of course, this doesn't mean that it is easy. Still, this information can provide guidance to help you make decisions regarding your child's youth sport experience.

NURTURING YOUR CHILD

Talent blossoms across a continuum that has three phases. These three phases have been labeled the early years, the developing (or middle) years, and the elite years. Even though your child may be well on the road to adulthood by the time he reaches the elite phase, you will play an important role across all of the phases. While the phases are described as "years," this does not indicate a set age or age range for any of them. The early years often occur at a young age when children begin to get involved in organized activities, but it can also describe the new days when someone has just discovered a sport. The developing or middle years occur when a child or young adult becomes more serious about participation and about athletic pursuits. Not all athletes go beyond this phase, but in a healthy environment this decision will be by choice.

The Early Years

In the initial phase of talent development, or the early years, children need to be introduced to lots of different experiences. Successful elite athletes indicate that when they were young, influential adults such as parents and grandparents provided them with a variety of opportunities. These individuals were also very involved in their children's activities. They attended practices and competitions and played supportive roles in their sport activities. The emphasis was on having fun, and there was no pressure placed on the child or the sport performance.

As children move out of the early years (and there is no time limit on these things), they will begin to express more interest in some activities over others. As their interest grows, parents can help to make sure the emphasis is now placed on skill development and mastery of skills. Parents should stay involved; in fact, staying actively involved without being overly involved is very important. Positive involvement still includes attending events and helping out with volunteer duties. You don't have to be proficient in the activity itself—for example, if your child is into swimming or BMX racing, you don't have to be a great swimmer or cyclist. Let your child's interests and efforts guide her participation. And when possible, let her begin to take responsibility for her participation. You can help by putting your child in charge of filling out race applications for you to sign or by asking your child to research travel directions before going to races. Remember, this is your child's activity, and her development, psychological as well as physical, is the number one priority.

The Middle Years

The middle years involve a phase when some children persist in an activity and others lose interest. What causes this? It turns out that the key factor for a child's continued participation in an activity throughout the middle years is whether the participation continues to be fun. This isn't the same kind of fun that children experience with activities in the early years. The definition of fun in the middle years will make a subtle shift, with the help of parents and coaches. During this phase, the young person will learn how to take personal satisfaction in his achievements. Pride in effort develops. This internal sense of accomplishment becomes the key motivation and part of how the young person defines fun. Parents can help their athletes develop the healthy mindset and approach that will sustain them in whatever activity they choose to pursue by emphasizing growth, development, and personal enjoyment in athletic endeavors.

A lot of kids don't participate in sports beyond the middle years. They discontinue their involvement for a variety of reasons, even with a fantastic sport experience. In adolescence, kids discover all sorts of new possibilities and options. They learn more about themselves and begin to look for ways to explore and express their individuality. Many young men and women leave activities they enjoyed because they discover dating, driving, and the power of making their own money. This doesn't mean that the sports experiences were wasted. A healthy youth sport experience will have provided the skills necessary to be successful in other activities—teamwork skills, ability to practice and persevere to reach a goal, and other positive results of participating in athletics will be transferable to other areas of life. Early participation in sports also makes it more likely that an individual will remain physically active, even if it isn't in an organized sport. If your child decides to pursue other interests, you can be sure that a positive youth sport experience will always serve him well. The goal of parents and coaches should be to see that a young athlete leaves a sport because something else seems shinier, not because that sport has lost its shine.

Leaving the Door Open

Many youth athletes who leave a sport, particularly those who had a positive experience, will return to it at some point in their future. Some may leave for a while to pursue other interests or experiences, but a positive, strong youth sport experience can leave a positive mark on an individual that lasts a lifetime.

A developmental sport experience that puts more pressure on a young athlete than she can handle, or that emphasizes winning over all else, or that is no longer enjoyable, will lead to dropout or burnout. A burned-out athlete may not quit right away, but her attitude, level of enjoyment, and performance will suffer. If your child is going through this type of burnout, she may continue to participate out of fear of angering or disappointing you. If caught early, burnout can sometimes be reversed, but it is always a challenge. The worst part of a negative youth sport experience is the lifelong effect it can have. In some cases, it can affect long-term attitudes about physical activity and competition.

In the middle years, it is important to let your child's enthusiasm be the guide while you remain the voice of reason. You cannot create a drive to pursue sports that just isn't there. Don't try to be the competitive force for your child. This almost always backfires. On the flip side, some young athletes chomp at the bit to do more and more, and their parents are worried that it's too much. It can be hard to know where to draw the line. In cases like this, parents should take their child's skills (emotional as well as physical) and long-term development into consideration and weigh the costs and benefits of the situation at hand. Your child may be able to handle a century ride, or hang in a Testosterone Tuesday ride, but what kind of load does that place on a developing body? Consult with a knowledgeable Juniors coach or sports medicine specialist to determine appropriate training and racing volume guidelines for your growing athlete to ensure long-term health and wellness.

Siblings and Talent

If you have more than one child, talent development can be a more complex equation. Help each child develop his or her own identity, even if both children are in the same sport. Avoid comparisons, which only leads to competition that pits one against the other, or sets only one up to be successful. Instead, help each see the other as a personal cheering section, offering the kind of support that is unique to family. Help them challenge each other in positive ways, teach each other, and learn from each other. A little competition between siblings isn't necessarily a bad thing, provided that it is done in good humor and that both siblings are comfortable with it. Above all, make sure they know that each family member is valued and important for who she is, not what she accomplishes.

Somewhere along the line during the middle years, the issue of specialization may come up. It is important to carefully weigh the pros and cons of focusing on just one thing at a young age. The decision to specialize needs to be made on a case-by-case basis. For an athlete who is still developing skills and learning the ins and outs of the sport, doing multiple activities is a great way to ensure balanced physical development and a well-rounded sense of self. A person is worth more than just his or her physical accomplishments. Knowing this at a deep level is a key element of a healthy sense of self-confidence that can withstand the occasional frustrations associated with competition. So, on the one hand, you don't want to push your child too hard into one activity to the exclusion of all others. And if you see your child becoming so obsessed with cycling—or one discipline within cycling—that other aspects of his or her development are suffering, it's time to gently intervene.

Athletes who specialize in a sport at an early age, particularly those who are at the front of the growth curve, often experience a lot of success. This can be a great ride and lots of fun. However, experience tells us that these same kids typically do not ultimately succeed at the elite level. Some find new interests to pursue and drop out of sports, but more often than not, athletes who are successful early are not well equipped to handle competition as their peers catch up and the playing field levels out.

But Mom, I'm a Cyclist!

Teenagers struggle with many things, including creating a sense of identity. Developing a healthy, balanced sense of self includes feeling worthy and competent. Teens also need to feel like they fit in. Identifying strongly as an athlete is a great advantage for pursuing the sport of cycling. Some young athletes may focus on cycling as their sole source of who they are, which can have them flying high when things go well, but can lead to many issues when things aren't going so well. The time for concern comes when your child's happiness or mood seems to depend solely on his performance in practice or competition. As a parent, remember to praise effort over outcome; let your unconditional support and love for your child and all her activities shine. Enlisting the help of a sport psychology consultant can help your young athlete develop a healthy sense of balance.

The Elite Years

After successfully navigating the middle years, an athlete who is interested in pursuing his or her talent will move from local competition to the elite level. In cycling, the move to the elite ranks is often signified by an earned license upgrade to a category 2 on the road or track or to a semipro ranking on the mountain bike. In addition to racing at a higher level of competition, in the elite years athletes have an opportunity to race in bigger, longer events, with more at stake.

In the elite years, athletes are self-driven and self-motivated. Their main efforts center on being a student of their sport and being a 24/7 athlete. Although athletes may also be students or employees during these years, the majority of their efforts are focused on supporting their athletic goals. Individuals in the elite years of their sport often follow a very different path from their nonathletic classmates, but they do so willingly and without a sense of loss. Keep in mind that many athletes may stay in the middle or developmental phase of cycling without ever graduating to the more intense elite years. As we will see, moving into the elite years should be carefully considered; in order for the experience to be a positive one with the best possible chance for success, the early and middle years need to be carefully constructed and supported.

If a strong effort and climate of skill and mastery were established in the middle years, and if the theme of intrinsic motivation (personal pride and self-satisfaction) was emphasized, athletes will be able to continue emphasizing them. As a parent, it is important that you remain involved at the start of and throughout the elite years of competition, although it is likely that you will now be more of a spectator and less of a chauffeur, gear washer, and head chef.

For young cyclists, true elite-level competition is rarely available until the very end of the Junior years (typically 18 and older), except at the highest international competitions. However, this does *not* mean that all young cyclists should move to the elite level just because they are 17, or even because they are nearing the end of high school or moving into the U-23 Espoir category. The move to the elite level also should not be assumed just because an athlete has earned the minimum points required to move up to the next race level (category 2 or higher for road and track and semi-pro for mountain biking). This is particularly true for athletes under the age of 18 or with less than two or three years of riding experience.

The decision to move to higher, more intense competition and into the elite phase must be carefully considered. Because of the ego element, many athletes rush to get the minimum points needed to upgrade as soon as possible. As a result, young riders start to race at a level that is far above them physically, emotionally, and in terms of their maturity and commitment level. Before athletes decide to cut out other activities and invest their time, finances, and energy in pursuing elite competition at a higher level, parents, coaches, and athletes should weigh the pros and cons. Most Junior and Espoir coaching experts recommend that young cyclists not take the category upgrade until they have earned enough points for a mandatory upgrade (see the USA Cycling rulebook for details on category upgrade points). This move requires emotional maturity and social skills as well as physical strength and race smarts.

Keep in mind that doing well in a few large competitions does not mean a young athlete is ready to transition to the level or lifestyle of elite competition. It is also crucial that the decision to make that investment and enter an elite phase of competition be made by the person who will be investing the most—the young athlete. Parents and coaches should carefully monitor their own behavior and expectations to ensure they do not overtly or inadvertently put undue pressure on a young athlete who is not yet ready, capable enough, or willing to make the investment necessary to compete in the elite phase. This is a recipe for disappointment, a sense of failure, and potentially disaster.

Once your child is beyond high school and at the U-23 level or in university sports, no matter what level of competition or investment he has made, your level of involvement will probably taper off a bit, especially if travel issues make it difficult for you to attend events. Obviously, you will not be as involved on a day-to-day basis once your child has moved away from home. However, even as your child transitions into competing as an adult, you can continue to be a great source of encouragement and unconditional support. No matter how old or how elite your child is, the pride in your eyes, your voice, and your words in who he is (not just what he has accomplished) will always be incredibly valuable.

POSITIVE PARENTAL PUSH

When researchers examine the developmental paths of successful people in business, sports, music, and science, they nearly always find that parents play a crucial role in fostering talent development. The most important thing is to give your child unconditional support and love. Parents also teach key lessons, both directly through their words and indirectly through their actions as role models, such as:

- Finish what you started.
- Focus on fun and development over outcome/winning.
- Pull yourself up by your bootstraps.
- Be respectful of your coach, teammates, competitors, and most importantly, yourself.
- Set high standards for yourself and believe you can achieve them.

Once in a while it will be your role to provide a "positive parental push." Being a teenager is hard work, especially for those who are pursuing a goal. While most of their peers are hangin' out, kids who are dedicated to their sport are already living a very structured life. This is especially true of young cyclists, given the hours in the saddle they will put in. As an adult, you know that day-in and day-out structure, even when you are doing something you love, can get tough. For a teenager, managing this can be challenging: Even the most dedicated young athlete can have days when the couch is more inviting than training. It is at times like this that a little positive parental push can make all the difference.

A positive push is that extra little nudge you give your child every once in a while. It is subtle, well timed, and motivated by the needs of your child. There's no exact science to it, and no one can tell you exactly what form it should take. That depends on your personality, your child's temperament, and your relationship. In a way, it's hard to pin down; it's probably easier to look at what it isn't than to define what it is. Here are a few general guidelines:

- A positive push isn't something that is needed all the time. If you are finding that your child is frequently unmotivated to race or train, it's probably time for a serious discussion.
- A positive push isn't based on your dreams for your child. Often parents get starstruck by visions of state titles, college scholarships, and

Olympic rings when their child picks up a sport. Your child may not be as starstruck as you are, however. Be sure the push you give is based on her dreams, not yours.

- A positive push isn't given because you think your child can accomplish more or hasn't done enough. Initiating a positive push for this reason can make your child feel inadequate; a child may feel like he can never satisfy you. It is usually the coach's job to push. Your job is to be proud unconditionally.

- A positive push isn't loud, in one's face, or negative. Remember, it is a *positive* push, not nagging.

Parents can tailor their positive pushes by asking their child, when she is motivated, what they can do to help on those days when getting up at 6 A.M. is tough or when she is dragging on rides.

COACHING AND YOUR CHILD

It can be tempting for parents to want to be alongside their children for every step they take (or mile they ride) in their talent development journey. There are plenty of great examples of elite athletes who did have their parents by their side. Unfortunately, there are many more stories of well-intentioned parents who pushed too hard and hovered too close. These stories rarely get highlighted during the sports hour or featured in glossy magazines. But ask around just a little and you will hear all sorts of stories about kids who never reached their full potential and the parents who thought they were doing what was best but got in the way.

As you contemplate and build your role as a youth sport parent, the most important motto you can adopt is "Athlete first," and the most important question is "What is best for the development of my athlete?" The answer will be different for each child based on his or her stage of development and personality, your personality, the relationship you already have, and the impact on other family members. As with so many other things we have discussed about parenting an athlete, there is no perfect answer here. But the fact that you are thinking about these issues and asking questions will help keep you on the right path.

How to Be a Youth Sport Parent

- Encourage your child to set his or her own goals. Self-selected goals are always the most powerful.
- Be careful not to let your goals or unfulfilled dreams get mixed in with your child's goals. You can support the ambitions of children, but you cannot dream their dreams for them.
- Sincerely praise effort no matter what the outcome is. Effort matters, and persistence and "sticktuitiveness" are wonderful skills to nurture in your child.
- Encourage your young athlete to seek out and face new challenges.
- Make sure your child knows that you value her regardless of her accomplishments, not because of them. This may seem obvious to you, but is it obvious to her?
- Let the coach do his or her job. Constantly adding your two cents' worth on strategies and training theories can confuse your athlete and reduces the coach's ability to be effective. The coach's job is to coach and push. Your job is to support and love unconditionally, and no other role is more important on your child's road to personal success.
- Show your love and pride verbally and nonverbally, both publicly and privately (just be careful not to be too embarrassing or gushing in public, especially with teenagers).
- Provide a positive parental push when necessary. This is an occasional nudge or reminder to help an athlete get through a lapse in motivation or handle a tough spot.
- Back off from time to time. Your young athlete will experience many distractions and stressors before and during a competition—don't be one of them. If you are unsure, ask your child how you can best help.
- Be a role model by having a positive attitude, being physically active, focusing on skill mastery and effort, enjoying life, and being a good sport.
- Proceed with caution, if you coach your own child. It can be difficult for a young person to separate unconditional parental love from coaching attitudes and advice.
- Remember that this experience belongs to your athlete. As a parent, your job is to facilitate this journey. If you are seeking cycling glory, then work for your own Masters title.

You know your child better than just about anyone else. So coaching your child may seem only natural. Coaching a family member presents several unique challenges that you should consider, however. As a parent, you need to provide unconditional love and support; but as a coach, you may at times need to be honest and say things that an athlete might not want to hear. While these role changes may be easy for you to navigate, your child may not be able to distinguish between the two. This can be especially true for younger kids, for those who strive to please you, for overachievers, and for kids with lower self-confidence. Remember that children and even young adults do not think and process information like adults do, no matter how mature they may sometimes act.

As your child becomes more focused on cycling, hiring a coach can be an excellent move. A coach can provide your young athlete with the specific training that is crucial in the middle stage of talent development. A qualified coach (see Chapter 14) has the knowledge and skills necessary to understand the unique needs of the devo athlete, the changing physiology of athletes in this stage of life, and the culture and opportunities available in youth cycling. And another positive adult role model in your child's life can free you up to be unconditionally supportive.

Involve your child in choosing the right coach. You will, of course, be paying the coach, so you need to feel that your money is being well spent, but your child will be the one working with the coach closely, so his preferences and comfort matter here as well. Before you begin to interview coaches, consider your expectations. What are you hoping for in a coach? Then, ask your child what things he likes best about his favorite teachers. This can help guide your search. You probably already have a sense of the type of teacher who inspires and motivates your child to do well. Draw upon this sense of intuition when interviewing potential coaches. Make sure your child has an opportunity to interview the coach as well. Then compare notes before you make a decision.

USA Cycling also provides a coach-finder service on its website (www.usacycling.org) that sorts coaches by level and lets you search by region. In the USAC system, Level 3 coaches are club or beginning-level coaches who have passed a base exam. Level 2 coaches have done further training and passed the Level 2 exam. Level 1 is the highest. These

Key Questions to Ask a Potential Coach

When seeking out a coach for your child, both of you could start by asking other parents and Junior cyclists about the coaches they know and have worked with. What did they like about them, and what did they not like? Check the USAC website to find qualified coaches in your area and ask at your local bike shop for recommendations. Then be sure to interview several coaches to get a sense of different approaches and personalities. Don't assume that someone is the best coach for your child just because he or she has worked with a successful Junior. Here are other tips for the interview:

- Find out about the coach's training and educational background. Do your homework to confirm that the coach has the credentials he or she claims to have.
- Ask about coaching philosophy, especially as it pertains to Junior development. A coach who can't tell you what he or she believes in, or who only talks about winning, is not the best choice for a devo athlete.
- Ask whether the coach has a current USA Cycling license or is licensed by some other organization.
- Make sure the coach has passed a background check. (In order to obtain a USAC coaching license, coaches must first pass a background check; if the coach does not have a USAC coaching license, you may want to consider running a simple background check yourself. Many organizations offer background checks for around $25–$30.)
- Ask the coach about his or her riding history. Having been an elite rider does not automatically mean someone will be a good coach, but it's still an important consideration.

coaches must have at least five years of experience and further training before passing the Level 1 test. Additionally, USA Cycling offers a special certification in power-based coaching, which indicates that a coach has demonstrated a high level of competency in using power and power meter training methodologies.

When you interview coaches, be sure to talk about their coaching philosophy and see if it matches up with your beliefs. Do you agree on key points? And for the things you don't see eye to eye on, can you still respect his or her coaching principles? You probably won't agree on every single issue, but if you start out with the same basic ideas, most of the details should take care of themselves. If you hire a coach for your son or daughter, it is crucial that you feel you can stand back and let the coach do his or her job. Constantly interfering with, questioning, or contradicting your child's coach, either directly or indirectly, can seriously undermine the coach-athlete relationship and the trust your child develops in the coach.

Just as a coach shouldn't try to be a parent to your child, you should leave the coaching to the person you hired. However, this doesn't mean that you should step out of the picture entirely. You are still responsible for making sure the environment is safe and healthy (and your child still needs your unconditional support). You can do this by observing practice and competitions, paying attention to how your child talks about practice, being alert for behavior changes, and staying in touch with the coach. The following list includes situations or concerns that should raise a red flag. Take action if you notice any of the warning signs. Your response depends on the situation. In some cases, you may want to have a discussion with the coach; other situations may call for more serious intervention. You must not tolerate physical reprimands, use of physical activity as punishment, or verbally abusive or degrading comments, for example. Be on the lookout for:

- Abusive coaching—physical or emotional
- Unrealistic expectations for time commitment, effort, or performance
- Intolerance of involvement in other activities, particularly for a young athlete who has not voluntarily made a commitment to the level of training that the coach seems to expect
- Lack of structure in workouts or long-term training plans
- Lack of appropriate teacher/learner interaction or age-appropriate boundaries
- Lack of individualization in team situations
- Overemphasis on winning over effort and learning
- Poor sportsmanship
- A sudden change in your young athlete's enjoyment or interest in training

Your child's coach is another advocate and role model for your child's development, both as an athlete and as a person. Working together and following the "Athletes first, winning second" model will create a strong, positive learning environment for your child. This nurturing environment won't happen by accident. Strong communication and a professional relationship between you and your child's coach are essential. The bottom line is that you should expect the same guidance and care for your child's well-being from a coach as you would from her teachers at school.

Making the Most of the Coach-Parent Relationship

- Recognize and respect the commitment your child's coach has made to the sport and to your child.
- Allow your athlete and his or her coach to build their own relationship. Discuss your expectations and the boundaries of this with the coach before the professional relationship begins.
- Communicate frequently with the coach. Don't wait until you have a concern or problem to touch base. Set up the boundaries of this communication with the coach so you don't overstep the relationship.
- Don't forget to let the coach know that you appreciate the work he or she is doing. Often we are quick to point out when things go wrong, but we forget to praise when things go well.
- Observe practice (but don't interfere!) whenever possible—especially with younger children.
- If you disagree with the coach, don't put your child in the middle. Deal with the coach privately and in a professional manner. Never ask a child to deliver messages about your concerns.
- Support and reinforce the coach to enhance what your child learns.

COMMUNICATING WITH YOUR CHILD

The term "teen communication" may feel a bit like an oxymoron at times. While the post-child, pre-adult years may not be the easiest to negotiate, good communication techniques can ease the way. As a parent, it is up to you to help create and foster good communication and to guide your teenager. Often we focus on the messages we want to send when we communicate. But sending a message is only a small part of the equation. We need to be sure that our message is sent in such a way that it will be received as we intended. Do your nonverbal signals (voice quality, body language, and so on) match the words you are saying? Saying you are proud does not ring true if your voice seems sarcastic, your body posture indicates frustration or anger, or you seem distracted. Watch carefully to see if your message was received as you intended, and follow up with open-ended questions to be sure your child understands what you were trying to get across, especially if the message is really important or contains instructions.

Many times, the most effective communication occurs when you don't say anything at all. Listening is one of the most powerful communication tools that we have. And proper, active listening is actually an art. When you listen, really listen, it is important that you not be distracted by other tasks. But sometimes, especially with adolescents, they are most comfortable talking when the situation isn't face-to-face. Side by side in the car, in the kitchen when prepping dinner, and in the garage when you are doing bike maintenance are all excellent times to listen. It is always tempting to share our wisdom, but one of the best ways to learn about the needs of teenagers is to hear what wisdom they are generating for themselves. Encourage your child to share by asking about his or her opinions, using open-ended questions, and reflecting back what you learn.

Of course, as a parent, you will need to share criticisms and critiques occasionally. Being unconditionally supportive doesn't mean not correcting and guiding. The key to effective and meaningful feedback is in the delivery. If all of your comments are criticisms and critiques, it can be hard for your child to separate the actual message from the culture of disapproval. Even though you mean them in the very best way, corrections have a way of putting people on the defensive or of being misinterpreted. Make sure your critiques are focused on behaviors that can be changed and not aimed at who your child is. Try saying, "It looked like the corners in today's race were tough. How did they feel to you?" rather than "You are a lousy cornerer."

Key Communication Points

We all communicate each and every day, but that doesn't mean we do it well or effectively. Like everything else, good communication skills are the result of practice and hard work. The following tips are designed to help you enhance your ability to communicate effectively with everyone, even teenagers.

- *Listen!* One of the most empowering things you can do is listen. Develop an interest in finding out what your child has to say. People feel important and valued when they know someone else is listening to them.
- *Ask rather than tell.* You have raised a smart child. Kids feel empowered when you let them share what they know, think, and experience.
- *Practice good attention.* Avoid multitasking when talking to your athlete. Perceived lack of interest is a sure way to shut down communication.
- *Let your athlete lead.* Keep in mind that the emotional age of a child may not match his or her chronological age. Keep the child's communication level in mind, and remember, you are the adult in the relationship.
- *Connect through activity.* Very few people, especially adolescents, are comfortable with one-on-one, face-to-face talks. How about riding with your child during the warm-up or cool-down or on a recovery day? If you are not comfortable cycling, choose some other activity you can enjoy together. Even painting the house side by side or walking the dog can help to foster communication.
- *Praise the good stuff.* Don't forget to tell your child what you like, what you are proud of, and what was well done. Kids need to hear these things said out loud. Don't just assume they know.

If you create a positive learning environment, it will be much easier for your child to accept constructive criticism when it is needed. Experts suggest that most people (adults as well as children) need to receive five positive messages for every one criticism in order for the learning environment (and relationship) to remain positive. This doesn't mean that you have to count or keep track. The positives can be both verbal and nonverbal, so hugs and smiles count toward creating that positive environment. Keep in mind that if your child has a coach, it's the coach's job to provide critique and criticism about cycling. You can help create a better learning environment by adding positives to the environment. In this way, you can help to balance out the working part of the relationship the coach is focused on.

How to Give Feedback

Everyone needs feedback: An employee needs it to improve in a job; a student needs it to learn; and cyclists—even at the top—need it to keep building their cycling skills. But the time is not always right for feedback. Here are some other tips to make feedback appropriate:

- First, ask yourself, "Am I an expert on this?" or "Am I qualified to give advice in this matter?"
- Avoid nonteachable moments. Your message will be lost if the timing is wrong. The drive home after a race might not be the best time to chat.
- Ask first if your child is ready to talk. Allow your athlete a chance to say "No, not right now," or "Sure, I'm ready to listen." Then respect his or her choice.
- Communicate useful, improvement-focused information rather than pointing out faults or errors. Just saying "That was wrong" is not helpful. Provide specific guidance, and if you can't, either don't say anything or work together to find the answers.
- Give criticisms and/or critiques in private. No one likes to be called out in a group or in front of friends or people they admire.

As a parent, it is only natural to want to help and nurture your child as much as possible. Keep in mind that your role is to be unconditionally supportive. It is your coach's job to provide feedback and criticism. Too much from you and it may undermine your ability to be the supportive parent your child needs.

THE JUNIOR CYCLIST AND SCHOOL

Unless your child's school is year-round, competition will not require a lot of missed class time. However, as your child progresses in cycling, training time will increase, and as training increases through high school, so will your child's academic workload. Set clear academic expectations and standards for your child to ensure that his studies do not suffer. No matter how far cycling takes someone in life, the value of a solid education cannot be overemphasized. Instill the importance of being a disciplined student athlete. For a young person, being successful in school is part of being a truly successful competitor.

In addition to academics, school affords many extracurricular and social opportunities. Encourage your child to explore and pursue different interests; after all, high school happens only once. Theater performances, band, debate club, and the yearbook or student newspaper staff all provide valuable life skill–development opportunities. Additionally, there are dances to go to, community service projects to do, and other social opportunities to be part of. Help your child weigh the pros and cons of different activities and encourage her not to miss out on these worthwhile experiences.

Finally, some high schools offer cycling as a sports option, but most do not. If your child has an interest in participating in multiple sports, do not let his cycling coach or school coach discourage this. Multisport participation can balance an athlete's physical strengths and provide a mental break from the demands of cycling. At the same time, help your athlete balance his schedule so he is not overbooked and stressed-out. And as always, the decision to specialize in cycling should be your athlete's decision only after careful consideration.

Even Elite Athletes Have to Bring in the Trash

Athletes, no matter how talented, are most successful when they are well grounded. One of my favorite stories is of the young Olympian who, returning home with his first gold medal, discovered that it was his turn to take out the trash. Help your children to keep their talents and strengths in perspective. Yes, they have skills that make them special, but so does everyone else. Some people can win bike races; others can teach, or sell, or bring people together with their leadership or diplomacy skills. This is a very valuable lesson to learn.

ENHANCING YOUR CHILD'S SELF-CONFIDENCE

With a healthy dose of self-confidence, a young person can both feel good about herself at a deep level and achieve her personal best. Some individuals naturally have a better sense of self-confidence than others, but the teenage years are enough to shake even the most self-confident among us. If your child lacks confidence in her abilities, she will be tentative and conservative and have higher levels of anxiety, all of which can undermine her ability to train or race well. If he is overconfident, he may actually be cocky, not confident. This means he is overestimating his abilities and may be improperly prepared for the challenge ahead. As a parent, you can help create an environment that will foster healthy self-confidence in your young athlete.

You are in an excellent position to identify and deal with small self-confidence issues before they grow into bigger problems. Think about the following:

- Does my teen seem to have excessive concerns regarding other people's beliefs in her? Does she seem overly concerned about what the coach thinks, what I think, or what other key adults think? (For example, does she wonder, "What will Mom and Dad think if I don't win?")
- Does my teen seem to believe that a problem or mistake in one area (for example, hill climbing) is a fatal flaw or a sign of lack of worth?
- Does he have self-doubts regarding his ability? (For example, does he ask, "Can I really do this?")
- Does she compete not to fail rather than to achieve or improve?
- Does he worry about the outcome (winning) rather than the performance (making a strong personal effort)?

Some of these questions may be hard to answer because you cannot read your child's mind. It is important to listen closely to how she talks about racing and to ask open-ended questions to learn more about her feelings. If what a child is saying is negative, or you think the answer to some of the questions in the list above might be yes, it doesn't automatically mean there is a serious problem with your child's self-confidence. It might, however, indicate that this is an area worth discussing and watching. Unfortunately, the things athletes say to themselves are often far worse than what they ever say out loud, so listen carefully with a supportive, nonjudgmental ear.

Every rider experiences lapses in confidence from time to time. Fluctuations are normal, but as a parent you can help ensure these normal dips don't become bigger holes. Consider your language and your own confidence level. It is important that you set an example by talking the talk and walking the walk. If you put yourself or your own abilities down, it will be hard for your athlete to learn to value himself.

Parenting: Athlete Self-Confidence

- Use language focusing on skill growth rather than deficiencies.
- Encourage positive thinking and practice it yourself.
- Help your athlete be honest and realistic with herself.
- Focus on performance accomplishments, not just outcome, and encourage the athlete to identify them.
- Let your athlete know it is okay to doubt himself or be nervous sometimes.
- Model confidence through your language and actions.

As a parent, you have certain expectations for your child and his actions. Even when you don't tell him what you expect, your child knows that you expect something. When these expectations are unclear, unspoken, or misunderstood, kids often err on the side of assuming you have harsh and unrealistic expectations. Clearly and frequently discuss what you expect in terms of effort, sportsmanship, and other behaviors that are important to you. If all you talk about is winning, then your child may overemphasize this area as well.

RECOMMENDED READING AND RESOURCES
Great Books for Parents
Champions Are Raised Not Born: How My Parents Made Me a Success, by Summer Sanders (Delacorte Press, 1999).

Good Sports: The Concerned Parents' Guide to Competitive Youth Sport, 2nd ed., by Rick Wolff (Sagamore Publishing, 1997).

Motivated Minds: Raising Children to Love Learning, by Deborah Stipek and Kathy Seal (Holt Paperbacks, 2001).

Positive Coaching: Building Character and Self-Esteem Through Sports, by Jim Thompson (Warde, 1995).

Raising Winners: A Parent's Guide to Helping Kids Succeed, by Shari Kuchenbecker (Three Rivers Press, 2000).

Why Johnny Hates Sports, by Fred Engh (Square One, 2002).

Key Youth Sport Organizations

Center for Sports Parenting, www.sportsparenting.org

Institute for the Study of Youth Sports, http://ed-web3.educ.msu.edu/ysi

Mom's Team, www.momsteam.com

Positive Coaching Alliance, www.positivecoach.org

14 COACHING JUNIOR and *Espoir Riders*

Besides racing, kids also have to be kids—they have to be hungry when they get
to the race.

—Dag Selander, father of Bjorn Selander, 2004 Junior National Cross Champion

Coaching Junior and Espoir riders can be very exciting and rewarding.
In French, *espoir* means "hope," a fitting description of the potential and
power of these young racers. However, with this opportunity also comes
responsibility. Coaching young men and women puts you in an important role in their lives, and it is part of your job to live up to that. Coaching has always been about more than just the X's and O's, the miles and
the tactics of when to attack. And in the case of devo riders, it is even
more important that you, as a coach, recognize the potential power of
your role. If you are mindful of what you are doing, you have a great
opportunity to help the young men and women you work with become
successful. Not all of them will go on to win Junior nationals or get Senior
pro contracts, but you will help them develop the skills to be successful,
and you can help them develop a lifelong love of cycling and being physically active. In this chapter we'll explore some things that devo coaches
should consider beyond the workouts.

SO YOU WANT TO COACH JUNIORS

The coach who decides to oversee the development of a young rider has
a lot more to think about than just training. No matter how talented they
are or mature they seem, young riders are not mini-adults on bikes. And
unlike adult riders, Juniors often come with one or more parental figures
attached. Successful devo coaches learn how to consider and work with
these additional variables. See Table 14.1 for a list of things that happen
to adolescents during this developmental stage.

Key Talent Development Tips for Coaches

- No matter how talented, precocious, or enthusiastic a young athlete seems to be, avoid pushing too hard or placing emphasis on outcome during the early years. The emphasis should be on a strong foundation based on enjoyment of the sport and skill development.
- When working with devo athletes, be mindful of all aspects of their development. Can they handle success and the frustration of failure? Do they know what it takes to achieve their best performance? What about developing skills and tactics? Contact USA Cycling for their guidelines on coaching young athletes and the key skills they need to acquire.
- Always individualize. No two athletes, even those from the same family, are exactly the same or have the same needs. Adjust your approach and training plans accordingly.
- Because of the individual nature of the sport of cycling, the athlete gets more out of a coaching experience if there is a good fit between the coach and the athlete in terms of personality and style. What you have to teach should match up with what the athlete needs to learn. Before taking on a new athlete, ideally you should sit down for an interview with the child and the parent. They may not know what to ask you in order to find out whether you will be the right coach for them. You can help them out by telling them about your coaching philosophy and methods. Find out about the athlete's needs and prior experience in cycling. Listen carefully to the answers (or lack of answers) from both the parent and the athlete. If possible, speak to each one individually. Be clear about how you work and how the coaching relationship will be structured. Will you explain the training plan to both parent and athlete? Will you speak to both of them with the same frequency? If you feel you are not the right coach for an athlete because his or her needs don't match up with your methods or skills, be frank about this, in a positive way, and help them find a coach who will be a better fit.

The emphasis of youth sport coaching should always be "Athletes first, winning second," a motto made popular by the ASEP, the American Sport Education Program. This message is also espoused by the Positive Coaching Alliance, a nonprofit group that focuses on improv-

TABLE 14.1	Key Areas of Junior Development
Physical	• Onset of puberty • Rapid physical growth • Changes in fat, muscle mass, bone length, etc.
Motor skills	• Moving from general to specific interests • Improving fitness and motor skills • Greater differences among individuals due to growth
Intellectual	• Growing awareness of the world • Beginning to synthesize information and improve critical thinking
Emotional	• Teenage turmoil • Changing parental relationships • Hormonal influence
Psychosocial	• Greater awareness of physical differences • Impact of peer group • Increased desire to fit in • Increase in life and activity options and opportunities

ing the quality of the youth sport experience. The PCA also emphasizes being a "double goal coach," with the key goals being the development and well-being of the athlete first and winning second. With this approach, coaches are always aware of the importance of working with individuals and putting their health and wellness (physical, psychological, and social) above all else. Competition and winning are still important, but when there is a concern or a choice to be made, the athlete's well-being—both short- and long-term—is considered before any decisions are made. As you read through this chapter, consider how this philosophy matches up with your own beliefs and how it might be reflected in your actions.

Kids Have Rights, Too

Appendix I contains the "Bill of Rights for Young Athletes," an important list of rights that should be guaranteed to every youth who chooses to participate in sports. It is a great document to share with parents. Parents and coaches can work together to ensure that children enjoy these rights.

Sports offer so many opportunities for physical, social, and emotional development. Lots of research has been conducted about what kids can get out of sports, and perhaps the most important of these—as it pertains to you, the coach—is the role you play in making their experience a successful one or a less than successful one. Research on the youth sport environment has provided insight into the potentially positive and negative impacts of sport participation. A well-constructed sport experience will boost a child's self-confidence and teach meaningful skills, such as how to handle both success and failure, how to set goals, how to manage time, and how to discipline oneself and persevere. A sport environment that focuses on winning at the expense of having fun and being a good sport, or that does not support the athlete in his or her overall development, can damage self-esteem and set up a lifelong aversion to physical activity and challenges of all kinds.

As you know, teenagers go through changes in every aspect of their lives as they move from adolescence to young adulthood. What you may not have thought about much is that they develop at very different rates: One 15-year-old may have exceptional motor skills but be at an earlier stage of development emotionally or intellectually. Another may be advanced emotionally, but catching up physically. While all of these changes are going on, it can be very difficult to remember that the boy before you is still a child psychologically, or that the girl who still looks quite young may be very mature in her cognitive skills. Every child develops at his or her own rate, and his or her development in each area will progress at its own rate as well. Figure 14.1 shows how different several athletes of the same age can be at different stages in their development across the various categories.

As you get to know each child through coaching, take note of what you learn about his or her maturity level in different areas. Knowing where each child is developmentally can help you communicate with your charges effectively. You may be surprised by the disparities. For example, one young teenager I worked with had just won a national-level race against a very strong field of Senior riders. He had just entered high school and was quite advanced in his motor skills. Later in the day, when we were discussing various things, he mentioned his love of a popular

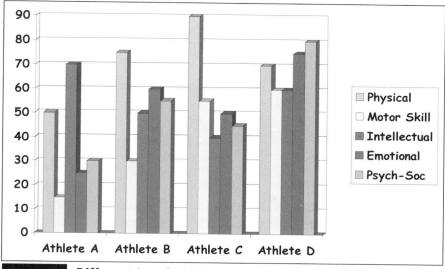

FIGURE 14.1 Different Levels of Development

book series. I was a bit taken aback, as I would have thought this series was too young for him. I expressed my surprise, and the young man responded that of course he loved the series; he looked forward to his mom reading him a chapter each night before bed. It was a strong reminder of the vast differences in maturity levels across the different areas of development. As coaches of Juniors, we always need to keep this variability in mind as we develop training techniques and work with this impressionable population.

Checklist for Coaching Excellence

The statements below have been identified as key points for successful coaching relationships. Consider your relationship with each of your Juniors and answer each one of the questions honestly. If you aren't sure you could honestly say some of these things, these are great places to start if you want to improve your coaching. You might begin by choosing one statement that does not yet reflect you and brainstorming about how you might improve, writing down your ideas on a sheet of paper. Try to think of concrete things you can do to improve in each area. Just as training is a constant process of

(continues)

working to improve, coaching should be a process of striving to find ways to be better and more effective. One of the things that makes great coaches great is the ability to honestly look at themselves and be confident enough to seek ways to improve.

- There is a mutual sense of trust between my athlete and myself.
- I have confidence in my athlete's abilities and I let him know this.
- My athlete has confidence in my abilities as a coach.
- There is good communication between my athlete and myself.
- I take an interest in my athlete beyond her athletic performance.
- There is a good fit between my athlete's personality, style, and needs and mine.
- I have a balance between being strict and kind with my athlete.
- I have a passion for my sport and coaching this athlete.
- I have a professional style with my athlete and his parents.
- I demonstrate my sports knowledge in my coaching.
- I strive to keep my sports knowledge up-to-date.
- I have different goals for each athlete based on her individual strengths and weaknesses.
- I have fun-based goals for this athlete.
- I have developmental-based goals for this athlete.
- I tailor the goals I have for each athlete depending on the stage of his career.
- I expose my athlete to high levels of competition and training.
- I provide a positive training and learning environment for my athlete.
- I provide appropriate challenges for my athlete's skill level and abilities.
- I individualize my approach with this athlete.
- I provide this athlete with unconditional support.
- I am present at practice (both physically and mentally).
- I let my athlete know I am proud of her, not just her accomplishments.
- I support the decisions and goals of this athlete.
- I have high but reasonable expectations for this athlete.
- I am a good role model for healthy skills and characteristics.
- I provide positive and constructive feedback and critique.
- I help my athlete find balance between his sport and life.
- I emphasize high standards in and out of athletics with this athlete.

Source: Modified from D. Gould, K. Dieffenbach, and A. Moffett, "Coaches' Roles in Olympic Championship Development," *Olympic Coach* 12, no. 3 (Spring 2002), 1–9.

COACHING PHILOSOPHIES AND PRINCIPLES

Whether you are just considering coaching devos or you've been working with them for years, take a moment to consider what you believe is important. Do you have a coaching philosophy? Have you taken the time to write down a list of the things you value and that you feel should be a part of the youth sport experience? If not, make one. Simple bullet points are fine. As I tell my students, this isn't English class, so incomplete sentences are fine, but incomplete thoughts aren't. If you have made a list, get it out now and review it. Having a clear, well-designed personal philosophy does several key things: It provides you with a set of personal guidelines that can ground you when you have to make tough decisions; it can help you stay in touch with what matters most (a key factor in avoiding coach burnout); and it provides something you can share with parents to help bring everyone onto the same page.

What will they say?

Take a moment and jot down a few things you would like your athletes to say about you when you retire from coaching. What would you want them to put on your plaque or say at the roast to reflect your work? I'm serious: Write them down.

Now look at your philosophy. Do the two lists line up? Can you think of specific ways you coach or things you do that directly tie in to your philosophy or that you want to be your coaching legacy? If not, brainstorm how you might change this.

Role of the Devo Coach

A devo coach can play a lasting role in the lives of young men and women by helping them develop into happy, healthy adults. Expert devo coaches know that developing champions isn't about finding the perfect athlete; rather it is about helping individual athletes find and develop the champion within themselves. Every athlete, with proper guidance, has the ability to experience personal success, and a healthy sport environment will help her achieve both on and off the bike. Studies of great coaches have found that they have several things in common. In their work with young people, great coaches do the following:

- Emphasize hard work and development
- Create a culture of positive achievement and personal pride
- Directly teach positive mental skills
- Keep an eye on fun
- Facilitate trust
- Encourage and support
- Give constructive criticism
- Model positive skills
- Understand athletes
- Share their enthusiasm and passion
- Understand that it is about the athlete's journey and achievement

Mentor, Role Model, Friend?

Coaches are really teachers. But unlike the traditional teaching setting, which could be summed up by the slogan "I talk while you sit and absorb," coaching is much more dynamic. We talk, interact, and spend more one-on-one quality time with our students than a classroom setting often allows. This environment provides a fantastic opportunity for learning. It also means that the coach-student relationship is often a closer one than the traditional teacher-student relationship. As a coach of young people, you need to recognize the powerful impact this kind of relationship can have on the life of a young person and to handle the dynamics of the relationship properly.

We tend to use the word "friend" casually and for just about everyone we know, whether they are superficial acquaintances or close buddies. But this is a term that really doesn't define your relationship with your athletes very well. In any situation where one person has the more senior position (team manager, employer, coach, teacher, and the like), a "power dynamic" is present. This isn't a bad thing, unless it isn't understood or used properly. In a power dynamic, the participants in the relationship aren't quite on equal footing. Instead, someone is in charge. In a true adult-to-adult friendship, ideally things are equal; both people have similar responsibilities in the friendship. In a situation with a power dynamic, like coaching, where the parties aren't on equal ground, the greater responsibility lies with the one holding the power—in this case, you, the coach. This responsibility is even greater when the athlete is young and the coach is older: It's one thing to hold the power of a coach when your athletes are well into adulthood themselves and have jobs and children of their own; it's another when your athletes are kids and you are an authority figure to them. You need to be aware of the influence you have over your young riders and the decisions they make. You must be sure that they clearly understand you when you communicate with them and that the lines of communication are always open. As your athletes grow up, your relationship with them may grow and evolve into a more true adult friendship, but this takes years to occur.

As a coach, you will be in the unique and sometimes awkward position of being part authority figure, part parent, and possibly part training partner, part counselor, or part confidant to young people who are not only trying to excel in their chosen sport but also trying to figure out who they are becoming. That can be pretty intense for both of you. Athletes will look to you for reassurance, advice, recognition, and approval. To them you are in a different category from teachers and parents: They will often see you more as a friend and someone they can "talk to about stuff." This isn't a bad thing, but it does mean that you have special responsibilities in the relationship. While it is tempting to promise confidentiality, keep in mind that if you are working with minors, this is not a good idea. Recognize that you will, at times, struggle with issues of trust, confidentiality, conflicts of interest, and possibly even athlete well-being and safety. Be sure to make it clear to athletes that you have a responsibility to make sure they are safe. You should also address this issue with your athletes' parents. Let them know what your principles are on confidentiality. While a certain amount of day-to-day confidentiality is important to help build athlete trust, you need to be clear with both the athlete and the parents that there are certain topics and issues that may impact an athlete's safety or well-being that you would have to share.

Setting clear boundaries and determining the scope of the coaching relationship you are comfortable with from the beginning will reduce problems that can arise from confusion over multiple roles. Think about potential role conflicts and how you might handle them. For example, if an athlete wants to confide in you about his relationship with his girlfriend, are you comfortable with this? If not, be a resource guide, pointing him (or nudging him) in the direction of those who are better equipped to help. Talk to other Juniors coaches about how they have handled these types of dilemmas, and work to build a network of professionals in other fields with whom you can consult on tough issues. Be open and up-front with your Junior athlete and with her parents about the job and the roles that go along with being a coach. This will not only help everyone better understand your role as a coach, but also foster the kind of trust necessary for a successful coaching relationship.

Terms that *do* apply very well to the coaching situation are "role model" and "mentor." Have you considered how you fill these roles? Being a role model means doing and being the things you want to see in your athletes. If you are still racing and you are a nervous wreck before races, what does your athlete see? If you talk about goal setting and emphasize process, but after a race all you talk about is winning, what message does that send? Consider carefully what it means to be a role model and how much the little things you do matter, even when you don't have your official coach hat on.

Being a mentor is the heart of teaching or coaching. You decide that you want to be a part of the lives of the young people in your charge, and you choose to actively guide them. You must understand whom you are guiding. This means you must understand the special developmental and other challenges of adolescents in general, and get to know each athlete as an individual with his or her own unique challenges and concerns. You must also understand your own strengths and weaknesses. All of this will give you the information you need to provide the guidance and structure that each individual needs. This can be a challenge when you work one-on-one with athletes, and it can feel impossible when you have a whole team to handle. But be patient. Being a great coach is not about being perfect. Great coaches develop over time and are always learning.

To have successful Junior coaching relationships, you must practice what you preach. Kids are very sharp; as anyone who has ever sworn around 4-year-olds knows, they pick up on, repeat, and emulate everything you say or do. Teenagers and young adults are no different. They notice what we say and do—including all the subtle and glaring inconsistencies between what we say and what we do—with sometimes embarrassing accuracy. Pay close attention to being consistent with your actions and words. If your coaching philosophy extols the virtues of performance efforts, yet all you praise or talk about is winning, then your athletes will believe that what really matters is whether or not they win, no matter what you say your philosophy is. You also need to be aware of how you treat your young athlete in different situations. Inconsistencies in different settings (for example, treating the athlete like an adult in one-on-one situations, but treating her like a child around parents) will undermine the trust you are trying to build and compromise the nature of the coaching relationship. Make it a habit to strive to be the type of athlete and person you would like your young charges to become someday.

Provide Other Role Models

Elite athletes often say that exposure at an early age to successful athletes inspired them and helped them to succeed. When young hopefuls see higher-level athletes compete live—or meet them in person—they are able to see that these heroes are really just people after all, which means that their own dream is achievable. If at all possible, set up situations where your athletes can meet elite cyclists, talk with them, and ask questions. Check local race schedules in your region well in advance to see what opportunities might be coming up. If a great cyclist is coming to your area to compete, he or she may be willing to set aside some time to inspire your team. Keep in mind that "elite" is relative, and it is not necessary to rub shoulders with Olympians for young athletes to get inspired.

What to Do If an Athlete Confides Something Serious

Suppose an athlete trusts you so much that he decides to confide in you about a serious issue—like confusion over sexuality, sexual abuse, eating disorders, sexual assault, anxiety, or one of a wide range of other concerns and problems that teenagers encounter. This is not uncommon, given the kind of relationship that develops in a coach-athlete situation. But the fact that it is not uncommon does not make it easy to know what to do. Remember, you do not have to go it alone when dealing with these things. And if you are not a licensed or certified counselor, you should not even consider going it alone. Keep in mind that you may have legal obligations as well, depending on the situation. In situations of abuse, you may be legally obligated to report it to the proper authorities, and trying to handle a problem alone that you are not qualified to handle may have serious legal repercussions. Seek counsel from individuals who specialize in the area of concern before you proceed. Not all situations will require intervention or outside counsel, but seeking advice confidentially is never a bad idea. When in doubt, ask a professional, such as an attorney or qualified counselor. Whatever you do, if a young athlete comes to you for help or advice, do not ignore the situation or hope it will just go away. The athlete's trust in you is a very valuable gift, but it is also very fragile and should be protected. As you proceed, follow these guidelines for handling serious and/or uncomfortable situations:

- Encourage your athletes to speak to their parents or an appropriate person at their school.
- Help them seek out the appropriate resources.
- Don't judge the situation.
- Don't try to solve the problem for them.
- Don't cut yourself off from young athletes. They trusted you enough to confide in you, and your unconditional support will be very important. This is even more important if athletes get outside help or must leave the sport for a while.

Seek out professionals who can provide you with advice and guidance before you decide how to handle a difficult situation. A list of qualified advisers with whom you can consult will be a valuable tool in all sorts of situations.

Coaching Champions

People often assume that great coaches have either a special talent for sniffing out talent or some secret formula for developing it. When we study great coaches across sports, we find that these men and women actually do have special knowledge. They have figured out how to help individuals make the most of the talents they have, and they treat all their athletes with respect. This provides the ideal environment for cultivating talent and allowing great things to happen.

Dr. Benjamin Bloom, an expert in talent development, has divided athletic development into three phases. Coaches can play an important role in all three. First is the early phase. This is the phase when beginners get introduced to a sport, and ideally to many sports. They are free to have fun and explore, and few training restrictions are set. As a cycling coach, you normally wouldn't be coaching young folks in this phase. You may, however, have the opportunity to run camps, clinics, and even kids' races that are geared toward providing them with early skill-development opportunities and a chance to fall in love with a sport. In some cases, you could be working with young children who literally have never ridden a bike before—in families where both parents work, taking time to teach children how to ride a bike and then practice with them is becoming surprisingly rare. You may also encounter individuals who have never had an opportunity to own a bike because they live in an area where riding isn't a safe or available option. When working with children in this age group, make sure the structure and activities are age-appropriate. Take into account their typical attention span and physical skill level, and provide plenty of encouragement. Help each young person feel successful.

From the early phase, athletes move into the middle years, or developmental phase. Even with fantastic experiences, not all kids move from the early to middle phase in the same sport. But positive early experiences will set a solid foundation for whatever they move on to next. The majority of Junior and Espoir riders you encounter will be in the middle years of their talent development. Your knowledge and expertise will provide skill, tactical, and technical guidance. You will also, as we noted, be a mentor and role model for the their overall development. It is natural for some young athletes to lose interest in this phase as the world opens up around them, but more often than not, when they burn out or drop out during this phase it is because the sport is no longer fun. You can prevent this outcome by helping athletes develop a sense of pride and satisfaction in their achievements and by maintaining some of the youthful fun of the sport. Keep in mind that even if young people leave cycling, you have been successful if they leave because something else seems more exciting, and not because cycling has lost its luster. And if you have helped them develop healthy skills and self-confidence that they can use throughout life, you have certainly made a worthwhile contribution.

Young athletes, today more than ever, are involved in lots of different activities. School programs, band, art, theater, Scouts, and often multiple sports crowd their schedules. Although it is during the middle years when young riders start to specialize, it is important for coaches and parents to be careful about the timing of this specialization. Young athletes who specialize too soon are more likely to experience burnout and other problems or to leave the sport permanently. Studies of elite athletes in the U.S. national ski program found that skiers who specialized later in their young lives had longer adult sport careers. Specialization should be the choice of the athlete, and it is up to parents and coaches to make sure that the athlete maintains a healthy, well-balanced sense of self. Individuals with a limited sense of self—in this case, a sense of self that is dependent on athletic performance—will experience more negative short- and long-term stress and difficulties when in a performance slump or when injured.

Research tells us it takes many years, possibly ten or more, to truly develop talent. We also know that in cycling, physical talent takes many seasons of riding to build. The third and final stage of the talent development journey is the elite phase. During the elite years athletes move to the next level of competition and involvement. Most athletes have specialized toward the end of their middle years. As they transition into the elite years, other life activities will take a backseat to the primary sport. These other interests do not disappear. They are excellent off-season activities and can play a crucial role in keeping athletes fresh and balanced by providing in-season breaks. Encouraging your athletes to maintain a healthy, balanced sense of self and activities, even in their elite years, can help to set them up for a long, healthy career. As a coach, you may move from the teacher role to more of an advisory role as athletes become more invested in their training.

Bloom's Three Phases of Talent Development

Dr. Benjamin Bloom, author of *Developing Talent in Young People*, has described three stages of talent development. He discusses different types of talent: athletic, musical, artistic, and even the talents of top scientists and mathematicians. Here's a summary of the phases as they apply to athletes:

Early Phase The child develops a love of sport, participates for fun, is free to explore, and receives encouragement.

Middle Phase A master coach helps with skill improvement, and the athlete works on long-term skill development. The sport remains fun for the athlete, and he or she begins to specialize more.

Elite Phase The athlete spends many hours practicing and honing technical skills and developing expertise, aiming for personal excellence, and the participation is still enjoyable and satisfying.

Perhaps the next obvious question would be "At what age does each phase occur?" As you may have guessed, it isn't quite that simple. While age can provide a rough gauge of the developmental phase, there are many exceptions to the rule. Most young athletes under ten are in the early phase of developing their talent. But older athletes who discover cycling for the first time also often go through an early phase (or discovery phase). For some people this phase is just fine; they are not participating for talent development but simply to enjoy bicycling, and they may not go on to the next phase. The middle phase often takes place during the adolescent years, and the elite phase may begin in late adolescence or young adulthood. The movement through the phases, and the length of time spent in each phase, will be influenced by each athlete's age, maturity level, physical development, and age when getting started.

Keep in mind that these things, and other external factors in athletes' lives, are out of your control. Your best energies are spent on creating the best training environment that you can.

COACHING PARENTS

Many times the first person to approach you about coaching a minor is the gushing parent. You hear all about the amazing talent, unlimited potential, endless dedication, lofty goals, and virtues of the young rider. No matter what wonderful things the parents say or what the athlete's resume looks like, spend some time talking to the athlete away from his parents before agreeing to a coaching arrangement. This will help you evaluate his interest level and your compatibility as coach and athlete, and it will give you a better feel for the potential relationship. Beware of the young athlete who is driven by fear of disappointing her parents or by a parent's ambition. This doesn't mean you shouldn't coach such a rider; it does mean that you will have to consider how to approach the situation properly. You can begin to gently educate the parent, for example, about the talent-development principles described in this book and the need for intrinsic motivation in the child.

Parent Pledge

Appendix J contains a "Youth Sport Parent Pledge." Use this pledge, or make up your own, to help ensure that you and the parents of your athletes are starting with the same ideas about parental involvement in the sporting experience. Ask both parents to review and sign it before you begin to work with their child. If problems occur later in the season, you can refer to this document to reinforce the original agreement. You can also get creative and create a three-way pledge among you, the athlete, and his or her parents. This can help the athlete feel he or she is more in control of scheduling and other matters. The "Bill of Rights for Young Athletes" (Appendix I) can also be brought into the discussion at this time. We encourage you to use the pledge and bill of rights with any underage athlete/parent group you work with to help set a healthy foundation for the relationship.

Riders, even college-age Espoir riders, usually have parents. The contact you have with them will depend on the young person's age, who is paying the bill, and the setting. Parents' expectations for your relationship with their child will vary as well. The most important thing you can do before you begin any Junior or Espoir coaching relationship where the parents will have any involvement is to have a frank discussion. This introductory meeting is a must to help clarify expectations and set the parameters of the coaching relationship you are going to establish with their young athlete.

The Parent-Coach Meeting

At your initial meeting with the parents of an athlete, you will want to clarify expectations and set the ground rules for the relationship. Having a typed agenda or list of key areas, plus a formal coaching contract, can also help you lay out your policies and concerns and set a professional tone. Your standard agenda for these types of meetings might include the following:

- Clearly explain your philosophy of coaching.
- Ask the parent to clearly explain what he or she hopes the child will gain from the coaching experience.
- Help the parent get a clear understanding of the time and financial investment involved.
- Address any red flags or items of concern.
- Explain how the parent can best help you and the young athlete by being unconditionally supportive—and leaving the coaching to you.
- Request that the parent discuss any coaching-related concerns directly with you and explain that you hope to work in a partnership, rather than having the parent second-guess you or discuss training in depth with the athlete, as this can lead to loyalty confusion for the child.
- Give the parent a clear role.
- Outline how you will communicate with the parent and how often.
- Keep lines of communication open so that the athlete never becomes the go-between. Even simple everyday messages have a way of getting lost and garbled when they travel via teenager.

- Develop a system for continuing the open communication beyond the first meeting.
- Outline your standard coaching policies.

Be sure to talk with other Junior coaches to pick up other ideas, and revise your parent meeting strategies over time to best suit your style and your experiences.

When you are working with a Junior, parents can be your greatest ally, as they see the athlete on a daily basis. But often you need to educate them about how they can best help you and help their young athlete. Discuss the different phases of training, explaining signs and symptoms of burnout or overtraining that they should look for in the athlete's behavior, and anything else you feel is crucial. Be clear regarding what you expect from the athlete and parents and about what they can expect from you. Explain what skill and process goals you are working on, and ask them to help reinforce these lessons. Enthusiastic parents without a place to channel their energy can wreak havoc, but with a little creativity you can put their energy to a very productive use.

The more worrisome parental issues might be a toss-up between the overinvolved and the underinvolved parent. Obviously the overinvolved parent is more of a bother to you, but styles of parenting can have a harmful impact on a young child. A child who is proud of her accomplishments can be hurt by a parent who doesn't value or acknowledge them. It is not your role, as a coach, to replace the parent or the support that the parent should be providing. But be aware that you have the potential, particularly in this situation, to have a profound positive impact on the child by being unconditionally supportive. You can also help surround her with other supportive adult role models by introducing her to other riders.

Overinvolved parents are the ones I typically hear the most about from other coaches. Sometimes called "stage parents," they can be driven by all sorts of things: love of their child, desire for him to have the best, and even their own unrealized dreams. Figuring out why they do what they do is far beyond the scope of this book. Instead, let's focus on some

Sample Coaching Policies

At your initial coach-parent meeting, you might want to go over your standard policies and expectations. Think about including the following:

- Please respect the fact that you hired me to coach your child. If you have concerns about how I am doing this, please schedule a time to speak with me about it privately. If angry about something, please allow a twenty-four-hour cool-off period before discussing any concerns.
- Please do not undermine my credibility or role when I am not around, or in front of the athlete.
- My ultimate goal is the same as yours: the health and well-being of your child. Please be supportive of this effort by allowing me to provide the push your child will need to excel while you provide the unconditional love, support, and acceptance of who he or she is.
- Do not vilify or speak ill of other competitors. I want to build a healthy respect and appreciation for the sport and for competition.
- Please keep your anger in check when at competitions, especially in feed zones. Sometimes unfair things happen at races. I expect my riders to conduct themselves according to the highest standards of sportsmanship, and it helps when we surround them with models of good behavior.
- Please check with me before making any major changes or modifications to your child's bike or equipment.
- Please notify me if you have any concerns over changes in your child's weight, appearance, sleep patterns, pre-race anxiety level, schoolwork and grades, or mood. These changes can occur due to adolescence or training load, but they can also be warning signs of overtraining, too much stress, or other potential problems. I will notify you if I see any points of concern. Together we can work as a team to ensure the best for the athlete.

of the things you can do to help minimize the negative impact and enhance the parents' positive influence.

Keep in mind that we are talking about the behavior of another adult, and you were hired to coach the child. This means you don't necessarily have to like the parent. For the well-being of the athlete, however, mutual respect is a must. How you set up your initial meeting can go a long way toward stemming many stage-parent behaviors. A football team doesn't allow parents on the sidelines with the coach during a game; likewise, the parents of your athletes should not be interfering with the workouts and vying with you at races. You may want to have a standing policy with all your athletes about when and where they meet up with their parents at races. Such policies can be hard to carry out in some settings, but try to craft guidelines that will allow for a predictable situation suitable for everyone involved.

Some parents are just really tough to deal with, or they hire you but then are constantly overinvolved. Before you give up on such a situation, consider carefully what you can do to improve it for the athlete. Keep in mind that you are working with a young person, and it would be unfortunate to terminate your coaching relationship with the child because of the parent's behavior. More than likely, if the parent has frustrated you to the extent that you can no longer work with the family, the child is feeling some stress or pressure as well. If you do terminate the relationship, do so in a professional manner to help ensure that you can continue to be a supportive contact for the athlete, if possible.

AVOIDING IMPROPRIETY

It is a shame that impropriety needs to be mentioned at all, but not to mention it would be a disservice to both you and the young men and women who want to be better cyclists under your direction. Legally, morally, and ethically, as a coach you have a responsibility to avoid any actions or words that might be considered physical, verbal, or emotional assault. This includes a wide range of behaviors, from berating an athlete to manipulation to sexual misconduct. Many organizations, including USA Cycling, now conduct criminal background checks to help ensure that licensed coaches have a clean record. While this is not blanket protection from all things, it does provide some peace of mind. These policies help protect you as a coach as well by creating a professional standard of conduct.

It should be obvious that you should not become romantically or sexually involved with a minor, and that hitting is assault. The issues can become less black-and-white when you consider things like a consensual relationship between an athlete in the Espoir age range (18–23) and a coach. This is a very tricky situation and one that you would be wise to avoid. Even if you are a young coach and the Espoir athlete is only a few years younger, a power dynamic still occurs. These relationships are fraught with potential problems. Many organizations, such as the U.S. Olympic Committee and the NCAA, frown so much on these sorts of relationships that they have formal policies against them.

Carefully consider how you approach subjects like weight loss, body fat, and other sensitive subjects. Offering comments without providing proper support or educational material, such as telling athletes to lose weight without putting them in touch with resources appropriate to their age, will leave them trying to sort through all the science and information alone, a prospect that can have many unintended and negative consequences.

SUCCESSFUL COMMUNICATION

In a coach-athlete relationship, as in any relationship, good communication is vital for success. As a coach, are you sure the messages you send are being correctly received? Are you sure that you are accurately receiving the information your cyclists send you? What kind of first impression do you present to new and prospective clients? Do your verbal or nonverbal communications convey the same message? These important questions remind us that communication is not as easy as it may seem. Like all skills, the art of effective communication can be improved through self-awareness and practice.

In his book *The Seven Habits of Highly Effective People,* Stephen Covey says, "Seek first to understand, then to be understood." This is good coaching advice.

Communication occurs through a variety of media. If you are coaching Juniors, the best way to reach them about training sessions and other matters is by e-mail and cell phone, and if you are not already into text-messaging, you soon will be. But the mode of communication doesn't matter unless your communication style is clear and effective.

Communication is a two-way street. You need to convey ideas and training instructions clearly. Your athletes need to receive the message properly and be able to send messages back. Here are some ideas to think about:

- Be credible.
- Be positive and upbeat.
- Strive to send messages that are high in information, not just fluff.
- Keep your messages consistent.
- Listen effectively.
- Be aware of both your verbal and nonverbal messages.
- Remain calm under pressure.
- Be aware of how your emotions impact your communication and messages.
- Speak from knowledge and avoid speaking of things you are not knowledgeable about.
- Be honest.
- Strive to be dynamic and engaging. If you aren't passionate, why should they be?
- Speak the same language. Don't use technical terms unless you first explain them to your athletes.
- Check for understanding. Ask athletes to explain what they heard or repeat the directions to ensure they understood the message as you meant it. And make sure you confirm your understanding.

Listening is always important for effective communication. One of the most effective teaching tools a coach has is listening. Often, listening is more important than anything you can say, and too many of us underestimate this skill. By listening, a coach can learn what is going on in an athlete's head, figure out how the athlete is processing information, and determine how to better help the athlete learn. Strive to ask open-ended questions. Give your athletes an opportunity to tell you about a race or an effort before you give your assessment. These opportunities not only show them that you value their opinions and ideas (a powerful positive reinforcer) but also give you a chance to provide better guidance.

When to Talk to a Junior

After a frustrating or upsetting workout or race, your rider might not be in the best frame of mind to talk. Actually, the same can be said about anyone, not just young athletes. If the matter isn't urgent, consider just saying something like "I have some thoughts on how things went today. Let me know when you want to talk." This approach is nonjudgmental and gives the athlete an opportunity to cool down and speak when he or she is ready to listen. It also invites the athlete to be an active part of the conversation rather than just a passive listener while you launch into your analysis.

Whenever possible, listen to other coaches speak; read what top coaches have written—even if they are in another sport. You may not agree with everything they say, but there is always something to learn about coaching style. There are excellent biographies and autobiographies of some of our best coaches.

Providing Healthy Feedback

As a coach, you know that providing feedback to athletes is a daily requirement. Feedback provides criticism, critique, and useful learning points. It also provides encouragement and praise. Being able to provide useful and accurate feedback effectively will speed learning and strengthen the coach-athlete relationship.

The most effective means of providing feedback is to use the "positive feedback sandwich" approach. When a correction or critique needs to be made, putting it between two positive observations or remarks helps the listener remain positive and open to the information offered. For instance, a coach might tell an athlete, "Marc, you are doing a really good job with body position. Now as you approach the log pile, consider your gear choice far enough out to make changes if necessary. Keep up the great effort."

When providing feedback, try to be as specific as possible. Generic feedback like "nice work" or "good job" can feel like fluff if it is used too often or if no specifics are given. Instead, try to follow up these general remarks with comments that are specific and positive. For example: "Good job, way to make use of Phil's wheel in the last lap." And always strive to be sincere. Insincere praise and feedback are visible from space, and athletes feel it. Insincerity can do tremendous damage to both credibility and trust.

Motivating Juniors

It is a common question: How can I motivate this child? What can I do to light a fire under her? Parents will ask you this, you will ask this of yourself, and at times it will drive you crazy. First and foremost, it is important to realize that you cannot be someone's source of motivation. Ultimately every person's motivation needs to come from within. This intrinsic or inner motivation is the source of pride, enjoyment, and satisfaction that each of us gets out of participating in our favorite activities. No amount of cajoling, hair-tearing, or promises will provide sustainable motivation for someone who isn't internally motivated. And although you don't have the power to create intrinsic motivation, you do have the power to build a small flicker of motivation into a roaring fire—or to snuff it out. You do this by the culture and coaching environment you create. Your enthusiasm, interest, and attentiveness—or lack thereof—will be noticed.

To create a team culture or environment that fosters strong intrinsic motivation, focus on skills and skill mastery. Your words and actions should emphasize and teach the elements that athletes need to focus on, and you should provide both feedback and praise about athletes' progress. Help them appreciate the small improvements. Pay attention to your athletes, and find out why they like to ride. If playing on trails is fun, make sure that playing on trails is a part of their program every now and then. If you have a track rider who also happens to love to swim, the occasional swim workout is a great way to keep it fun.

It's okay to use rewards and exciting sources of external motivation. These are powerful motivators. Just be sure to use them carefully so that they are always supported by activities that build a sense of confidence and mastery over skills and efforts.

Ways to Foster Positive Motivation

Effective and long-lasting motivation comes from within, not from sources outside of us. It is grounded in pride, enjoyment, and self-satisfaction. To fan a spark of internal motivation into a flame, use the following principles:

- Use realistic, challenging, performance-based goals.
- Help athletes understand why they ride.
- Provide successful experiences in training.
- Help athletes set goals contingent on performance, not outcome.
- Help athletes see and value the progress they make.
- Involve athletes in decision-making about training.
- Keep training from becoming routine.

COACH, HEAL THYSELF: HANDLING STRESS AND BURNOUT

Coaching is a rewarding profession. However, it can also be very stressful. Unlike most jobs, there really is no 9 to 5 in coaching. You will not be off on weekends, and the relationships you forge may in some cases last a lifetime. Unfortunately, many coaches succumb to burnout and frustration over time and leave a profession they were once passionate about. In order to be an effective and fulfilled coach for many years, it is important for you to take care of yourself and your own stress levels. Stress, if allowed to accumulate, may not only reduce your enjoyment but also negatively impact your family, friends, and athletes. The following ideas are designed to help you keep your stress to a minimum.

- Don't try to be "all things to all people." Know your strengths and your limitations. There are only twenty-four hours in a day. Learn and practice the word "no."
- Avoid becoming overworked. All work and no leisure is a recipe for disaster. Plan and carefully protect your downtime the same way you honor your other commitments.

- For many, coaching is not only a job, but a passion and a lifestyle. Be careful not to let it become all-consuming. Develop unrelated hobbies or interests.
- Coaching isn't your only role; you may also be a parent, spouse, or sibling, and you have friendships to nurture as well. Make sure you identify your other roles and take time for them.
- Know your own sources of stress and identify the resources you have to help you cope with them. Being aware of what makes you tense can help you handle these everyday stressors.
- Be realistic. We all like to believe we can do it all. Not only is this not possible, it is also counterproductive. Trying to do too much often makes us ineffective.
- Seek out resources to learn effective time-management techniques.
- E-mail, BlackBerries, and cell phones put us in constant contact, and it is easy to fall into the trap of coaching 24/7. Set regular business hours and communicate your expectations to your athletes.
- Connect with other coaches. Many coaches work in isolation from others in the profession. Seek out relationships with others who understand coaching—people with whom you can share ideas and frustrations. Attend coaching clinics and workshops whenever possible, not only for the information you will learn but also for the networking relationships you will develop.
- Exercise! Even if you are no longer competitive, keep up your activity level. Regular exercise will keep you healthy and moderate the impact of stress. (By maintaining a workout schedule of your own, you will also be setting an excellent example of lifetime fitness for your young athletes!)
- Delegate whenever possible. Not everything in training is your responsibility. Help your athletes understand what their responsibilities are in the coaching and training relationship. Provide clear expectations and guidelines about how they can best help you be an effective coach. (For example, they should notify you promptly about changes in their work or school schedules so that you don't have to rush and figure out last-minute changes in training plans.)

WHEN TO LET GO

As your young athletes grow, so will their needs. A young person's developmental issues will change as adulthood approaches, and as an athlete becomes more proficient in cycling, there may come a time when he or she needs a more advanced level of coaching than you can provide. Coaches must recognize that they cannot be all things in all phases. Successful devo coaches have the best interests of their athletes at heart and know there is a time to let go.

Think of it this way: An elementary school teacher specializes in laying the foundation for reading and math. Although this teacher may be able to do algebra or read Shakespeare, his specialty lies in working with younger students and fostering early growth. Coaching and coaching specialties are much the same. Coaches need to know their own limitations and must recognize when an athlete needs more than they can provide. The well-being of the athlete and her overall growth demands that you master the sometimes extremely difficult art of letting go.

Keep in mind during this letting-go process that you will always play an important role as a mentor, supporter, and friend. Successful devo coaches often report that even after their athletes have gone on to higher levels of competition, they will check in for advice and guidance. In this advisory role, you will provide your athlete with a key ally for further success.

Preparing Athletes to Be Coachable

One of the greatest skills you can impart to your young athletes as they climb the ladder of competition is how to be coachable. Being coachable means that an athlete has a healthy sense of self-awareness, can listen to constructive criticism, and can provide important feedback about her own experience. Being coachable doesn't mean that the athlete rolls over and does whatever a coach says no matter what. Coachable athletes are respectful and responsive. They take responsibility for their own actions and are willing to work with others. For some athletes, this will come naturally because of their personality and home environment. For others, learning to be coachable may take time. As a coach, you can help foster coachability through your actions and coaching style.

Here are some tips for fostering coachability:

- Provide your athletes with the opportunity to evaluate their own training or performance. Before you share what you saw, ask an athlete to tell you about his experience. This can provide you with valuable feedback. It will also help the athlete develop an "eye" for better understanding his training progress or competitive approach.
- Use positive feedback and constructive criticism. Be specific and sincere. Point out what athletes do right, not just what went wrong.
- Listen to constructive criticism and feedback well. If you get bent out of shape, how will your athlete learn how to take it in stride?
- Create an environment where mistakes are seen not as failures or screw-ups but as an opportunity to go back to the drawing board to figure out how to meet a challenge or solve a puzzle.
- Be clear on your expectations about boundaries and guidelines. Teach athletes what it means to be an athlete (the healthy model, not the pro-sport "bad boy" model). Athletes may not have expectations about respect for others. Let them know how you expect them to treat officials, teammates, competitors, their parents, and you. Do not tolerate anything less, and certainly not temper tantrums.
- Encourage your athletes to ask questions when they don't understand your instructions, and to respectfully share their opinions, even if they are different from yours. Create an environment where it is safe to ask questions and disagree. Provide clear rationales and explanations when an athlete does ask a question, and avoid the "because I said so" or "I am the coach" approach.
- Instead of telling your athletes what their race strategy should be, encourage them to discuss their own plans first. You cannot be in the peloton with your athlete, and you want her to develop into a rider who can think fast and make snap decisions on the bike. You may not always be available to help her decide what to do in a given race situation. If your athletes get all their instructions from you,

they will be lost when they are confronted with a situation alone. By allowing them to come up with their own strategies, you are fostering this decision-making ability.

COACHING FOR THE NEXT PHASE

What do you do when your athlete makes a regional or national team? This step marks a big transition for an athlete, and as a responsible coach you will need to prepare him for this new level of competition. That preparation actually begins long before the transition is about to occur.

USA Cycling is always watching and monitoring Junior and Espoir cycling in the United States to spot young athletes who show developmental promise. They carefully select athletes based on physical skill, coachability, and maturity for participation in a variety of national and international competitions to help provide athletes with exposure to high levels of competition. If one of your athletes gets an opportunity to participate, here are some ways you can help make the most of the experience:

- Consider and coach the skills and mindset of being a good traveling teammate, even before your athlete is in a position to make such a team. It is very difficult to suddenly instill self-reliance and responsibility in anyone, let alone a teenager. Your athlete should be gaining these skills long before she is invited to join a squad.
- Encourage and help your athlete to be responsible. The team director will expect him to act appropriately. Have a discussion about what this means, as he may not clearly understand what appropriate behavior is.
- If possible, talk to the team manager as early as possible to learn about what the competition will entail. This will help you structure training and will enable you to tailor your conversations with the athlete to prepare her for the experience.
- Talk with your athlete about performance and experience expectations. Don't just discuss expected outcomes; also review the other benefits he might gain from the experience.

- Talk with the athlete's parents about trip expectations, athlete responsibilities, and the value of the experience for the athlete.
- Make your athlete responsible for the details. What paperwork is needed? When is it due? When are key deadlines? If you do everything for the athlete, she will not learn valuable skills that will come in handy later on, both on and off the bike.
- When traveling with a team, athletes are usually expected to be able to do basic mechanics. Your athlete should be able to put his bike together, for example, or box it up, or change a tire. He should be capable of getting ready on time, so as not to delay the group. Make sure these skills are in place.
- Once the experience is over, be sure to discuss lessons learned, both good and bad, with your athlete. Allow her to lead the discussion, as the more an athlete can clearly identify what should be done differently next time and what was done well, the better these lessons will stick over time.

RECOMMENDED READING AND RESOURCES

Coaches' Guide: Sport Psychology Mental Training Manual (U.S. Olympic Committee, 2006).

Coaching for Character, by Craig Clifford and Randolph M. Freezell (Coaches Choice Books, 2003).

Coaching for the Inner Edge, by Robin Vealey (FIT, 2005).

Coaching Mental Excellence: It Does Matter Whether You Win or Lose, by Ralph Vernacchia, Richard T. McGuire, and David Lamar Cook (Warde, 1995).

Creative Coaching, by Jerry Lynch (Human Kinetics, 2001).

Developing Talent in Young People, by Benjamin Bloom (Ballantine, 1985).

The Double Goal Coach, by Jim Thompson (Collins, 2003).

The Seven Secrets of Successful Coaches, by Jeff Janssen and Greg Dale (Janssen Peak Performance, 2002).

Sport Psychology Mental Training Manual (U.S. Olympic Committee, 2002).

Talented Teenagers: The Roots of Success and Failure, by Mihaly Csikszentmihalyi, Kevin Rathunde, and Samuel Whalen (Cambridge University Press, 1996).

Training Games: Coaching and Racing Creatively, 3rd ed., by Eric Anderson (Tafnews, 2006).

Why Good Coaches Quit and How You Can Stay in the Game, 2nd ed., by John Anderson and Rick Aberman (Coaches Choice Books, 2005).

Why Johnny Hates Sports, by Fred Engh (Square One Publishers, 2002).

The American Sport Education Program (ASEP) offers a wide variety of coaching education courses online. See www.asep.com.

The Positive Coaching Alliance (PCA) is a not-for-profit youth sport organization that educates youth sport coaches, parents, and administrators. While much of its programming is geared to youth team sports, PCA provides excellent resources and ideas for creating a positive sport culture and for handling parents. See www.positivecoach.org.

Also, Level 1 cycling coach and tactics expert Steve Thordarson has created fantastic materials for teaching tactics. Check out his website at www.smartcyclinginc.org and click on the link for tactical games.

15 GETTING
Started in Racing

You learn the most from bad races.

—Katie Compton, 2007 Cyclocross
World Cup winner, CTS Pro coach

Competition is a lot of fun. It gives you a chance to pit yourself against others and dig deep to see what you can really do. The world of bike racing is full of fantastic people and can take you both to new places and to new heights of accomplishment. Let's talk a little about what it means to be a competitive Junior racer and how you can make the most of the opportunities that lie ahead as you begin to take on the excitement and challenges of a racing career.

If you are interested in racing and know how to handle your bike safely around other riders, then you are ready to give racing a try. Riding with more experienced riders on group training rides will also give you an indication of both your skills and your readiness to race. Some of the basic skills and abilities that will help make your entry into racing go smoothly are:

- Being able to ride in a straight line. This may sound simple enough, but many new riders only think they are riding straight when they actually are weaving around a bit, creating a hazard for both themselves and other riders.
- Being able to ride close to other people comfortably and safely.
- Having a few training efforts under your belt that are as long as the race will be, if not a bit longer. In other words, don't do a race that will be 50 miles if the farthest you have ever ridden is 30 miles. You are a devo athlete, so your focus should be on doing what it takes to become a smarter, stronger racer, not just a rider who races a lot.

If you live in or near a major metropolitan area, you will be able to find plenty of road and off-road events to participate in. If you live in a rural area, races will probably be farther away, which makes getting started a little more challenging. Either way, you will want to know what to expect as you enter the strange new world of bicycle racing. This chapter is designed to help you navigate your first racing experiences.

FINDING A RACE

Learning to ride a bike is a rite of passage for many young kids. When they start to get involved in baseball, soccer, and other "traditional" sports, the bike might even be their mode of transportation to and from practice. But most young riders ride their bikes simply because they enjoy it. Meanwhile, they are building confidence in their bike-handling skills and developing a love of riding. Then, at some point, they become aware that cycling is a sport in its own right, and they may begin to think about racing. But because bike racing isn't as common as other sports, figuring out how to get involved can be a challenge. So where do you start if you want to start racing?

If you happen to live near a velodrome and want to check out track racing, it should be pretty easy to take this step. Most tracks have programs especially designed for beginners and Juniors, with an opportunity to learn to race. They even have bikes you can rent, because most people don't want to invest in a track bike of their own until they are sure they like racing on the track. If you don't live near a velodrome, check out websites for different velodromes and look for camps and other opportunities that the various velodromes offer.

If you are interested in mountain biking or road racing, there are Junior development camps and Junior racing series that you can sign up for. The Lance Armstrong Junior Olympic Racing Series (for road biking) and the Alison Dunlap Junior Olympic Racing Series (for mountain biking), for example, can help you gain experience and learn racing skills. Many area clubs also offer training series races that provide riders of all levels with an opportunity to practice racing skills. This is most common in road clubs, which may meet weekly at a local business park after hours or on weekends for training criteriums.

Once you decide to check out the racing scene in your area, you'll need to find the races. There are a few places you can go to find information. Many big cities have a sports-dedicated free publication that lists cycling races. You can usually find these at sporting goods stores. See if the biggest city near you has a print and/or Web publication of this type. Racing- and training-related magazines, such as *Bicycling, VeloNews,* and *Dirtrag,* list upcoming events and provide more detailed race calendars on their websites. *Dirtrag* is dedicated to mountain biking. Check out the websites of local bike shops or racing teams, or look at the registration sites listed at the end of this chapter. And of course, ask your local shop. Many area clubs and shops sponsor local races and know about other events in the area, and will be able to tell you the best place to look for events. They may even be able to give you the inside scoop on the best races, or the pros and cons of different events, which is something that you probably won't find on any website.

Once you figure out what events are coming up in your area, be choosy. As a Junior rider or new Espoir rider, you must be careful not to overdo it right out of the starting gate. Packing your calendar with tons of races may seem like a good idea at the start of the season because you are excited and revved to race. But "windshield miles" (that is, travel miles), as Gunner Shogren, an elite mountain bike and cyclocross racer, calls them, can be very draining. In the first few seasons of your career, it is much more important to get in quality training than to race in every event you can find. The top sport scientists at the U.S. Olympic Training Center agree that one of the biggest mistakes that racers of all levels, especially beginners, make is overracing and undertraining. Racing every weekend might be fun in the short term, but it actually does more harm than good to your development as an up-and-coming athlete. And overracing contributes to training fatigue, reduced enjoyment, and diminished performance. These things can all add up to a short racing career instead of the type that just gets better over time. Consider racing only a few times a season at first (for example, pick just two or three days to race each month), and make sure your emphasis is on getting stronger and learning how to race smarter. As your skills get better, you will be able to add more races to your schedule with confidence.

RACING OPTIONS

As a Junior or Espoir rider, you will have the option of racing by age group or by ability. New riders often benefit from racing in their age-group category. This is an excellent way to begin. It provides a good introduction to racing, and at local events it can be less intimidating than racing by category because it usually means competing against a smaller field of racers. Keep in mind, however, that at larger events and nationals, age-group racing is among the most competitive and challenging out there.

If a race doesn't offer specific age-based categories, you will still be able to race. At the Senior level (over 18 years old), racers are separated by ability level and advance by proving their ability at each progressive level and earning upgrade points. At any event where a USAC racing license is required, you are allowed to race in the category you are qualified for. If an event has both age-group Junior races and category-based races, you are allowed to do both—racing twice on the same day, if the timing works. Unfortunately, it doesn't always work because several groups may be out on the course at the same time. It is more common in criterium racing and track events than in road or mountain biking events. Doing multiple races within an event can be a great way to get in a full day of training and practice skills, if your fitness and training level are good enough. However, brand-new racers should focus on just one race at a time and should not try to do too many events in a given day.

Female riders have additional racing options because they may sign up for age-group women's events and category women's events as well as the men's age-group and category events. Boys and men are not allowed to race in the women's categories or age-group races.

No matter what race event or category you choose to compete in, you can make the most of your racing experience by approaching the race with a clear plan and knowing ahead of time what you want to work on. Review the goal-setting information in Chapter 10 and apply the same

SMART principles to setting your racing goals. Racers need to consider what they can learn from each event. But above all, focus on having fun when you race. It's easy to get discouraged if you're not winning and you're not sure if you're even making much progress. But remember, training is cumulative, and many of the best Senior riders had pretty unremarkable records when they were Junior riders. The important thing is to race smart, have patience with yourself, and keep learning.

Race Frequency

In many countries, devo athletes may enter only a certain number of races each year. These limits help to ensure healthy athletic development. In the United States, the predominant model of racing is to race as much as possible. At the more elite levels, riders know that this is not the best way to get peak performance, but at the lower levels many cyclists overrace and undertrain. Racing takes a certain level of intensity and tears the body down, and unfortunately it is not the same kind of systematic breakdown that you can get from training. As a result, too much racing means you never get an opportunity to really develop your talents to their full potential. Be careful not to race too much in your first year or two of racing. As you move beyond your early years, you can reassess and find the right balance of training and racing for you.

You also need to consider how long the season is. There are enough races on the calendar that you could race almost year-round, going from road to track, from mountain biking to cyclocross. While racing in different disciplines is fun, be careful about going from one racing season right into the next. As we saw in Chapter 7, the science of periodization shows that optimal training benefits happen only when periods of work are matched by periods of stress. These periods occur both on a small scale (for example, in a week of training) and on a bigger scale (across the training year).

THINGS TO KNOW BEFORE YOU RACE

Know the rules of racing. It is your responsibility as a racer to know the guidelines for racing in your category. USA Cycling posts its entire rulebook for racers on its website, www.usacycling.org. You don't have to read the whole thing, but definitely take a look at the sections on Juniors. You'll also need to know the rules that the race promoter has set up. For example, is it an open race, meaning anyone can ride, or is it for licensed riders only? This information is often on the race flyer or website.

Read everything you can about a race beforehand. Read all the materials you receive when you sign up, and look through everything on the race website. Make sure you understand the directions to the race site. There's nothing worse than missing the start of a race because you didn't really pay attention to the directions! Check out how long the race is and what the course is like. Most race websites post maps, course profiles, and other useful information. Does the race promoter make recommendations for gearing? (Don't forget that you have gear restrictions if you are under 18.) The more you know beforehand, the better.

Bigger races, such as national mountain bike events or multiday road race events, have a "race bible." Depending on the size of the event, the race bible may be a single sheet or a small book. It contains all the logistical information, prize listings, and other necessary details. If you are given a race bible at an event, be sure to check it out carefully—that is part of your responsibility as a racer.

On the day of the race, pre-ride the course or drive it ahead of time, if possible. Keep your eyes open for landmarks, marked turns, and potentially dangerous spots. Make sure you are thoroughly familiar with the layout of the course: About the only type of racecourse you can't get lost on is a track. For road or mountain bike events it is possible to get off-course. Knowing the course like the palm of your hand can reduce your chances of making a costly navigation mistake.

Licensed to Ride

USA Cycling, the largest racing-based cycling organization in the United States, operates a racing license system for all levels in road, mountain bike, track, cyclocross, and BMX racing. To race in any USAC-sponsored event, riders must have a current USAC license. Individuals can apply for membership and a seasonal license or a one-day racing license.

With a one-day license, you will only be allowed to race in the beginner category.

Small, regional cycling organizations also exist around the country, and they may sponsor racing events as well. These organizations typically have their own membership fee and racing license program, which may or may not correspond to the USAC license. Be sure to find out who is sponsoring a race before you compete so you can be sure that you have the right type of license.

Some races also allow unlicensed racers to race in a special category known as "citizen." This is usually an all-comers' race that is shorter than the other events, and the main purpose is to involve the community. These races are therefore not as competitive as the races that require a license. No records or points can be earned, for example, in a citizen's race, so these events will not count toward racing license upgrades.

As soon as you get your racing license, make a photocopy. Roll it up, remove the bar plug or end plug from your handlebars, and slip the copy of your license inside. This will ensure that you never go to a race without your license. It will also provide further identification if your bike is ever stolen.

RACE DAY LOGISTICS

Every race is a little different, but there are some things that generally stay the same across disciplines and levels of competition. Races commonly require pre-registration, for example, and as racing becomes more popular, many events fill up before race day even arrives. Even if you have pre-registered, on the day of the event (or sometimes the night before, if events start very early) you will need to check in to let the race officials know you are present. The people at the registration table will check to make sure your paperwork is in order and that your racing license is current, and will provide you with your race number and any new race instructions. They will also take your money if you haven't already paid.

After you have signed in, pin your number to your race jersey. Most races do not allow you to alter your race number, and USAC rules forbid you to damage your number. This is to ensure that your number is readable; the officials will need to be able to identify you if there is a tight finish.

Always double-check the start time, and stay close enough to the start area before the race so that you will hear any changes announced. Find out where the wheel pit/mechanical help area is, and locate the feed zone. Many races have a start or lead vehicle, and for longer road and circuit races there may be a follow vehicle as well. The lead vehicle may stay out in front of the group the whole race, or it may not. Or it may stay only in front of the group until the riders are close to the finish. You should know what these vehicles look like.

Pinning on Your Number

Your race number should be pinned to your jersey properly so that it is easy for others to see. To get it just right, either remove your jersey and pin it on yourself or let someone else pin it on for you. If you are given only one number, be sure to ask which side the officials would like it placed on. If you are given two numbers, one goes on each side of your back. Do not wrinkle up or fold your race number because this makes it hard for officials to read. Riders can actually be disqualified for improperly placing their numbers.

Try to plan your warm-up so that you are back and ready to begin the race as close to the start time as possible. You don't want to cool down again before the race: Arriving at the starting line after you've already broken a sweat will help you put forth your best effort once the race is under way.

In most racing events, your starting position is an important factor. Before the race, scope out what might be the best starting position for the course you are facing. Does one side of the field or the other set up better for the first corner? Is it a course where you might get trapped or slowed down by other riders if you are in a certain position for the early curves or turnoffs? Thinking about these things can help you determine your best lineup position.

Before you line up, make sure you have your number pinned on properly, that your bottles are full, and that you have the repair gear and your race will require. Many longer races have feed zones where hand-ups are allowed. These are special designated areas where coaches, parents, and other riders can pass water and extra food to riders as they pass. Riders are not allowed to get this type of support anywhere else on the course. If you have someone feeding you in a race, make sure you talk about what you may need at different feed zones and how the bottles and other supplies should be handed to you. You can label the items ahead of time with a permanent marker, if necessary, to avoid the frustration of getting the wrong bottle as you make this exchange. Keep in mind that feed-zone accidents do occur. If you communicate effectively with your pit crew and practice handoffs, fewer problems will occur.

There is nothing worse than showing up at a race and discovering that you are missing something important. Have a designated race bag that you take to every race. See Appendix C for a complete race bag checklist.

MAKING THE MOST OF YOUR RACING MILES

Take stock of what your strengths are so you can look for ways to make the most of them. Also take some time to consider the areas you need to work on. Think about ways you can use your skills during a race and how you can use the race to practice things that you aren't as good at.

Stay positive. Mid-race is not the best time to dwell on why something went wrong. When emotions are running high, tanks are running on empty, and nerves are wearing thin, it can be difficult to determine what went wrong in a rational way. More importantly, focusing on what went wrong takes away from your ability to focus on what you need to do to keep racing well.

Have realistic expectations. You can't go into every race all season at the peak of your fitness. And sometimes it is important to jump into a race above your head to push your limits. In these situations, focus on the things you want to accomplish based on your current training needs and fitness level.

Race Day Tips

1. Pre-register for the race to avoid late fees.
2. Pre-ride the course and do a good warm-up before the race begins.
3. If there is a hole shot, or wide start area that narrows down to a single track, do your best to make it there first when the race begins.
4. Know where to pass on the course (in case you don't make the hole shot).
5. Know how long the climbs are and gauge your speed when climbing accordingly.
6. If it is a mountain bike or cyclocross race, know the sections where it may be quicker to dismount and run.
7. Know where you can drink and eat on the course, then drink and eat! Keep yourself hydrated.
8. Pace yourself—most riders start too fast and can't finish strong.
9. Draft whenever possible.
10. Never give up—finishing a race on a bad day is always better than quitting.

Evaluating Your Race

If you ride and race just because it is fun, that is fantastic! If you love to race but you also want to see how far you can go in the sport—if you have dreams of a World Cup title, Tour podium spot, or Olympic medal—you need to have a method to your madness. Even if you just enjoy racing, having a plan will help you make the most of your efforts. Take a look at the information in Chapter 10 about goal setting and apply this to your racing. When you first start out, you will probably just be having fun; once you feel more serious about meeting certain goals in cycling, you will need to learn how to train more effectively. And once you know how to train, both training and competition will be focused on building skills. You should go into every training session and every race with a purpose. Ask yourself before each event or session what you are going to work on and what you want to learn from the experience.

Whether you did well or not in a race, review how it went for you. You aren't replaying it to get upset with yourself—that isn't very productive. You want to review the race and learn from it. This is how top athletes in all sports make consistent improvements. Everyone, absolutely everyone, makes mistakes sometimes, and that is okay! The problem comes when you don't learn from your mistakes and improve. Think through what happened, what you could learn from it, and what new skill or understanding you can take to the next race. The next race will be different—no race plays out in exactly the same way as another race—but you will use the same skills over and over again in different ways. So look for ways to improve your skills. Only when your fitness *and* your skills are on a very high level will you truly be ready to train to compete. It takes several years for most racers to reach this stage. You can be very successful during this period, however—we are not saying you have to wait to be good. But if you want to reach the highest levels and make the most of your talents, you need to become a student of the sport, train smart, race smart, and be committed to being a thinking, learning athlete throughout your career.

JOINING A TEAM

Even though bike racing seems like an individual sport, joining a team can really boost your level of enjoyment. It can also provide you with more racing opportunities. And in some disciplines, like road and track, teammates work together for team success. Cycling teammates can be your training partners, help to motivate you, and provide support. Teams also often have sponsors that support the team. This support can be financial, or it can provide discounts on certain products. Choosing a team is an important decision. So carefully consider your team options. Ideally, you want to find teammates who will make good training partners and friends. It's nice if you have similar interests, and it is certainly a good idea if at least some of your teammates are more experienced than you so that they can help you learn the ropes. Teammates should also have the same level of commitment and sense of drive for achievement in racing. Some teams are very high-pressure and focused on winning,

TABLE 15.1 **Teams Versus Clubs**

Team	Club
• A group of riders specifically focused on competition. A team may be part of a larger club or may be independent of any other group.	• A larger group that usually has a range of riders at all levels.
• Usually focuses on bringing together riders with similar skills for both individual and team success.	• Anyone who pays the membership fee can join.
• In races, teammates are expected to work together for the good of the team and to promote team success.	• More casual than a team and often more centered on the social aspects of riding.
• Some teams have membership dues and others don't.	• Teammates may be of different levels, so there is less teamwork in races and less emphasis on team success.
• The perks associated with riding for a team depend on the level of racing and the sponsorship the team has.	• Low-key, less competitive environment.
• Riders may be expected to use or endorse specific sponsor products.	
• Teammates are usually expected to compete in a set number of events each season.	

while others are more laid-back. Make sure your attitudes are compatible; otherwise there are sure to be conflicts.

The USA Cycling website, your local bike shop, or a quick Google search can help you locate teams and riding clubs in your area. Many new riders begin by riding with a local club. Even local clubs can sometimes work out a few local sponsorship perks (such as a discount at the local shop or reduced race-entry fees). Team membership has lots of perks. Teams usually have nice team kits, and teammates may train or travel together.

Keep in mind that not all teams are created equal. Some teams are all-comers' clubs that allow anyone with an interest in racing to join. Others require an invitation to join. Teams may be selective, allowing only Juniors or only road riders on the team, for example, or only riders ranked category 3 or higher (or any combination of elements). Some teams may expect you to do a set number of races or to help out at a local event. Make sure you understand what your responsibilities would be before joining a team.

CLIMBING THE RACING LADDER

Once you have your racing license and have started racing, the next step is to move up into higher categories. Each USA Cycling discipline has several levels, starting with an entry level for beginners and going up through the ranks to the professional level. The first step up from beginner is very often the easiest transition. Simply doing a number of beginning races will qualify you for your first upgrade. After that, riders earn points to move up to the next category based on how they finish in sanctioned events. Once you start racing, it is important that you keep an accurate record of the races you do so you can submit your request for an upgrade when you have met the requirements.

Keeping Track of Race Results

Starting and keeping a personal file for your race results and race resume is a fantastic idea, even if you aren't concerned with getting an upgrade. In a simple Word or spreadsheet file, or on a piece of paper, keep a log of race date, time, and location. Note the size of your field (number of racers who started), the type of race, the race category, the length of the race, and how you finished. You will be able to use this document in a number of ways. This is the information that USA Cycling will request when you file for an upgrade, and the higher you go in the sport, the more important this record is. You can also share this log with team managers when you are looking for a team to join. All of the USA Cycling–sanctioned races that you compete in will be listed as a part of your racing account in the personal My USACycling page that you can log on to once you get a racing license and become a USAC member.

When is the right time to upgrade to the next level of competition? Young cyclists who want to pursue a career as a bike racer are often very anxious to achieve upgrades as soon as possible. Though upgrading is an important part of climbing the racing ladder, upgrading too quickly, particularly in your first two or three years of racing, is not the best idea. Bike racing in all disciplines is much more complex than just being strong or fast. Early success at the lower levels of competition and fast upgrades often put a racer at a level of competition that is over his or her head. At the higher levels of competition, the fitness levels of the competitors are no longer spread out across a wide range; instead, everyone is fit, fast, and strong. There are many factors that support success at the higher levels: knowledge of race tactics; competitors' strengths, weaknesses, and habits; your technical skills; and your understanding of the politics of sport. If you advance too quickly through the ranks, you do not have a chance to develop a working knowledge of these things, and you cannot learn many of them from training alone. Every year, young riders who have climbed the ranks too fast get blown off the back of the big road races, not because they aren't strong riders but because they don't know the "game" at the new level. Making steady progress that is based on constant improvement and learning is the best way to reach the highest ranks and stay there in the sport of cycling.

It is recommended that Junior and devo racers stay at their current category of racing until they have earned the maximum number of points allowed and the rules require a mandatory upgrade. By then, you will have done well consistently over the course of a season or perhaps two, not just in a few races. And this means you will have developed both the fitness and the skills you need to do well at the next level. A slow, steady progression helps to ensure that you are really ready, both physically and mentally, for the challenges you will face at the next level.

Getting into the Pipeline

The organizations that govern sports have a term for the pathway that a beginning athlete takes to reach high levels of competition. This path is called the "pipeline." In an ideal world, athletes would enter the pipeline as little kids and would train and be well supported throughout their entire journey along the pipeline. Unfortunately, the real world isn't quite that neat and organized. USA Cycling tries to correct for this by having a way for coaches to identify young riders with talent so they can nurture and guide them toward elite performance. But don't sit around and wait for the pipeline to notice you—this is a big country, and even though cycling isn't a huge sport, there is a lot going on. You can be proactive. Here's what you can do to put yourself in the path of the pipeline:

- Attend the USAC Lance Armstrong and Alison Dunlap Junior Olympic development events (for road and mountain biking, respectively). These events are designed specifically to help USAC coaches identify budding talent. (For more information, visit www. usacycling.org.)
- Attend one of the USA Cycling Junior and Espoir training development camps. Information about these camps is posted on the USA Cycling website (www.usacycling.org). Scholarships are available. Your local cycling club may have scholarship money available as well, so don't hesitate to check.
- Work with a coach who has a good track record—not just working with Juniors, but working with Juniors who are still racing as Seniors.
- Join a team that emphasizes Junior or Espoir development. Make sure the team not only talks the talk but also actually provides opportunities for development. Does the team do workshops and clinics? Does it do training races? How can they contribute to your growth? Where have other young cyclists from the team gone after they graduated from the Junior or Espoir ranks? These are all important questions to ask when finding a program that will help you make the most of your riding career.

Don't be discouraged if it takes a while to get noticed by the pipeline, and don't assume that not being in the pipeline means you don't have what it takes. Due to the nature of the sport, there are very limited opportunities for Juniors to race at the highest levels of the sport. The most successful elite athletes are those who have forged their own path, not those who waited for someone to notice them. Train smart, train hard, take care of yourself, be good to your sponsors, learn, and keep looking for new racing challenges, and you will be on the best path toward achieving your personal racing success.

A LOOK AHEAD: RACING IN EUROPE

As a new racer, you may think it's a bit premature to bring up the subject of Europe. But racing in Europe or on the world circuit is the goal of many young racers, so let's take a moment and make sure you know what racing in the bigger field is like. Although the U.S. racing scene is getting better and more competitive every year, racing in Europe still provides some of the best competition in the world. When you are ready for it, spending time overseas can be an important step in your development. We do not recommend going to Europe early in your career, before you have at least three or four years of experience in your body. You need physical depth and excellent pack, trail, or track skills before you consider going. Racing at that level before you are ready will not provide you with the experience you need to improve, because you will be off the back or out of the race before the fun even begins.

Once you are ready, racing in Europe is one of the best ways to take your game to the next level. There are two main ways that young riders can go to Europe. The first is getting into the USAC pipeline. Once you are in the pipeline, you have a good chance of getting selected to go to Europe with the national team. The second way is to pay a fee to take part in a program such as the Johan Bruyneel Cycling Academy (see

---

Racing Outside the United States

If you plan to do any racing outside the United States (including Canada), you will need to do your homework, and that means getting some red tape out of the way. It can take a while for the government and cycling organizations to process these documents, so be sure to begin well ahead of your departure date. Before you race outside the United States, you will need the following:

- *A passport.* All international travel now requires a passport, so be sure you have one and that it is current.
- *A UCI license.* This is the international cycling license (apply for it at www. usacycling.org).
- *A letter of release* to race outside the United States from our main cycling governing body, USA Cycling. The request form is available in the My USACycling section of the USAC website, www.usacycling.org. (Once you become a USA Cycling member, you will have an account that is accessible on My USACycling.)

www.cyclingcenter.com). There are very few spots available with the national program, so most young riders who go to Europe follow the fee-for-service model. Another option is to go by yourself, but this is only really feasible if you have connections who can help you get set up with housing, travel, and racing opportunities.

Once you decide to race in Europe, make a smart training and racing plan for getting the necessary experience, and start the process for the paperwork you will need, there are other things you can do to prepare for a great experience:

- Follow the blogs and online posts of riders racing in Europe. Young riders share their experiences at www.cyclingnews.com and www.cyclingcenter.com.
- Talk to other riders who have been to Europe recently.
- Have a detailed plan for improving your technical and tactical bike skills.

Making the Most of Europe

Your first trip to Europe will be a huge learning experience, no matter how well prepared you think you are. Here are some ideas to make the most of your experience and ensure the trip goes as smoothly as possible:

- If you are under 18, make sure you have the proper paperwork from your parents to allow the trip chaperone, coach, or manager to be responsible for your care. This will protect you if you become ill or injured.
- Always have some cash with you in the local currency when you travel abroad. Whenever possible, exchange some of your money for the local currency before you travel. But it's not wise to travel with a large amount of currency. Consider taking traveler's checks (from a large, widely recognized company). You can also use ATM machines or prepaid traveler's check cards overseas. Credit cards are another option. But you may be subject to extra fees when using your credit card or a traveler's check card,

(continues)

so check with the company before you go on your trip. Each one of these methods has drawbacks: You may end up someplace where an ATM machine is not available, for example, and some hotels and restaurants in other countries do not accept traveler's check cards or credit cards. If you plan to use your debit card or credit card, you will need to inform the company that you will be traveling overseas; otherwise the charges may be rejected and your card canceled. This is because the company has safeguards to prevent someone else from using your card, and sudden unusual activity on the card raises a red flag. Plan ahead, and check the details for the country (or countries) that you will be visiting.

- Make sure you bring along your medications and prescription information (this includes your contact information). And if your medication is on the U.S. Anti-Doping Agency's list of banned or regulated items, make sure you have copies of your approval paperwork with you.

- Take some healthy, simple snacks for the journey. It can be difficult to find healthy foods in airports. Include a few packages of instant oatmeal, granola bars, and other simple foods in your pack. (Note: Be aware that most foreign governments will not let you bring fruit or other nonpackaged foods into their country.)

- Stay in contact with your family. You may not think you will get homesick, but many young athletes do, especially on trips that last longer than a week, or when they are at a low point from hard racing or struggling with an unexpected problem. Calling from overseas can be expensive, but many companies, such as Skype (www.skype.com), offer free computer-to-computer calling or very low-cost computer-to-phone calling. American cell phones typically do not work in Europe.

- Bring something to do that will occupy your free moments: Work on learning the language, read a good book, or take an online class. Keep a detailed training log or blog. And whenever possible, explore and learn about the culture or area you are in. Make your travels about more than just the racing. This will enrich your mind and might even enhance your racing performance.

- Most importantly, have clear goals for the trip. Outcome goals are great, but really think about what you want to learn and the personal gains you would like to make.

Do you feel ready to race? In this chapter and throughout this book, you have learned a lot about the different aspects of training, riding, and racing. It can all seem a bit intimidating. But all of this information has been presented to make you a smarter, stronger racer, not to scare you away. When you begin to race, you will learn some lessons the hard way. We hope these lessons will be easier to learn because you read about them here. Sometimes things will come easy, and sometimes you will feel like you are trying to bike through a brick wall. All of this is part of the process. The more you know about that process, the better prepared you will be to weather the ups and downs, and the more likely you will be successful.

RECOMMENDED RESOURCES

www.bikereg.com
www.uci.ch (international race calendar)
www.usacycling.org
www.usantidoping.org

16 HIGH SCHOOL and
Collegiate Cycling

Collegiate cycling is a great way to compete and also to build bonds that will last a lifetime.
—Gary Achterberg, cycling coach, Midwestern State University

High school or collegiate team bike racing is an incredibly fun way to participate in the sport of cycling, regardless of your skill level. Experts and beginners are both welcome when it comes to team racing in high school and college, and racing is a great way to make friends and develop camaraderie. The sport at these levels is equally rewarding to parents, coaches, teachers, and other mentors who become involved. Since high school team racing is much less prevalent than collegiate cycling in the United States, we'll start with an overview of the high school mountain bike and road scene. If your school or district does not have a cycling program and you are interested in developing a team, you'll find tips here on how to get started. (See also Appendix K for an example of a successful club and more tips on setting up a club.)

HIGH SCHOOL CYCLING

The biggest obstacle facing high school riders is the lack of nationwide racing and organizations. This could change over the next few years as more young people become attracted to the sport and more adults realize the benefits that a cycling club can have for high schoolers. There are good models for cycling programs in the United States that other clubs can learn from, and USA Cycling is set up to assist new clubs with resources and guidance. USA Cycling in fact hired someone to work specifically on developing high school and collegiate racing. This staff member is a resource for any rider who would like to organize racing in his or her area.

Mountain Biking

The concept of promoting or organizing high school mountain bike team racing is fairly recent. Rules were not put to paper until 2001, and there are only a handful of schools and a few areas nationwide that have really seized the idea and developed teams. The way it works is pretty simple: Riders race cross-country bikes for their school team on a closed course. A combination of low scores from the top finishers of each school determines the team outcome in a way that is similar to scoring cross-country running. Usually events are scored with both individual and team points, but the fun is really in the team. You could have three solid riders on your team and beat the team who has one superstar and ten other riders who are not quite so fast. The team event encourages each individual to perform at his or her best regardless of the level of skill or speed the rider has achieved.

High school cross-country running and cross-country mountain biking are very similar and can both be varsity sports. It takes more planning to choose racecourses for mountain biking events and training, and at first, more work may go into setting up high-quality races. An actual cross-country running course may make for a great mountain bike racecourse, although the bike course may need a bit more length and possibly more diverse terrain. Ideally, a lap in a mountain bike course will take the top riders 12 to 15 minutes to complete, and for high school athletes, a race of four or five laps is more than enough. If middle school riders are included, their races should be shortened by at least one or two laps, depending on the course. It is best to run middle school riders separately in their own time slots so they have the course to themselves. And with large fields in a high school race, it may be advantageous to run the junior varsity riders separately from the varsity team, and women separately from the men.

Keep in mind that mountain bikes can tear up wet ground. A well-designed course is what distinguishes a good race from a mediocre one, so if you are organizing races, make sure you keep your trails in good shape for training and competition. The International Mountain Bike Association (www.imba.com) is the leading organization for mountain biking and provides advice and guidelines for trail design and maintenance.

There are only a few small pockets of organized middle and high school mountain bike racing programs. The biggest of these is the NORCAL High School Mountain Bike League in the San Francisco Bay Area of California. This league has grown to a membership of more than 300 riders and 25-plus schools, with organized coaching and dedicated races for the students. There are also movements in Colorado, Arizona, Tennessee, and a few other states. Every state with access to riding and racing venues should have state championships for high school teams. We look forward to seeing the sport grow.

Road Biking

When it comes to high school road racing, there are only two areas of the country where there is activity: New England and Texas. A network of private schools in New England has a private school league of road racing, but because it is "private," you must be enrolled in one of the participating schools to gain access to the events. A league was formed in the Dallas–Fort Worth area by a former collegiate racer, called the Texas High School Cycling League, and as of this writing was in its third year of competition and steadily growing. Visit http://www.texashighschool-cycling.org to check out the details.

Starting a Program

If you are a Junior rider with no racing in your area, convincing a teacher, coach, or other interested adult mentor to help put on a race or start a club may not be as hard as you think. There have been cases where students actually organized a state championship, assuming all the responsibility for race production and organizing adult volunteers to help with the race. There are guidelines and rules in the USA Cycling Mountain Bike Rulebook to help potential race organizers understand the basics.

If you are interested in establishing a program at your school, here's how to get started:

- Study the NORCAL league webpage at www.norcalmtb.org.
- Find out if any of your teachers or coaches are cyclists and speak with them about helping you organize a school club.

- Contact local clubs, if there are any in your area, and ask for help organizing your first training rides and races. Check the USA Cycling webpage at www.usacycling.org to find cycling clubs near you.
- Contact the USA Cycling high school/collegiate manager to discuss additional steps to get things started in your area.

COLLEGIATE CYCLING

Many Juniors wonder what comes next as they cross over from racing age 17 to racing age 18. In addition to advancing into the Espoir category, these young men and women are figuring out what to do after high school. Making a decision about college is very personal. College provides wonderful opportunities to learn, meet new people, and expand your view of the world. But if you're wondering whether you will have to put cycling on the back burner for four years if you choose college, rest assured that you will not. Many colleges and universities provide fabulous opportunities to begin or continue a cycling career. Far from reducing your cycling opportunities, the right college can provide you with new ones. In fact, many of our best Senior riders started their cycling careers in collegiate programs. You may discover that one of the best things about college is the cycling and the cycling friendships that develop.

Benefits of Collegiate Cycling

- Travel
- Friends
- Fun
- Opportunity to serve as a club leader
- Opportunity to gain excellent self-driven time-management skills
- Opportunity to grow in your sport experience while you continue to develop

If you're not sure whether you want to go to college, or if you're sure you want to go but don't know how to choose a college, you have some work to do in considering your goals and how best to achieve them. This is a decision that will be influenced by many factors. Let's look at a few:

- What would you do otherwise? If you don't continue your education after high school, what will you do next? Bike racing is expensive, and the types of jobs you can get when you're just out of high school typically don't pay well. Plus, working from nine to five certainly can put a crimp in your training plan. College schedules and term papers can be demanding, but usually not so demanding that you can't go out for a spin on the bike between classes.
- What do you want to do down the road? No matter how successful your cycling career is, it won't last forever. You may be a lifetime rider, but there are many factors that can limit your elite competitive days, including age, though that may be hard for you to believe now. It is important to consider your long-term future, no matter how far away it seems. To put it bluntly, no matter how great a start you have in cycling, you need to prepare to make a living beyond racing.
- How far from home do you want to be? (Or how close, depending on how anxious you are to be out on your own.)
- How much can you and your parents afford to spend on college (including room and board)?
- What size campus do you think you would like best? A big university may have more opportunities to do different things, and is more likely to have a cycling program or offer community cycling opportunities. On the other hand, small colleges offer a more personal setting where you may have more leadership opportunities.
- What size city would you like to be in during college? Bigger cities may have more to offer in terms of cultural and social events, but smaller cities and towns have a charm all their own and can be easier to navigate when you are out on your own for the first time.
- Which colleges and universities within these parameters offer programs you are interested in?
- Is it safe to ride your bike in the area near the school? Is there trail access or a track? Think about what you will need to pursue your

cycling discipline and see if these things are available at the colleges and universities you are interested in. Is the coach for the cycling club highly experienced or just a beginner? Before you apply or commit to attending, can you meet with or talk to the coach?

- There are some programs that offer cycling-based scholarships, although they are not the same as National Collegiate Athletic Association (NCAA) program scholarships. Check to see if any of the schools you are interested in offer these.

- If possible, visit each of these "finalists" with your parents. You will get a better feel for the place if you can tour the campus. You may want to schedule interviews with an admissions counselor, a professor in a subject you are interested in, and, if there is a cycling program, the cycling coach. Talk to some students in the academic programs you are interested in and in the cycling program while you are there as well.

It is best to apply to several colleges and universities, so pick the ones that seem most suitable for you and make sure you get your applications in on time. Even if you're sure that one particular college is your favorite, apply to others as well so that you have a backup plan.

Once you've made a decision to pursue college, and completed your applications, you have every reason to be excited about all the new op-

Alternatives to Consider

Universities and colleges have really changed since your parents' day. In addition to the traditional four-year programs, colleges now offer a wide variety of ways to earn a degree. Classes are offered both the old-fashioned way (living on or near campus and attending classes) and online. This new flexibility makes it easier for competitive young athletes to train, travel, and keep up with studies. Both traditional colleges and universities and online-only programs are available. Competitive cyclists can even set up their coursework to allow for a normal classload and on-site learning in their training off-season, and a lighter load and online classes when they are busy during racing season. It may take a bit more time to earn your degree this way, however, so it is important to discuss the options with your parents.

portunities you will be encountering. The collegiate cycling scene has much to offer. College programs are a part of the National Collegiate Cycling Association (NCCA), which was formed in 1985. The NCCA is part of USA Cycling and is responsible for the collegiate racing system. Colleges can participate in mountain bike racing (both downhill and cross-country), road racing, and track racing. These programs are organized within the school and run by a student board. The cycling team or club must be affiliated with the school, usually through the recreation department, and the students are responsible for running meetings, raising funds, organizing the season, and submitting the right paperwork. The NCCA has its own rulebook, and this and other regulations are posted on the USA Cycling website.

Who coaches collegiate cyclists?

Cycling is considered a club sport by colleges and universities. The coach is typically a volunteer or someone who receives a small stipend for helping out the team. This coach could be someone with just a beginning coaching certification—maybe even another teammate—or someone with many years of experience coaching cyclists. Between these two extremes, there are many other possibilities. When you visit the campus, meet the coach, if possible. At the very least, find out who the coach is and what kind of experience he or she brings to the job.

Collegiate cycling is a true team sport. Unlike traditional cycling, where racers work together to help the strongest rider go for the win, collegiate racing is concerned with team score. It is similar to cross-country running in that the finish place of each rider counts toward an overall team score, and the team with the lowest score wins. And even though men and women compete in separate races, their points are added together to calculate the team score. This scoring system pulls together collegiate cycling teams and creates a unique experience.

From humble efforts by college students who simply loved riding, collegiate cycling has grown into a sport with more than 215 participating schools and some 2,500 licensed collegiate riders. During the regular season, collegiate teams get to travel to different colleges and events around their conference region. National collegiate championships are held for road, mountain bike, cyclocross, and track racing. Qualifying athletes and teams compete against other elite racers from around the country at these championships, and they have an opportunity to earn a national collegiate title.

One of the most common questions that young riders ask is "Should I just race and not go to college?" Maybe the thought has crossed your mind that it might be a lot of fun to just skip college for now and go to Europe to race instead. After all, you're young now, and you can always do college later, right? Before you jump across the pond with both feet, however, consider the drawbacks carefully. Going to Europe to race is a crucial step in becoming a successful racer, but it doesn't automatically guarantee you an awesome cycling experience. Ideally, you should go when you are in top form and ready to maximize your experience. Remember that a young person's development as an athlete takes a long time. While you are building your fitness and cycling experience level, you are in the best possible situation for at least starting your college education. Talk over your options with your parents and an experienced coach as you weigh your development as an athlete against the pros and cons of going to Europe now. Maybe you're not quite ready for Europe and would benefit more from a European experience if you developed your skills as a cyclist first—while going to school to prepare for your long-term future.

Being a Student Athlete

What exactly does it mean to be a student athlete? A basic answer would be that it is about pursuing a sport while attending school. But what else does it mean?

First, notice that the term is "student athlete," not "athlete student." If you have made the commitment to go to school, you are a student first, so keep your grades up. Some programs (and many parents) will not allow athletes to train or compete with the team if they have failing grades.

Being a smart, well-educated athlete should be a source of personal pride. Second, notice that another word follows "student," and this means you have more to fit into your schedule than other students do. As a student athlete, you can expect to have a busier lifestyle than most, and you will need to build good time-management skills. Third, since you will be part of a team, you will be expected to be an ambassador for the school program. And finally, you will need to take better care of yourself than nonathletes do. Drinking and staying out late on Friday night is out, because it would affect Saturday training or racing. Even if you have a rest day the next day, these kinds of things will affect your overall health and your ability to stay on top of grades and training. As a student athlete, you will be demanding more of yourself and setting higher standards than the average party guy or gal.

Another important difference between collegiate and regular season racing are the categories. On both road and track, the U.S. Cycling Federation separates athletes by ability using categories 1 through 5. For mountain bikers, racers are divided into beginner, sport, expert, semipro (men only), and pro. On the collegiate circuit, athletes are divided, based on ability, into levels A through D, where D is the lowest. The level you race at will depend on your team's needs and your regular season license.

RECOMMENDED RESOURCES
Collegiate Conferences

The collegiate cycling conferences were established on a regional basis. If you are planning to go to college in a certain region and have questions about the collegiate cycling clubs in that region, check out the appropriate conference listed below.

Atlantic Collegiate Cycling Conference (ACCC), www.usacycling.org/accc
Eastern Collegiate Cycling Conference (ECCC), www.usacycling.org/eccc
Midwestern Collegiate Cycling Conference (MWCCC), www.usacycling.org/mwccc
North Central Collegiate Cycling Conference (NCCCC), www.usacycling.org/ncccc
Northwestern Collegiate Cycling Conference (NWCCC), www.usacycling.org/nwccc
Rocky Mountain Collegiate Cycling Conference (RMCCC), www.usacycling.org/rmccc
South Central Collegiate Cycling Conference (SCCCC), www.usacycling.org/scccc
Southeastern Collegiate Cycling Conference (SECCC), www.usacycling.org/seccc
Southwestern Collegiate Cycling Conference (SWCCC), www.usacycling.org/swccc
Western Collegiate Cycling Conference (WCCC), www.usacycling.org/wccc

Cycling Scholarships

USA Cycling offers two annual John Stenner Collegiate Cycling Scholarships for collegiate cyclists who demonstrate excellence as student athletes. For details, see the USA Cycling website, www.usacycling.org. Interested students must fill out an application and submit an essay.

Some individual scholastic programs also offer scholarships to incoming or returning cyclists who fit specific criteria. These scholarships are typically small, nonrenewable amounts designed to help with training or educational expenses. Check out each program's website to see what is currently available.

APPENDIX A

Contacts and Resources

MAJOR SPORTS GOVERNING BODIES AND ORGANIZATIONS

American Bicycle Association (ABA BMX)

Website: www.ababmx.com

Phone: 480-961-1903

This is a national-level organization for BMX racing. ABA works together with USAC, which oversees the Olympic BMX program. It sanctions events, provides resources, and promotes the sport to youth racers across the country. Its headquarters is in Gilbert, Arizona.

International Mountain Bicycling Association (IMBA)

Website: www.imba.com

Phone: 303-545-9011 or 888-442-4622

This is a nonprofit international organization that is not involved with competitive cycling. However, it does provide excellent resources and guidance for mountain bike trail management and mountain bike riding. It is based in Boulder, Colorado, but has many affiliated local clubs in the United States and around the world. See the website for local contact information.

National Bicycle League (NBL)

Website: www.nbl.org

Phone: 614-777-1625 or 800-886-BMX1

This is a national organization for BMX and bicycle motocross racing. NBL works together with USAC, which oversees the Olympic BMX program. It sanctions events, provides resources, and promotes the sport across the country. Its headquarters is in Hilliard, Ohio.

Union Cycliste Internationale (UCI)

Website: www.uci.ch

This is the international governing organization for bicycle racing. The UCI governs international road, mountain bike, BMX, and track racing. With its headquarters located in

Switzerland, this organization oversees the international racing calendar, the ranking of riders, and rules and regulations of the sport. Additionally, the UCI issues licenses for riders and coaches for participation in international competitions.

U.S. Anti-Doping (USADA)

Website: www.usantidoping.org

Phone: 719-785-2000 or 800-601-2632

The U.S. Anti-Doping Agency, based in Colorado Springs, Colorado, oversees anti-doping efforts across Olympic sports in the United States. It provides education, testing, and recommendations for sanctions when individuals test positive. Its website has excellent resources for coaches and athletes about banned medications and drugs and testing procedures.

USA Cycling (USAC)

Website: www.usacycling.org

Phone: 719-866-4581

USA Cycling, located in Colorado Springs, Colorado, is the official national governing body for cycling in the United States. It provides coaching education, certification for mechanics, training and certification for officials, and racing licenses. The USAC oversees track, road, mountain bike, BMX, and collegiate cycling. Additionally, it coordinates the road, mountain bike, and track national calendars; provides race permits; and oversees national teams.

World Anti-Doping Agency (WADA)

Website: www.wada-ama.org/en/

WADA was formed in 1999 in response to growing concerns about the misuse of drugs and other substances in athletic competitions around the world. Its basic purpose was to create guidelines for anti-doping efforts and drug testing of athletes and to coordinate and monitor these efforts on an ongoing basis. WADA is not directly responsible for testing athletes but provides organizational guidelines and guidance to all Olympic-officiated sports and many beyond. Its headquarters are in Montreal, Quebec, and it has regional offices in Lausanne, Switzerland; Tokyo, Japan; Cape Town, South Africa; and Montevideo, Uruguay.

REGIONAL ORGANIZATIONS

Although the organizations listed below are not affiliated directly with USAC, they can provide information and opportunities for racing within your local area. Many run local racing circuits. Many states also have cycling organizations. Some of these are general cycling associations, and some concentrate on a specialty such as off-road cycling. Check with the national organizations or your local bike shop to find out about cycling organizations and clubs active in your state or local area.

American Bicycle Racing (ABR)

Website: www.ambikerace.com

Phone: 708-532-7204

This is a national organization that is not affiliated with USAC or the U.S. Olympic movement. It provides race permits, coaching education, and race licenses for the events it sponsors. The ABR is largest in the Midwest and focuses mostly on road and track events. It is headquartered in Tinley Park, Illinois.

American Cycling Association (ACA)

Website: www.americancycling.org

Phone: 303-458-5538

This is a national organization that is not affiliated with USAC or the U.S. Olympic movement. It provides race permits, coaching education, and race licenses for the events it sponsors. The ACA emphasizes road racing and cyclocross. It is based in Denver, Colorado.

APPENDIX B

Glossary of Common Cycling Terms

Aerobic: Cellular metabolism that happens in the presence of oxygen during a low to mid-range level of activity.

Aerodynamic: Shaped to cut through the air with little to no wind resistance. An aerodynamic bicycle or helmet design reduces drag and increases the cyclist's speed.

Anaerobic: Literally, "without oxygen," referring to cellular metabolism or energy creation that does not use oxygen in the process. When an athlete works at high intensities that demand more oxygen than the heart and lungs can supply, muscle cells produce energy anaerobically. They cannot do this as long because anaerobic metabolism "costs" more and produces waste products that eventually slow one down.

Anaerobic endurance: The ability to maintain a high speed for an extended period of time using anaerobic metabolism. This is a key element for anyone training for endurance events, and it builds over time with smart training.

Attack: A strategy whereby a rider suddenly accelerates to try to generate enough force to leave the pack, often using the element of surprise. *See also* Counter (or Counterattack).

Base period: An early training period within a periodized training program. In this period the basic abilities of endurance, speed, and force are emphasized. *See also* Mesocycle; Periodized training.

Berm: A banked section of a mountain bike trail perfect for fast corners.

Block: A team tactic designed to allow a teammate to gain an advantage. One or more riders on a team may get in front of another rider or in front of the pack to manipulate the pace so that a teammate can get away or gain the edge in a sprint.

Blow up: What happens when an athlete has ridden so hard and exerted all he has and can't ride anymore.

Bonk: A sense of fatigue that a cyclist suddenly feels while training or racing, due to glycogen depletion as the body attempts to conserve energy and vital organs. Often a bonk affects the cyclist's thinking (the cyclist may feel muddle-headed and confused or may even become angry or weepy), or may feel as if someone has suddenly put lead into her limbs. It can take time to recover from a bonk, and the fatigue can affect racing or training for several days. The solution is to eat enough carbohydrates to support one's training load each day, and to always carry extra food to keep fueled on rides. Good examples of food to take along are gels, granola bars, and bananas.

Break (or Breakaway): An attack or jump off the front of a pack in an attempt to get away. This can be done by a solo rider or a group of riders working together. The timing and placement of a breakaway effort are crucial to its success.

Bridging the gap (or Bridging): Closing up the distance to catch up with a rider or group of riders ahead of a cyclist on the track or road.

Build period: A specific phase within a periodized training plan during which high-intensity training in the form of muscular endurance, anaerobic endurance, and power are emphasized while force and speed are maintained. *See also* Mesocycle; Periodized training.

Bunny hop: A maneuver used to get over an obstacle such as a log or hole in the road while minimizing loss of speed. When executing a bunny hop, the rider pulls the bike wheels up to allow the obstacle to be cleared. Bunny hops are used most often in mountain biking and cyclocross, but skilled road riders use them as well.

Burnout: A condition wherein athletes feel mentally drained. Burnout can be mild to severe. It can affect performance, mood and attitude, riding, and training enjoyment and may even lead to quitting the sport. Burnout is usually related to overtraining and/or underrecovery but can also be related to experiencing too much pressure to win and/or unrealistic expectations. Many who experience long-term burnout or who quit due to burnout are not able to return. *See also* Overreaching; Overtraining; Underrecovery.

Cadence: Revolutions per minute of a cyclist's pedal stroke, often abbreviated as "rpm."

Caravan: The pack of vehicles that follow behind a road race. The caravan may include neutral support as well as team support vehicles. In some races, riders are allowed to drop back into the caravan to pick up food or water.

Chase group: A group of riders working hard to catch the lead pack or breakaway that is in front of it. There can be several chase groups in a race, and the members of a good chase group work together to maximize their efforts. Riders from different teams often work together in a chase group.

Circuit race: A mass-start race that usually involves riders doing two or more laps on a road course that is 2 to 20 miles long.

Clinchers: Wheels that have rims designed to hold the tire on using a hooked bead. They use an inner tube and can be used in both training and racing. *See also* Tubular.

Closed course: A racing course that has been closed to traffic. Only racers and official vehicles are allowed on the course. Always find out before a race whether it will be an open or closed course; however, even if it is closed, it is critical to remain alert for traffic in case a motorist slips onto the course. Usually race officials, volunteers, and police are placed along the course to help maintain a safe environment. An entire course or just a section of the course may be closed (for example, the start, a dangerous section, or the finish). *See also* Open course.

Commissaire: The highest-level cycling official for the Union Cycliste Internationale.

Counter (or Counterattack): When a rider or group of riders attacks immediately following another attack that was attempted unsuccessfully. The cyclist who initiated the first attack may have gained the lead briefly but is fatigued by the attempt and unable to retain it. *See also* Attack.

Counter-steer: A steering technique to control the bike while executing a turn.

Criterium: Also called a "crit," this is a mass-start, multiple-lap race on a course that is half a mile to a mile long. The number of laps depends on age and race category. Crits usually last 30 to 90 minutes and are a great spectator sport.

Cross-country: A style of mountain bike racing whereby racers ride on single- and double-track trails, fire roads, and paved roads on mountain bikes. *See also* Double track; Single track.

Crosstraining: An approach to training that involves doing different types of activities. For example, a cyclist might swim or run instead of biking for the variety and training benefits these sports provide. Crosstraining can keep training fresh and fun and can reduce injuries that occur from repetitive overuse. Too much crosstraining, however, can reduce the specific gains needed within a single sport.

Cyclocross: An off-road multiple-lap race, usually held in a park or around a school, where racers ride on grass, dirt, roads, and trails using a road-style bike with knobby tires. Riders may have to dismount and carry their bikes over barriers or up steep hills, and races typically last 30 to 60 minutes. Cyclocross racing is a great spectator sport.

Domestique: A French term for a rider on a team whose job is to sacrifice for the benefit of teammates. For example, a domestique may give up a wheel to a teammate who has a better chance in the race, or may push the pace so the lead sprinter can sit in the pack and save her energy for the final sprint.

Double track: Mountain biking trail that is wide enough for a car and typically has two car-tire-like parallel tracks. *See also* Single track.

Downhill: A gravity-based individual downhill time trial event on mountain bikes wherein riders follow a set course down a mountainside to see who can record the fastest time.

Draft: A technique for reducing wind resistance by riding close behind or near another rider to take advantage of the windbreak and the pull created by the other rider.

Drop: Leaving other riders behind by pulling into the lead. When a rider or group rides away from other riders, those left behind have been "dropped."

Echelon: A specific formation for a paceline that stretches sideways. An echelon provides maximum draft when there is a side wind. An echelon should not be attempted on a busy road, as it takes up a good bit of road area, depending on the size of the group. *See also* Paceline.

Endurance. The ability to persist and resist fatigue over time.

Espoir: The French term for "hope"; in cycling it refers to the category of riders ages 18 to 23, the best and brightest getting ready to race in the Senior ranks.

Etch-a-Sketch (or Squirrel): A rider who doesn't know how to "hold a line," or who puts other riders in a pack in danger because of his poor handling skills.

False flat: A road that looks flat but in reality has a slight uphill grade, usually 1 to 2 percent.

Field: The main group of riders. Also called "the pack."

Field limit: The maximum number of racers allowed in a race or on a course at any time. Most races have a field limit for safety reasons.

Field sprint: The main group or pack sprint at the end of the race. Positioning in the field is very important for a shot at a good finish in the field sprint.

Fixed-gear: A bike whose chain mechanism is controlled completely by pedal rate. When a rider pedals, she drives the chain and the bike moves forward. When she stops pedaling, the bike's chain, and thus the wheels and the bike, immediately stop. A fixed-gear bike does not coast, and it is not uncommon for a first-timer on a fixed-gear bike to get "bucked off" because she inadvertently stops pedaling. Track riders are required to use single-speed bikes without brakes (they control speed and stopping directly through pedal speed). *See also* Single speed.

Flier: When a rider "takes a flier," he makes or attempts to make a breakaway or attack. A flier is usually short and often not expected to work.

Float (1): Short for "pedal float," freedom of movement between the cleat and pedal. A small amount of float allows the cyclist to move her foot in the twist motion that occurs naturally when pedaling without disengaging or unclipping the cleats. This helps protect the cyclist's knees from injury or strain.

Float (2): Pedal with little to no pressure on the pedals. Floating on the pedal stroke requires little to no energy.

Force: The strength evident in a muscle or muscle group while exerting against a resistance.

Form sprints: Training sprints that focus on good posture and sprinting technique, not on absolute speed. They help a racer sprint properly so that he can make the most of a sprint when he does apply speed.

Fred: A common term for a new rider or someone who doesn't seem to know what he is doing. There is no equivalent term for women—the term isn't gender specific. Anyone can be a Fred.

Gap: The space that opens up between two riders or a rider and a group. A gap can be created at the front or back of a pack. Riders who have been gapped are no longer getting the benefit of the draft and are often at risk for being dropped if the pace picks up.

GC: General classification; refers to the ranking of riders by their accumulated time in a stage race.

Gear inches (GI): The measure of a gear being used. Junior riders and track riders use the term most often—Juniors because they have gear restrictions for races, and track riders because they change their gearing for different racing and training efforts. GI is calculated by multiplying the number of chain-ring teeth by the tire diameter (26 inches for a 650c tire and 27 inches for a 700c or tubular tire), then dividing it by the number of rear cog teeth.

Gear restrictions: The specific gear sizes that cycling governing bodies allow in certain kinds of events. Gear restrictions were created by cycling governing bodies to protect Juniors from injuries caused by pushing hard gears before developing muscles and joints can handle it.

Grimpeurs: French term for "climbing specialists," or riders who excel in the mountains.

Half-wheel: Riding so that one's front wheel is beside the rear wheel of another rider and overlapping a bit. This can be a dangerous position because if the wheels hit each other, both riders may crash. A rider should never half-wheel another rider in a paceline. Half-wheels or overlapped wheels do occur in races, but a good racer knows how to avoid them and how to deal with them when they occur.

Hammer: A verb meaning to ride really hard. A rider might hammer for fun, to push the pace on a ride, to complete a hard interval effort, or to shake up a pack in a race.

Handsling: A hand move used by track riders in the Madison event to move a teammate out onto the track.

Heart-rate training zones: Ranges for target heart rates during different types of workouts and for different individuals based on fitness level, age, and other factors. There are several methods of setting and using heart-rate zones to help a rider train different systems in the body.

Heat exhaustion: A serious medical condition related to heat and dehydration whereby an individual feels physically weak, nauseated, and dizzy and suffers from muscle cramps.

Prompt medical attention should be sought before the condition gets worse. *See also* Heat-stroke.

Heatstroke: A condition even more serious than heat exhaustion that is potentially life-threatening. Dehydration and continued exposure to high temperatures may lead to a high fever; headaches; hot, dry skin (due to loss of ability to sweat); physical exhaustion; and eventually physical collapse, coma, and death. *See also* Heat exhaustion.

Holding a line: Maintaining a smooth, straight line, especially around the curves, in riding. Often it is measured in terms of a constant distance from the side of the road or from the painted white line as the road curves. A rider who does not hold the line may be called a squirrel or an Etch-a-Sketch.

Hoods: On drop handlebars, the covers of the brake handles.

Hyponatremia: An imbalance that occurs in the body when water and electrolytes are lost but only the water is replaced. Hyponatremia may be life-threatening if it becomes severe.

Indoor trainer: A tripod-like device that clamps the rear wheel of a bicycle a few inches above the ground and applies resistance so that a rider can train in place.

Intensity: A measurement of training that refers to how hard a workout is or how much effort is required during the workout. It can be measured quantitatively, with numbers such as heart rate and power, or qualitatively, using perceived effort.

Interval training: A system of high-intensity work marked by short, regularly repeated periods of hard exercise alternating with periods of recovery. These efforts usually last for a prescribed distance or length of time and aim for a particular level of effort based on perceived exertion, power, speed, or heart rate. *See also* Recovery interval.

Jump: To accelerate hard for a few seconds, typically by getting out of the saddle. A rider may jump to close a gap, jump onto a break or attack, or jump just to mix things up.

Junior: A rider under the racing age of 18.

Kermesse: An exhibition race that requires riders to do laps on a relatively flat, 4- to 6-mile course. Kermesse races are more common in Europe than in the United States.

King of the Mountain (KOM, or Queen of the Mountain [QOM]: Title awarded to the rider who crests designated climbs first or who earns the most climbing points for a series of climbs within a race.

Lactate: The substance formed in the body when lactic acid from the muscles enters the bloodstream. *See also* Lactate Threshold (LT); Lactic acid.

Lactate Threshold (LT): The point during exercise of increasing intensity at which blood lactate begins to accumulate above resting levels. Also known as anaerobic threshold. There are several ways to estimate this point. *See also* Lactate; Lactic acid; Ventilatory Threshold (VT).

Lactic acid: A by-product of the lactic acid system resulting from the incomplete breakdown of glucose (sugar) in the production of energy. This is not a bad thing in itself, but may cause problems when the body makes it faster than it can clear it away. *See also* Lactate; Lactate Threshold (LT).

Lap the field: To overtake riders from behind and pass them in a circular lap event such as a criterium or cyclocross race. When the lead rider is able to do this, she is said to be "lapping the field." A breakaway of more than one rider may also lap the field.

Lead out: To ride hard, typically when getting ready for a sprint, so the rider behind can benefit from the draft, build up speed, and then sprint past for the finish. Typically a strong rider provides a lead-out to someone on his team who is a good sprinter.

Mash: To push a big gear. This is typically not good for a rider's knees, particularly in the case of young riders whose knees are still developing or riders with existing knee problems.

Mass start: A race in which all the competitors start at the same time.

Masters: The "old folks" of cycling. Anyone over the racing age of 30 or 35 may be called a Masters rider, depending on the event. *See also* Seniors.

Mesocycle: A training period of approximately two to six weeks in a periodized training plan. *See also* Base period; Build period; Microcycle; Peak period; Periodized training; Preparation (Prep) period; Race period; Transition period.

Microcycle: A training period of approximately one week in a periodized training plan. *See also* Mesocycle; Periodized training.

Minute man: The rider who starts ahead of you in a time trial. Riders are often sent at one-minute intervals.

Motorpace: Training done in the draft of a motorcycle or car to help a rider train at a pace faster than normal. Motorpacing can be very dangerous and should be attempted only by trained coaches with athletes who are prepared for the challenge and in a safe location.

Muscular endurance: The ability of a muscle or muscle group to perform repeated contractions for a long period of time while bearing a load.

Neutral support: Race-provided support available to all racers; sometimes called the "neutral wheel van" or "neutral vehicle." Neutral support may provide small repairs before a race, follow the race to help swap out flat wheels, or make minor repairs during a race. In some races, such as cyclocross events and criteriums, the neutral support or wheel pit is set up alongside the course; in others it is supplied by a van that follows the race.

Omnium: A competition that includes several types of racing events, where points are earned and combined for an overall winner. In a stage race, the overall winner is the racer who has the fastest cumulative time. In an omnium, the racer with the highest number of points wins.

Open course: A racecourse that is not closed to motorists. Riders need to be very careful on an open course. Usually race officials, volunteers, and police are placed along the course to help maintain a safe environment. *See also* Closed course.

OTB: An acronym for "off the back." This is the term for a rider who is so far behind the main race that she is no longer considered to be part of the race.

Overreaching: Pushing the body or specific physical systems in such a way as to stretch their capacity. If overreaching is continued and proper rest does not occur, it may lead to overtraining and injury. If overreaching is done right, an athlete gets stronger and faster. *See also* Burnout; Overtraining; Underrecovery.

Overtraining: Extreme fatigue, both physical and mental, that occurs as a result of heavy training when the body is not allowed to recover and/or does not get what it needs for proper recovery. Overtraining may lead to depression, injury, or illness. It can take weeks or months to recover from serious overtraining. *See also* Burnout; Overreaching; Underrecovery.

Paceline: A group of riders who ride and work together to maximize their efforts through the use of drafting. A paceline is usually done single or double file.

Pack: A group of riders. *See also* Field.

Peak period: The training phase in periodized training when the volume of training is reduced and intensity is proportionally increased to promote a higher level of fitness. Usually considered a mesocycle. *See also* Mesocycle; Periodized training.

Periodized training: A theory of training that uses work/rest cycles to place stress on different physical systems and allow for adequate recovery to help an athlete adapt and improve. The work/rest cycles occur on daily, weekly, and monthly schedules as different systems and skills are addressed. *See also* Mesocycle; Microcycle.

Pole: The area below the Sprinter's Line on a velodrome.

Power: The ability to perform work resulting from force and speed.

Power endurance (PE): A strength phase in training performed to develop the capacity to quickly recruit groups of muscle fibers for a movement and to sustain their use at a high power output.

Preparation (Prep) period: The mesocycle that marks the start of training for the racing season, usually involving crosstraining and low loads. *See also* Mesocycle; Periodized training.

Prime (pronounced "preem"): A prize that is not related to the final outcome. The prime varies according to the type of race.

Pull (1): To ride at the front of the paceline for a period of time, setting the pace and creating the start of the draft.

Pull (2): To take a rider or riders out of a race. Race officials sometimes do this to control the race and keep it safe, generally pulling riders who are off the back or out of contention. When a rider is taken out of a race, he has been "pulled."

Pull off: To leave the front of the paceline and move to the back of the line.

Pull through: To fill in the space left by someone who has rotated to the back of the paceline. *See also* Wheel suck (or "To suck a wheel").

Race period: The mesocycle during which the workload is greatly decreased, allowing the athlete to compete in high-priority races. *See also* Mesocycle; Periodized training.

Racing age: Age categories for race as determined by the organization that is holding the race or issuing racing licenses. For USA Cycling, a rider's racing age is the age he or she will be as of December 31 of the year for which the license is being issued. So if a rider will turn 16 on August 1, 2008, and is issued a racing license for 2008, his racing age will be 16 all year long, even before his birthday.

Racing license: The official document issued by the organization that governs or oversees the sport. Regional, national, and international organizations issue racing licenses for the different cycling disciplines. Some licenses can be purchased the day of an event, but most need to be purchased on a yearly basis.

Rail: The area at the top of the velodrome track closest to the wall and the railing.

Rating of Perceived Exertion (RPE): A subjective assessment of how hard one is working.

Recovery: A period of training when rest is emphasized.

Recovery interval: The relief period between work intervals within an interval workout. *See also* Interval training.

Relegation: A sanction from race officials that a rider may receive for a minor rule infraction. A relegation usually means the rider will be moved back in the race standings (lose places).

Repetition: The number of times that a task, such as a work interval or weight-lifting set, is repeated.

Repetition maximum (RM): The maximum load that a muscle group can lift in one attempt. Also called "one-repetition maximum," or 1RM.

Road race: A mass-start event usually held on open roads. There are three basic types of routes in road races: Point-to-point races start in one place and end in another. Other road races may require riders to go out to some point and back, or might involve doing multiple laps on a long loop course.

Roadie: A rider who prefers to ride and race roads.

Rock garden: A section of mountain bike trail that has multiple rocks to negotiate through and over.

Roll a tire: To have a tire come loose from the rim.

Rollers (1): The device on which a cyclist can balance a bike to ride indoors. Rollers provide no support and typically offer little resistance unless they incorporate a resistance device. They provide excellent training in bike-handling skills.

Rollers (2): Small rolling hills.

Rollout: The procedure done, usually before an event, to ensure that a Junior rider is using the proper gear inches based on the Junior gear restrictions. Rollouts are usually conducted by an official. If a rider fails rollout, she must correct the problem and pass the test before being allowed to race.

Rotate: The term used to indicate when someone comes off the front of the paceline and moves to the back. Riders may yell "Rotate!" when it is time for the lead rider to move.

Rpm: *See* Cadence.

Sandbagger: A negative term used to describe someone who is racing in a category lower or easier than he should be.

Seniors: Racers age 19 to 30 or 35 during the year of the race (*see also* Racing age). Masters riders can race in their special categories or in Senior races. But Seniors cannot race in Masters events unless they are old enough to qualify. Unless a race is designated as Senior or Espoir only, Juniors can race in Senior events; however, they still must follow the gear restrictions for their age group.

Set: A group of repetitions.

Sew-ups: *See* Tubular.

Short track: A fast mountain bike race done on a short dirt course, typically less than a mile long. These races are very spectator-friendly.

Single-speed: A bike buildup with only one gear option. A single-speed bike is different from a fixed-gear bike because it allows the rider to coast; if the rider stops pedaling, the bike still moves forward from momentum. A single-speed bike requires brakes in order to stop and is often used for a challenging workout on mountain bike trails or in training for maintaining a steady pace on the road. *See also* Fixed-gear.

Single track: Mountain bike trail that is wide enough for only one bike and has a single trail or path. *See also* Double track.

Sitting in: Hanging out at the back of a pack or field and not contributing to the group effort. *See also* Draft.

Slipstream: The sweet spot in a draft where a rider saves the most energy. Usually the following rider is within just a few inches of the rider in front of her in order to take advantage of it.

Soigneur: An individual who works with racing teams and is often responsible for everything from filling and handing out water bottles to post-event massage. The sounjear may be a certified massage therapist and may have other sports-related credentials, and is often vital to the smooth functioning of the team.

Specificity, principle of: The theory that training must stress the systems critical for optimal performance in order to achieve the desired training adaptations.

Speed: The ability to move the body in ways that produce optimum performance. For example, the ability to turn the cranks quickly on the bike.

Spun out: A rider has "spun out" when she has hit a cadence or rpm that maxes out the power or speed she can produce. This happens more to track athletes who have selected too easy a gear than to other types of riders, since track bikes have only one gear. This isn't typically a problem in other types of riding because of the large number of gear options.

Squirrel: A rider who is unsteady in a group or who cannot hold a line.

Straights (or Straightaways): The two straight sections of the velodome track, typically where racers start and finish events. This is also where riders enter the velodrome to ride.

Strength maintenance (SM) phase: A weight-lifting phase of training that focuses on maintaining the basic strength established in the previous phases of strength training.

Stress: Mental, physical, or emotional strain due to something pushing a person beyond his comfort zone. Training creates physical stress on purpose so that the body will respond and grow stronger. Not all stress is bad. Typically, stress is only a problem when it exceeds the cyclist's ability to cope with it. Keep in mind that stress from all sources adds up, and it is the cumulative effect of stress that can become too much for an athlete to handle.

Take a flyer: To accelerate off the front of a group suddenly and without warning, as in "He is taking a flyer."

Taper: A reduction in training volume prior to a major competition.

Time trial: An all-out race effort wherein an athlete must cover the set distance in the fastest possible time. Time trials can be done by individuals (individual time trial, ITT) or a team of two to five riders (team time trial, TTT).

Tops: The portion of the handlebar closest to the stem.

Tow: When a strong lead rider pulls a group. There is no physical connection, but the front rider's speed and draft help the other riders keep up.

Track stand: A balancing maneuver in which one holds the bicycle in place without using a support or putting a foot down.

Trackie: A rider who prefers velodrome riding.

Training zone: A level of intensity based on a percentage of some measure of the individual's capacity for work, such as heart rate or power.

Transition period: The mesocycle during which the workload and structure of training are greatly reduced to allow for physical and psychological recovery from training and racing. *See also* Mesocycle; Periodized training.

Tubular: A style of tire that is attached to a wheel rim by means of a strong cement rather than via the hook-and-tire-bead system found in clinchers. Tubulars are also called "sew-ups" because their rubber casing is literally sewn around the inner tube. Relatively new to the market, a tubular clincher allows a tubular tire to be used on a clincher rim without glue. *See also* Clinchers.

Tuck: A riding position in which the rider gets small and low on the bike to become more aerodynamic. Typically riders tuck only on long descents.

Underrecovery: When athletes have not given their bodies enough time and/or resources to allow them to properly adapt and respond to training. It is closely related to overtraining but focuses on the lack of proper recovery rather than on the amount of training stress. Underrecovery can be made worse by stress in other areas of an athlete's life (emotional, social, and so on) and can result in the same negative consequences as overtraining. *See also* Burnout; Overreaching; Overtraining.

Upgrade: Moving up from one category of racing to the next. One must earn enough race finish points to qualify for an upgrade. Race upgrade points and systems are determined by the national governing bodies and individual race organizations.

Uptrack: The top rail position, the area closest to the wall on a velodrome.

Velodrome: Bicycle racing tracks that are closed to cars. They typically have high, banked sides and may have spectator bleachers. Riders use special track bikes that have a single fixed gear and no brakes.

Ventilatory threshold (VT): The point during increasing exertion at which breathing first becomes labored. It is closely related to Lactate Threshold. *See also* Lactate Threshold (LT).

VO₂max: The body's capacity for oxygen consumption during maximal exertion; also known as "aerobic capacity" or "maximal oxygen consumption." It is usually expressed as milliliters of oxygen consumed per kilogram of body weight per minute (ml/kg/min).

Volume: A quantitative element of training, such as miles or hours of training within a given time, that combines duration and frequency.

Warm-up: The period of gradually increasing intensity of exercise at the start of a training session. A good warm-up is necessary to properly prepare joints, muscles, and mental focus for the workout. A good warm-up routine helps reduce the likelihood of overuse injuries.

Wheel pit: *See* Neutral support.

Wheel suck (or "To suck a wheel"): To draft behind another rider; often used in a derogatory way to describe someone who is taking a "free ride" but who isn't contributing to the paceline or will not pull through.

Wind trainer (or Trainer): An indoor training tool that allows an athlete to use her own bike. The rear wheel is clamped into the trainer and rolls against a drum that provides resistance. The front wheel rests on the ground or on a small riser to keep the bike level.

Workload: Measured stress applied in training, taking frequency, intensity, and duration into account.

Yellow line rule: A crucial rule for safety in racing that prohibits racers from crossing over the yellow line in the middle of the road into the left lane. Racers are not allowed to cross the yellow line to pass or to move up in the pack. Violating this rule can result in disqualification or having one's finish place relegated (moved farther back).

APPENDIX C

Race Bag Checklist

Always in Your Race Bag

Health insurance information
List of important phone numbers
Safety pins (pin them to your bag so they are easy to find)
Spare clean water bottle
Ibuprofen, allergy medications, etc.
Dry T-shirt
Towel
Plastic bags for wet, soggy items
Patch kit and spare tube
Multitool or travel tool kit
Small bottle of chain lube
Warming gel
Waterproof sunscreen
Chamois cream

For Race Day

Team jersey (and a clean one for post-race events on the podium)
Undershirt
Team shorts
Gloves
Helmet
Shoes
Socks
Sports bra (if applicable)
Pre-mixed or ready-to-mix bottles/hydration system
Food (for before, during, and after the event)
Glasses and spare lenses
Rain jacket (even if the race looks like it will be dry)
Arm/leg/knee warmers

Warm jacket for warm-up
Tights
Warm hat

For After the Race

Dry change of clothes, including socks
Towel, rubbing alcohol, disposable moist wipes, etc., for cleaning up
Warm hat

Personal Items to Remember

Racing license
Medical insurance card or copy
Money and checkbook and/or debit/credit cards
Signed waiver (especially if minor)
Cell phone
Personal medications

APPENDIX D

Taking Care of Your Bike: A Checklist

Get in the habit of taking care of your bike, for your own safety as well as for top performance. Below you will find a basic tools list and a checklist of tasks that you will need to perform regularly. To get hands-on training from someone with experience, take a class in bike maintenance from your local bike shop, if available. There are also some great books to guide you, such as *The Bicycling Guide to Complete Bicycle Maintenance and Repair: For Road and Mountain Bikes* (5th ed.), by Todd Downs. Usually, mechanics in local shops welcome questions. Better yet, consider getting a summer job at a shop so you can receive one-on-one training and learn how to take care of your own gear.

Here are the items you should have in your beginning toolbox:

- Chain lube
- Allen keys
- Phillips head screwdriver
- Flat head screwdriver
- Clean rags
- Tire levers
- Floor pump
- Chain tool
- Syringe-type lube applicator and a thin lube (for example, Pro Link)

There are a few items you should have with you on every ride to equip yourself for the unexpected. Of course, you will need something to inflate a tire if you get a flat. Some pumps are frame-mounted, including the newer mini-pumps, but the CO_2 pumps with disposable cartridges are small enough to fit in your saddlebag. Here are some other items to take with you in a pocket and/or in your saddlebag:

- Tire levers
- Patch kit

- Spare tube
- A few dollars
- Names and phone numbers of emergency contacts
- Basic multitool or Allen key set

Do the following before each ride to ensure safety and minimize the number of repairs that must be done on the road:

- Check your tire pressure and do a visual check of the tires, looking for cuts or bubbles.
- Give each wheel a quick spin. They shouldn't be rubbing against your brakes.
- Make sure your flat repair kit is complete.
- Check your front and rear wheel skewers. First, make sure your wheel is in the frame straight. Then, make sure the skews are closed tightly. The skewers should start binding when perpendicular to the frame or fork and should be handtight by the time you have them closed against the frame or fork.

If you ride on trails or other muddy surfaces, be sure to clean your bike promptly after a ride. In addition, complete the following on a regular basis, weekly if you ride most days and monthly if you ride just on weekends:

- Routinely check all the screws and bolts on your bike. Things tend to loosen up over time. This is bad for the bike and can create a dangerous situation.
- Do the drop test: Raise your front wheel a few inches off the ground and gently drop it. If you hear any strange rattles or obviously loose parts, figure out what is wrong and take care of it. These problems need to be fixed right away to prevent injury to you and further damage to your bike.
- Do a visual check of the rims, looking for broken spokes or cracks in the rim around the spoke nipples.
- Give your brakes a couple of good squeezes to check for loose cables and to see how much play they have. Cables can loosen over time.
- Look at your brake pads and check the surface of each. If they look worn-down, replace them.
- Apply the front brake and rock your bike back and forth. If you feel a wiggle or any looseness, you may have a loose headset.
- Check your pedals to make sure they are tight in their cranks. The pedals are threaded differently, but always loosen by turning the wrench back and tighten by turning forward.
- Look at your shoe cleats to make sure they aren't damaged, and check the cleat screws for tightness.
- Do a visual check for frayed cables. Frayed cables should be replaced as soon as possible.
- Slowly roll your crank backward and do a visual check of the chain. Look for tight links (ones that don't wrap properly around the chain rings), links that are spreading or look like they are misshapen, or anything else that might interfere with a smooth rotation.

- Get a syringe-type lube applicator and a thin lube (for example, Pro Link). These are great for lubing pivot points (derailleurs, brakes) and cables. Clean, lubed cables make for nice shifting and predictable braking.
- Lubricate your chain and wipe off the excess lubricant. This is especially important after it rains.

Finally, get to know the mechanics at your local shop. They can help you take care of any problems you find. Until you are comfortable doing all your own maintenance, take your bike in for an overhaul at least once a year.

—Special thanks to Chris Baker

APPENDIX E

Using a Logbook

Make copies of the logbook page shown here or use it as a template to create your own. A regular notebook works just as well to keep track of your training progress. If you prefer to go high-tech, there are also online training logbooks, like the one at www.trainingpeaks.com, that you can purchase for a small fee. It doesn't matter which method you use so long as you keep track of your progress.

Here are a few reminders:

- Be as complete as possible when filling in workout details. Include whatever information may be useful to you. Greater detail will give you more information to assess your progress.
- Make a note of the days you lift, stretch, do plyometric exercises (plyos), or add any other workout components to your cycling program.
- Make sure to note when you get sick, when you have exams at school, and any other important event that might impact your training.
- Track your recovery efforts, too.

TRAINING LOGBOOK ENTRY FORM

Day/Date : _____ Mood Today: _____
Route: _____ Weather: _____

Overall, today I felt

1	2	3	4	5	6	7	8	9	10
Terrible		Poor			Okay				Wonderful

Planned workout:

Actual workout:

A.M. RESTING HEARTRATE	FOCUS (1–10)	INTENSITY (1–10)	TIME	DISTANCE

Recovery activities:

Comments:

SMART Stepping-Stone Goal Setting

My outcome goal for this season:

_____

_____

                          Goal evaluation date: _____

Performance goals:

◆ _____

◆ _____

◆ _____

Training goals for the week of _____

◆ _____

◆ _____

◆ _____

◆ _____

NOTE: You may do other workouts each week as well, but you will focus on reaching these specific training goals and evaluating your progress. Each month, you will set new training goals depending on your performance goal progress.

Is my outcome goal . . .	**Are my performance goals . . .**	**Are my training goals . . .**
_____Specific?	_____Specific?	_____Specific?
_____Measurable?	_____Measurable?	_____Measurable?
_____Action oriented?	_____Action oriented?	_____Action oriented?
_____Realistic?	_____Realistic?	_____Realistic?
_____Timely?	_____Timely?	_____Timely?

APPENDIX G

Race Planning

Race name, location, time, and date:_____

Am I going to pre-register?   No/Yes

Pre-registration due by: _____

Transportation to the race:_____

Before leaving for the race:
- Review race bag checklist to make sure I have all equipment.
-
-

Once I arrive at the race site:
- Check in and get race number.
-
-

My warm-up routine:
What I need to do to prepare properly and how much time I need:

My competition goals are (performance and outcome):

My race plan is (how do you plan to accomplish your goals?):

What are possible distractions and what will I do about them (for example, arriving late, flatting in the race)?

Post-Race Reflections

Consider your race as objectively as possible. Use this sheet to help further understand what helps you perform well and what aspects of training or preparation get in your way.

Race name: _____

Weather: _____

Length of race: _____

Field size:_____ Location:_____

How did you perform during the race? Were you able to accomplish your race goals?

What positively impacted your ability to perform?

What negatively impacted your performance, and what could you do to prevent or deal with this in the future?

What did you learn from this performance—physically, technically, tactically, mentally?

What would you do the same way to prepare for your next competition?

What would you do differently to prepare for your next competition?

Bill of Rights for Young Athletes

1. Right to participate in sports

2. Right to participate at a level commensurate with each child's maturity and ability

3. Right to have qualified adult leadership

4. Right to play as a child and not as an adult

5. Right to share in the leadership and decision-making of their sport participation

6. Right to participate in safe and healthy environments

7. Right to proper preparation for participation in sports

8. Right to an equal opportunity to strive for success

9. Right to be treated with dignity

10. Right to have fun in sports

Reprinted with permission from R. Martens and V. Seefeldt, eds., *Guidelines for Children's Sports* (Washington, D.C.: American Alliance for Health, Physical Education, Recreation and Dance, 1979).

APPENDIX J

Youth Sport Parent Pledge

As the proud parent of a young athlete, I pledge:

- To seek out qualified coaches who are focused on healthy growth and development and who understand the demands of being a young athlete
- To love and support my athlete unconditionally
- To encourage, reward, and practice good sportsmanship
- To let my athlete's interests, not mine, lead the way
- To provide a positive parent push that is focused on my athlete's needs rather than my own
- To honor the Bill of Rights for Young Athletes
- To have patience
- To always be a respectful fan
- To practice good communication skills with my athlete and with his or her coach
- To respect my athlete and to encourage all of his or her efforts, not just the outcome
- To support my athlete's coach through both my words and efforts
- To remember that this experience belongs to the athlete

_____   _____

Signature   Date

Successful Junior or Espoir Club Program

Successful club or team programs for Juniors or Espoirs are typically organized by parents of young riders or by other adults in an existing club or team as a way of expanding the current club. This is not always the case: Some great clubs have actually been formed by Junior or Espoir riders themselves; others are part of the growing high school club movement. If your area lacks a Juniors or Espoir club, you might consider getting together with other young cyclists and their parents to explore the possibility of setting up a program in your area.

Yes, setting up a Juniors or Espoir program would entail some hard work. What is the best format for such a program? How would you set goals and get funding? How would you prevent legal difficulties? All these problems are surmountable, especially if you have some models of good programs to look to for answers.

LEGAL AND MEDICAL CONCERNS

Successful clubs provide young riders with proper development opportunities as well as a healthy and safe experience. If you are thinking about setting up a club, try to cover all the bases:

- Have a clear safety policy for club rides and activities that is strictly enforced. Give prospective members a copy of safety guidelines that include such things as wearing a helmet at all times when on the bike and obeying all traffic rules and signs.
- Have the proper parental signature authorization for emergency medical attention on file. Coaches and ride leaders should always carry an up-to-date list of emergency contact numbers.
- Have up-to-date medical information on file. All young athletes should be required to get a medical physical before joining the club. Coaches and ride leaders need to be aware of allergies and other medical concerns for individual riders. If athletes have asthma or severe allergies (such as a bee allergy), coaches need to be aware of the medi-

cal treatment required in case of emergency and where to find the medication in the rider's bag. Medication should be kept on hand at all rides.

- Consider the culture you would like your team to have and the impression of your club you want the cycling community to have. Team leaders should develop a clear code of conduct for training, racing, and travel. Set clear expectations about road etiquette, curfew, handling frustrations (for example, no throwing bikes or other equipment), sportsmanship, and any other issues you feel are important. These guidelines will help reduce discipline concerns and will teach athletes proper athletic behavior. In your guidelines, consider describing what behaviors you expect and want to see, not just what you don't want to see.
- Explore medical and accident insurance issues and how to create proper legal parental release/disclaimer forms for your riders and club. Disclaimers do not release a team leader from a negligent action, but they do ensure that parents have acknowledged the nature of the sport.
- Consider registering your club or team with USA Cycling. Club affiliation affords club officers a degree of legal protection and gives you access to resources such as medical and event checklists that may be helpful in setting up a successful club.

OTHER CONSIDERATIONS

Successful Junior and Espoir clubs do more than just provide opportunities to race. The best clubs emphasize participation, development, and successful experiences. Interestingly, the clubs that do these things well also tend to help athletes achieve their best performances. Common characteristics of great youth programs include:

- A clear mission and program philosophy that is written down and shared with members.
- Activities that reflect the mission and philosophy of the program.
- Officers, coaches, and leaders who buy into the philosophy and mission. As in parenting, these individuals may not always agree; however, they strive to present a united front when working with devo athletes.
- An understanding of youth development issues, physical as well as psychological.
- Clear focus. Rather than trying to do lots of things well, successful programs pick a few key objectives to focus on.
- A genuine interest and desire to enrich the lives of young people.

You don't have to reinvent the wheel or start off with a complex structure. There are many great programs around the country and passionate devo coaches who are willing to share ideas and provide advice. Don't be shy about asking them for guidance.

For more information on one club that has been successful, check out the Front Rangers Cycling Club (FRCC) of Denver and Colorado Springs at www.frontrangersdenver.org and www.frontrangers.org, respectively.

ABOUT THE AUTHOR

Kristen Dieffenbach is an elite-level USA Cycling–certified coach and associate professor of athletic coaching education at West Virginia University. She holds a PhD in exercise science and sports psychology, and serves on the advisory board of the USA Cycling coaching committee. Dieffenbach has coached cycling for more than 10 years at the high school, collegiate, recreational, and elite levels. She is also a former collegiate runner and cyclist who now competes in ultraendurance events.

Steve McCauley is director of development for the USA Cycling Development Foundation and a certified USA Cycling coach. In his eight years with USA Cycling, McCauley has worked closely with the sport's up-and-coming talent, including USA Cycling's Junior Athlete Programs as well as its collegiate cycling, membership, and athlete programs.